KV-510-004

ALSO BY PAUL FLYNN

The Tannery Cookbook:
An Irish Adventure with Food

Second Helpings

Martin and Paul's Surf and Turf

Paul Flynn's Family Food

BUTTER BOY

For Máire

BUTTER BOY

PAUL FLYNN

collected stories & recipes

NINE BEAN ROWS

South Dublin Libraries
www.
libraries.ie

Contents

2021

2022

People want simple, tasty food that doesn't take hours to make. That's what I concentrate on: easy techniques that even the most novice cook can master. The most important thing is not to be afraid. Turn down the heat and keep calm.

27 FEBRUARY 2021

I'm a
butter,
pot,
cook,
eat
kind of
guy.

29 AUGUST 2020

Foreword

I first met Paul and Máire Flynn when I was an anonymous restaurant critic and travel writer. The anonymity was never a pose: I guarded it jealously. The thinking behind it was to ensure that I would get the same treatment as my readers wherever I went, not the VIP schmoozing doled out to the well-known faces who, whether they admitted it or not, always got the full bells and whistles.

Sometimes I'd get 'made' and, when I was, I always got a sense of it: either an amped-up atmosphere of nervousness in the room or the sudden offer of a better table or a flurry of extra dishes would start to arrive, unsolicited and undesired. Only once did I think I'd been clocked due to the sheer loveliness of everything: the food, the surroundings, the perfect table and, most of all, the genuine warmth of the welcome. This was in a much-loved independent restaurant called the Tannery in a County Waterford town that seemed to me to be so quintessentially Irish it was almost a pastiche.

As the night wore on, we became more and more mellow, suffused with the wellbeing that can only come with feeling you're in the right place at the right time, among the right people. So I thought I'd put an end to what I'd assumed to be our joint pretence — mine and the restaurant's — and said to Máire, 'Oh, it's okay. I know you know it's me.' She went quite pale: they genuinely had no clue. Turns out everyone was treated the same way there. Simply, every single diner at the Tannery was, and still is, a VIP.

This is a welcome that's been refined over the years. It's more than two decades since the couple opened their restaurant in, yes, an old tannery, where Paul's grandfather once worked, ignoring more 'foodie' locations and in defiance of an occasionally recalcitrant early-doors clientele. They wanted to put Dungarvan on the map. And they have, with resounding success, helped by Paul's columns and many TV appearances.

Paul worked on this book during lockdowns. I vividly remember, in our suddenly shrunken worlds, how much more important cooking and eating became, even for the likes of me, for whom the next meal is never far from my mind. At a time when we were all in a state of low-level trauma, sleepless and fearful and jittery, the comfort of good food was never so vital. The recipes that Paul has collected for this book are all about that comfort. And yes, butter has a starring role: lovely, comforting butter.

Paul's writing is always uplifting, with the same hilarious, infectious energy as the man himself. Few people could convince me of the pleasures of a turnip tortilla — school dinners left me with a lifelong fear of the neep — but Paul can. He takes you with him in a very real way, whether to his Irish childhood Christmases — he was the youngest of eight — or trips abroad punctuated by a constant curiosity and love for food. After reading the column on his rekindled passion for France, I'm now determined to visit Auberge de la Môle as soon as humanly possible, every bit as much of a pilgrim as the man himself on his treks along the Camino de Santiago.

That first night in Dungarvan ended with an invitation from Paul to a fabulous little boozer called Downeys where we drank and talked till some silly time in the morning. Yes, okay, maybe past midnight it degenerated a bit beyond intelligent chat; I might need to confess to some Dolly and Kenny renditions. 'Fungarvan', I was told by those in the know before I went there, often mistily. 'Fungarvan' was what I got.

We've kept in touch since and I've followed his increasingly high-profile career with almost proprietorial fondness. I last saw him in Lismore Castle, a setting of quasi-mystical loveliness, for a lavish dinner organised to celebrate his stellar career and role in attracting international attention to this beautiful part of Ireland. Máire, as ever, was by his side, an invaluable part of his success, from the days of helping rationalise his scrawled column when he started writing for the *Irish Times* to being the radiant face front of house at the Tannery. If anyone deserves the accolades, it's him — it's the pair of them.

This book is also a celebration. I want to eat everything within its sunny pages. But it's more than that, too: it's a celebration of Paul's riotous lust for life and his ability to behave like a big teenager, all the while happy to laugh at himself. (His recollection of the junior Butter Boy sporting a Christmas gift of a cowboy outfit had me properly laughing out loud.) It's also a celebration of his love for music and travel and people — all the things that make life worth living. In his kitchen, a background in some of London's most serious and ambitious restaurants has been distilled down into nothing but pleasure: all of the technique and respect for the finest ingredients, but with none of the po-faced attitude.

Over the years, the Paul Flynn empire has grown with his cookery school and chic rooms for the Tannery pilgrim who wants to make more than a night of it. Dungarvan is lucky to have him. We are too.

Marina O'Loughlin

Introduction

I was the food writer for the *Irish Times* from 2000 to 2004. When that ended, I thought that was it as far as my newspaper career was concerned. However, I had got the writing bug and that urge to put my musings down on paper wouldn't leave me.

That first stint was the birth of something. Those articles became my first book, which gave rise to my first TV series. Despite having a full-time job cooking in the Tannery, my restaurant in Dungarvan, County Waterford, I was determined to promote our name. We needed that push, as in the early days the winter months were chronically quiet. The PR from the articles and books became crucial to our survival. My goal wasn't to be a celebrity chef. In fact, I would scorn the very idea as I took a pompous pride in having earned my stripes the hard way.

Another few books came along that didn't particularly trouble the bestseller lists. I honestly thought there would never be another.

Then one lazy Monday in 2019, I got a call from Marie Claire Digby asking me to return to the role of food writer for the *Irish Times*. A brief chat with my wife, Máire, sealed the deal. It was a no-brainer. I was back in the saddle, baby.

My second stint lasted from November 2019 to October 2022. In compiling all the recipes for this book, it became apparent that if we separated the articles from the time they were written, the book would make no sense. It was a case of all or nothing. This means it's a beast of a book, with 152 articles and over 450 recipes.

Of course, that period wound up being a unique and challenging time. I am left with a chronicle of the three most unusual years of our lives. It was as if someone pressed a very surreal pause button. Our girls went into covid as children and came out as young women. We lost a dear friend to cancer and bad news seemed to lurk around every corner.

The closure of the restaurant during the covid lockdowns wasn't all bad. Indeed, as a family we quietly regarded it as a time to be with each other. We walked, cooked and read. Máire turned into Mary Berry and baked every day, the consequences of which I'm still trying to deal with.

We had no staff worries as they were all taken care of by the government. Nothing could break down as nothing was being used. We all stayed in touch to make sure we were okay and good to go when it all kicked off again.

My brief for writing my column was to keep it to 350 words, to include a description of the recipes. This turned out to be a challenge as I'm a bit of a warbler. In my previous time with the paper I was allowed to waffle away. This time, however, I had to fit in my musings but also make sure to give the recipe some relevance for the reader.

I was disciplined. Every week's article would normally take four to five hours to write. Up early before anybody stirred was always the best time. Once it got into the bones of the day, I could never find the focus and restaurant duties took over.

I would always work from my notes from the photography days with Harry Weir, who was a joy to work with. Prep for the column and the shoot days always had a system. First, I'd send the ideas for 12 new dishes for the coming month to Marie Claire for approval. I shopped on the first day, tweaking my recipes in my head as the ingredients landed in the basket. The next day I prepped each dish, making initial notes. On the third day I completed the recipes as Harry styled and photographed them. It was always a hectic day as I cooked and scribbled.

In the mornings I'd tap one-fingered into my phone from my sometimes indecipherable notes, then email my piece to Máire, who would do a word count. Afterwards, we would both huddle around the desktop to edit. She would correct my appalling spelling and punctuation, then submit the piece. It was a self-inflicted, laborious process, for I am a caveman with a very patient wife.

So here it is, the complete collection of those columns and recipes in all its glory. I do hope it's a book that finds a place in your kitchen and on the stack of books you may have in your bedroom for curling up with. The recipes are for the most part simple and family oriented. All I can hope for the writing is that it gives you the odd laugh.

I've interspersed the book with some casual essays, mostly about my gallivanting. It's my dream for the future to do more. Who knows, I might even write about it.

Notes on the recipes

All the recipes in this book originally appeared in the *Irish Times* on the date listed. If you would like to see a photo of the dish, you can look it up online on the *Irish Times* website.

All the oven temperatures in the book are for a fan oven. If you are using a conventional oven, just increase the temperatures by 20°C.

All eggs are large unless stated otherwise and ideally free-range.

All butter is salted unless stated otherwise.

Salt and pepper are not included in the ingredients lists unless a specific amount is called for, but all dishes should be seasoned to taste.

Glad to be back

02 NOVEMBER 2019

It's been the bones of 15 years since I regularly wrote the food column for the *Irish Times*. Back then I used to write in indecipherable longhand, then pass the sauce-stained A4 tragedy to my wife to figure out and type through gritted teeth.

I've become a little more self-sufficient with the advent of smartphones. My finger cautiously stabs the letters onto my notes. I curse my varifocals, eventually abandoning them altogether in utter frustration. I eventually get it done but I still have to run it by the boss because apparently my punctuation leaves a lot to be desired. It's around now that I would use the eye-roll emoji that I have become addicted to on social media but that is not appropriate for proper grown-up writing.

I'm thrilled to be back. Those articles all those years ago literally made us at the Tannery, our restaurant in Dungarvan, Waterford. We were cooking good food, but we needed people to travel to us to sustain a year-round business.

We opened rooms and a cookery school, as I was evangelical about passing on my love of cooking to others. Over the years, the food I teach there has become less cheffy and more family orientated — the arrival of our own two girls focused my mind.

In the early years of the Tannery, our home took second place. We never got to spend much time there. It was just a place to sleep and do some serious couch surfing on our day off, usually with a dodgy takeaway as I simply could not chop another onion.

There were times set aside, of course, for fantastically wild parties, for everyone knows that restaurant people know how to work hard but are also adept at letting off steam. The house became a Mecca for off-duty restaurant people. This was around the time Dungarvan was rechristened Fungarvan. I frequently wrote about those great times and the people we encountered to ensure I had some sort of catalogue of the shenanigans. I still have every copy of the *Irish Times Magazine* that I contributed to during that time. It was three and a half years of great memories and the great food that went with them.

Years later, the same friends still come but now I love to cook at home. We have some wine and watch the telly, and by 11 p.m. we're all nodding off. How times have changed.

Children change the dynamics of a house. They give it life and a purpose. All of a sudden it's not about us anymore, but that's okay. The hours that we grasped for ourselves before are now the hours that we spend ferrying children to piano lessons or swimming. Every parent knows what it's like. Cooking at home is far more important than any complicated creation that any chef can make. It literally shapes our children and can make every house a home.

These articles will focus on seasonality. I know it's a cliché, but for someone who loves to cook it is as important as a painter's palette. I'll be doing simple recipes that give comfort, whatever the time of year. I will try to give you a little giggle whenever I can, but this might depend on there not being any drama in the restaurant that day.

I still love food. I suppose I've slowed down a bit, although I would categorically state that I haven't got any more sense (cue eye-roll emoji).

So stay with me when you can and let's see what happens.

BAKED EGGS WITH CHORIZO, CREAM AND PARMESAN

SERVES 4

melted butter, for greasing
8 medium eggs
12 thin slices from a small chorizo
8 tbsp cream
a little grated Parmesan cheese

Preheat the oven to 180°C. Brush four decent-sized ramekins with melted butter.

Crack one egg into each ramekin, drop in three slices of chorizo, then crack another egg on top. Season with salt and pepper, then spoon 2 tablespoons of cream on top and sprinkle over a little grated Parmesan. These can be done ahead of time and refrigerated.

Bake in the oven for 12 minutes, until there is just a little jiggle in the middle.

Serve with a grilled wedge of buttered country bread or even better, sourdough.

FLYNNY'S LAMB HOTPOT
(FOR LONG-TIME FANS OF *CORONATION STREET*)

SERVES 4

350g diced lamb shoulder

3 tbsp country relish

1 tbsp prepared English mustard

a few sprigs of fresh thyme

200g broth mix (widely available in supermarkets in the health food aisle – a mix of barley, lentils and split peas)

400ml water

400ml cider (optional but nice – replace with water if you don't have it)

1 chicken stock cube

5 medium Rooster potatoes, peeled and thinly sliced

a knob of butter

3 bay leaves (fresh if possible)

1 cinnamon stick

Preheat the oven to 160°C.

Put the lamb in the bottom of a medium-sized pot or casserole with high sides. Add the relish, mustard and thyme, season with salt and pepper and mix well. Sprinkle the broth mix evenly over the top.

Pour the water and cider into another pot, add the chicken stock cube and a little salt and pepper. Bring to a simmer briefly, whisking to dissolve the stock cube.

Cover the lamb and broth mix by overlapping the sliced potatoes on top. They should make two layers or so. Pour the cider stock gently over the top – your potatoes will be immersed, but don't worry. Dot butter over the top of the spuds, then intersperse the bay leaves and cinnamon stick with the potatoes.

Cover the pot or casserole tightly with a lid or foil and cook in the oven for 1 hour 15 minutes. Turn the heat up to 190°C. Remove the lid or foil and cook for 25 more minutes, until the potatoes are golden and crisp.

This would be lovely with a generous blob of redcurrant jelly and a crisp green salad.

CROISSANTS WITH HOT APPLES, PEARS, BROWN SUGAR AND CREAM

SERVES 4

a knob of butter, for greasing

3 pears, peeled, cored and cut into quarters

2 Gala apples, peeled, cored and cut into quarters

2 fresh bay leaves or a few sprigs of fresh thyme

2 tbsp golden brown sugar

150ml cream

4 croissants, cut in half lengthways

Preheat the oven to 180°C. Rub a baking dish with a little butter.

Put the pears, apples and bay leaves or thyme in the dish and scatter over the brown sugar. Cover the dish tightly with foil. Cook in the oven for 15–20 minutes, depending on how ripe the pears are — the fruit should be soft and tender.

Peel back the foil and add the cream. Put the dish back in the oven for a further 5 minutes, until the cream starts to bubble and thicken.

To serve, carefully scoop out the hot fruit and cream and spoon it over the croissants.

Keep calm and cook

09 NOVEMBER 2019

I'm in training to be a hipster. I'm not quite sure if I'd fit in or not. I'm probably too old and I've no tattoos. I have the hair, though, and I give thanks for that every day, even if it rarely stays sculpted. It behaves itself for a while on the day that it's cut, but that's about it. I'm the permanent custodian of the Crazy Wild Man look. I've even cooked at the Big Grill Festival a couple of times in an effort to join a different, cooler tribe, but I don't think I fit in there either. So I suffer on with an incurable case of cool envy.

I'm fascinated with hipsters because they all seem so unflappable. I, however, invented flappable. I love a good panic. Observing a hipster making a hand-crafted coffee makes me nervous. I shuffle and fidget as I'm always in a rush, forever edgy, thinking about my day. Steam inevitably comes out my ears, but I am not a complainer, I remind myself (cue loud guffaws). Serves me right for stopping in that sort of joint anyhow.

My calm time comes on a Sunday evening. I get home from work after lunch, and once I've ensured my teenage girls' rooms are reasonably tidy, I can relax (it's my OCD and they love me for it). The restaurant doesn't open on Sunday evenings in the winter, so it's all about the hygge. I can't describe how much we look forward to it.

We follow a routine. It works best in the winter months, especially on cold, wet days, as there's no guilt about not going for a walk. There is always music, lots of papers with the food sections open and perhaps a G&T. The girls watch some TV and my wife and I read in contented silence.

I can't make complicated food on a Sunday night. The effort wilts me and I can't be bothered with a mountain of washing up. Sometimes I make a lame attempt to Instagram the process under the stern eye of my 14-year-old, as I'm utterly stupid when it comes to technology. An earlier Insta effort turned into a car crash when the wine caught up with me while cooking a lengthy roast duck dinner. Apparently it's important to show the finished dish, the money shot. Another lesson learned.

GRAPE AND PARMESAN RISOTTO
SERVES 6

1.2 litres chicken stock

80g butter

1 tbsp olive oil

1 onion, finely chopped

2 bay leaves (fresh if possible)

400g Arborio risotto rice

1 glass of white wine

100g Parmesan cheese, grated

30 mixed seedless grapes, cut in half

a drizzle of your best olive oil (optional)

Heat the stock to just below the simmering point.

In a separate large saucepan, melt the butter with the oil over a medium heat. When the butter starts to foam, add the onion and bay leaves, cover the pan with a lid and cook slowly for about 20 minutes, until the onions are tender.

Add the rice, stirring until it's coated with butter. Add the wine, stirring until it has all been absorbed by the rice.

Pour half of the hot stock over the rice and bring to a gentle boil, making sure there is no rice left up the sides of the pan or it will stay hard and fall in later. You only need to stir once or twice until the stock is absorbed.

Add the rest of the stock one ladleful at a time from now on, stirring until it's all been absorbed before you add the next ladleful. You might not need to use all the stock.

When the rice is just tender but still a little runny, stir in most of the grated Parmesan, keeping a little back for garnish. Remove the bay leaves, then season.

Spoon the risotto onto warm plates. Scatter the grapes on top, sprinkle over the rest of the Parmesan and away you go. If you have fancy olive oil, you could drizzle a little over the top at this stage too.

CONFIT DUCK WITH SWEET POTATOES, APPLES AND GINGER

SERVES 4

800g sweet potatoes, peeled and cut into large, even-sized chunks

a small piece of ginger, peeled and finely chopped

2 tbsp sunflower oil

2 Granny Smith apples, cored and each cut into 6 wedges

a few fresh sage leaves or sprigs of fresh thyme

4 confit duck legs

Preheat the oven to 180°C.

Put the sweet potatoes and ginger in a roasting tin. Drizzle over the oil and season with salt and pepper, tossing to coat. Roast in the oven for 20 minutes.

Remove the tray from the oven and turn the potatoes over, then add the apples and fresh herbs.

Scrape off the excess fat from the duck legs, then put them on top of the sweet potatoes and apples, skin side up. Put the tray back in the oven and cook for 20 more minutes. Serve hot.

ROAST BUTTERNUT SQUASH WITH SPROUTS AND PARMESAN CREAM

SERVES 4

1 butternut squash, halved lengthways and deseeded

a drizzle of olive oil

a few sprigs of fresh thyme, plus extra to garnish

300g Brussels sprouts

FOR THE PARMESAN CREAM:

250ml cream

2 garlic cloves, crushed

½ vegetable stock cube

80g Parmesan cheese, finely grated

a squeeze of lemon

Preheat the oven to 180°C.

Score the flesh side of the squash 1cm deep. Put the two halves in a roasting tin, cut side up, then drizzle over some oil, scatter fresh thyme leaves on top and season with salt and pepper. Cover the tray tightly with foil and roast in the oven for 1 hour. Remove the foil and cook for 30 minutes more, until the squash is soft and tender and has a little colour. Once cooked, you can keep it warm or reheat to serve.

Bring a pot of lightly salted water to the boil. Add the sprouts and cook for 3–4 minutes, until just tender. Drain and refresh in iced water until cold, then set aside.

To make the sauce, bring the cream to a gentle simmer in a medium-sized saucepan. Add the garlic and the stock cube and continue to simmer until the cream has reduced by one-third. Whisk in most of the Parmesan, then add a squeeze of lemon juice and season with salt and pepper.

To serve, warm the sprouts gently in the Parmesan cream. Spoon the sprouts and the sauce into the cavity of the squash and around the plate, then dust with the remaining Parmesan and garnish with a few sprigs of thyme.

PAUL FLYNN

I wish I was
Antonio Banderas

16 NOVEMBER 2019

I've fallen head over heels in love with Spain. I'm totally smitten. In my ignorance I avoided it for years after having a couple of unimpressive experiences in my early twenties in Fuengirola that left me as cold as an uneaten all-day English breakfast.

It was Majorca that broke the impasse. One large family holiday unlocked something in me. I shopped, swam, then cooked in the sun. I drank cheap wine and revelled in all the deep, garlicky flavours. I had lots of bad, predictable tapas that made me want to cook good Spanish food.

Then came Barcelona, many times. I had my 40th there. The Boqueria market thrilled me time and time again, but then Las Ramblas began to bore me.

Madrid, with its history and majesty, gave me more than just food. It opened my eyes to the greatness of this incredible country.

A trilogy of cities in dusty, ancient Andalusia was the best education we could have ever given our girls for that week. The Alhambra in Granada filled us with awe in the proper sense of that much-abused word. An argument with my sat nav led me down the tiny, terrifying streets in the Jewish quarter in Córdoba. The locals enjoyed my efforts to extract my car. The episode has gone down in family history.

Watching my daughters eat clams in El Rinconcillo in joyous Seville filled my heart with quiet pride. The restaurant has been there since 1670. It reminds you that we are indeed just passing through.

Galicia came next. I walked the Camino with a friend from Vigo to Santiago de Compostela. It was a life-changing experience that had nothing to do with religion.

The tiny sparkling coves of the Costa Brava this last summer showed me yet another side of Spain. It was one of our best family holidays in this overexposed but most surprising part of Spain. We were beginning to wonder if we'll ever go anywhere else. Each trip shows us something new. It was clear I had become addicted.

A pilgrimage with friends to San Sebastián and the famous grill restaurant Extebarri was another delirious excursion. They both deserve the plaudits.

Then just a few weeks ago, another Camino, but not to Santiago this time. It was a walk from Bilbao to Santander with my brother Declan, who has just retired. All our lives we have been like ships in the night, always too busy to spend proper time together. It was a series of delicious encounters along the Cantabrian coast. We walked and talked all day and talked more into the night over many small cervezas. I'm very glad we went together.

You will have guessed by now that I don't need any encouragement to go to Spain. I love a Spanish influence in my food. I can be ultra-traditional or sometimes I change it around and make it my own, like this slightly eccentric turnip tortilla. The chicken dish is total lusty comfort food and is very easy to make. The chickpea dish is a staple that I use with so many things. It's particularly brilliant with this chicken dish, but it can also be used with fish, roasted veg or even served over rice on its own. Saffron is a luxury, of course, but it's the heartbeat of Spanish cooking and a staple of the keen cook's cupboard.

If I don't cook Spanish food for a period of time, I miss it. It won't be long before I go back. I feel drawn to Spain and its wonderful, gregarious people. I dream of conversing with them in their own language like some mystical Celtic Antonio Banderas. One day, perhaps.

TURNIP TORTILLA

SERVES 6

a splash of olive oil
½ turnip, roughly grated
1 large onion, sliced
350g potatoes, peeled and very thinly sliced (a mandolin is best for this)
4 garlic cloves, thinly sliced
1 sprig of fresh rosemary, finely chopped
100ml cream
8 eggs, beaten

Preheat the oven to 180°C.

Heat the oil in a large, non-stick, ovenproof frying pan on a low heat. Using your hands, squeeze all the water out of the grated turnip. Add the onion and turnip to the pan and cook for about 15 minutes, until soft. Add the potatoes, garlic and rosemary. Mix well, cover and cook for a further 15–20 minutes, then check to see if the potatoes are cooked through. If not, give them a bit more time. It's important that they are fully cooked.

Add the cream to the beaten eggs, then stir this through the potato and turnip mixture. Smooth out the top and transfer the pan to the oven. Cook for 20 minutes, until just set.

Remove the pan from the oven and loosen around the sides with a spatula. Turn the tortilla out onto a plate. This is lovely served warm or at room temperature with a generous blob of aioli.

CHORIZO, CHICKEN AND BUTTER BEAN BAKE

SERVES 4

8 skinless chicken thighs, bone in

1 sprig of fresh rosemary

a drizzle of olive oil

1 x 400g tin of butter beans, drained and rinsed

200g chorizo, cut into chunks

2 garlic cloves, sliced

juice of ½ orange

200ml cream

½ tsp smoked paprika

Preheat the oven to 185°C.

Put the chicken thighs and rosemary in a roasting tin. Drizzle some oil over the top and season. Cook in the oven for 20 minutes, then add the rest of the ingredients. Stir everything together, making sure it's all coated, but leave the chicken thighs skin side up.

Return the tray to the oven to cook for a further 15 minutes or so, until the chicken is completely cooked through. Season and serve over rice.

SAFFRON CHICKPEAS WITH SULTANAS AND ORANGE

SERVES 4

1 heaped tbsp sultanas

1 orange

a small pinch of saffron

1 x 400g tin of chickpeas, drained and rinsed

1 garlic clove, crushed

1 tsp honey

a pinch of chilli flakes

150ml light olive oil

Soak the sultanas in a bowl of just-boiled water for 15 minutes to plump them up, then drain.

Zest half of the orange, then squeeze out the juice of both halves. Warm the orange juice and zest in a small saucepan, then add the saffron and allow to infuse for 5 minutes.

Add the soaked and drained sultanas and the chickpeas, garlic, honey, chilli flakes and oil. Season to taste. This is delicious served warm.

Turnip head

23 NOVEMBER 2019

I never got the allure of baby vegetables. In fact, they always annoyed me and turned me into a grumpy old man. In my mind, they were jumped-up, overpriced little upstarts that required tweezers to pirouette them onto the plate. Not my style of cooking, I would pompously harrumph. I will suffer the occasional baby beetroot but only to indulge the frilly vanity of gravadlax.

I like my vegetables big, something that can take the hardships of an Irish winter. Cutting them into manly chunks gives me enormous satisfaction and makes me feel even more masculine. I invariably roast them, bathed in cider, butter, cinnamon and a bit of fresh thyme or a bay leaf. Their dusky, nutty glaze awaits to comfort and soothe you.

I want to be brave enough to change the way I cook. We are driven by the consumption of meat and we are conditioned to the idea of meat and two veg being a meal. This is both primal and traditional. I love meat but sometimes I feel that relegating vegetables to the supporting act grossly underrates them and doesn't challenge me. I would be happy to sit down to a plate of glistening roasted roots punctuated with sticky oxtail or duck with a cooling river of horseradish cream to complete the picture.

This week's dishes are favourites of mine because they are a mixture of everyday and fancy. I like to have the parsnips with almost anything, especially roast chicken. This quirky cheese dish can be anything you like: a starter, a lunch or a cheese course. It dignifies the turnip and is robust enough to stand up to the Crozier Blue, a beautiful blue cheese.

Jerusalem artichokes make me happy. They are unsung heroes of mine. Unfortunately they aren't all that easy to get, but if you do come across them, this is a wonderful dish. I usually scrub the knobbly roots, then slowly roast them in duck fat, thyme and skin-on garlic with a whisper of golden brown sugar at the end, but here I've given them an olive oil treatment. They are sweet, crispy and gooey, all in one mouthful. This, to me, is cooking: the transformation of a humble ingredient into something surprising just by being thoughtful and curious.

STICKY PARSNIPS WITH SHERRY AND SMOKED BACON
SERVES 4

6 medium parsnips, peeled
100ml water
100ml cream sherry (optional)
1 sprig of fresh thyme or sage or a few bay leaves (fresh if possible)
125g smoked bacon lardons
a large knob of butter
a drizzle of olive oil
a drizzle of honey

Preheat the oven to 180°C.

Cut the tops off your parsnips, then cut them in half lengthways. Put them in a roasting tin, cut side facing down. Add the water, sherry (if using) and herbs, then scatter over the bacon and dot the butter on top. Drizzle with oil and season.

Cover the tray with foil, making sure it's nice and tight so no steam escapes. Cook in the oven for 20 minutes. You can do all this in advance and finish the dish later.

Take the foil off, drizzle over the honey and turn the parsnips in the juices. Return to the oven to cook for another 15 minutes, until the parsnips are tender and the bacon is crisp. Serve hot.

CIDER-GLAZED TURNIP WITH CROZIER BLUE AND CHARD

SERVES 4

1 small turnip, peeled and diced into 1cm pieces (you will need a good knife for this, as it can be a little tricky)

a knob of butter

300ml cider

1 sprig of fresh thyme

1 tbsp Demerara sugar

a pinch of ground allspice

200g Crozier Blue cheese, broken into uneven chunks

a handful of chard (this can be hard to get, so use whatever greens you can find)

a drizzle of olive oil

a few drops of red or white wine vinegar

Put the turnip, butter, cider and thyme in a frying pan set over a medium heat. Cover and cook for 10 minutes. Remove the lid, then add the sugar, allspice and some salt and pepper. Gently cook the turnips until the cider becomes a sticky glaze and the turnips are tender.

Dress the greens with the oil and vinegar and season. Scatter on top of the warm turnips along with the Crozier Blue to serve.

WARM SALAD OF JERUSALEM ARTICHOKES, LEEKS AND PARMA HAM

SERVES 4

100ml olive oil

8–10 large Jerusalem artichokes, peeled and halved

2 small leeks, cut into slices 1cm thick

2 garlic cloves, sliced

16 walnut halves

8 fresh sage leaves

juice of ½ lemon

2 tbsp red wine vinegar

1 tbsp maple syrup

8 slices of Parma ham

Preheat the oven to 180°C.

Add a drizzle of the oil to a roasting tin. Add the artichokes, tossing to coat, and cook in the oven for 10 minutes. Stir in the leeks, garlic, walnuts, sage and the remaining oil, then return to the oven to cook for a further 15 minutes. Stir in the lemon juice, vinegar and maple syrup, then season to taste.

Serve warm with two slices of Parma ham draped on top of each serving.

Hello again, my love

30 NOVEMBER 2019

I have a conflicted relationship with France. In recent years, I have foolishly abandoned her in favour of Spain and Italy. It was an accidental drift rather than something premeditated.

I went back to France recently for a quick trip with friends. I hadn't been to Provence in 25 years, even though Provençal food is something I know well and very much love. I wanted to eat bouillabaisse, pissaladière and aioli by the bucketful, washed down with as much pastis and rosé as I could get into me. I was determined to live out all the clichés in a few short days. The mistral was puffing intermittently and I was in her lee.

One restaurant in particular piqued my interest. I had been told about it many times and I'd seen the photos of the gargantuan feasts eaten in dappled sunlight. I badly wanted to go.

Auberge de la Môle is the restaurant of my dreams. It's been there for decades, by the side of the road in a dusty old village about 30 minutes inland from St Tropez. An ancient bar tabac nestles in the corner with a simple awning over the generous terrace. Apparently it's not unusual to see Joan Collins lunching there, as ageless and starry as ever.

They have two simple menus: €35 or €55 at night. There is limited choice, but unfathomable portions of French country classics spill onto the table. They don't take credit or debit cards but considering that the wine list goes up to €4,000, I wondered how this was dealt with. Do you simply stuff your pockets with notes? Or discreetly ask your minder to hand over the cash on your behalf? Both, I suppose.

I knew the menu by heart. A selection of terrines, rillettes and pâtés to start. A small choice for main course: duck confit or magret, a heaving cassoulet or a cèpes omelette. There was also wild boar on as a special that day. It was somewhat dull of us, but we all had the confit. It came with sauté potatoes, a green salad and a bowl of eye-watering mustard. It was perfect.

Next came cheese. That's the way it should be. Then a rippled trough of chocolate mousse to share, accompanied by a terrine of deep, dark creme caramel. Lastly, a bowl of prunes in Armagnac was quietly placed on the table. It was a memorable afternoon.

French food is my first love. Of course it has its regal haute cuisine, but I'm drawn to the simple cuisine paysanne, the recipes that are rooted in time, regionality and tradition. If you're fortunate enough to eat French food in such a bucolic setting as I did that day, it's something you will never forget. These recipes are a short and simple homage to a great culinary tradition.

LAMB AU VIN

SERVES 4

a good knob of butter

3 red onions, peeled and quartered

125g smoked bacon lardons

250g chestnut mushrooms, cleaned and halved

4 garlic cloves, sliced

1 tbsp plain flour

1 chicken stock cube dissolved in 400ml boiling water

250ml red wine

a few sprigs of fresh thyme or sage

1 tbsp golden brown sugar

8 gigot lamb chops

Preheat the oven to 160°C.

Melt the butter in a large, heavy-based casserole over a medium heat. Add the onions and cook for 2 minutes, then add the bacon, mushrooms and garlic. Cook for 3 minutes or so, then add the flour and cook for a couple of minutes more. Add the stock, wine, herbs and sugar and bring to a simmer.

Season the chops and add them to the casserole, making sure they are covered with the liquid as much as possible. To help, put a piece of greaseproof paper or baking parchment on top and press everything down.

Transfer the casserole to the oven and cook for 1 hour 15 minutes, until the lamb is tender and the sauce has thickened. There may be some lamb fat sitting on the surface. You can mop this up with kitchen towel if you wish, but I eat it. Now there's a surprise.

Serve with mash.

MY TARTE FLAMICHE

SERVES 4

a drizzle of olive oil

1 x 320g packet of ready-rolled puff pastry, thawed

100ml sour cream

5 new potatoes, cooked and sliced

1 onion, very thinly sliced

125g smoked bacon lardons

a few fresh thyme leaves (optional)

Preheat the oven to 175°C.

Brush a baking tray lightly with oil. Unwrap the pastry onto the tray. Pierce it numerous times with a fork but leave an edge all round, unmarked.

Smooth the sour cream evenly over the pastry, almost to the edges. Add the cooked and sliced potatoes, then scatter over the onion slices, followed by the bacon and thyme. Cook in the oven for 20 minutes, until glazed and golden.

Serve with a green salad.

MUSSELS WITH FENNEL AND PERNOD
SERVES 2

1kg fresh mussels
a drizzle of olive oil
1 fennel bulb, outer leaves removed, then halved lengthways and thinly sliced
2 shallots, sliced
2 garlic cloves, sliced
200ml cream
50ml Pernod (or substitute with 100ml white wine and 2 star anise)

To prepare the mussels, immerse them in a clean sink of cold water. Agitate. Debeard them one by one into a clean bowl, discarding any that are open and won't close when you gently tap them on the counter. Drain and clean the sink, fill it with cold water again and re-immerse the debearded mussels. Agitate the mussels once more, then lift them from the water, leaving any sediment behind.

Heat the oil in a large saucepan over a medium heat. Add the fennel, shallots and garlic and sauté until soft. Add the cream and Pernod, then the mussels. Cover the pan with a tight-fitting lid, raise the heat to high and cook, stirring once or twice, until all the mussels are open (discard any that are still closed).

Serve with crusty bread.

How to roast a cauliflower like a pro

07 DECEMBER 2019

I make time to leaf through my cookbooks, not to write my menu, as this had to be done long before now. Such is the nature of things, as people plan their Christmas parties months ahead. People who truly love food cherish their cookbook collection. Delia is a Christmas goddess to me, if any further proof were needed that I am old-fashioned at heart. Her Christmas and winter cookbooks are unsurpassed. Diana Henry is another hero. Her books are inspirational treasures. I always have Nigel Slater close by too. His book *The Christmas Chronicles* is a fairy tale of the Christmas we all wish we'd had.

I am a compulsive list maker. These weeks approaching Christmas are all about preparation. Chutneys, pickles, jellies, fudges and mulled fruit are all made and stored in the quieter days before the run-up to the madness. The home cook can do this too. Planning what you cook is half the battle.

For example, I start mulling pears in the first days of December. I cheat by using prepared mulled wine from a supermarket, then pimp it up by adding star anise, cloves and cinnamon. A hint of orange peel, two fresh bay leaves and a spoonful of redcurrant jelly enhance it beyond belief. Get in early, though, as it sells out quickly.

I've treated this cauliflower like a roast dinner. I wanted a meatless centrepiece that could be the star of the show, even on Christmas Day. I've come late to Middle Eastern flavours — a result, no doubt, of my rigid and sometimes insular classical French training — but thankfully I've always been curious and hungry both for knowledge and the food itself. Dukkah is a wonder. Its nutty, fiery crunch enhances dishes when the mood takes me. It's particularly good with roast root veg, salads and this cauliflower dish.

The apple and cinnamon butter is a brilliant thing to have in the fridge for pâtés, cold meats or even grilled cheese sandwiches.

A CHRISTMAS CAULIFLOWER
SERVES 2

zest and juice of 1 lemon

4 tbsp olive oil

3 tsp paprika

1 tsp ground cinnamon

1 whole cauliflower

300ml vegetable stock

80g butter, diced

250g chestnut mushrooms, left whole

1 garlic clove, thinly sliced

a splash of port or sweet sherry

2 handfuls of baby spinach

a handful of salted almonds

20 seedless black grapes, halved

Preheat the oven to 165°C.

Put the lemon zest and juice in a bowl along with the oil, paprika, cinnamon and some salt and pepper. Mix into a paste, then rub it all over the cauliflower, making sure you get it into every nook and cranny.

Put the cauliflower in a shallow casserole or baking dish and pour the stock all around. Transfer to the oven and cook for 1 hour 15 minutes. Add the butter, mushrooms, garlic and port or sherry, then return to the oven to cook for a further 10 minutes.

Remove the cauliflower, then add the spinach to the casserole or baking dish, tossing to coat in the cooking juices. Allow to wilt a little for 1–2 minutes over a gentle heat. Season.

To serve, spoon the spinach onto the centre of a serving plate. Put the cauliflower on top, then scatter over the almonds and grapes.

DUKKAH

SERVES 4

50g sesame seeds
50g butter
2 tsp coriander seeds, roughly ground
1 tsp cumin seeds, roughly ground
80g roasted cashews, roughly chopped
a pinch of chilli powder

Lightly toast the sesame seeds in a dry saucepan over a low heat, stirring regularly, until they begin to colour. Set aside.

Melt the butter over a low heat, allowing it to brown a little. Add the ground coriander and cumin and cook, stirring, for 2 minutes, then add the nuts and toasted sesame seeds. Reduce the heat and cook for 2 minutes more, still stirring. To finish, add the chilli powder and season with salt.

This will last for two weeks in the fridge. Its nutty, fiery crunch enhances dishes, particularly roast root veg, salads and even a sultry roasted cauliflower.

APPLE CINNAMON BUTTER

250g butter

3 large cooking apples, peeled, cored and diced

1 tbsp ground cinnamon

80g light brown sugar

200ml cider

Melt the butter in a saucepan. When it starts to foam, add the apples and cinnamon and cook gently for 2 minutes. Add the brown sugar and cider and simmer gently for 20 minutes, until the apples have mostly broken down and the cider has evaporated. Blitz with a hand blender and put in clean jars. Cool, cover and refrigerate.

My secret for perfect roast turkey

14 DECEMBER 2019

We occasionally wonder what Christmas would be like if we didn't have it at home. There are many fine hotels around the country offering packages that would pamper us into bigger pants within hours of arriving.

It's always hectic. The restaurant is heaving on Christmas Eve and somehow we have to get things ready at home for our own family. We always manage it, though. I go home and set things up. I light the candles and the fire. I set the all-important mood.

When it comes to it, we couldn't move from the house. We love Christmas at home too much. There are usually 12 of us, including the cousins from Zurich. They are as close as brothers and sisters. The house trembles with excitement and anticipation. There are lots of presents despite the sensible Kris Kindle.

There's very little sleep over these few days. Christmas morning bustles while it's still dark outside. 'They're up already,' we groan, but we're excited for them so we haul ourselves out of bed. Did Santa eat his biscuits? Did Rudolph eat his carrot? Then it's a simple, lazy breakfast, the teenagers lounging around the house in their Christmas PJs.

The turkey is in by now. (I'm allowing 35 minutes per kilo for a room temperature bird.) The ham was done the day before. I'm busy cooking but I do have help, plus I always get a few sneaky jobs done in the restaurant in the preceding days. This is an advantage of having your own chefs.

I feel like turkey has been inflicted on me, even though I've written recipes for it as my duty. The only reason it graces my table at Christmas is because others want it. Sure, I get the symbolism of it all, but for the most part, turkey just leaves me cold — they don't use that expression for nothing.

So if I have to have it, I like to break with tradition and I cook the bird with cider. It imbues an appley moistness to the meat and goes wonderfully with the stuffing. I use the cooking juices to form the gravy. It isn't brown but I'm not one bit worried.

This is my favourite stuffing. I've been making it for years to stuff inside many a bird. It has a Spanish accent and the flavours combine to lift even the most pedestrian of turkeys.

Sprouts are heaven. I even eat them cold, like stinky little gobstoppers, much to my wife's delight. This gratin is different — crunchy and lovely. You can prepare stage one with the breadcrumbs on top and finish the baking when you're ready to eat.

I hope these recipes help. Don't get too stressed. Delegation is the way to go. The cook should be the first on the couch with a little glass of something. Then have the inevitable snooze knowing that the leftovers will do for tomorrow.

CHORIZO, ORANGE AND ALMOND STUFFING

MAKES ENOUGH FOR 1 X 5–6KG TURKEY OR SERVES 10–12

100g raisins

200g butter

2 medium onions, finely chopped

200g chorizo, finely diced (use the kind that's already sliced, it's very handy)

500g fresh white breadcrumbs

100g toasted flaked almonds

zest of 1 orange

a handful of fresh parsley, finely chopped

Soak the raisins in a bowl of just-boiled water for 15 minutes to plump them up, then drain.

Melt the butter in a large frying pan over a medium heat. When it starts to foam, add the onions and cook slowly for 20 minutes, until soft and translucent. Add the chorizo and cook for a further 5 minutes, until its oil renders out. Remove the pan from the heat, then add the drained raisins, breadcrumbs, almonds, orange zest, parsley and seasoning. Reserve for stuffing the turkey.

This is also a lovely stuffing for chicken – the amount made is enough for at least two. Freeze what you don't need for another time.

CIDER ROAST TURKEY

SERVES 6–8

1 x 5–6kg turkey

4 onions, cut into thick slices

125g smoked bacon lardons

2 cinnamon sticks or a pinch of ground cinnamon

2 large sprigs of fresh sage or thyme

2 x 440ml cans of cider

250g butter, melted

Preheat the oven to 170°C.

Remove the neck and giblets from inside the turkey and set aside. Trim any excess fat from the opening and stuff the turkey with the chorizo, orange and almond stuffing (page 35), taking care not to pack it too tightly.

Put the onions and smoked bacon lardons on the base of your roasting tin along with the turkey neck, cinnamon and herbs. Perch the turkey on top of the onions, then pour one can of cider around. Brush the turkey liberally with the melted butter and season well.

Cover the tin tightly with foil, making sure to seal around the edges. Cook in the oven for 2 hours 45 minutes.

Remove the tin from the oven and turn the heat up to 185°C. Remove the foil, then pour in the other can of cider. Put the tin back in the oven to roast for another 30 minutes. Baste the turkey a few times in this last phase to give the bird a lovely golden sheen.

When cooked, transfer the turkey to another tray, cover it loosely in foil and allow to rest.

Strain the cooking juices from the tin into a saucepan and let it settle. Any fat will rise to the top – ladle this off. Bring the juice to the boil and reduce by one-third. This is your gravy.

BRUSSELS SPROUT GRATIN

SERVES 6

125g smoked bacon lardons

1 tbsp duck fat

750g Brussels sprouts, shredded

a pinch of caster sugar

250ml cream

3 tbsp water

150g fresh white breadcrumbs

80g Gruyère cheese (or similar), grated

50g butter, melted

zest of ½ orange

6 fresh sage leaves, chopped

Preheat the oven to 170°C.

Sauté the bacon in a little of the duck fat until golden. Transfer the bacon to a shallow casserole or baking dish along with the sprouts, the remaining duck fat, a pinch of sugar and a little salt. Pour the cream and water over the top and mix well. Bake in the oven for 15–20 minutes, until the sprouts are just tender.

Mix the breadcrumbs with the Gruyère, melted butter, orange zest, sage and some salt and pepper, then sprinkle over the top of the sprouts. Return to the oven and bake for 12–15 minutes more, until crusty and golden. Serve hot.

Foolproof starters for Christmas Day dinner

21 DECEMBER 2019

The festive season is now upon us. It's been a long run-up. By now your fridge is probably bulging at the seams and your house will be blinking and twinkling like a constellation of stars.

As a cook and a food writer, Christmas always tugs at my heartstrings. I write about abundance, comfort and luxury and the creation of wonderful memories with your family while being acutely aware that we are the lucky ones. We work hard to create a safe and happy home for our children, but we also know that not everyone has had our chances in life. We try to instil in our children how fortunate we are.

Others make Christmas seem easy. Chefs like me are omnipresent, making it all look so simple, but there are so many expectations of the cook. It can be stressful and onerous. Some of us are delegators while some can't bear to have people around them. The most important thing for me is organisation, but then, I'm always on the edge of my precipitous OCD cliff.

If you're still stuck for a starter, I'm giving you three foolproof and elegant options. The crab claws are a festive and delicious version of crab claws in garlic butter. The pomegranate seeds settle like jewels on top. I like to serve this dish family-style so everyone can help themselves. Make sure you use an oven-to-table dish. You can prepare it ahead of time and just warm it through when you need it.

The blue cheese soufflé is undoubtedly a little more technical, but you can make it the day before, turn it out, then reheat it in a matter of minutes. It's lovely and not too heavy, as the name suggests. You can use any ripe blue cheese. For extra indulgence, make a quick Parmesan cream by bringing 250ml cream to the boil. Add 100g grated Parmesan, a twist of black pepper and a squeeze of lemon juice.

The potted salmon is a dream. It's soft and silky, perfect with pickled cucumber for a stress-free starter that you can make a day or two ahead.

CRAB CLAWS WITH ORANGE, POMEGRANATE AND ROSEMARY BUTTER

SERVES 4

125g butter
2 garlic cloves, crushed
zest and juice of 1 orange
1 sprig of fresh rosemary, finely chopped
400g cooked crab claws
4 spring onions, finely chopped
seeds and juice from 1 ripe pomegranate

Melt the butter in a frying pan over a medium heat. When it starts to foam, add the garlic, orange zest and juice and rosemary and cook for 1 minute. Add the cooked crab claws and spring onions. Warm everything through the butter and season.

Scatter the pomegranate seeds on top and drizzle over a little juice. Serve with crusty bread.

TWICE-BAKED CASHEL BLUE SOUFFLÉS

SERVES 8

FOR THE MOULDS:

50g butter, melted

100g panko breadcrumbs

FOR THE SOUFFLÉS:

30g butter

30g plain flour

240ml milk

4 egg yolks

300g Cashel Blue cheese, crumbled

6 egg whites

Preheat the oven to 190°C.

Brush eight soufflé moulds with the 50g of melted butter, then coat with the breadcrumbs, tipping out any excess. Set aside.

To make the soufflés, melt the 30g of butter in small saucepan, then whisk in the flour. Cook gently for 3 minutes to make a roux. Heat the milk in a separate pan, then gradually whisk it into the roux a little at a time to make a béchamel sauce. Remove the pan from the heat, then stir in the egg yolks and blue cheese.

In a separate clean, dry bowl, whisk the egg whites until firm. With a spatula, gently fold one-third of the egg whites into the cheese mix to introduce it, followed by the remaining egg whites.

Spoon the mixture into the ramekins until they are two-thirds full. Put the ramekins in a roasting tin and boil the kettle. Pour the boiling water around the ramekins until it reaches halfway up the sides. Transfer to the oven and bake for 16 minutes.

Remove the ramekins from the roasting tin. While still warm, run a knife around the edge of the ramekins and turn out the soufflés onto a buttered baking tray. These are now ready to be reheated just before serving. To reheat, cook in an oven preheated to 180°C for 10 minutes.

Serve with chutney or some diced apple and a little dressed salad.

POTTED SALMON

SERVES 6

1 egg
3 egg yolks
100g smoked salmon, skinned and finely diced
300ml cream
200ml milk
1 tbsp horseradish sauce

Preheat the oven to 140°C.

Whisk the eggs and egg yolks in a bowl. Add the smoked salmon, cream, milk and horseradish, then season.

Ladle the mixture among six ramekins, making sure you stir while you ladle so that the salmon is evenly distributed.

Put the ramekins in a roasting tin and boil the kettle. Pour the boiling water around the ramekins until it reaches halfway up the sides. Put the tin in the oven and cook for 20–25 minutes, until the mixture is just set but with a little wobble in the centre. Remove the ramekins from the tin and allow to cool before refrigerating.

Serve at room temperature with pickled cucumber.

Cracking Christmas cooking tips

There were eight children in my house when I was growing up. We lived over my father's chemist in the square in Dungarvan. I was the youngest.

The smells and flavours of Christmas are my most abiding memories. They seem to linger as hungry thoughts long after Christmas has passed.

It began in October, when my mother made the cake (it needed all that time to mature). I was always sent for the stout in exchange for the rights to lick the mixing bowl, which made me yearn for Christmas to come more quickly. It certainly got the ball rolling in terms of me thinking about the presents I was going to ask for, much to my parents' annoyance, no doubt.

Christmas stressed my mother with so many people in the house, all of them demanding something. There was always too much food — mountains of it overflowing indiscreetly from the plates — with lots of waste, inevitably, my dad tut-tutting all the while.

On Christmas morning we queued in sequence outside the locked door of the sitting room, where all our presents were designated a special place. Naturally I was first, eagerly waiting to squeeze myself into a long-awaited cowboy suit. I usually needed help, for I was a chubby little fella.

My parents always delivered — not an easy thing in difficult times. Whether it was the latest Beatles or Rolling Stones album for the boys or Bay City Rollers scarves or Max Factor make-up for the girls, it was there.

There was never a starter with our Christmas dinner. It was always turkey and ham, sprouts, mashed carrots and parsnips, peas and two types of potatoes. We always deliberated over the stuffing, for that was the Holy Grail. We all loved it and inevitably compared it to the previous year's, sometimes to my mother's dismay. We always drank Cidona, even my father. No Blue Nun in our house! For dessert we had trifle, ignoring the long-laboured-over Christmas cake.

Boyfriends and girlfriends called over then and took over the sitting room, humming along to Simon and Garfunkel and stealing kisses. I was brought in for a laugh, for by now my cowboy outfit was at breaking point. I was okay with it, though, because they gave me Milk Tray. Then as now, I would do anything for chocolate.

Some of the eldest helped my mother with the washing up. There was a lot of it, but she smoked her way through it, then went into the sitting room with a glass (or two) of Baileys. She loved a party. I was an ordinary Irish boy in an ordinary Irish house.

I adore Christmas. It's time for family, friends, fun and forgiveness. Food is central to everything in our house. Starting in early November, we have family discussions about what we are going to eat over the course of the holiday.

Food has changed enormously. We have so much choice. People expect more and mothers still get stressed. However, I want to leave stress at the door and want to help you do the same. So here are a few tips:

· Draw up menus. Nothing fancy, but it will give you a good idea of what to shop for. This way, you put structure on your shop and minimise food waste.

· Buy enough cranberry sauce.

· For nights in front of the telly or with visitors, have a cheese and charcuterie board with the finest selection of cheeses, cold meats and pâtés with tasty chutneys, bread and biscuits — no cooking required.

· On Christmas morning, serve smoked salmon on toasted brioche with tangy crème fraîche.

· For Christmas dinner, more is not more. If you're having turkey and ham, prepare as much as you can in advance. Don't do too many types of vegetables, including potatoes.

· Delegate.

· The cook should never, ever wash up — they should sit, watch telly and eat chocolate.

· Get someone else to make the Christmas night sandwiches and tea.

· Don't be afraid to have the same dinner the next day. In fact, I love it even more. The work is done and the pressure is off. You don't always have to make turkey curry; it's just more work.

· Take a walk. Get some fresh air over the Christmas break or your little man won't be able to fit into his cowboy outfit.

With seasonal wishes,

Paul (John Wayne) Flynn

My recipe for a happy Christmas

Christmas for me is all about the spices that magically generate scents and flavours I wouldn't dream of encountering in the height of summer. In my kitchen, you would be able to tell it's Christmas even if you were blindfolded.

This is what seasons should be, each one with their own story. Cloves, cinnamon, star anise, juniper, mixed spice are all eager notes in our Christmas dishes, forming their own memorable part in our culinary concerto.

Citrus is important too. It cuts through the indulgence with great aplomb. The orange and its cousins, the mandarin and clementine, preside over Christmas like the three wise men, their scent mingling with the spice in perfect harmony.

Booze comes to the fore at Christmas in more way than one. Rum, mulled wine, brandy, whiskey, sloe gin — they all play a more prominent part than they normally do. I generally don't believe that abundant alcohol makes cooking better, but at Christmas, boozy generosity seems to work. After all, it's a celebrated time of excess that we all pay for in the rueful weeks that follow.

In the cookery school, I sagely dole out advice about how to manage Christmas. People get stressed. I'm not supposed to. I apparently have the answers. I tell them the key is not to cook too much, to make lists. Plan with military precision and you'll be assured of success.

However, one Christmas I succumbed to everything I said I would never do. My steely resolve evaporated in the realisation that my opinion was as useful as a chocolate fireguard. It became obvious that I fell between the cat and the dog in terms of the pecking order in the house, as I live with three determined and opinionated women.

My pared-down, elegant Christmas dinner became a lumbering monster of excess. We were having visitors, you see, treasured family over from Zurich. In my ladies' opinions it was important that everyone's whims were catered for, so we ended up with three types of spuds, five types of veg and a table that groaned under the sheer weight of the feast.

To be clear, I love having a crowd at Christmas, particularly this bunch. They are all, without exception, no trouble and great fun. The pressure to cook so much food came from within my own camp.

Fortunately, though, help was at hand in the form of a talented stray chef and buddy of mine who shall remain nameless. He was at a loose end for his dinner, so I gladly nabbed him, relieved to trade hospitality for his much-needed labour.

It started off well but steadily descended into farce as he chose this day to 'discover' white wine. Two bottles later, he was thoroughly buckled and in isolation in the back room with only me for company, where he could safely unleash the filthy jokes and colourful language out of earshot of the kids.

Fearful, and with jangled nerves, we summoned his girlfriend to collect him at 9:00 that evening, whereby he plunged to his knees, professed his love and asked her to marry him. It was worthy of an episode of *Father Ted*. In retrospect, it was really one of the best Christmases ever.

I also use it as a threat to my girls, promising to invite Jimmy (he's obviously not called Jimmy) again this year if they don't tidy their rooms. It works and I relish the look of terror on their faces.

Christmas is special, but all of us in the hospitality industry have to juggle feeding our customers and taking care of our own families. Our great fear as parents is our children telling us that we were never there, we were always working. We have two days off, but that's okay. We're used to it and the nature of our business means that we have to be happily open when people want to eat and socialise. There have been enough tough times. It takes laughter and happy people to give a restaurant its soul.

Here's to a stress-free Christmas for everyone.

Bowled over

04 JANUARY 2020

I was a judge recently at the Euro-Toques Young Chef of the Year competition. Some of the techniques and cooking styles they used made my mind boggle. So much of it was new to me. Did you know that if you blend the dark part of the leek at 85°C with a little oil in a Thermomix, the chlorophyll sets and it won't discolour? Nope, me neither! Or have you ever smoked a chicken over birch twigs? Or drunk mushroom tea through reindeer moss? These young chefs were doing all this, and all under immense pressure too with us judges craning our necks, silent and looming.

I'm an old codger who cooks. I like simple, deep and pleasing flavours. The testosterone disappeared from my cooking a long time ago. However, I loved being with these young chefs. They are the future of Irish food. They inspired and invigorated me. I was proud to be in their company, and to be honest, I felt like a bit of a fraud judging them. Perhaps I was intimidated by all the machines – I'm a bang-it-in-the-oven-with-a-load-of-butter kind of guy.

I also got to judge with Michel Roux, a real food hero from an undeniable dynasty of culinary demigods. My eyelids and heart fluttered. I'm a fanboy and it showed. As he was leaving, I hugged him. I suspect he would have preferred a handshake. It was a great day.

I'm going to stick to what I know this week: heart-warming comfort food that's easy to make. To eat on your lap watching telly, perhaps; it's allowed once in a while. This kind of food is also handy for feeding a gang, no knife necessary. Some might call it a fork supper, but I'm rarely asked to those kinds of shindigs.

There's a little bit of prep with the pork meatballs, but once they're made, you can sit back while they cook in the oven. The lamb ragù is a favourite of mine, robust and wintery. I use a packet of gnocchi to make it easy. The chickpeas and black pudding is a classic Spanish tapa that is dear to my heart.

MEATBALLS WITH CHILLI, GINGER AND COCONUT
SERVES 4

500g pork mince

100g fresh white breadcrumbs

1 egg

3 spring onions, chopped

3 garlic cloves, chopped

2cm piece of ginger, peeled and grated

1 small fresh red chilli, deseeded and chopped

1 small bunch of coriander with the stalks, roughly chopped

1 chicken stock cube

200ml boiling water

1 x 400ml tin of coconut milk

3 tbsp soy sauce

75g cashew nuts

½ cucumber, peeled and diced

Preheat the oven to 180°C.

Put the pork, breadcrumbs, egg, spring onions, garlic, ginger, chilli, most of the coriander and some salt and pepper in a food processor. Pulse a few times, just until everything comes together. Don't over-blend or it will become pasty. Form into meatballs.

Crumble the stock cube into the boiling water in a large Pyrex jug, then add the coconut milk and soy sauce. Whisk together and pour into a baking dish. Add the meatballs, turning to coat them in the liquid. Cook in the oven for 25 minutes, until the meatballs are cooked through.

Scatter the cashews, cucumber and the remaining coriander over the top. Serve with jasmine rice.

RAGÙ OF LAMB AND STICKY ONIONS WITH GNOCCHI

SERVES 6

3 tbsp plain flour
750g diced lamb shoulder
3 tbsp olive oil
4 onions, sliced
4 garlic cloves, sliced
1 chicken stock cube
350ml water
4 tbsp balsamic vinegar
1 x 500g packet of gnocchi

FOR THE SALAD:
1 x 100g bag of rocket salad
25ml extra virgin olive oil
juice of ½ lemon
80g Parmesan cheese, grated

Preheat the oven to 160°C.

Put the flour in a large bowl and season with salt and pepper. Add the lamb and toss it in the seasoned flour, shaking off the excess.

Heat the oil in a heavy-based casserole over a medium-high heat. When it's gently smoking, carefully add the lamb and onions. Cook for 10 minutes, stirring occasionally to make sure everything caramelises evenly. Add the garlic and cook for a minute. Crumble in the stock cube, stir in the water and balsamic vinegar and bring to a simmer. Cover the casserole and cook in the oven for 75 minutes.

Cook the gnocchi as per the packet instructions, then drain and add to the lamb.

Dress the rocket in the oil and lemon juice, season and scatter the Parmesan on top. Serve the salad alongside the gnocchi.

CHICKPEAS AND BLACK PUDDING WITH GARLIC AND PARSLEY

SERVES 4

2 tbsp sultanas
2 tbsp olive oil
½ large onion, thinly sliced
1 garlic clove, crushed
1 x 400g tin of chickpeas, drained and rinsed
280g black pudding, cut into 1cm dice
1 tbsp pine nuts, toasted
a splash of sherry (if you have it)
a good pinch of chopped fresh parsley

Soak the sultanas in a bowl of just-boiled water for 15 minutes to plump them up, then drain.

Heat the oil in a saucepan over a low heat. Add the onion and garlic and sauté for about 15 minutes, until softened. Add the drained sultanas along with the chickpeas, black pudding, pine nuts and sherry (if using) and heat through, stirring all the time.

Add the parsley, season to taste and serve.

A delicious attempt to be good

11 JANUARY 2020

For a grown man it might seem ridiculous, but I'm fairly obsessed with my weight. It's always been so, for I was a plump little fella that got his own way most of the time, greedily feeding myself with biscuits and butter. I lost it in my teens and twenties but started to put it on again in my thirties, much to my wife's delight.

It came to a head when I saw a particularly copious photo of myself in the Aer Lingus *Cara* magazine – an international audience, what a coup. The next day I bought an exercise bike and noticed the weighing scales lurking in the bathroom. It took a lot of work and newly discovered restraint but I lost the guts of three stone over 18 months, thus heralding The Jeggings Years.

My self-confidence soared. I felt better and I started work on becoming the style icon I always knew I could be, Ireland's Gok Wan.

I lost the run of myself a bit. A lot, really. I didn't know jeggings were a thing until the women at a meeting told me. It was time to rein myself in a bit. I like to refer to that time as Peak Paul.

The jeggings still hang there forlornly, never to be worn by any sane man again. A reminder of more vainglorious times, a personal fall of Rome.

I still yo-yo and it disturbs me. My chins are like the rings of an oak tree – the older I get, the more I have.

These recipes are a post-Christmas redemptive effort to lose weight. Máire, my wife, is the determined woman in question. When she wants to lose weight, she approaches it with military precision and unwavering determination. I just hope she never wants to lose a husband.

Beetroot with feta is a classic but healthy and warm (you can use pre-prepared beetroot if you're under pressure). The soup is easy and lovely, with the avocado giving a richness to the young peas. The curry bursts with vegetables, goodness and satisfying flavours.

WARM BEETROOT SALAD WITH SMASHED FETA, ORANGE AND PUMPKIN SEEDS

SERVES 4 AS A STARTER

4 medium-sized beetroot
200g feta cheese
4 tbsp low-fat natural yogurt
1 tsp honey
a small pinch of chilli flakes
2 oranges – 1 squeezed, 1 segmented
50ml olive oil
2 tbsp pumpkin seeds, toasted
lots of fresh dill

Preheat the oven to 140°C.

Scrub the beetroot and wrap each one in foil. Cook in the oven for 1½ hours, until soft (test with a knife). When they are cool enough to handle, peel and cut into chunks.

Smash the feta with a fork and mix in the yogurt, honey, chilli flakes and seasoning.

Put the orange juice in a saucepan set over a medium heat and whisk in the oil. Add the beetroot, season and cook until warmed through.

Spoon a pool of the feta in the middle of each plate. Put the beetroot on top, followed by orange segments, pumpkin seeds and dill fronds. Drizzle the orange vinaigrette around the edge and serve.

SPICED PEA AND AVOCADO SOUP

SERVES 6

700g frozen petits pois
1 chicken stock cube
1.2 litres water
2 ripe avocados, diced
½ fresh green chilli, deseeded and diced
4 tbsp low-fat natural yogurt
½ tsp garam masala or mild curry powder

Bring the peas, chicken stock cube and water to the boil and cook for 5 minutes. Blend the soup with the avocados and chilli. Season.

Mix the yogurt with the garam masala or curry powder.

To serve, ladle the soup into bowls and add a spoonful of the spiced yogurt on top.

A DETERMINED WOMAN'S CURRY

SERVES 4

1 tbsp sunflower oil

2 garlic cloves, grated

3cm piece of ginger, peeled and grated

1 onion, finely chopped

½ small fresh red chilli, deseeded and finely diced

200g dried red lentils

2 tsp curry powder

1 carrot, cut into slices 5mm thick

1 cauliflower, broken into florets

1 vegetable stock cube

700ml water

1 x 400ml tin of low-fat coconut milk

1 bunch of fresh coriander, chopped

Heat the oil in a large casserole over a medium heat. Add the garlic and ginger and gently fry for 1 minute. Add the onion, chilli, lentils and curry powder and cook over a low heat for 5 minutes.

Add the carrot and cauliflower, then crumble in the stock cube and pour in the water. Bring to the boil, then reduce the heat and simmer for 20 minutes, until the vegetables are all cooked.

Turn off the heat, then stir in the coconut milk and season.

Serve with plenty of chopped fresh coriander.

Feeding teenagers

18 JANUARY 2020

I sometimes think back to what my favourite thing to eat was when I was at school. We ate dinner in the middle of the day back then. Everyone did.

The food in the house was always very simple — having cooked for seven other children, my mother was simply tired of cooking. Breakfast was unintentionally cursory. Sometimes the milk bottles were polished off on the doorstep on the way to school, much to my mother's chagrin.

As with many other families in the 1970s, you knew what you were getting every day of the week; it simply followed a rota. Monday was always beef stew. I used to mop up the juices with buttered sliced pan. Another day would be fish fingers and peas, which I still love to this day. Bacon and cabbage would always feature. I still crave this Irish staple with lashings of English mustard. Roast chicken on Sundays with new potatoes and more butter than was good for me. A fry on a winter's evening was a special treat. I was 18 and working in London when I had my first Chinese meal. Unthinkable now.

My girls are now 13 and 14, tall and hungry. The hormonal maelstrom has begun. I'm hanging on tight. We try to give them good food. I'm not dictatorial, but I am careful. They love burgers and pizza, like any teenagers. Family dinners can still be a bother, though. One girl eats everything and the other still doesn't eat veg, so there's always a compromise. My stubbornness won't allow me to do two dinners.

Here are a few crowd-pleasing staples from the Flynn household that might come in handy. The pasta bake is an easy little twist on macaroni cheese. Make it ahead and bake it when you want. Gnocchi is a trusty fallback in our house. Paired with sausages and some hopeful onions, it makes a hearty dinner. Duck quesadillas are brilliantly tasty. You can substitute the pickled cabbage for red onion jam if your little Johnny won't eat cabbage; I'd totally understand.

BAKED PASTA WITH CHORIZO AND PARMESAN

SERVES 4

300g fusilli, penne or rigatoni
1 x 240g tin of tomatoes
150ml cream
3 garlic cloves, chopped
1 chicken stock cube
a pinch of caster sugar
100g sliced chorizo, roughly chopped
100g Parmesan cheese, grated

Preheat the oven to 180°C.

Cook the pasta as per the packet instructions.

Meanwhile, blend the tomatoes, cream, garlic, chicken stock cube and a pinch of sugar together.

When the pasta is cooked, drain and put it back in the pot along with the sauce, chorizo and grated Parmesan. Season to taste and stir to combine, then transfer to a baking dish.

Bake in the oven for 15–20 minutes, until hot and bubbling. Serve with a green salad.

SAUSAGE, GNOCCHI AND RED ONION ROAST

SERVES 4

8 large sausages – use your favourite

3 red onions, quartered

4 garlic cloves, skin on

2 sprigs of fresh thyme

a drizzle of olive oil

1 x 500g packet of gnocchi

50g butter

80g Parmesan cheese, grated

Preheat the oven to 185°C.

Put the sausages, onions, garlic, thyme and oil in a roasting tin, turning to coat everything in the oil. Cook in the oven for 20 minutes, stirring once or twice, until the sausages and onions are golden and cooked through.

Meanwhile, cook the gnocchi as per the packet instructions. Reserve a small mugful of the cooking water, then drain.

Add the gnocchi and reserved cooking water to the roasting tin along with the butter and some salt and pepper, stirring to combine.

Divide among warm plates and scatter over the Parmesan to serve to serve.

DUCK QUESADILLAS

MAKES 4

80g butter, melted

8 plain tortilla wraps

4 tbsp sour cream

4 confit duck legs, skin removed and the meat shredded

200g mature Cheddar cheese, grated

4 heaped tbsp pickled red cabbage or red onion jam

Off the heat, brush a large non-stick frying pan with some of the melted butter, then put one tortilla on top. Spread a tablespoon of sour cream evenly over the tortilla, then scatter over some shredded duck, grated cheese and a tablespoon of pickled red cabbage or red onion jam. The objective is to make sure the quesadillas are thinly filled and don't fall apart. Put another tortilla firmly on top and brush with a little more melted butter.

Put the pan on a medium heat and cook for 3–4 minutes. Take a peek at the underside to make sure it's not browning too fast. When it's golden brown, turn deftly with a fish slice to flip it over and cook for another 3 minutes. Keep warm in a low oven and repeat with the remaining tortillas and filling.

Slide the quesadilla from the pan onto a chopping board and cut into wedges to serve.

It's not always all about spuds

25 JANUARY 2020

The best rice dish I ever ate was at a welcome dinner in France with the Scouts when I was 14: chicken a la crème, generously flecked with tarragon, nestling on buttery rice. I lapped it up like a happy little hound. The other boys were bewildered and disdainful and worried that this was the sort of food they we going to be forced to eat for the rest of the trip. I, however, was hopeful that this would be the case. More for me.

Although I didn't know it at the time, that was a lightbulb moment in my life. It sparked my curiosity about food. Just three years later, I was happily ensconced in the kitchen of a local restaurant with a life of cooking ahead of me.

I pity the blinkered cook and eater. Curiosity and appetite are such happy bedfellows. They make life so much richer.

Rice carries spice in a warm, comforting embrace. From a saffron-hued paella or a crisp-bottomed Iranian tahdig to a comforting risotto or just a simple rice pudding, I love them all. So many, all wonderful.

I use a rice cooker for this chicken pilaf. I'm not presuming everyone has a rice cooker, but it's the same timings if you cook it on the hob. The salad is a mushroomy winter version of that Italian staple, panzanella. We have it with steak. The bread carries all the flavours of everything else in the dish.

The lentils are a Tannery staple in the winter. They go with practically every main course, but sometimes I like to warm them gently and serve them with a soft, creamy goat cheese. An earthy, nutritious delight. A brilliant shortcut for lentils – and one that I use when I'm feeling lazy at home – is to take a tin of lentils and warm them through with a clove of crushed garlic, a little balsamic vinegar and a touch of olive oil, salt and pepper. Instantly delicious.

CHICKEN PILAF

SERVES 4

a large knob of butter

3 chicken breasts, cut into 2cm chunks

1 large leek, cut in half lengthways and thinly sliced

125g smoked bacon lardons

350g basmati rice

a pinch of ground cinnamon

700ml chicken stock

1 x 200ml tub of sour cream

1 tbsp spicy mango chutney

Preheat the oven to 170°C.

Melt the butter in a heavy-based casserole over a medium heat. When the butter starts to foam, add the chicken and brown it gently for a couple of minutes. Add the leek and bacon and cook for another minute or so. Add the rice and cinnamon and mix well, then add the stock and some salt and pepper.

Bring to a simmer, then cover with a lid and cook in the oven for 25 minutes. When the time is up, fluff the rice gently with a fork, then put a clean tea towel over the top of the casserole, without the lid, and leave it for a few minutes. This will remove any excess moisture.

Mix the sour cream and mango chutney together and serve it with the pilaf.

MUSHROOM, ROASTED BREAD AND SPINACH SALAD

SERVES 4

½ baguette, torn into pieces

150ml olive oil

250g button mushrooms, halved

250g chestnut mushrooms, halved

6 shallots, sliced

4 garlic cloves, thinly sliced

2 tbsp red wine vinegar

1 tbsp honey

250g baby spinach

Preheat the oven to 180°C.

Put the bread on a baking tray and drizzle with a little of the oil. Roast in the oven for 10–12 minutes, until golden and crunchy.

Put the remaining oil in a large pan (I like to use a wok) set over a medium-high heat. Heat until gently smoking, then add the mushrooms, shallots and garlic. Cook for 3–4 minutes, then add the red wine vinegar, honey and spinach. Season and turn the spinach through the mushrooms until it starts to wilt. Finally, add the toasted bread and fold it through.

Eat warm or at room temperature.

LENTIL VINAIGRETTE

SERVES 4

150g dried Puy lentils
1 slice of smoked streaky bacon
2 sprigs of fresh thyme
50ml olive oil
1 stick of celery, finely diced
1 small carrot, finely diced
1 shallot, finely diced
1 garlic clove, crushed
20ml red wine vinegar
1 tsp Dijon mustard
1 tsp honey

Put the lentils in a large saucepan and cover generously with cold water. Add the bacon and thyme and bring to a simmer. Cook for 15–20 minutes, until the lentils are soft but not broken up.

Meanwhile, heat half of the oil in a frying pan over a low to medium heat. Add all the diced vegetables and the garlic, cover the pan and gently sweat until just cooked – they must still have some bite.

Strain the lentils, reserving a little of the cooking water. Remove and discard the bacon and thyme.

Add the vegetables to the lentils along with the rest of the oil and the vinegar, mustard, honey and some salt and pepper.

Serve straightaway or reserve until needed – it will keep for up to a week in the fridge. Best served warm.

Beefy Flynn

01 FEBRUARY 2020

I have a farmer friend who I go out of my way not to disappoint. It's just not worth the guilt. His whole body curls with a sense of betrayal. His tone and expression suck at your very soul. It could be something as simple as not being able to meet him for a pint when you said you might, although those who know me know this doesn't happen very often.

Some weeks back, I wrote about cauliflower. I wanted to give a Christmas alternative. He sent me a text to say he was disappointed.

We met for a pint and discussed Cauliflowergate. He thinks I use too many vegetables. He was getting agitated. His hands were beginning to flap and his expression was tightening. He was well and truly piqued, something I'd rarely seen before. Although he's a metrosexual, disco-dancing farmer, Pat has been working with the land and animals since he was 14. He worries that as food gets cheaper, the farming community is getting squeezed out and underappreciated. He feels that food has little value these days and that the people who produce it have even less, it seems. Dungarvan is an agricultural town. We are surrounded by the people who produce our food and we need to support them.

This week is a tribute to the ways I like to cook our stunning, precious Irish beef. For me, it's never just about steaks or roasts. I love exploring different cuts, transforming them with simple techniques and sometimes unusual flavours.

I'm using beef shin in the osso buco. It might be hard to get, but if you ask your friendly butcher in advance I'm sure they would get it for you. Otherwise use chunky pieces of chuck. I use blackcurrant cordial to deepen the flavour, which goes well with the cabbage. To serve, I'm nicking the garnish of the glorious Austrian dish Tafelspitz, where apple and pungent horseradish are paired with the beef to delightful effect.

I also wanted to make derivatives of this lovely dish in case you have leftovers. One is a deeply flavoursome beef sandwich. The other is a pappardelle dish made with the slippery scrapings of the pan.

I'm an old codger who cooks. I like simple, deep and pleasing flavours.

04 JANUARY 2020

OSSO BUCO OF BEEF AND RED CABBAGE WITH APPLE SAUCE AND HORSERADISH CREAM

SERVES 4

50ml sunflower oil

2 tbsp plain flour

4 x 3cm pieces of beef shin cut across the bone (1.5kg) or 4 large pieces of chuck (1kg)

½ head of red cabbage, cut into 8 pieces

2 red onions, halved

4 garlic cloves, halved

500ml chicken stock (from a cube is fine)

350ml red wine

100ml blackcurrant cordial

2 star anise

2 strips of orange peel

1 cinnamon stick

FOR THE APPLE SAUCE:

2 cooking apples, peeled, cored and diced

50ml water

1 tbsp golden brown sugar

FOR THE HORSERADISH CREAM:

200ml cream

1 tbsp finely chopped fresh chives

1 tbsp hot horseradish sauce

Preheat the oven to 150°C.

Heat the oil in a wide, deep, heavy-based casserole over a medium-high heat until it's gently smoking.

Meanwhile, put the flour in a large bowl and season with salt and pepper. Add the beef and toss to coat, then shake off the excess.

Add the beef to the hot oil. When it's brown on both sides, transfer the beef to a plate, then carefully pour off the excess oil and leave the casserole off the heat.

Return the beef to the casserole along with the rest of the ingredients. Cover tightly with a lid or foil and bring to a simmer, then transfer to the oven to cook for 2½ hours, until the beef is soft and tender.

Meanwhile, to make the apple sauce, put the apples, water and brown sugar in a saucepan set over a medium heat. Cook for 10 minutes, until the apples break down into a deliciously lumpy purée. Serve warm or at room temperature.

To make the horseradish cream, whip the cream until it's slightly stiff, then fold in the chives and horseradish.

When the beef is done, carefully strain off the juices into a separate clean saucepan. Bring to the boil and reduce by half, then pour it back over the beef and cabbage.

Serve with the apple sauce and horseradish cream.

BEEFY CHEESE MELTS

MAKES 2

60g butter
1 onion, sliced
a pinch of caster sugar
a little leftover beef from the osso buco on pages 64–65
2 tsp Dijon mustard
a few slices of mature Cheddar cheese
4 slices of wholemeal bread

Melt the butter in a small saucepan set over a low heat. Pour a little out to brush the outside of the bread with later on.

Add the sliced onions to the butter in the pan. Cover with a lid and cook slowly for 15 minutes, then remove the lid, turn up the heat, add a pinch of sugar and cook until they turn golden. Season with salt and pepper, then fold in the leftover beef.

Spread the mustard on two slices of bread. Add the onion and beef mixture on top, followed by the cheese. Sandwich together with the other slices of bread and brush melted butter on the outside.

Put a non-stick frying pan over a medium heat. Add the sandwiches to the hot pan, buttered side down, then brush the top of the other slices. Cook until golden, then flip over and cook the other side until that's golden too, making sure the filling is soft and gooey. Serve hot.

PAPPARDELLE WITH BEEF AND RED CABBAGE

SERVES 4

500g pappardelle

50g butter

leftover juices, cabbage and beef from the osso buco (pages 64–65) – but don't worry if there's no meat, you will still have the beefy juices

leftover horseradish cream from the osso buco

lots of grated Parmesan cheese

Cook the pasta as per the packet instructions. Drain and add it back to the pot along with the butter, juices, cabbage and beef leftovers. Season with salt and plenty of freshly ground black pepper.

Divide among four warm plates. If you have horseradish cream left over, add a sneaky little dollop on top along with lashings of grated Parmesan to serve.

Stay home and cook something delicious

08 FEBRUARY 2020

Every 10 days or so I'm on the *Today Show* in RTÉ's Cork studio. Sometimes I go early to amble around and soak up the spirit of Cork. On one such morning last month, a woman stopped me and pressed a 20 cent coin wrapped in a note into my hand. It was Handsel Monday, a tradition I had never heard of before. She kissed me on the cheek and wished me good luck for the coming year. It warmed me.

I went to the English Market. In Coughlan's I watched an elderly butcher teach his apprentice how to perfectly roll a beef brisket. I bought sparkling prawns from Ballycotton Seafood and fillets of plaice from O'Connell's, the well-honed chat and banter from Pat and Paul ever present. I bought olives for home and ate a sample of Medjool dates stuffed with a hint of Gorgonzola and wrapped in Parma ham – a delicious bomb of pleasure. I urge you to try it at home.

I'm always drawn to the kind, caring and innovative brother–sister combination at O'Mahonys Family Butchers. Their spiced buffalo was a revelation, a logical twist on traditional Cork spiced beef.

The Farmgate Café is the jewel in the market's crown. The late AA Gill gave it five stars for its taste and integrity. Then there is the Mutton Lane Inn. Nestled in a shy capillary of a lane that leads to the heart of the market, it's one of my favourite places in the world.

Valentines is upon us and it's not only men who are placated when they're well fed. If you've had enough of the clichéd table for two, stay home and cook something delicious, maybe fish, for a change. Try coating plaice in crème fraîche before grilling it. This protects it and gives it a creamy coating. In truth it only needs a squeeze of orange or lemon, but I added this sauce for a bit of easy luxury.

Chicken, mushrooms, bacon and sour cream are all great friends. Serve with basmati rice for a bowl of delicious comfort food. This apple pie is my version of a strudel. Even the most reluctant of cooks will impress their partner with this easy dish full of familiar flavours.

GRILLED PLAICE WITH GARLIC AND PARSLEY BUTTER

SERVES 4

4 large double fillets of plaice, skin on and trimmed
2 tbsp crème fraîche
a drizzle of melted butter, plus extra for greasing

FOR THE BUTTER SAUCE:
50ml olive oil
4 garlic cloves, very thinly sliced
100g butter, diced
a few baby plum tomatoes, halved
a squeeze of orange
a good pinch of fresh flat-leaf parsley, finely chopped

To make the sauce, heat the oil in a saucepan over a low heat. Add the garlic and cook it gently just until it's evenly golden brown. Add the butter and let it bubble up, then remove the pan from the heat. Add the tomatoes to soften, then add the orange juice and parsley. Set aside until the fish is ready.

Preheat the grill to high.

Put the plaice on a lightly buttered grill tray, skin side down. Brush the fish evenly and liberally with the crème fraîche, then drizzle over the melted butter. Put under the grill for 5–6 minutes, until cooked through (this depends on the thickness of the fish).

Warm the sauce for 30 seconds.

Serve the fish on heated plates and spoon the sauce over the top. I like to eat this with boiled potatoes and green veg, tomatoes or salad, depending on the time of year.

CHICKEN WITH BACON, MUSHROOMS AND SOUR CREAM

SERVES 4

30g butter

2 tbsp olive oil

1 onion, finely diced

125g smoked bacon lardons

1 sprig of fresh thyme or 1 bay leaf (fresh if possible)

3–4 chicken fillets (depending on size), diced into 2cm cubes

250g button or chestnut mushrooms, sliced

150ml chicken stock

1 x 200ml tub of sour cream

Heat the butter and oil together in a saucepan over a low heat. When the butter starts to foam, add the onion, bacon and thyme or bay leaf. Cover the pan with a lid to keep all the flavour in and sweat for 10 minutes.

Add the chicken and mushrooms, increase the heat to medium and cook, uncovered, for 12 minutes, stirring occasionally. Add the stock and cook for a further 5 minutes with the lid off. Stir in the sour cream and bring to a simmer, then remove the thyme or bay and season to taste.

Serve with basmati rice.

APPLE ROLY POLY PIE

SERVES 4

a knob of butter

3 Gala apples, peeled, cored and thinly sliced

3 tbsp brown sugar

1 x 320g packet of ready-rolled puff pastry, thawed and chilled

1 egg beaten with 1 tbsp milk

Preheat the oven to 180°C. Grease a baking tray with the butter.

Mix the apple slices with half of the sugar.

Lay out the chilled pastry on the countertop with the wider side facing you (if you work quickly, you won't even need to dust it with flour). Brush the pastry with the egg wash, then scatter the apples evenly over it, leaving room around the edge.

Roll the pastry away from you as tightly as you can — it should resemble a Swiss roll. Pinch the edges together to seal, then transfer it to the tray as carefully as you can.

Brush with more egg wash, sprinkle over the remaining sugar and put it straight into the oven. Bake in the oven for 20–25 minutes, until golden and crisp. Serve warm.

An Italian story

15 FEBRUARY 2020

I'm writing this at 11 a.m. on a Tuesday morning from the cinema. It's cold and rainy outside and it's busier than usual. I was hoping to see Guy Richie's latest Cockney blokefest, but it wasn't on. Instead I'm at *Little Women*. I'm the only man here and I'm also the youngest by a distance. I shouldn't be on my phone, of course, but I'm secreted in the uppermost dark corner so hopefully I won't be detected.

Today I'm in the mood for Italian food. In our cookery school, our Italian courses can be bigger than a gondolier's bank account. Everyone loves them.

We've been to Italy many times, most recently Umbria. Its quiet rolling hills were perfect when the girls were younger. We could rent a stylish apartment with our own pool for much cheaper than its brasher Tuscan neighbour. I'd spend my days exploring and food shopping while they were all in the pool. The evenings were spent quietly cooking, listening to my beloved JBL speaker and exploring the wines of the region.

There is unending exploring to be done in Italy. Last year I was brought on a little trip with a couple of other chefs — a dangerous proposition if you know what chefs are like. We flew into Innsbruck at night, then travelled south to the Italian Dolomites to attend a conference about cheffy stuff and ski. I can't ski so they put me on a grandad's pony and trap. My blushes nearly melted the snow. Thunderstruck by the beauty of the region, we discovered Ladin, an Italian—German series of valleys with its own proud and prosperous culture, food and language.

I've two pasta dishes this week and one deeply delicious starter. In this Italian-inspired starter or light lunch, mozzarella is given depth and dignity by sticky, smoky aubergine and an artfully applied slice of Parma ham. The orecchiette is something we do at home. It's perfect for the teenage cook. The cheat's ravioli makes fabulous use of wonton pastry (for those not inclined to make their own pasta), which is found in the freezers at Asian shops. A simple goat cheese filling and a nutty butter sauce are all that's needed to turn this into a great dinner.

MOZZARELLA WITH PARMA HAM, STICKY AUBERGINE AND RED PEPPERS

SERVES 4

4 tbsp olive oil

2 red peppers, cut into 3cm chunks

1 aubergine, cut into 3cm chunks

3 garlic cloves, thinly sliced

2 tbsp red wine vinegar

1 tbsp light brown sugar

½ tsp smoked paprika

1 sprig of fresh rosemary

juice of 1 clementine

4 good-quality balls of mozzarella

4 slices of Parma ham

Heat the oil in a saucepan over a medium heat. Add the peppers, aubergine and garlic, stirring to coat them in the oil. When they're sizzling, turn the heat down to low, cover with a lid and cook for 20 minutes, stirring once or twice.

Add the vinegar, sugar, smoked paprika and rosemary. Cover with the lid again and continue to cook on a low heat for a further 20 minutes, checking it from time to time and giving it the odd stir to make sure it's not catching on the bottom of the pan.

When all the vinegar has evaporated and the mixture is jammy, remove the rosemary. Add the clementine juice and season with salt and pepper. This will keep in the fridge for up to three days at this stage.

Serve warm or at room temperature with a ball of mozzarella on top of each portion and a slice of Parma ham artfully draped around it. It's also great folded through pasta.

ORECCHIETTE WITH CHORIZO, LITTLE TOMATOES, CREAM AND PARMESAN

SERVES 2

50ml olive oil

80g dry-cured chorizo, peeled and sliced

1 garlic clove, sliced

1 sprig of fresh rosemary

12 mixed cherry tomatoes, halved

10 stoned green olives, roughly chopped

250g orecchiette (penne or rigatoni will also work)

100ml cream

50g Parmesan cheese, grated

Heat the oil in a large saucepan over a medium heat. Add the chorizo, garlic and rosemary and cook gently for 3–4 minutes, until the oil renders out from the chorizo and the garlic is golden.

Remove the pan from the heat and remove the rosemary. Add the tomatoes and olives. This can all be done ahead of time up to this stage.

Cook the pasta as per the packet instructions and bring the chorizo mixture up to a simmer.

Drain the pasta, reserving half a cup of cooking water. Stir the pasta and the cooking water through the chorizo mixture, add the cream and season to taste.

Divide between warm bowls and sprinkle the grated Parmesan over the top to serve.

CHEAT'S RAVIOLI WITH GOAT CHEESE, SAGE, LEMON AND PARMESAN

SERVES 4

200g soft rindless goat cheese

1 egg yolk

1 packet of wonton wrappers, thawed

1 egg beaten with 1 tbsp milk

75g Parmesan cheese, grated

FOR THE SAUCE:

100g butter

20 fresh sage leaves

a squeeze of lemon

Mash the goat cheese with the egg yolk and some black pepper.

Line up four wrappers at a time. Put a teaspoon of the goat cheese filling in the middle of each one — it's important not to overfill them, otherwise they will burst open when they cook.

Lightly brush the edges of the wonton wrappers with the egg wash. Fold the wontons to form a sealed triangle, pressing firmly to make sure there are no air pockets. Repeat with the remaining wrappers and filling.

Line a baking tray with greaseproof paper. Put the filled wontons on the tray, leaving space between them so they don't stick together. You can use them straightaway or put them in the fridge if you want to cook them later.

To make your sauce, melt the butter in a saucepan over a medium heat. When the butter starts to bubble and foam and turn golden brown around the edges, swirl to mix, then carefully observe it — you want it to turn a light hazelnut colour. Add the sage leaves and cook for 30 seconds to allow them to crisp a little, then add the lemon juice. Your sauce is now ready. This can be done ahead of time.

Bring a pot of salted water to the boil. Add the ravioli — they will rise to the top after 2 minutes. Separate them gently and cook for 1 more minute. Lift them out with a slotted spoon to drain off all the excess water and put on warm plates.

To serve, stir the sauce well, then spoon it on top of the ravioli. Sprinkle generously with Parmesan.

The perfect chowder

22 FEBRUARY 2020

In our cookery school, I talk about weather a lot. It's not banter. It's because weather and the seasons determine what we eat and when we eat it. What you eat also has everything to do with mood. When you're soaking and miserable after walking the dog on a cold, rainy day, you don't want a tomato salad. What you want is a bowl of chowder. Eating is logical if we listen to our bodies.

What makes a chowder work is the magical combination of smoke and cream. That hint of familiarity is instantly reassuring. I like simplicity in my chowder, which is why the base is just leek and potato. This combination might not engender much excitement — it's normally the lazy man's soup — but when it's cooked with care, it's seafood's best friend. And I don't use flour, as many a nicely flavoured chowder has been ruined by having the texture of wallpaper paste.

The first dish I ever learned to make was gratin potatoes. A part-time job in a local restaurant gave me skills that allowed me to help at many a party where my gratin went down a storm.

I don't know anyone who doesn't love gratin dauphinois. What you might not know is that it makes a tremendous feed if you nestle something within it — in this case, smoked mackerel and a bit of turnip. This recipe is adapted from the emperor of food writing, Nigel Slater. If you leave out the mackerel, try adding celeriac, sweet potato or parsnip. It's a tasty revelation.

I'm picky, though, when it comes to smoke. I don't like smoking for the sake of it; it needs to be subtle, not overbearing. I wouldn't eat smoked cheese even if Scarlett Johansen desperately wanted to feed it to me while staring at me lustfully at a post-Oscars party. The gentle, silky notes of perfectly smoked chicken make me swoon. Ummera makes an amazing smoked chicken. I pair it with a creamy blue cheese dressing, crunchy leaves, grapes and toasted almonds for some diversion. It's like a Caesar salad's more interesting cousin.

Cook these, rub your belly and think of me.

GRATIN OF SMOKED MACKEREL AND TURNIP WITH SPICED PICKLED CUCUMBER

SERVES 6

600g potatoes, peeled and thinly sliced

½ turnip, thinly sliced

3 garlic cloves, crushed

400ml milk

200ml cream

1 tbsp horseradish sauce

2 fillets of smoked mackerel, skin and bones removed

100g Cheddar cheese, grated

FOR THE PICKLED CUCUMBER:

100g caster sugar

100ml rice wine vinegar or white wine vinegar

100ml water

1cm piece of ginger, peeled and finely chopped

1 cucumber, peeled, halved lengthways and thinly sliced

To make the spiced pickled cucumber, put the sugar, vinegar, water and ginger in a saucepan and bring to the boil. Allow to cool completely, then add the cucumber.

Transfer to a jar and keep in the fridge until needed. This will keep for up to a week in the sealed jar. I use the pickling liquid as the basis for a salad dressing with a little hint of cream to thicken it.

Preheat the oven to 180°C.

Put the potatoes, turnip, crushed garlic, milk, cream and some salt and pepper in a large saucepan and slowly bring to the boil over a low heat. Stir a few times to make sure the potatoes are evenly coated with the milk and cream. Simmer for at least 20 minutes, until the potatoes are just tender, taking care that the potatoes don't stick to the bottom of the pan. Stir in the horseradish.

Turn half of the potato mixture into a baking dish. Flake the mackerel and scatter it over the potatoes, then spoon the remaining potato mixture on top and sprinkle over the grated Cheddar. Bake in the oven for 35–40 minutes, until golden and bubbling.

Serve the gratin straight to the table with the spiced pickled cucumber on the side.

SEAFOOD CHOWDER

SERVES 4

1 medium leek, cut in half lengthways and sliced

50g butter

3 large potatoes, peeled and diced into 2cm chunks

800ml chicken or vegetable stock

1 fresh bay leaf, lightly crushed (if you have it)

250g mixed fish, ideally salmon, smoked haddock and one white fish

250ml cream

chopped fresh chives or dill

Put the leek in a large saucepan with the butter. Cover and cook on a low heat for 5 minutes to allow the leeks to steam in their own buttery juices.

Add the potatoes, chicken stock and bay leaf (if using). Bring to the boil, then reduce the heat and simmer for 15–20 minutes, until the potatoes start to break up. Add the fish and cream and cook gently for 5 more minutes before seasoning.

When you're ready to serve, scatter over the chives or dill.

SMOKED CHICKEN, GRAPE AND CROZIER BLUE SALAD

SERVES 2

50ml apple juice

2 heaped tbsp crème fraîche

4 heads of Little Gem lettuce

1 smoked chicken breast, thinly sliced

16 seedless grapes, halved

80g Crozier Blue cheese (or anther soft blue cheese), crumbled

a good pinch of flaked almonds, toasted

Whisk the apple juice with the crème fraîche in a large bowl and season.

Break the heads of lettuce into individual leaves. Turn the leaves in the dressing, making sure there is a light coating on every leaf.

Assemble the salad with the leaves on the base, followed by the chicken, grapes, blue cheese and finally the almonds.

Spice bag roast chicken is a bit bonkers but a lot of fun

29 FEBRUARY 2020

Our friend Eunice went to Morocco on her holidays recently. There were a lot of tantalising photos on Instagram. I've never been but have always loved the food. The closest I've been is Tunisia, which is like saying Wexford is fairly close to St Petersburg. I started to blame my wife, silently accusing her for not wanting to go there.

At one stage, my food in the Tannery was brimming with Middle Eastern influences. But then the recession made me more conservative. I was afraid to lose even one precious customer to any flights of fancy. I was braver before then, I think somewhat regretfully.

Crippled with Insta-envy, I craved my own little bit of Morocco while wading through the biting wind and frigid rain to buy couscous and a half leg of lamb for our dinner. Food has always soothed us, both in the cooking and the eating.

It wasn't all plain sailing, though, as the two teenagers aren't fond of couscous. Or lamb. This touches on a point. Many a keen cook's enthusiasm is neutered due to their unadventurous offspring, and the drudgery of cooking two dinners is unappealing. They are banished to the land of spaghetti and meatballs until the offspring hopefully come round. On this occasion, however, I insisted. I wanted my couscous.

I found prunes in the press. I love them but I know that Irish people associate them with exploding bottoms. I had a dinky matchbox of saffron that I bought in a health food shop for around €6 and I bought a trilogy of herbs and peppers. The lamb went on the barbecue, but I don't presume you have one. I use mine throughout the year.

Continuing with the spice theme, I'm giving you this slightly eccentric chicken dish. It's a bit bonkers but a lot of fun — a bit like me. You can buy spice bag spice blends handily enough these days. Chef Kwanghi Chan makes one in his ChanChan sauces range.

Lastly there's something to go with both the lamb and the chicken here and lots of other things too — a cucumber and orange raita. Perhaps unnecessarily pimped, but it's good to break out once in a while.

ROAST LAMB WITH PRUNE, PEPPER AND SAFFRON COUSCOUS

SERVES 4

½ leg of lamb (approx. 1kg)

1 tbsp duck fat

75ml olive oil

2 red peppers, cut into 2cm pieces

3 garlic cloves, thinly sliced

½ teaspoon smoked paprika

a pinch of saffron

zest and juice of 1 orange

250g instant couscous

10 ready-to-eat prunes, each one cut into three

a handful of fresh mint, leaves picked and roughly chopped

a handful of fresh coriander, leaves picked and roughly chopped

a handful of fresh basil, leaves picked and roughly chopped

Preheat the oven to 220°C.

Put the lamb in a roasting tin, rub the duck fat all over it and season generously. Roast it in the oven for 15 minutes, until it starts to brown, then turn down the oven to 180°C and continue to cook for a further 30 minutes. Remove the tin from the oven, cover loosely with foil and allow the lamb to rest.

Heat the oil in a frying pan over a medium heat. Add the peppers, garlic and smoked paprika and cook for 10–15 minutes, until the peppers are somewhat sticky. Add the orange zest, season and remove the pan from the heat.

Boil a kettle of water. Put the saffron in a small heatproof dish or mug, pour over approx. 50ml of the boiling water and allow to sit for a little while.

Put the couscous in a large heatproof bowl. Wait for a couple of minutes before measuring out 350ml of the hot water and adding it into the couscous (boiling water makes it clumpy). Add the saffron and its soaking water and the orange juice. Season and cover the bowl with cling film. Allow to sit for 10 minutes.

Fluff up the couscous with a fork. Add the pepper mixture, prunes and chopped fresh herbs and fold them through the couscous.

This is perfectly lovely at room temperature — all you need to do is carve the lamb and sit it on top. If you don't fancy making the raita on page 83, serve it with shop-bought hummus.

ROAST SPICE BAG CHICKEN WITH BUTTERNUT SQUASH, BABY SPINACH AND CASHEWS

SERVES 4

1 x 1.7kg free-range chicken

1 lemon, cut in half

2 garlic cloves, halved

100ml olive oil

1 heaped tsp spice bag seasoning

1 large butternut squash, peeled, deseeded and cut into 6cm chunks

1 x 200g bag of baby spinach

70g cashew nuts

FOR THE YOGURT:

2 spring onions, finely chopped

200ml natural yogurt

Preheat the oven to 180°C.

Stuff the cavity of the chicken with half a lemon and the garlic, then put it in a large roasting tin. Drizzle over the oil, followed by an even sprinkling of the spice bag mix. Massage it into the chicken, making sure you get it into all the nooks and crannies.

Roast in the oven for 30 minutes, then add the butternut squash to the tin, making sure you turn the chunks in all the lovely juices. Cook for another 50 minutes, turning the squash once or twice.

Meanwhile, mix the chopped spring onions with the yogurt and set aside.

When the chicken is cooked, drain all the juices from the cavity into the roasting tin. Transfer the chicken to a chopping board and cover with foil for 15 minutes.

Add the spinach and cashews to the squash and roasting juices still in the tin. Put the tin over a low heat on the hob to wilt the spinach. Season and stir in the juice of the remaining lemon half.

Carve the chicken and divide everything among warm plates. Serve with the spring onion yogurt.

CUCUMBER AND ORANGE RAITA

SERVES 4

½ tsp black mustard seeds (optional)
250ml natural yogurt
½ cucumber, peeled and finely diced
zest of ½ orange

Toast the mustard seeds (if using) in a hot, dry pan for 2 minutes over a medium heat, until they start to pop. Allow to cool, then fold into the yogurt along with the cucumber and orange zest. Keep in the fridge until needed.

I could never be a hipster

07 MARCH 2020

I'm in the bar of a hipster hotel in Hoxton, London, waiting for the boss. We've had two squeezed days in a city that I lived in for 10 years. I feel strange, like a tourist. I need to feel my way around as the city has changed so much since the 1980s and 1990s.

I've no tattoos and I'm a good bit older than everybody else here. I'm visiting restaurants that I've loved from afar. Narrowing them down was torture, a truly First World problem. I veer towards good, simple cooking. Nothing fancy, no tweezers involved. It's an age thing.

Cooking over fire has been here for a while — a really long while, you could argue. A whole John Dory eaten in Brat was a stand-out dish. It came with a little butter and its own gelatinous juice pooled around it. It was like a still life.

We were fed until we popped in Daffodil Mulligan. There was fire there too, but among many lovely things a humble mackerel stood out. Louche and full of literary history, the French House was a tiny joy. Its freshly baked madeleines would melt the hardest of hearts.

So I'm here waiting to go to the last of our chosen restaurants. I don't need any more food, to be honest. My buttons are groaning but we're going to the Quality Chophouse tonight. I've had my eye on it for a while. Its robust, simple cooking belies a wealth of considered craft.

We're meeting a true food and journalism hero of mine at the restaurant, the food critic of the *Sunday Times*. A surreal encounter some years ago in Dungarvan that involved much craic, a lock-in and Fleetwood Mac sealed an unlikely friendship. When AA Gill passed away, Marina O'Loughlin became a more than worthy successor. I'm a delirious fanboy.

The sweet potato is creamy and deeply savoury. The spinach truly shines. The mackerel dish is a bowl of springtime. The wilted lettuce in this is a welcome success — just don't overcook it. The croissant pudding is easy and works with strawberries too.

BAKED SWEET POTATOES WITH FETA AND SPICED PUMPKIN SEEDS

SERVES 4

4 tbsp olive oil

2 large sweet potatoes, scrubbed and halved lengthways

a generous knob of butter

2 garlic cloves, thinly sliced

a pinch of chilli flakes

2 tbsp pumpkin seeds

250g baby spinach

200g feta cheese

Preheat the oven to 180°C.

Drizzle the oil into a roasting tin, season the oil with salt and pepper and add the sweet potatoes to the tray, cut side down. Cover with foil and cook in the oven for 60–75 minutes, until the sweet potatoes are soft.

Melt the butter in a large frying pan over a medium heat. Add the garlic and chilli flakes, followed by the pumpkin seeds. Cook gently for 3–4 minutes.

When you're ready to serve, add the spinach to the pan and wilt for 1 minute. Season.

To serve, transfer the sweet potatoes to plates, cut side up. Spoon over the wilted spinach, then crumble the feta on top.

GRILLED MACKEREL WITH PEAS AND LITTLE GEM

SERVES 4

2 tbsp olive oil

4 large butterflied mackerel fillets, bones removed (feel free to substitute with another fish if you like)

300ml vegetable stock

500g frozen petits pois, thawed

4 spring onions, cut into 3cm pieces

1 Little Gem lettuce, shredded

a knob of butter

1 tsp Dijon mustard

Preheat your grill.

Brush a baking tray with a little of the oil, season the oil with salt and pepper and add the mackerel fillets to the tray, skin side up. Brush the skin with a little more oil and season. Put the tray under the hot grill and cook for 4–5 minutes, until the mackerel is cooked through.

Meanwhile, bring the stock to the boil in a saucepan, then add the peas and spring onions. Put a lid on the pan and bring it back to the boil, then reduce the heat and simmer for 3 minutes. Add the lettuce, butter and mustard, then season.

To serve, spoon the vegetable mixture into warm bowls along with some of the pan juices, then put a mackerel fillet on top of each portion. Lovely with some boiled new potatoes.

RASPBERRY CROISSANT PUDDING

SERVES 4

4 egg yolks
125g golden caster sugar
250ml milk
250ml cream
2 croissants, torn into chunks
125g fresh raspberries
whipped cream, to serve

Preheat the oven to 150°C.

Beat the egg yolks and sugar together. Add the milk and cream and whisk vigorously.

Scatter the torn croissants evenly over the base of a baking dish, followed by the raspberries. Pour the egg mixture over the top, scraping the bowl thoroughly. Press the croissants down to make sure they are well soaked.

Put the dish in a snug-fitting roasting tin to make a water bath — this will prevent the eggs from scrambling and will help to keep the pudding light. Boil a kettle and pour the hot water into the tin until it comes halfway up the sides of the baking dish. Bake in the oven for 40 minutes, by which time the custard will have set and the top will be lightly crisp.

Serve at room temperature with a little whipped cream.

I always eat my greens

14 MARCH 2020

My cooking changes in March. I'm happy to leave slow cooking and comfort food behind for a while. I embrace the hopeful green of spring. I start to gather wild garlic. In truth, it's one of the only things I forage for. It's fashionable to forage but it's not a habit I ever adopted.

Anyhow, in the interest of self-preservation, it's wise for me to rely on my many wonderful and hardworking suppliers. I'm spectacularly ungainly and have a recently acquired fear of heights, so I'm better off indoors in the confines of my kitchen.

The waters warm up and I look forward to cooking, eating and serving more fish to our customers in the Tannery. We start grilling instead of stewing. Our food becomes more immediate and lighter.

It's harder to get chefs these days. Everybody's crying out for them. Interviews now involve me selling myself to some young hopeful who might turn into the next kitchen sensation. But I love working with a young, eager team. They fire me up and give me life.

Here are a few springtime ideas, dishes that might appear in the Tannery or at home. Lemon and greens are firm friends — I tend not to have one without the other. This salad has petits pois at its heart. It's vibrant and lovely.

I collect wild garlic by the bagful. Pick it when it's young, before it flowers. Wash and dry it before blending it with light olive oil and it will keep in the fridge for two weeks. Think of it as pesto's dusky cousin. Mussels are easier to find than clams, so don't worry if you can't get clams for this broth.

This soup is wholesome and healthy. The broth mix is available in most supermarkets. It makes the soup filling, delicious and worthy.

SPRING SALAD WITH GOAT CHEESE AND MINT

SERVES 4

1 bunch of asparagus
700g petits pois, thawed
1 red onion, very thinly sliced
1 small bunch of fresh mint, leaves torn into small pieces
150g soft rindless goat cheese, crumbled

FOR THE DRESSING:
100ml olive oil
juice of 1 lemon
1 small fresh red chilli, deseeded and finely chopped
a good pinch of caster sugar

Bring a big pot of salted water to the boil.

Meanwhile, trim 3cm from the bottom of each asparagus stalk, then cut the rest of the stalk into chunks, leaving the tips intact.

To make the dressing, whisk all the ingredients together in a large bowl with some salt and pepper.

Add the asparagus and peas to the boiling water and bring it back to the boil as quickly as you can. When just boiling, add the sliced onion, stir, then immediately drain through a colander. Run cold water over the veg and throw in some ice if you have it to cool them as quickly as possible.

Shake off the excess water thoroughly, then add them to the dressing in the bowl, tossing to coat. Season and add the fresh mint.

Serve in one of your best bowls with the goat cheese crumbled on top.

MUSSELS AND CLAMS IN WILD GARLIC BROTH
SERVES 4

1kg mussels
500g clams, cleaned
300ml cider
a pinch of chilli flakes
a good knob of butter
juice of ½ lemon

FOR THE WILD GARLIC PURÉE:
2 large handfuls of wild garlic leaves
enough sunflower oil to make it all turn around in the food processor

To make the wild garlic purée, wash and pat dry the leaves. Cut them roughly with a sharp knife. Put into a liquidizer or food processor and blitz with enough sunflower oil to make the leaves all turn around in the food processor, blending until fine. This will keep for two to three weeks in a sealed jar in the fridge. Just make sure there is a thin layer of oil on the surface to protect the purée.

To prepare the mussels, immerse them in a clean sink of cold water. Agitate. Debeard them one by one into a clean bowl, discarding any that are open and won't close when you gently tap them on the counter. Drain and clean the sink, fill it with cold water again and re-immerse the debearded mussels. Agitate the mussels once more, then lift them from the water, leaving any sediment behind.

You will need a pot with a lid for this or a large wok would be great. Put the mussels, clams, cider, chilli flakes and butter in the pot. Cover with the lid and bring to the boil as quickly as possible, stirring once or twice with a wooden spoon.

When the mussel and clam shells begin to open, add 2 tablespoons of the wild garlic purée, the lemon juice and a few twists of black pepper. Cook for 1 minute, until all the shells are fully open (discard any that remain closed).

Divide among four large bowls. Serve with crusty bread to mop up the juices.

CHICKEN, LEEK AND BACON SOUP

SERVES 4–6

a knob of butter

125g smoked bacon lardons

2 medium leeks, thinly sliced and rinsed (keep a little water on the leeks)

1 sprig of fresh thyme

200g broth mix (widely available in supermarkets in the health food aisle – a mix of barley, lentils and split peas)

2 litres chicken stock

2 chicken breasts, cut into 1cm pieces

1 large apple

Melt the butter in a saucepan over a medium heat. When it starts to foam, add the bacon lardons and cook gently for 3 minutes, then add the leeks and thyme. Stir to coat in the bacony juices, then cover the pan with a lid and cook gently for 5 minutes, turning once or twice.

Add the broth mix and stock. Bring to the boil, then reduce the heat and simmer for 30 minutes, until the broth mix is tender. Add the chicken and cook for 10 more minutes.

Peel and grate the apple, then add it to the soup. Remove the thyme, season to taste and serve.

I'm such a caveman

21 MARCH 2020

Some people have seemed to blossom during this lockdown. I spend my time poring longingly over social media. All this amazing food but we can't get to it.

It's all about Instagram these days. I've mentioned before that I've been getting lessons from my 14-year-old but I still can't crack it. The visual nature of it is instant and compelling, of that there is no doubt. It allows people with no discernible talent to make a fortune from their own narcissism. Am I ranting?

The magnificence of the food on Instagram draws you in. You hunger for what's in those images. Every undulation of that buttercream icing drives me wild with lust (I'm looking at you, Jess Murphy). I'm just jealous. I'm notoriously untechnical.

Sunday night is our favourite family night. It's also when I have the time to be Insta-friendly. We always have a nice dinner. I take my time over the preparation. The lighting is just right. So, too, is the music and I have some wine open. I cook and read the papers. Nobody bothers me until they're hungry.

I start off keen and meticulous, recording every step. I'm fine with short, sharp recipes. I get it done, but not without the help of one or other of my daughters. The longer recipes are more difficult. I lose interest. Maybe it's the wine.

Roasting asparagus concentrates the flavour. Plus it's all done on one tray. This asparagus recipe evaporated into the cloud some time ago. I put it on Instagram and wrote the recipe diligently, and much to my delight, Diana Henry told me it was lovely. That was a high. When I went to look for it, though, the gremlins had run off with it.

I adore leeks and I also have a big crush on smoked haddock (try to get undyed, but not to worry if you can't). This is an easy bake for the family.

The salad is an adaptation of a dish we once ate in Carmel Somers's wonderful Good Things Café. The Parma ham over the top gives it sweet and salty satisfaction. Make sure you buy good, firm courgettes, though — it's pointless otherwise.

ROASTED ASPARAGUS AND FENNEL SALAD WITH TOONSBRIDGE MOZZARELLA

SERVES 2

1 bunch of asparagus

1 large fennel bulb, thinly sliced

1 red onion, thinly sliced

2 garlic cloves, thinly sliced

1 small fresh red chilli, deseeded and finely chopped

100ml olive oil

100g baby spinach

juice of 1 lemon

2 balls of Toonsbridge mozzarella

Preheat the oven to 200°C.

Snap the woody stems off each asparagus spear and discard. Put the asparagus in a roasting tin with the fennel, onion, garlic and chilli. Drizzle over the oil, tossing to coat everything evenly. Roast in the oven for 12–15 minutes, depending on the size of your asparagus, turning once or twice during cooking. Everything should be slightly charred.

Remove the tin from the oven. Immediately add the spinach, lemon juice and some salt and pepper and stir together thoroughly.

Serve on warm plates with the mozzarella artfully torn on top.

SMOKED HADDOCK, LEEK AND POTATO BAKE

SERVES 4

50g butter, melted

16 baby potatoes, cooked and halved

1 leek, finely shredded

2 tbsp raisins

4 x 120g fillets of smoked haddock (undyed if possible)

250ml cream

100ml milk

1 tsp prepared English mustard

1 tsp curry powder

Preheat the oven to 180°C.

Brush a shallow casserole or baking dish with the melted butter. Put the cooked and halved potatoes on the bottom, then cover with the leek and raisins. Put the fish on top.

Whisk your cream, milk, mustard and curry powder together, then pour this over the fish and season with salt and pepper.

Cover tightly with a lid or foil and cook in the oven for 30 minutes. Serve straight to the table.

ROASTED COURGETTE, ROCKET AND PARMA HAM SALAD

SERVES 4

3 large courgettes, cut into 3cm chunks
2 garlic cloves, thinly sliced
1 small fresh red chilli, deseeded and finely chopped
50ml olive oil
juice of ½ lemon
1 x 100g bag of rocket salad
8 slices of Parma ham
lots of Parmesan shavings

Preheat the oven to 200°C.

Put the courgettes, garlic, chilli and some salt and pepper in a roasting tin. Drizzle over the oil, tossing to coat. Roast in the oven for 10–15 minutes, until the courgettes are soft and yielding. Divide among four plates.

Squeeze the lemon juice into the roasting tin and mix with the cooking juices. Use this to dress the rocket.

To serve, put the dressed rocket on top of the courgettes, then drape the Parma ham over the rocket. Scatter the Parmesan shavings generously over each dish.

Cooking like my heroes

28 MARCH 2020

I'm a bit of TV addict, but now, for obvious reasons, I have too much time to watch TV. I have to force myself to get a bit of structure into the day and to get some exercise so I'm trying to keep it to night-time only, starting with the six o'clock news, which is invariably scary.

I always gravitate towards food TV. You might think I'd have enough of it as that's all I do during the day, and the night too for that matter. I look forward to a new series from Rick Stein like a flushed Juliet hovering on her balcony waiting for Romeo.

Rick is the best. I look at his life and travels through my rose-tinted glasses and wish I was him. He's urbane, likeable and has a mischievous glint in his eye. He's a curious, educated traveller who always appreciates where he lands. His love of literature separates him from other shouty chefs. Quotes emanate easily from him. My eager ears soak them up, like soft, sweet rain over parched land. He loves Spain and so do I, so I am doing a simple paella as an homage.

Meanwhile, Nigel Slater is one of the most gifted natural cooks I've ever seen. His ability to do so much with so few ingredients is pure alchemy. His body of work is phenomenal. He's a one-man cookbook industry that has eased many a reluctant cook into the kitchen. He is all about comfort food and deep, delicious flavours. Eating his food is like a warm hug from an old friend. This pork dish is an easy and apt tribute to a wonderful cook and communicator.

I also have to mention Darina. She doesn't need a surname. She lives for food and not only talks the talk but walks the walk. The reputation of Irish food would not be the same without her. We are now enjoying a young, dynamic food culture in Ireland that is rooted in the traditions that Darina always championed, even when it wasn't fashionable. I think she would approve of this white onion, Cheddar and apple soup, which shows that humble ingredients, cooked well, can be stunning.

AN EASY PAELLA

SERVES 4

50ml olive oil

1 red onion, sliced

2 garlic cloves, sliced

100g dry-cured chorizo, sliced

1 tsp smoked paprika

300g long-grain rice

1 x 400g tin of chopped tomatoes

200g frozen petits pois

300ml chicken stock

250g cod fillets, bones removed and cut into 2cm cubes

250g prawns (shelled) – frozen are fine but make sure they are defrosted

Heat the oil in a large, wide pan over a gentle heat. Add the onion and garlic and cook for 5–6 minutes, then add the chorizo and smoked paprika and cook for 2 more minutes.

Add the rice, stirring until it's completely coated in oil and glistening, then add the tinned tomatoes, peas and stock. Bring to a gentle simmer, season with salt and pepper and cover with a lid.

Cook for 15 minutes, then scatter the cod and prawns evenly over the top, gently pushing them into the rice. Cover once more and cook for a further 5 minutes or so, making sure that the rice is tender, all the stock has been absorbed and the fish is cooked through.

Serve straight to the table.

PORK CHOPS WITH ROASTED PEARS, SAGE, RED ONIONS AND GORGONZOLA

SERVES 4

4 pork chops (on the bone if possible)

4 medium Rooster potatoes, unpeeled and cut into slices 5mm thick

4 small red onions, halved lengthways

2 pears, quartered and deseeded

10 fresh sage leaves

75ml olive oil

2 tbsp maple syrup

2 tbsp red wine vinegar

150g Gorgonzola cheese

Preheat the oven to 190°C.

Put the chops, potatoes, onions, pears and sage leaves in a roasting tin. Drizzle over the oil, then season. Scrunch together so the oil coats everything. Bake in the oven for 20 minutes, turning once or twice.

Add the maple syrup and vinegar, then pop the tin back in the oven to cook for another 10 minutes, until everything is caramelised and golden and the pork is cooked through.

Divide among four warm plates with a piece of melting Gorgonzola on each for a creamy kick.

CREAM OF WHITE ONION, CHEDDAR AND APPLE SOUP

SERVES 4

80g butter
4 large white onions, thinly sliced
1 sprig of fresh thyme
750ml chicken stock
250ml cream
150ml good-quality apple juice
1 tsp prepared English mustard
100g Cheddar cheese, grated

Melt the butter in a large heavy-based saucepan with a tight-fitting lid. When the butter starts to foam, add the onions and thyme, stirring to coat. Reduce the heat right down, cover with the lid and cook for 30–40 minutes, until the onions are soft, melting and tender.

Pour in the stock and bring to the boil. Add the cream, apple juice and mustard and bring back to a simmer. Cook gently for another 10 minutes. Season and remove the thyme sprig.

To serve, ladle into warm bowls and sprinkle the Cheddar on top.

A big night in

I'm sitting outside. It's sunny but cold. The dog is beside me but at any time she might catch a glimpse of the cat and bolt. She took off three times yesterday. It's as if she's milking every moment of us being at home. She's like a one-dog Disney movie, a fluffy blur in the fields below us with the girls chasing after her. We thought we had her trained but she's gone rogue all of a sudden.

Something special is happening tonight in the Flynn household. It's a kitchen takeover.

There was an Insta-row last night and the youngest one threw the toys out of the pram. You would think it was us berating them, but no — it was the other way around.

For some reason I don't find Instagram easy. Like maths, I've made up my mind that it's beyond my intellectual capacity. I co-opted Number 1 to help me for an intermittent weekly wage, but we've spent so much time on it in the last few days that the tension is palpable and combustive.

Last night we sat around a stodgy toad in the hole, glaring at each other, when Number 2 said she wanted us all off the phones the following day. She was going to open a restaurant, cook dinner and we all had to eat and be happy about it. Drinks were at six (we have her well trained).

Before you say 'Oh, how wonderful', this has never happened before. I'm happy but nervous. My back is to the kitchen. I suspect I won't be able to go in for some time as I'll pass out from the mess.

My girls are no different to other children — or am I deluding myself? When they were very small I was thrilled when they slurped up mussels in Honfleur. They developed a long-lasting love of sushi that continues to make other children gag and gasp. They can wield chopsticks like little ninjas. Back when we could travel, we brought them to Il Rinconcillo in Seville, purportedly the oldest restaurant in Spain, where we fought over almejas, little clams in garlic and olive oil.

We are always in our restaurant, in other restaurants or talking about restaurants. It's been in their blood since they could walk.

In saying all this, I'm keenly aware that I'm in danger of raising entitled caviar-eating monsters. This is where we meet reality. The early promise of gastronomic greatness has withered like an unwanted truffle. Number 1 will pretty much eat anything, but Number 2 will automatically gag at the sight of a green vegetable.

The affinity for brown food is embedded in every Irish child, it seems. I was no different. Burgers and pizza would be in the top three of my girls' favourites, with chips and pasta close behind.

They have loved baking ever since they were tiny, though. I learned to put my OCD aside for the greater good. Coming home to two flour-coated cuties after a hard day made me forget any tribulations. Their little efforts made our house a home.

They do home economics at school, but in truth they don't seem to have much interest. I've seen the recipes they are given and I always think, perhaps unfairly, it's no wonder they're not interested. Then I realise not every house is as obsessive about food and cooking as ours.

They have no interest in learning from me either. They just ask what's for dinner and arrive when it's ready.

Frustratingly, I see them eat things on holiday like a famous onion risotto in we had in Lake Garda. I recreated it at home and it was a resounding thumbs down: 'It's not like the one in Campagnola.' I know what you're thinking. I think the same as I grit my teeth.

'Wait until you're in college,' I often say. 'You will long for Daddy's dinners as you eat your beans on toast.'

So back to tonight. I can hear them beavering away.

Number 2 has written a menu. It's sweet. She's also the master of ceremonies, maître d' and main course chef. Number 1 is on dessert, wash-up and general bouncer duties if things go pear shaped. We had to make a reservation. That's when we found out how she planned to deal with intolerances and life choices. We have to dress up. We can't give out or fight.

The menu reads like this: selection of 'snackie' bits. I'm led to believe this will consist of olives, salami, crisps, pâté and roasted chicken skin (okay, the last one was me; I couldn't throw it in the bin).

The main course is chicken alfredo pasta. Vegetarian? Don't eat the chicken! Gluten free? Don't eat the pasta! I really love her approach here.

Dessert is a raspberry chocolate brownie, then 'maybe cheese, it depends' (hopefully she doesn't mean it depends on how much wine we drink).

I have a gin and tonic in front of me now. The dog is calm and so am I. Is that the time? I must hurry and get changed for dinner.

Food has always soothed us, both in the cooking and the eating.

29 FEBRUARY 2020

Oh, Switzerland

04 APRIL 2020

At the beginning of the year I was on holiday in Switzerland, where we have family. It's scary to think how much has changed in such a short time. The gang skiied into blissful exhaustion. I ate cheese. The alpine beauty was expected but still took my breath away.

I took the Bernina Express from Davos through chiselled mountain passes. I felt like I was in a Fellini film, the maroon livery of the train set against the snow like a little boy's dream. It wound its way up to the sky, stopping by a glacier where we got off at a chocolate box station. I was in the middle of my very own snow globe.

Our descent trundled towards Italy. A whisper over the border in Tirano, we stopped for lunch in a sunny square, delighting in the cheaper wine and looking back at the mountains. At last, I was Paul Theroux.

Everything works in Switzerland. There is commitment and a confidence that I haven't seen before. Perhaps there is an aloofness, but only because they simply don't need anyone else. There are also lots and lots of rules.

We ate wonderful food, designed for people who have spent all day skiing, hiking or casually creating momentous feats of engineering. I have never witnessed a more outdoorsy bunch.

Röstis are ubiquitous in Switzerland and very satisfying. I'm combining mine with the breakfast I had every morning in the hotel: shards of crisp bacon, honeycomb and young, creamy goat cheese. Don't judge me, I was front loading.

Fondue is the ultimate comfort food, easy and theatrical. I was blown away one evening in a special cheese bubble on the terrace of our hotel. It was like eating your dinner in a deliciously stinky glasshouse. We watched the snowploughs clinging perilously to the slopes, their lights twinkling in the darkness. The most memorable meals are often about time and place.

To alleviate any guilt, I had Bircher muesli one day. It's as close as I'll ever get to being a hunky Swiss ski instructor.

RÖSTI WITH CRISPY BACON, HONEY AND GOAT CHEESE

SERVES 4

3 large Maris Piper potatoes (850g), peeled and coarsely grated
1 egg, beaten
1 tbsp plain flour
¼ tsp baking powder
a few fresh thyme leaves
12 rashers of smoked streaky bacon
75ml sunflower oil
100g mild, creamy goat cheese, such as St Tola
4 tbsp comb honey (runny honey will do)

Squeeze any excess water out of the grated potatoes, then transfer to a bowl with the egg, flour, baking powder, thyme and some salt and pepper.

Cook your bacon on a tray under a hot grill until very crisp. Set aside, keeping any bacon fat to cook the rösti.

Divide the grated potato mixture into four equal portions and flatten each one into a circle.

Heat the oil and bacon fat in a non-stick frying pan set over a medium heat. Add the rösti and fry for about 5 minutes on each side, until golden. You may have to cook them in batches, depending on the size of your pan — just keep the cooked ones hot in the oven.

To serve, smear the goat cheese over the top. Add the honey and top with the bacon.

A BLISSFUL FONDUE

SERVES 4

1 small ciabatta, torn into chunks

a drizzle of olive oil

2 bunches of asparagus

225g Crozier Blue cheese or another soft blue cheese

75ml cream

75ml good-quality apple juice

Preheat the oven to 185°C.

Scatter the ciabatta chunks on a baking tray and drizzle with a little oil. Bake in the oven for about 10 minutes, until golden and crunchy. Set aside.

Trim one-third from the base of each asparagus spear and discard.

Bring a large pot of salted water to the boil. Add the asparagus and cook for 2 minutes, but this entirely depends on the thickness of the asparagus — it needs to be slightly crisp. When cooked, drain and plunge the asparagus into iced water. This keeps the colour and stops the cooking. Pat dry on a clean kitchen cloth.

Take a handsome little pot (you will be eating from this). If you have a fondue pot, that would be amazing. Crumble in the cheese, then add the cream and apple juice. Warm through until gently bubbling, stirring now and again.

Serve in the centre of a platter with the asparagus and toasted bread arranged around. Dip and dredge to your heart's content.

BIRCHER MUESLI WITH HOT BLUEBERRIES

SERVES 4

200g porridge oats

125g natural yogurt

2 apples, peeled and grated

375ml good-quality apple juice

2 tbsp of your favourite nuts, roughly chopped

1 tbsp honey

1 small punnet of fresh blueberries

Mix all the ingredients except the blueberries in a bowl. Cover the bowl and leave it in the fridge overnight.

When ready to serve, heat the blueberries in a microwave for 1 minute, until they burst and release their juices.

Serve the muesli in bowls and pour over the hot blueberries.

Cooking in colours

11 APRIL 2020

I think about cooking in colours and those colours always reflect the changing seasons. Earthy tones for autumn and winter — the turnips, beetroot, carrots and parsnips that favour the slow cooking that I love. These make the ultimate comfort food that we crave in the cold, dark winter months.

Summer is all glorious red. I lighten my cooking to reflect a hopeful summer of sunny days on the beach. I let Mediterranean flavours dominate my cooking. Fruity olive oil replaces butter as my staple, teasing the flavour from the summer's bounty.

Spring is a revelation, all green. Asparagus, peas, broccoli, spinach, broad beans. It's all fresh and determinedly perky, a welcome brightness after the long months of slow cooking.

My mind turns to lamb, and Easter. Not that I'm giving you a lamb recipe today. There's an abundance of those this time of year, but all these recipes can be served around it.

There are certain times of the year that are all about family, Christmas being the obvious example, but people love Easter too. Easter Sunday for us Irish meant the end of Lent. There was always a big dinner. I personally celebrated by eating as many Easter eggs as I could lay my chubby little hands on. Competition with my siblings for the eggs was fierce.

My dad usually took us to Whitechurch House hotel as a treat at Easter. The food was reliably lovely but of course we could hardly eat a thing because we were queasy from all that chocolate. Dad got annoyed — these were not times when people could afford to waste money — but he always forgave us.

The potato cake is a real centrepiece. Sometimes I add salami, mortadella or smoked bacon. You could serve it with lamb or it's equally good on its own, warm, with a lovely salad.

You don't have to make the goat cheese mousse to go with the caponata but it's an extra-fancy starter if you do. Just use your favourite soft goat cheese instead.

These carrots can be served as a side or add feta cheese and toasted sunflower seeds to make a complex-flavoured, warming vegetarian main course.

POTATO, PARMESAN AND RED PEPPER CAKE

SERVES 4

3 tbsp olive oil

2 red peppers, cut into 1cm chunks

2 garlic cloves, thinly sliced

1 sprig of fresh rosemary, finely chopped

1 tsp smoked paprika

850g potatoes, peeled

100g butter

150ml milk

a pinch of ground nutmeg

4 eggs, beaten

150g Parmesan cheese, freshly grated

1 ball of mozzarella, sliced

FOR THE BASE AND THE TOP:

40g butter

4 tbsp fresh white breadcrumbs

Preheat the oven to 200°C.

Heat the oil in a saucepan over a low heat. Add the red peppers, garlic, rosemary and smoked paprika and cook gently for about 15 minutes, until the peppers become soft and jammy. Season and set aside.

Meanwhile, cook the potatoes in a pot of boiling salted water until tender, then drain. While still warm, mash the potatoes with the butter, milk, nutmeg and some salt and pepper. Allow to cool a little, then add the beaten eggs and grated Parmesan.

Use some of the remaining 40g of butter to grease a 20cm springform cake tin, then sprinkle over some of the breadcrumbs. Spoon over half of the potato mixture.

Layer the red peppers on top, followed by the mozzarella slices, then the remaining potatoes, smoothing the top with the back of a spoon. Sprinkle the remaining breadcrumbs on top and dot over the rest of the butter.

Bake in the oven for 30 minutes, until golden and crisp. Allow to stand for 10 minutes before unclipping the tin and cutting into wedges to serve.

CAPONATA BREAD SALAD WITH GOAT CHEESE MOUSSE

SERVES 4

2 slices of white bread, cut into 1cm dice

5 tbsp olive oil

1 aubergine, cut into 1cm dice

1 red onion, cut into 1cm dice

2 celery sticks, diced

1 red pepper, diced

1 yellow pepper, diced

2 garlic cloves, chopped

1 x 400g tin of plum tomatoes

4 tbsp red wine vinegar

2 tsp caster sugar

20 stoned black olives, roughly chopped

1 tbsp capers

½ bunch of fresh basil, leaves torn

FOR THE MOUSSE:

1 x 12g sachet of powdered gelatine

200g soft rindless goat cheese

275g crème fraîche

125ml cream

1 tbsp honey

To make the goat cheese mousse, dissolve the gelatine in a little warm water. Whisk the goat cheese into the crème fraîche, making it as smooth as you can.

In a separate bowl, whip the cream to smooth peaks, then add the honey and some salt and pepper. Fold the crème fraîche and goat cheese mixture into the whipped cream along with the gelatine. Chill in the fridge for 4 hours.

Preheat the oven to 185°C.

Scatter the bread on a baking tray and drizzle with a little of the oil. Bake in the oven for 10 minutes, until golden and crisp.

Heat the rest of the oil in a saucepan over a medium heat. Add the aubergine, onion, celery, red and yellow peppers and garlic and cook slowly for 15 minutes, until soft.

Add the tinned tomatoes, red wine vinegar and sugar. Reduce until thick and syrupy around the vegetables, then add the olives and capers. Take the pan off the heat and allow to cool, then season and add the basil leaves.

To serve, fold the crispy bread through the caponata and serve with the goat cheese mousse on the side. A little tip: heat a spoon before scooping the goat cheese to give it a lovely professional finish.

ROASTED HERITAGE CARROTS WITH CARDAMOM AND ROSEMARY BUTTER

SERVES 4

1kg mixed heritage carrots, scrubbed and cut into 3cm chunks (if you can't find heritage carrots, use organic carrots)

100ml water

50ml olive oil

a thumb-sized piece of ginger, peeled and grated

a few sprigs of fresh mint

FOR THE BUTTER:

juice of 1 orange

10 green cardamon pods, crushed

1 sprig of fresh rosemary

200g butter, diced and chilled

Preheat the oven to 185°C.

Put the carrots in a roasting tin with the water, oil and ginger. Roast in the oven for 20 minutes or so, until caramelised and cooked through.

For the cardamom butter sauce, slowly reduce the orange juice by half in a saucepan with the cardamom and rosemary. Whisk in the butter a few cubes at a time over a low heat. Pass through a fine mesh sieve to discard the solids.

To serve, warm the carrots and divide them among four serving bowls. Drizzle the butter sauce over the carrots, then tear the mint leaves over the top.

Posh bacon and cabbage

18 APRIL 2020

We normally hold the Waterford food festival this weekend, but sadly not this year. We've had a blast being part of it over the years, proudly hosting many famous chefs in the Tannery.

There are some great stories about the food, the people and the after-hours shenanigans, most notably a late night with Fergus Henderson watching a recording of the 2004 Munster final between Cork and Waterford. I was determined to show him the glories of hurling. The crowd watching with us roared as passionately as they did on the day of the match. Bewildered, he was like a man trapped in a joyous, smoky Twilight Zone.

My favourite part of the festival is the Sunday market in the square. We miraculously almost always get good weather and the town feels like the centre of the universe.

April for me is all about wild garlic. Its delicious funk permeates the kitchen and its distinctive flavour heralds the summer. I gather it by the bagful, ideally before it flowers, then give it a gentle wash and blend it with light olive oil. The result is a verdant, heady mixture that we keep in the fridge for up to two weeks. It's ubiquitous in my kitchen for about a month. It's stunning in a broth with mussels and clams (page 90) or crab. It lifts a roast chicken with a little squeeze of lemon. It even finds its way into our mashed potatoes.

I'm keeping it local this week as an homage to the West Waterford Festival of Food. In 2021 the festival will be back, bigger and better than ever.

Roast rack of bacon is a real treat. Cooking anything on the bone always gives extra flavour and the cabbage is a bit of a one-pot wonder. The Caesar-dressed purple sprouting broccoli is a quick fix. Use tenderstem if you wish and substitute Parma ham, sliced roast beef or even leftover roast chicken for our local corned beef. It's a lovely starter or it can be more substantial with some boiled new potatoes. Frittata is a crowd pleaser. Eggs, potatoes, cheese and onion: flavours as familiar to us as a bag of Tayto. The wild garlic elevates it but don't fret if you can't get it.

ROAST RACK OF BACON WITH CREAMED CABBAGE, MUSTARD AND APPLE

SERVES 4

1 x 4-chop rack of bacon (approx. 1kg)

250ml water

1 small head of Savoy cabbage, thinly sliced

1 red apple, cored and sliced

300ml chicken stock

170ml cream

1 tbsp prepared English mustard

1 tbsp maple syrup or honey

Preheat the oven to 175°C.

Put the rack of bacon in a roasting tin, skin side up. Pour the water into the tin and cook in the oven for 45 minutes.

Meanwhile, put the cabbage in a pot with the apple, stock and some salt and pepper. Put a lid firmly on top and bring to a fierce boil. After 3 minutes or so, add the cream and mustard and continue to cook with the lid off so that the liquid reduces and makes a sauce around the cabbage. Reserve and set aside.

To finish the bacon, pour the maple syrup or honey over the top and put it back in the oven for a further 15 minutes or so to caramelise.

Allow to rest a little, then serve with the creamed cabbage and some boiled potatoes.

CAESAR-DRESSED PURPLE SPROUTING BROCCOLI WITH MCGRATH'S CORNED BEEF

SERVES 4

1 small ciabatta, torn into chunks

12 vine-ripened cherry tomatoes

a good drizzle of olive oil

400g purple sprouting broccoli or tenderstem

170ml cream

80g Parmesan cheese, grated

juice of ½ lemon

1 garlic clove, crushed

12 slices McGrath's corned beef (if you can't get corned beef, you can happily substitute Parma ham, sliced roast beef or leftover roast chicken)

Preheat the oven to 180°C.

Put the bread and tomatoes in a roasting tin, drizzle with oil and season. Cook in the oven for 10–12 minutes, until the bread is golden. Keep an eye on the tomatoes so they don't overcook.

Bring a pot of salted water to the boil. Add your broccoli and cook for 3 minutes or so, depending on the thickness of the stems – it's important to retain the colour and a little bite. Plunge into iced water, then pat dry on a clean tea towel.

Put the cream in a bowl. Stir in half of the grated Parmesan along with the lemon juice and crushed garlic. Season.

When you're ready to serve, turn the broccoli in the dressing. Serve everything together in a pretty way and scatter the remaining Parmesan on top.

CHEESE, ONION AND WILD GARLIC FRITTATA

SERVES 4

50g butter

a splash of olive oil

1 red onion, thinly sliced

2 spring onions, roughly chopped

8 new potatoes, cooked and sliced

8 eggs, beaten with a little milk and seasoned with salt and pepper

1 tbsp wild garlic purée (page 90)

100g Cheddar cheese (I used red), grated

Preheat the oven to 200°C.

Heat the butter and oil in a non-stick ovenproof frying pan over a medium heat. When the butter has melted and starts to foam, add the red onion and spring onions and cook gently for 10 minutes, until softened. Add the cooked, sliced potatoes and cook gently for 1 minute or so.

Add the beaten egg mixture and the wild garlic purée. Turn up the heat a little and start to fold everything together, preferably with a rubber spatula. Scatter the cheese evenly over the top.

Cook in the oven for around 12 minutes, until golden and puffy. Remove from the oven and allow to rest for 3–4 minutes.

Carefully turn the frittata out onto a plate to be eaten warm.

Give a man a few tins of butter beans and he can conquer the world

25 APRIL 2020

In a crisis, I am good at feeding people. I can make a silk purse out of a sow's ear at the drop of a hat. I love opening the cupboard to see what's in it when the fridge has let me down. Give a man a few tins of butter beans and he can conquer the world.

I have a dinky little book called *Cupboard Love* by Tom Norrington-Davies. He was seminal in creating the legendary Eagle in Farringdon, London's first gastropub. I love the title and I love his ethos. Sometimes good things are right under your nose.

This week I'm cooking from my own cupboard. I hope it doesn't come across as glum and frugal. Cooking by its nature is hopeful, and we all need some hope at the moment. A bit of magic can be created with everyday things. Andy Warhol did it with tins of soup and you can do it too, albeit in a simpler way, without the fame, notoriety and fortune.

I'm a big fan of traybakes. They're easy and sensible. I'm also a champion of fennel. It's grossly underappreciated. We're just not used to cooking with it. I like it raw in the height of summer, but roasting it makes its aniseedy loveliness shine. It becomes mellow and sweet. The butter beans add easy heft and soak up all the other fantastic flavours in the tray.

A tin of tomatoes can become something deep and complex. This mozzarella dish is based on the tomato sauce I make at home all the time. The partnering with chickpeas is obvious, while the mozzarella adds cream and comfort. The orange brings everything together.

These flatbreads are pukka. I'm using that word because the man who came up with the recipe, Jamie Oliver, uses it. They are so easy to make that it would be a crime to change the recipe because the simplicity encourages people to make them. I'm using crab and avocado here. It's a little bit posh but these could accompany a curry or a simple smear of wild garlic butter would lift them into the stars.

CHICKEN, BUTTER BEAN AND FENNEL BAKE

SERVES 4

8 skinless, bone-in chicken thighs

4 tbsp olive oil

2 large red onions, quartered

2 fennel bulbs, quartered

125g smoked bacon lardons

8 garlic cloves, unpeeled

2 sprigs of fresh rosemary

1 x 400g tin of butter beans, drained and rinsed

250ml cream (optional)

a squeeze of lemon juice

Preheat the oven to 185°C.

Put the chicken in a roasting tin, drizzle it with the oil, season and cook for 15 minutes.

Add the onions, fennel, bacon, garlic and rosemary. Stir everything together and put the tin back in the oven for another 20 minutes, stirring once or twice.

Add the butter beans and the cream (if using), lemon juice and some salt and pepper. Put the tin back in the oven for a further 5 minutes, until golden and bubbling.

Serve with some boiled new potatoes.

MOZZARELLA WITH CHICKPEAS, TOMATOES AND BASIL

SERVES 4

2 tbsp olive oil

2 garlic cloves, thinly sliced

1 x 400g tin of chopped tomatoes

½ chicken or vegetable stock cube

½ tsp smoked paprika

a squeeze of honey

1 x 400g tin of chickpeas, drained and rinsed

1 orange, peeled and sliced

4 balls of mozzarella

extra virgin olive oil, for drizzling

a few fresh basil leaves, torn

Heat the oil in a saucepan over a low to medium heat. Add the garlic and gently fry just until it starts to colour, then add the tomatoes, crumble in the stock cube and add the smoked paprika and honey. Cook gently for 10 minutes before adding the chickpeas and seasoning. Keep warm.

To serve, put two orange slices on each plate. Tear open the mozzarella balls and put one on top of each plate. Spoon the warm chickpea mixture over each ball of mozzarella. Drizzle a little extra virgin olive oil over the top, followed by torn basil.

FLUFFY CRAB AND AVOCADO FLATBREADS

SERVES 4

2 ripe avocados
½ fresh red chilli, deseeded and finely diced
juice of 1 lime
100g picked crab meat
a few sprigs of fresh coriander

FOR THE FLATBREADS:
350g natural yogurt
350g self-raising flour, plus a little extra for dusting
1 tsp baking power
2 tbsp olive oil

To make the flatbreads, mix the yogurt, flour, baking powder and a pinch of salt together until it becomes a dough. Cover with cling film and let it rest for 20 minutes before cutting into eight even pieces.

On a lightly floured surface, press the dough into rounds 0.5cm thick. Heat the oil in a frying pan until it's gently smoking. Working in batches, add the flatbreads to the hot oil and cook for 3 minutes on each side, until golden and puffy. Drain on kitchen paper and keep warm.

Crush the avocados with the chilli, lime juice and some salt and pepper, then fold through the crab meat.

To serve, spoon the crab and avocado on top of the warm flatbreads. Garnish with a few coriander leaves.

A springtime barbecue feast

02 MAY 2020

I had an emergency visit to the dentist last week. I woke up one morning with a wobbly tooth and a chipped filling. I was like a fella who'd been in an altercation in his dreams.

A check-up determined that the tooth had to go. Apparently it was a baby tooth anyhow and I shouldn't be worried. 'Tell that to the hole in my mouth,' I said as I felt the last vestiges of my youth pulled from me. I was diagnosed as a teeth grinder, brought on by anxiety. 'What's there to be anxious about?' I said smartly.

I've more time on my hands than I've ever had, except perhaps for when I was studying for my Leaving Cert. However, I'm getting used to the routine. I'm finding that scary in and of itself. It's like being retired but without a pension.

As with everybody, the cooking at home is constant. We are sitting down for more meals as a family than was ever conceivable before. The moods around the table ebb and flow. I acutely avoid information overload, as sometimes I think my frazzled brain will pop out of my head like a piece of toast from a toaster.

The weather has been tantalising — the perfect spring — so I've been using the barbecue as much as possible. I need no encouragement. Perhaps deep down it makes me feel more manly but I just love the ease of it.

I cooked these lamb chops, rubbed and adorned with nothing but salt. The lick of the flames did the rest, the fat crisp and charred in an almost primal way.

This week's dishes are meant to go together. The agrodolce of soft onions complements the earthiness of the roasted beetroot in the salad. The feta, yogurt and mint dressing adds piquancy and the seeds provide pings of interest. The hot herbiness of the spuds give life to the chops. It's a lovely springtime feast.

Those of us with gardens are lucky. We can sit, eat and watch everything blossom as the year ticks on. Is it just me or do the birds seem louder? Perhaps they are singing for us.

LAMB CHOPS WITH SWEET AND SOUR ONIONS AND RAISINS

SERVES 4

1 x 8-bone rack of lamb, cut into chops

FOR THE ONIONS:
50g butter
2 large onions, thinly sliced
1 sprig of fresh thyme
1 tbsp raisins
1 tbsp golden caster sugar
2 tbsp red wine vinegar

Melt the butter in a saucepan over a medium heat. When it starts to foam, add the onions and thyme, cover the pan and cook gently for about 15 minutes, making sure the onions don't take on any colour. This will ensure a sweet, thyme-y butteriness.

Add the raisins, brown sugar and vinegar. Cook for another few minutes, until thick and syrupy. Season and set aside.

To cook your chops, set your barbecue to a high heat, then turn it down a little. Season the chops well and put them on the barbecue. Do not move them for 5 minutes, then turn them over. After another 3 minutes, try to balance the chops on their fatty side to get the fat crisp. They won't take much longer to cook at this stage, depending on how you like them.

Turn off the barbecue. Let the chops rest for a few minutes in the coolest spot.

Warm the onions and serve the chops on top along with your two lovely salads on the following two pages.

A LOVELY BEETROOT SALAD

SERVES 4

4 large beetroot, scrubbed

250g natural yogurt

100g feta cheese

1 tbsp mint jelly

2 mandarins, peeled and segmented

50g sunflower and/or pumpkin seeds, lightly toasted in a hot, dry pan

a few sprigs of fresh dill

a drizzle of extra virgin olive oil

Preheat the oven to 150°C.

Wrap each of the beetroot in foil and roast in the oven for around 2 hours, until soft — you can test them with a knife.

When they're cool enough to handle, peel and cut into chunks. Put them in a pretty bowl and season.

Blend the yogurt, feta and mint jelly together, then spoon it over the beetroot. Scatter over the mandarins, seeds and dill. Finally, give everything a lick of good extra virgin olive oil and it's ready to serve.

GREEN AND PERKY SPUDS

SERVES 4

juice of ½ lemon
75ml sunflower oil
a pinch of rock salt
1kg new potatoes, cooked, cooled and peeled if you fancy
½ fresh red chilli, deseeded and very finely diced
1 tsp nigella seeds, toasted in a hot, dry pan (optional)
lots of chopped fresh mint

In a large bowl, whisk the lemon juice into the oil with a pinch of rock salt and some freshly ground black pepper.

Add the cooked and cooled potatoes, followed by the rest of the ingredients. Mix well and serve in a pretty bowl.

Simple dishes are often the best

09 MAY 2020

I've finally realised that I suffer from tsundoku (Google it, reader). I was a voracious reader but my powers of concentration are shot. The phone has ruined me. I can only absorb information in short bursts, never allowing relaxation to replace the fretting. I chastise everyone else in the family for their phone usage but I'm just as bad.

Pictures help. I've taken solace in beautiful garden books. We have quite a few. Perfectly snipped foliage and verdant lawns keep me distracted for a while, but the glow of admiration is replaced by envy as I stare out the window.

My cookbooks give me the most comfort, especially the ones with beautiful writing. The best books give me an understanding of the cook's wishes and the dishes' origins. I'm left wistful, longing to travel to the place of their birth.

I came across some lovely oxtail and couldn't leave it behind. It's not something most people are used to cooking, but I urge you to try it. Your butcher will get it for you; after all, every cow has a tail. It's early summer, so I needed to make it lighter. It longs to be with mash and a deep gravy, but I experimented with star anise, cardamom and sesame. It's a more involved recipe than usual, but it's a technique worth knowing. By the way, you can use beef shin for this if you can't get oxtail — just leave it in big chunks and cook it for 3½–4 hours.

Smoked haddock and egg are best friends. This is the simplest of dishes, but they are often the best. The key is to cook the eggs until they just set, keeping a runny yolk. This becomes your sauce, helped along with a little cream.

We've been living off pasta. This was one of many dinners we made quickly and cheaply. I had all the ingredients handy but the dill was an eccentric addition. I worried about it slightly, but the lime, dill and Parmesan work surprisingly well. These unlikely but newfound friends would go wonderfully with grilled fish if you wanted to make it a little bit more sophisticated.

OXTAIL WITH STAR ANISE, LITTLE GEMS AND SESAME

SERVES 4

plain flour, to coat

2kg oxtail or beef shin, cut into pieces

100ml sunflower oil

a knob of butter

2 onions, roughly chopped

2 carrots, roughly chopped

3 celery sticks, roughly chopped

1 fennel bulb, roughly chopped

1 head of garlic, cut in half around the equator

3 star anise

2 sprigs of fresh rosemary

750ml chicken stock

1 heaped tbsp redcurrant jelly

FOR THE PICKLED CARROTS:

2 carrots

juice of 1 orange

1 tbsp golden caster sugar

1 tbsp red wine vinegar

6 green cardamon pods, crushed

FOR THE SALAD:

200g natural yogurt

2 tbsp toasted sesame oil

2 heads of Little Gem lettuce, leaves separated

1 tsp toasted sesame seeds

a few sprigs of fresh coriander

Preheat the oven to 140°C.

Put the flour in a large bowl and season with salt and pepper. Add the oxtail, tossing to coat. Pat off the excess.

Heat half of the oil in a large, heavy-based casserole until it's gently smoking. Working in batches, add the oxtail and sear it over a medium heat until it's golden brown all over, then transfer to a plate with a slotted spoon while you sear the rest.

Carefully pour off the hot oil. Put the casserole back on a medium heat with the remaining oil and the butter. When the butter has melted, add the onions, carrots, celery, fennel, garlic, star anise and rosemary. Cover and sweat for about 15 minutes, until soft.

Add the oxtail back to the casserole, then add the stock and redcurrant jelly. Bring to a simmer, cover and put in the oven. Cook for 4–5 hours, until the meat is falling off the bone.

Meanwhile, to make the pickled carrots, peel the carrots, then continue to peel into ribbons down to the base of the carrot. Bring the orange juice, sugar, vinegar and cardamon to the boil in a saucepan, then add the carrot strips. Immediately remove the pan from the heat and allow to cool.

When the oxtail is ready, lift it out of the casserole and set aside. Strain the cooking liquid into a fresh saucepan through a fine mesh sieve, pushing through any juices from the vegetables with the back of a ladle.

Bring the liquid to the boil and reduce by half, carefully skimming any fat from the surface all the while. When the sauce reaches a coating consistency, put the oxtail back into the sauce until you need it.

To serve, heat the oxtail in its juices, then divide among four wide, shallow bowls.

Mix the yogurt with the sesame oil in a large bowl, then add the Little Gem leaves, tossing to coat, like a Caesar salad. Put on top of the oxtail, followed by pickled carrots, the sesame seeds and fresh coriander leaves.

Serve with plain basmati rice.

SMOKED HADDOCK WITH NEW POTATO, EGG AND SPRING ONION SALAD

SERVES 4

1 tbsp raisins

6 eggs

10 new potatoes, cooked, peeled and lightly crushed

4 spring onions, chopped

100ml cream

1 tsp red or white wine vinegar

250ml milk

1 sprig of fresh thyme or 1 bay leaf (fresh if possible)

4 x 125g portions of smoked haddock, bones removed

a little rapeseed or extra virgin olive oil

Soak the raisins in a bowl of just-boiled water for 15 minutes to plump them up, then drain.

Meanwhile, cook your eggs in boiling water for precisely 6 minutes, then drain and run under cold water to cool. Peel the eggs and crush them into the cooked, crushed potatoes with the back of a fork. Add the drained raisins to the mix along with the spring onions, cream, vinegar and some salt and pepper.

Bring the milk and herbs to a simmer in a saucepan. Add the smoked haddock, cover and cook gently for 6 minutes or so, until cooked through – this will depend on the thickness of the fish.

Spoon the egg and potato salad onto warm plates. Drain the haddock and serve on top. Add a drizzle of good oil for a lustrous sheen.

LITTLE EARS WITH PEAS, LIME AND PARMESAN

SERVES 6

500g conchiglie

450g frozen petits pois, thawed

1 red onion, thinly sliced

100g Parmesan cheese, grated

250ml cream

150ml vegetable stock

zest and juice of 1 lime

2 tbsp chopped fresh dill

Bring a large pot of salted water to the boil. Cook the pasta according to the packet instructions, until al dente.

When the pasta is still slightly firm, add the peas and sliced red onion. Bring back to the boil and cook for 1 more minute.

Drain the pasta, peas and onion and put them back in the pot. Stir in the Parmesan, cream, stock, lime zest and juice and dill. Season and serve.

∞

The arrival of better weather flicks a piscine switch in me

16 MAY 2020

I was in the RTÉ studio in Cork doing a furtive in-and-out recording for the *Today Show*. I made a trip to the English Market before I went home. It felt so good to be there, almost normal. I went to all my usual spots, as there were many requests from my hungry chicks back home.

The fish, of course, was the highlight. The counters glistened and shimmered with hope. They made me happy. I couldn't resist. Filleted brill was paired with tenderstem broccoli and a buttery onion champ that evening. The world was perfect for an hour.

It's normal for me to shift my focus at this time of the year. The bright evenings call for it. The arrival of better weather flicks a piscine switch in me. I have great difficulty understanding people who don't like fish. I just can't get my head around it. Often it's not about posh fish for me — I like to champion the unappreciated and ugly. However, a pile of tangled langoustines is one of my many death row meals.

When thinking of this seafood roast, I imagined I had access to the most perfect fish counter. In reality I scrambled for my catch, but that's okay as the best cooks have the confidence to adapt. Freshness is key, but so is the cutting of the fish. Being all the same size is crucial to the perfect result, no matter what the fish.

I wanted to show you a simple butter sauce, the sriracha being a bold but removeable addition. A sprig of fresh rosemary would be a pleasing substitution.

This salmon dish is a perky delight. The Asian twist gives vigour and interest to its rich flesh. We usually eat it with steamed basmati rice and greens for a guilt-free midweek dinner.

I love hake as much as the Spanish do. Its yielding creaminess marries perfectly with darker flavours — the black pudding stands up to it admirably.

The garlic sauce is a little cheat and a pure luxury, a great addition to your repertoire. Try it with lamb, steak or chicken and you might never go to a restaurant again — although I should hardly be saying that, even in jest.

A SEAFOOD ROAST

SERVES 4

200g mussels

4 tbsp olive oil

1 x 250g piece of monkfish, trimmed and cut into 3cm chunks

4 x 80g fillets of hake or cod

1 bunch of asparagus, trimmed

1 small leek, washed and cut into rounds 1cm thick

12 new potatoes, cooked and halved

180g shelled prawn tails

8 vine-ripened cherry tomatoes, halved

FOR THE SAUCE:

juice of 1 orange

100g cold butter, diced

1 tbsp sriracha sauce

chopped fresh chives (optional)

Preheat the oven to 200°C.

To prepare the mussels, immerse them in a clean sink of cold water. Agitate. Debeard them one by one into a clean bowl, discarding any that are open and won't close when you gently tap them on the counter. Drain and clean the sink, fill it with cold water again and re-immerse the debearded mussels. Agitate the mussels once more, then lift them from the water, leaving any sediment behind.

Drizzle the oil in a large, shallow roasting tin. Put your monkfish, the hake or cod, asparagus, leek and cooked potatoes in the tin, season and turn carefully to coat it all in the oil. Even everything out and cook in the oven for 10 minutes.

Meanwhile, to make the sauce, bring the orange juice to a gentle simmer in a saucepan. Whisk in the butter a few cubes at a time until fully emulsified, then add the sriracha and remove the pan from the heat.

When the 10 minutes are up on the oven timer, add the mussels, prawns and tomatoes to the roasting tin in an even layer, making sure they are all covered in a little bit of oil. Return to the oven to cook for another 10 minutes.

Once the roast is cooked, add the chives to the sauce (if using). Drizzle the sauce over the top and serve straight to the table.

SKINNY SALMON WITH SOY, GINGER AND CABBAGE

SERVES 4

2 large garlic cloves, grated

a thumb-sized piece of ginger, peeled and grated

75ml dark soy sauce

75ml water

1 tsp honey

4 x 140g skinless salmon fillets

1 small head of cabbage, trimmed

1 tbsp toasted sesame oil

Preheat the oven to 200°C.

Mix the grated garlic, ginger, soy, water and honey together.

Put the salmon in a baking dish, then pour in the garlic and soy mixture. Turn the salmon in the mixture, then tightly cover the dish with foil. Bake in the oven for approximately 15 minutes, then check to see if the salmon is cooked through. If it isn't ready, pop it back in the oven for another couple of minutes.

Meanwhile, cook your cabbage in boiling salted water for 2 minutes. Drain, drizzle with the sesame oil and keep warm.

Plate up the salmon with the cabbage, with the garlicky, gingery juices from the baking dish poured over. Serve with rice.

HAKE WITH GARLIC CREAM AND BLACK PUDDING

SERVES 4

4 x 140g skinless hake fillets, bones removed

8 thick slices of black pudding

1 tbsp olive oil

a few apple batons, for crisp freshness

FOR THE GARLIC CREAM:

1 tbsp olive oil

4 large garlic cloves, very thinly sliced

250ml cream

1 sprig of fresh rosemary

½ chicken stock cube

a generous squeeze of lemon

Preheat the oven to 185°C.

Heat the oil in a small saucepan over a low heat. Add the sliced garlic and cook it VERY gently in the warm oil. The objective is to achieve an even golden colour without overcooking the garlic, which would make your sauce bitter.

When the garlic is golden, add the cream, rosemary and stock cube, then bring it up to a gentle blip. After 5 minutes or so, when your sauce has reduced a bit to a coating consistency, remove the rosemary. Add a squeeze of lemon juice to lighten. Season and keep warm.

Put your hake and black pudding in a shallow roasting tin. Drizzle over the tablespoon of oil, season and turn the fish and pudding in the oil to make sure it doesn't stick to the tin. Bake in the oven for 12 minutes before checking to see if the fish and black pudding are cooked through. The fish may need to cook for a little longer depending on its thickness.

Divide among warm plates with the sauce spooned over generously. Artfully add some apple batons. Serve with some boiled new potatoes.

Grown-up pasta, straight from Venice

23 MAY 2020

These days, I always seem to be looking backwards. The future has been postponed, so I find myself reminiscing more than ever. A friend posted a live picture of St Mark's Square in Venice recently. It was devoid of any life. It was eerie, almost apocalyptic

We visited Venice one crisp, bright January, when restauranteurs take holidays. This historic beauty had been on my bucket list for some time. It was love at first sight. The steps from the main train station in Venice descend into Canaletto. The Grand Canal assaults you with its bustling, breath-taking beauty.

As ever, I had food on my mind. My guide for the city was Russell Norman, owner of the Polpo restaurant. His *Polpo* cookbook contains an essential list of all the places he loves in the city. Narrowing it down to his favourites was a conundrum. Busy even in the off season, Venice's network of tiny streets can be daunting. We spent most of our time lost, as my quest to find the Holy Grail increasingly became a chore.

The Rialto fish market was base camp. A man trimming artichokes with preposterous speed caught my imagination. We found All'Arco. In a tiny space, it delivers some of the best food in the city. We ate delectable little toasts and desperately tried to fit in. I have been dreaming about it ever since.

The first two dishes today are an homage to All'Arco. The bigoli is a grown-up pasta. It divisively contains anchovies, the brown salted ones. I adore them but have pared my version back for any sensitivities.

We also ate cod brandade on toast there. I've adapted it a little into an easy, creamy delight. Incidentally, if you didn't want this on toast, it's wonderful with a summer salad and boiled potatoes or served as a gentle sauce for pasta.

This gratin honours the artichoke and the craftsman from the market. I'm using tinned or jarred artichokes. They are not the same, but they are easy and quick. If you can't get them, don't worry — substitute a tin of butter beans. I've also added salami. I love its fatty saltiness — or maybe it just takes me back to Venice.

BIGOLI IN SALSA

SERVES 4

4 tbsp olive oil
2 large white onions, thinly sliced
10 brown anchovy fillets
1 small glass of white wine
300g wholegrain spaghetti
a generous knob of butter
a twist of black pepper

Heat the oil in a large, heavy-based pan over a low heat. Add the onions and gently sweat for 20–30 minutes, until they are really soft and nearly falling apart.

Add the anchovies and wine. Continue to cook gently until the wine reduces, mashing the anchovies into the onions until you have a thick, chunky sauce.

Cook the pasta as per the packet instructions in lightly salted water, making sure you keep it authentically al dente. Drain but retain 100ml of the cooking water.

Add the pasta, reserved cooking water, butter and pepper to the sauce and mix well, coating the spaghetti thoroughly.

Serve straightaway in warm bowls.

CREAMY COD BRANDADE ON TOAST

SERVES 6

½ tbsp salt (rock salt if you have it)
1 x 250g cod fillet
2 garlic cloves, crushed
100ml cream
50ml extra virgin olive oil, plus extra for drizzling
a squeeze of lemon
6 slices of bread from a good crusty loaf, toasted

Sprinkle the salt over the fish, cover with cling film and put in the fridge for 4 hours. Rinse thoroughly in cold water.

Bring a medium pan of water to the boil. Add the cod, then immediately remove the pan from the heat. Allow the cod to cool in the water.

Remove the cod from the water and flake the flesh into a bowl. Add the crushed garlic and cream and start to whisk and break up the fish. When it starts to thicken, drizzle in the oil and lemon juice.

Serve the cod brandade on toast with a drizzle of extra virgin olive oil over the top.

CRUSTED SUMMER GREENS WITH LEMON, ARTICHOKES AND SALAMI

SERVES 4

2 courgettes

200g tenderstem broccoli, trimmed

6 artichoke hearts (from a tin or jar), halved

1 small fresh red chilli, deseeded and thinly sliced

120g sliced salami, cut into strips

60ml olive oil

200g fresh breadcrumbs

50g Parmesan cheese, grated

zest of 1 lemon

2 garlic cloves, finely chopped

50g flaked almonds

Preheat the oven to 180°C.

Top and tail your courgettes, then slice them at an angle, 1cm thick. Put them in a large, shallow roasting tin along with the broccoli, artichoke hearts, chilli and salami. Add half of the oil, season, mix well and spread everything out evenly.

Mix the breadcrumbs, Parmesan, lemon zest, garlic, almonds, some salt and pepper and the remaining oil in a bowl. Sprinkle this over the vegetable mixture in the roasting tin.

Bake in the oven for 15–20 minutes, until everything is cooked, golden brown and crunchy. Serve immediately.

After too much lockdown eating

30 MAY 2020

So we're back to work, sort of. We're doing a simple takeaway at weekends. It's just as well as I'm not good at doing nothing. Despite plenty of walking, the pounds are creeping on. It's not surprising, really, as the whole focus of the day was what we were going to have for lunch and dinner. I was constantly cooking, then inevitably it was couch time. I could feel myself getting more bootylicious by the day.

I tried doing a bit in the garden, but digging holes isn't my forte. It's not great when your tetchy wife banishes you to the kitchen with an ill-concealed roll of her eyes as a result of your general uselessness. I've always been a good worker, but my body refuses to obey my mind once it goes outside. It only operates full belt in the warm confines of the kitchen.

The food this week isn't what we're serving from the Tannery kitchen, but rather the food I'll be having at home after this bank holiday weekend to help with the battle of the bulge.

The whole thing about lighter food is that it shouldn't resonate of penury, misery and guilt. Otherwise you won't be satisfied. I love lemon sole, but if you can't get it, use plaice. I'm cooking double fillets that are brushed with crème fraîche and drizzled with a little olive oil. This prevents the fish from drying out while cooking. The crunchy fennel salad is one I use a lot in the summer, often paired with burrata or goat cheese.

This broth is given body by roasting ciabatta with a little olive oil. It's kind of a soupy version of panzanella, the classic Italian bread salad. The smoky, pungent juice seeps into the bread to make it ultra-satisfying. This salad is simple but it requires good leaves and ripe tomatoes, otherwise don't bother.

A salad with a light dressing of gazpacho, pert courgette and Manchego cheese will give us a gentle nudge towards the Iberian peninsula. This recipe makes more dressing than you need, but it happily freezes.

BAKED LEMON SOLE WITH FENNEL, ORANGE AND CHILLI

SERVES 4

4 large double fillets of lemon sole, skin on (use plaice if you can't get lemon sole)

2 tbsp crème fraîche

75ml olive oil

2 fennel bulbs, sliced as thinly as you can (a mandolin works well for this) – keep any fronds to chop through the salad

1 orange, peeled and segmented

½ fresh red chilli, deseeded and finely diced

a little pinch of sugar

Preheat the oven to 185°C.

Put the sole on an oiled baking tray, skin side down. Spread the crème fraîche in an even layer over the top. Drizzle with some of the oil, then bake the fish in the oven for 8–10 minutes, until cooked. The cooking time will depend on the thickness of the fish.

Meanwhile, mix the fennel with the orange segments, chilli, sugar and the remaining oil. Chop any fennel fronds you may have and stir them through, then season.

Serve the fish with the fennel and orange and some boiled new potatoes.

TOMATO BROTH WITH ROASTED BREAD AND PARMESAN

SERVES 4

1 small ciabatta, torn into chunks

6 tbsp olive oil

1 fennel bulb, quartered and sliced

1 red pepper, quartered and sliced

2 garlic cloves, sliced

1 tsp smoked paprika

500ml chicken or vegetable stock

2 pieces of orange peel

a few sprigs of fresh basil, leaves and stalks kept separate

250g baby plum or cherry tomatoes, halved

1 tsp honey

50g Parmesan cheese shavings

Preheat the oven to 185°C.

Put the bread on a baking tray, then drizzle over a little of the oil and toast in the oven for 12–15 minutes, until golden and crisp.

Meanwhile, heat the remaining oil in a saucepan over a gentle heat. Add the fennel, red pepper and garlic, cover the pan with a lid and sweat for 15 minutes or so, until soft and sweet. Add the smoked paprika and cook for 3 more minutes.

Add the stock, orange peel and basil stalks. Bring to a simmer and cook for 5 minutes before adding the tomatoes, honey and some salt and pepper. Remove the basil stalks.

Divide the toasted bread among warm bowls, then ladle the soup over the top. Finish with Parmesan shavings and the fresh basil leaves.

SUMMER LEAVES AND COURGETTE WITH GAZPACHO DRESSING AND MANCHEGO

SERVES 4

400g salad leaves
1 courgette, peeled into strips
100g Manchego or Parmesan cheese, shaved
little plum tomatoes, halved

FOR THE DRESSING:
500g vine-ripened cherry tomatoes, halved
1 red pepper, sliced
½ cucumber, peeled and diced
2 garlic cloves, sliced
8 stalks of fresh basil
300ml water
200ml olive oil
2 tbsp red or white wine vinegar
a pinch of sugar

To make the dressing, blend all the ingredients in a food processor until smooth. Season and put in the fridge – like a true gazpacho, it's better chilled.

When ready to serve, turn your leaves and courgette strips in the gazpacho dressing, then transfer to a large serving platter. Scatter over the cheese shavings and tomatoes and serve.

Retro boy

06 JUNE 2020

I used to be the head chef of a restaurant called La Stampa in the early 1990s. It was a pretty rock 'n' roll place at the time, with wall-to-wall celebs and giddy weekly reportage in all the gossip columns.

It was a great place to work. It bustled with people, like the best Parisian brasseries. There was always a frisson in the air, especially on the walk from the bar through the corridor that opened up into a room of breath-taking beauty. Bagging a Saturday night table was like being given a golden ticket by Willy Wonka.

Ireland was on the cusp of the mad years — things were on the up and people were flashing the cash. Everybody was glamorous, as befitted the room. It was a million miles away from the staidness of the restaurant I'd come from in Park Lane in London. Here, for the first time, I cooked what I wanted. I had to find my own way.

That restaurant taught me a lot of things, most importantly that a great restaurant is not all about the food. Front of house is every bit as important. The waiters were famously the highest tipped in Ireland and the managers, Declan Maxwell and Pat Gath, ran the place like a Las Vegas show. I kept the food simple and tasty. I had to — we were doing 250 people a night. It was all about the infamous buzz and the happy punters clamoured to return.

I still have all my menus from La Stampa. One dish stands out: bang bang chicken. I had eaten it at Marco Pierre White's Canteen and loved it. So did the people of Dublin. It's deliciously retro, as are the other dishes here. The prawn cocktail is super-easy. You could cheat even more and buy decent hummus to replace the butter bean dip to make a snazzy little starter. I'm using shop-bought shortcrust pastry for the quiche, but fire away if you want to make your own. I've added dark sherry and a few raisins to the onions to give it robustness.

BANG BANG CHICKEN

SERVES 8

6 heads of Little Gem lettuce
1 whole cooked chicken, shredded
a few sprigs of fresh coriander
toasted sesame seeds

FOR THE CARROT AND CUCUMBER PICKLE:
1 carrot
½ cucumber
100ml rice wine vinegar
100ml water
100g caster sugar
½ fresh red chilli, deseeded and finely diced

FOR THE DRESSING:
1 x 400ml tin of light coconut milk
3 tbsp crunchy peanut butter
a thumb-sized piece of ginger, peeled and grated

To make the dressing, bring the coconut milk up to a gentle simmer in a saucepan, then whisk in the peanut butter and ginger. Set aside to cool, then chill in the fridge.

To make the pickle, peel and trim the carrot, then cut it lengthways into four pieces. Peel the cucumber, then cut it lengthways into four pieces too.

Bring the vinegar, water and sugar to the boil in a saucepan, then add the carrot and chilli, take the pan off the heat and set aside. When cool, add the cucumber and chill in the fridge.

To serve, scatter the Little Gem leaves over a serving platter. Turn the cooked, shredded chicken in the dressing, season and put on top of the lettuce. Drain the carrot and cucumber pickle and scatter the veg over the salad, then sprinkle fresh coriander and toasted sesame seeds over the top.

A NEW PRAWN COCKTAIL

SERVES 4

1 head of Little Gem lettuce, shredded
a knob of butter
20 large prawn tails
4 tbsp sweet chilli sauce
4 lemon wedges

FOR THE BUTTER BEAN PURÉE:
juice of 1 lemon
1 tsp caster sugar
1 x 400g tin of butter beans, drained and rinsed
1 garlic clove, crushed
2 tbsp crème fraîche
2 tbsp olive oil

Bring the lemon juice and sugar to the boil in a small pan, then remove from the heat.

Put the butter beans and garlic in a food processor with the lemon syrup and purée until smooth. Add the crème fraîche, oil and seasoning, then scrape out into a bowl and set aside.

When ready to serve, divide the butter bean purée among four nice glasses. Top with shredded lettuce.

Melt the butter in a frying pan. When it starts to gently foam, add your prawns and cook for 1 minute on each side before adding the sweet chilli sauce. Remove the pan from the heat and let the sauce bubble around the prawns.

Spoon the prawns on top of the lettuce in the glasses and serve with a lemon wedge.

This, to me, is cooking: the transformation of a humble ingredient into something surprising just by being thoughtful and curious.

PEDRO XIMÉNEZ, CARAMELISED ONION AND COOLEA QUICHE

SERVES 6

50g raisins

30g butter

2 large onions, sliced

50ml Pedro Ximénez or another dark, sweet sherry

a few fresh thyme leaves

1 x 320g sheet of ready-rolled shortcrust pastry, thawed

plain flour, for dusting

a little oil, for greasing

3 large eggs

200ml milk

200ml cream

a pinch of ground nutmeg

150g Coolea, Gubbeen or a good Cheddar cheese, grated

Soak the raisins in a bowl of just-boiled water for 15 minutes to plump them up, then drain.

Melt the butter in a frying pan over a medium heat. When the butter starts to foam, add the onions and cook for 20 minutes, until soft and golden brown. Add the sherry and allow it to all be absorbed by the onions. Add the drained raisins to the onions along with the thyme and some salt and pepper.

Roll your pastry out a little on a lightly floured surface. Oil and flour a 25cm loose-bottomed tart tin. Line the tin with the pastry as best you can, making sure you leave a slight overhang around the edge of the tin. This will prevent shrinkage later. You may have to use some excess pastry to patch up any shortcomings – simply trim some off one side and press it into the less abundant side. Lightly prick the base all over with a fork and chill in the fridge to rest for 15 minutes.

Preheat the oven to 180°C.

Line the tart base with parchment paper and fill the base with ceramic baking beans or a good amount of rice. Bake in the oven for 20 minutes before removing the baking beans and parchment. Return to the oven for 10 more minutes, until the pastry base is golden and crisp.

Reduce the oven temperature to 170°C.

Spread the caramelised onion mixture over the base of the tart.

Whisk the eggs with the milk, cream, nutmeg and some salt and pepper, then pour this over the top of the onions.

Sprinkle the grated cheese over the custard mixture. Put the quiche back in the oven to cook for 25–30 minutes, until golden and the custard is set but still has a slight wobble in the centre. Allow to sit for at least 10 minutes.

To serve, trim away the excess pastry, carefully remove the quiche from the tin and cut into slices.

I'm a committed butter boy, but I've fallen for olive oil

13 JUNE 2020

I have a confession: I never fully appreciated good olive oil until frighteningly recently. I've always used it in my cooking but it was the workmanlike, everyday stuff, pleasant but unobtrusive. The dark, bitter, green oil scares me.

There are a few reasons for this. Some of it is ignorance on my part; some of it stubbornness, as I harbour a distain for elitism in food; and some of it is down to my roots, as I remain a committed butter boy. I bristle at the insistence of some food writers that only the olives harvested on the foothills of Mount Etna and pressed by the vestal virgins should be used to cook with. Food is simpler than that, more democratic. Delicious food can be made without breaking the bank or delivering a lecture.

I'm not going to tell you how recently my epiphany was. I bought a golden bottle of Extremaduran nectar one day when I was feeling flush. I drizzled it over Toonsbridge burrata with abundant flecks of sea salt and ate it with decent toast. I was transported. What a fool I had been to wait so long for such a joy. I always keep a bottle now, never for cooking with but for anointing something special like a beautiful piece of fish.

I love chicken wings. I could eat them all day long in all their manifestations. The true devotees will suck the garlic with as much enthusiasm as they devour their wings.

I should eat more aubergines. I never fell out with them but somehow in the past I needed others to convince me of their slippery glory. This dish is soothing, creamy and fiery at the same time. If you like aubergines, you'll love this. If harissa isn't your thing, smoked paprika would be a wonder.

Peperonata has been in my repertoire for a long time. I only cook it in summer. It's best friends with everyone, carnivore or vegetarian. More than anything else I eat it with rice or perhaps flatbread, something to absorb all its smoky goodness.

CHICKEN WINGS WITH ROASTED GARLIC, BALSAMIC AND ROSEMARY

SERVES 4

1.5kg large chicken wings

4 tbsp olive oil

2 tbsp honey

2 tbsp balsamic vinegar

2 bulbs of garlic, broken into cloves and left unpeeled

2 sprigs of fresh rosemary

Preheat the oven to 200°C.

Put your wings in a roasting tin, toss them in the oil, season and cook for 20 minutes.

Remove the tin from the oven and add the honey, balsamic, garlic and rosemary. Turn the heat down to 180°C and cook for 20 more minutes, turning once or twice in the tin until the wings are dark and sticky. Serve immediately.

BAKED AUBERGINES WITH HARISSA, ORANGE AND MASCARPONE

SERVES 6

3 aubergines

6 tbsp olive oil, plus extra for drizzling

250g mascarpone

1 egg yolk

zest of ½ orange

½ tbsp harissa paste

100g panko breadcrumbs (ordinary breadcrumbs will do too)

Preheat the oven to 180°C.

Cut the aubergines in half lengthwise. Score the flesh and put on a baking tray, cut side up. Drizzle over the oil, making sure it's rubbed well into the flesh, then season. Bake in the oven for 40 minutes, until soft and tender.

Meanwhile, mix the mascarpone with the egg yolk, orange zest and harissa, then season. Spoon the mixture evenly over the aubergines, then sprinkle over the breadcrumbs and drizzle with a little more oil. This can all be done ahead of time.

Bake for 20 minutes more, until golden and crisp. Serve with salad.

PEPERONATA

SERVES 6

50ml olive oil

2 onions, thinly sliced

3 red peppers, sliced

3 garlic cloves, sliced

½ fresh red chilli, deseeded and finely diced

1 tsp ground cumin

1 tsp smoked paprika

1 x 400g tin of chopped tomatoes

1 x 400g tin of kidney beans, drained and rinsed

2 pieces of orange peel

½ tbsp honey

Heat the oil in a saucepan over a medium heat. Add the onions, cover the pan and cook gently for 10 minutes.

Add the peppers, garlic, chilli and spices. Cover the pan again and cook on a low heat for another 20–25 minutes. I usually like to get things going over a medium heat, then cover the pan and turn down the heat until everything becomes soft and sweet.

Add the tomatoes, kidney beans, orange peel and honey. Cook over a medium heat for another 10 minutes with the lid off until it's all thick and syrupy. Season and set aside until needed.

The food of my dreams

20 JUNE 2020

I've just had the food of my dreams. My friend Ivan asked us over to his garden for lunch. The deal was he'd get the wine and I'd bring the food. 'I've got new spuds, though,' he said excitedly.

The anticipation of the coming of the new season potatoes is real — in the country, anyway. At home we binge on them for a full week before we tire of them. We never do anything fancy, just a simple steam, then a layer of butter, then some salt.

Our lunch was a classy one and my friend is one of the best cooks I know. I'm not calling him a chef. A chef is taught and the cooking is often strained. A cook is natural, instinctive, in harmony with the food. I've always wanted to be a cook.

To do the spuds justice, I brought a whole turbot. You can curse me for being a name-dropping fancy pants, but one of the advantages of having a restaurant is that I can order lovely things and have them delivered. It's annoying, I know.

When we arrived he'd already made a Tuscan bread salad then insisted on making a hollandaise for the turbot. I handed over the fish and all the responsibility. This doesn't happen very often, so I settled in and had some wine. It was a perfect day. We almost forgot about the you know what.

Fish cooked on the bone is a wonderful thing and nothing to be afraid of. It's the simplest of recipes. Turbot needs no gilding. The cooking time all depends on the size. I had a whopper and it took 25 minutes at 180°C. This method is suitable for other flat fish too.

I'm a bit weird. I loathe regular broccoli but love tenderstem. This is my favourite way of cooking and eating it, although when in a hurry at home I've often chucked the bag of broccoli straight into the microwave for two minutes. It works!

A Tuscan bread salad is a staple of our summer. It's also brilliant as a starter or light lunch with mozzarella, feta or goat cheese.

WHOLE BAKED TURBOT

SERVES 6

1 x 3kg turbot
200ml lightly salted water

Preheat the oven to 180°C.

Get your fishmonger to trim the head and the skirt of the fish, then to make an incision along the outside of the fillets and across the tail. This allows the skin to be lifted easily when cooked to expose the flesh.

Pour your lightly salted water into a large roasting tin, then add the turbot. Add a few twists of pepper, then bake in the oven for 20 minutes before checking. A smaller fish will take less time — don't be afraid to check.

The turbot is ready when the flesh is creamy, white and lifts from its central bone with ease. A slight touch of pink near the bone is expected and acceptable.

STEAMED TENDERSTEM BROCCOLI WITH HOLLANDAISE

SERVES 6

2 tbsp olive oil

3 garlic cloves, sliced

a knob of butter

2 x 200g packets of tenderstem broccoli

150ml water

FOR THE HOLLANDAISE:

4 egg yolks

juice of 1 lemon

a pinch of caster sugar

300g butter, melted and kept warm

To make the hollandaise, boil a saucepan of water, then put it on a kitchen towel to stabilise it. Put the egg yolks in a large-ish bowl and set the bowl on top of the saucepan, making sure the bottom of the bowl doesn't touch the water. Add the lemon juice, sugar and a pinch of salt and ground white pepper, then whisk over the pan of steaming water for 2–3 minutes, until the egg yolks start to thicken.

Slowly drizzle in the melted butter little by little, making sure it amalgamates all the while. I like to add the milk solids from the melted butter too, it's full of flavour.

For the broccoli, put the oil and garlic in a saucepan set over a gentle heat. Be patient and wait for the garlic to turn lightly golden, then add the butter to the oil to cool it down and stop the garlic getting brown and bitter. Add the broccoli and the water to the pan, season and cover. This can all be done ahead of time.

Bring the broccoli to a rapid boil and cook for 3 minutes or so, depending on the thickness of the broccoli stalks. The water will evaporate and cook down into a garlicky emulsion that will coat the broccoli like a dream.

Transfer the broccoli to a serving platter and drizzle over the hollandaise to serve.

TUSCAN BREAD SALAD

SERVES 6

2 red peppers
2 yellow peppers
150ml olive oil
½ loaf of ciabatta, torn into chunks
500g vine-ripened cherry tomatoes or other ripe tomatoes
1 red onion, thinly sliced
15 or so stoned large green olives, roughly chopped
8 salted anchovies, finely chopped (optional but lovely)
2 garlic cloves, crushed
1 tsp honey
a splash of red wine vinegar
10 fresh basil leaves, torn

Preheat the oven to 185°C.

Put the peppers on a baking tray, drizzle with a little of the oil and roast in the oven for 20 minutes or so, until soft and slightly charred (or you can buy roasted peppers in a jar for a quick cheat).

Put the bread in a roasting tin and drizzle with a little of the oil. Roast in the oven for 10 minutes or so, until golden and crunchy.

Cut the tomatoes in half and put them in a large bowl.

Put the sliced onion in a sieve and pour boiling water on top to soften them a little, then add to the tomatoes along with the toasted bread.

When the peppers are cool, peel, deseed and chop them, reserving any juices to sieve and add to the salad. Add the olives, anchovies (if using), garlic, honey, vinegar and the remaining oil.

Season, add the torn basil and serve.

I'm stepping back and taking a deep breath

27 JUNE 2020

I'm spoofing a bit in this one. These recipes are not so much family favourites, more what I *wish* were family favourites. My family likes all the ingredients in them, but it never follows that they will like the dish.

I won't repeat the foibles of my children to you, that would just be boring. They're not that fussy – I don't think. At least not in comparison to the other children they choose to tell me about. Maybe I'm gullible and they're fickle and we've all been cooped up together now for way too long. It's just as well things have loosened up. We were all flintily eyeing each other up by the end of the lockdown.

In truth, I also feel a bit taken advantage of over the past few months. Their in-house chef has done all the cooking except for the two times their mother made dinner, with great fanfare. I feel like an old pony that's been ridden once too often. I'm stepping back and taking a deep breath.

Ingredients don't make dishes. That's where common sense comes in. The dishes today all make sense and are lovely to eat. A chicken schnitzel has crunch and interest. It can make the most mundane chicken tolerable. It sits on a buttery, simple stew of green things. Eat it with mash for comfort.

Rigatoni is sturdy and reliable and here it's enveloped in a pea cream that has the faint smoke of a rasher. Crisp pieces of white pudding adorn it like a crown. (Top secret: I prefer white to black pudding.)

I never waste chicken skin; it's the essence of roast chicken. Anytime I'm cooking chicken thighs, I save the skins and make this butter. Sometimes I roast the skins on their own with some salt as a dreamy snack. This butter is great with pasta or baked potatoes or with bread. I whip it to make it lighter so I can eat more of it, but if you choose not to, that's okay. It's a staple in the Tannery – I can't imagine being without it. You will have butter left over, but that's a good thing.

CHICKEN SCHNITZEL WITH BUTTERED COURGETTES, RED ONION AND THYME

SERVES 4

4 chicken breasts

plain flour, for coating

2 eggs beaten with a little milk and seasoned

250g stale breadcrumbs

a drizzle of olive oil

2 medium courgettes, topped and tailed

a large knob of butter

1 red onion, sliced

1 sprig of fresh thyme

200g frozen petits pois, thawed

a squeeze of lemon

4 tbsp sour cream

Preheat the oven to 200°C.

To butterfly the chicken breasts, cut each one in half from the side without cutting all the way through, then open it out like a book. Put the chicken between two pieces of cling film and bash it with a rolling pin until it's thin and even.

Get yourself a system whereby the flour (seasoned with salt and pepper) is in one wide, shallow bowl, the beaten eggs are in another and the breadcrumbs are in a third. This is a messy business.

One by one, coat your chicken in the flour, shaking off any excess, then in the egg, then finally in the breadcrumbs, making sure they adhere to every part of the chicken.

Drizzle a large baking tray with oil. Put your breaded schnitzels on the tray, then drizzle more oil on top of them. (This can all be done ahead of time.) Bake the chicken schnitzels in the oven for 15 minutes before checking to see if they are cooked. They dry out really easily, so it's better to be safe.

Meanwhile, cut the courgettes in half lengthways, then slice them evenly.

Melt your butter in a pan over a low heat. When the butter starts to foam, add the onion and thyme and cook for 3–4 minutes, then add the courgettes. Put a lid on the pan, raise the heat to medium and cook for 5 minutes before adding the peas. Give it another few minutes – the vegetables need to be soft but mustn't lose their colour. Season.

When the chicken is cooked, add a squeeze of lemon. Serve the schnitzel with the vegetables, a dollop of sour cream and some boiled new potatoes.

RIGATONI WITH SMOKY PEA CREAM AND WHITE PUDDING

SERVES 6

80g butter

1 onion, sliced

1 garlic clove, sliced

2 rashers of smoked streaky bacon

1 sprig of fresh rosemary or thyme

350g frozen petits pois, thawed

150ml water

500g rigatoni (penne would be fine too)

300g white pudding, sliced

a drizzle of olive oil

a sprinkling of grated Parmesan cheese

Preheat the grill.

Melt the butter in a saucepan over a medium heat. When the butter starts to foam, add the onion, garlic, rashers and rosemary or thyme, cover the pan, reduce the heat to low and sweat for about 15 minutes, until the onion is soft and translucent.

Add the peas and the water and cook over a high heat for 5 minutes. Remove the rashers and the rosemary or thyme from the pan. Season with salt and ground white pepper, then blend until smooth.

Cook the pasta according to the packet instructions.

While that's cooking, brush the pudding with a little oil, then grill until crisp.

Fold the pea cream through the pasta, then season.

To serve, divide among warm bowls. Put the pudding on top along with some grated Parmesan and a few extra herbs for prettiness if you have them.

SWEETCORN WITH ROAST CHICKEN BUTTER

SERVES 4

4 ears of fresh corn (prepacked will suffice of course)
a little olive oil, for brushing

FOR THE ROAST CHICKEN BUTTER:
6 chicken thigh skins
250g butter, softened
2 tbsp Worcestershire sauce
1 tbsp Dijon mustard
fresh thyme leaves

Preheat the oven to 185°C.

Lay your chicken skins out on a baking tray and bake in the oven until golden and crisp – this should take 15 minutes or so. Allow to cool, then chop. Reserve any fat that might be on the tray for the butter.

Put the soft butter in the bowl of a stand mixer fitted with the paddle attachment. Add the chicken fat and skin, Worcestershire sauce, mustard, thyme and some salt and pepper. Whip the butter for 2–3 minutes, until light and fluffy.

Roll into a sausage shape in a piece of cling film, twisting the ends like a Christmas cracker. Keep in the fridge until needed.

If using fresh corn, peel and boil for 15 minutes before barbecuing or roasting in the oven (the corn must be brushed with a little oil before barbecuing).

Slather the cooked corn with the roast chicken butter to serve.

The hulking carnivore inside me is utterly bored

04 JULY 2020

There's a large part of me that wants to change. Not the late-night, festival-going, disco-dancing part, but the hulking carnivore inside me is utterly bored.

As long as I've been in charge of a kitchen, my menus have been constructed the same way: meat or fish in the centre with vegetables playing second fiddle. Seasons are adhered to, of course, for without that there is nothing but lumpen tediousness. I've long wanted to put the vegetables centre stage. How old do I have to get before I'm brave enough to do it?

These dishes put vegetables first with a little meat or fish to enhance them. Sometimes the agricultural side of the Irish man will only be satisfied by size. I'm qualified to comment as I've spent a large part of my life feeding them. Portion sizes grow bigger the further you move away from the capital. I'm not judging, but it's a fact.

Taste is the key with these dishes. Their full-on flavours are fab. No ethereal nuancing. Eating these is like getting an enthusiastic hug — remember hugs?

I like cabbage at any time of the year. I imagine eating this on an uncertain summer day. We all know those days, when you spend a large part of it staring at the sky, wondering if it will rain. The cabbage is rendered soft in buttery juices, while the fat silkiness of the salami is cut by vinegar and apple. As a treat, eat with mash.

I made the crab dish in the height of elderflower season. It would be lovely on a pert salad but I decided on toast. It was just the mood I was in. Elderflower, tomato and crab might not be obvious bedfellows but they've gotten on famously since I forced them together.

Yuan Ming Yuan on Prince's Street in Cork is our favourite Chinese restaurant. The anticipation of our visits there sends us all into an excitable babble. We always have a dim sum feast that includes four seasons green beans. We devour them silently, interspersed only by groans of happiness. I've made the beans with duck instead of pork because I love duck.

ROASTED SUMMER CABBAGE WITH SALAMI AND APPLE

SERVES 4

1 summer cabbage

100g butter

2 tbsp golden raisins

2 sprigs of fresh thyme

200ml chicken stock

2 tbsp apple cider vinegar

a drizzle of honey

1 Granny Smith apple, peeled, cored and cut into batons

200g your favourite salami (mine is Gubbeen), diced or sliced

Preheat the oven to 185°C.

Trim off the outside leaves from the cabbage. Cut the cabbage into four wedges, then wash and pat dry.

Melt the butter in a baking tray set over the hob. When the butter starts to foam, add the cabbage, cut side down. Cook gently until the cabbage starts to brown, then add the raisins, thyme, stock, vinegar, honey and some salt and pepper. Cover the tray tightly with foil and bake in the oven for 25–30 minutes, until tender.

Remove the cabbage and raisins to warm plates. Spoon the juices over the cabbage, then divide the apple and salami over the top. Serve with mashed potatoes.

BUTTERED TOMATOES ON TOAST WITH ELDERFLOWER AND CRAB

SERVES 4

100g butter

250g mixed cherry tomatoes, halved

½ fresh red chilli, deseeded and finely diced

100g white crab meat, picked

2 tbsp chopped fresh chives

1 tbsp elderflower cordial

4 slices of good white bread, for toasting

Melt the butter in a saucepan over a medium heat. When the butter starts to foam, add your tomatoes and chilli. Cook gently for 2 minutes, until the tomatoes start to soften, then add the crab, chives, elderflower cordial and seasoning.

Toast the bread and serve the mixture on top. This would also be lovely with brown bread.

FOUR SEASONS GREEN BEANS WITH CRISPY DUCK

SERVES 4

300ml sunflower oil

400g French beans, trimmed

2 garlic cloves, finely chopped

1 fresh red chilli, deseeded and finely chopped

3cm piece of ginger, peeled and chopped

2 cooked duck legs, meat removed and chopped

1 tsp spice bag spice

a handful of cashew nuts, roughly chopped (peanuts would be fab too)

4 spring onions, thinly sliced

4 tbsp dark soy sauce

Heat the oil in a wok over a high heat. To test if it's hot enough, drop in one bean to see if it sizzles. Carefully add the beans to the hot oil and fry for 5 minutes or so, until the beans cook and shrivel a little. Remove the beans from the oil with a slotted spoon or tongs, then drain on kitchen paper.

Very carefully pour out the hot oil, leaving a little in the bottom of the wok. Add the garlic, chilli and ginger and fry for 1 minute over a medium heat, then add the duck. Cook for 2 more minutes before adding the spice bag mix and the cashews, followed by the beans. Cook for a couple of minutes, then stir in the spring onions and soy sauce and serve.

⌐☐

This seafood dish might be a little controversial

11 JULY 2020

Food has always been a comfort to me, whether it was an unfeasible number of custard creams after another failed maths exam in my spotty, well-upholstered youth or a lovely Sunday evening dinner after a stressful week at work.

Good food doesn't have to be posh. A bowl of soup will give you pause and sustenance. It will rest your mind and give you strength to tackle the rest of the day.

At long last, the Tannery is open again. Those balmy May days in the garden are just a dream. It's full tilt and it's good to be back, even in these difficult circumstances.

There's been so much goodwill from the customers. After all these years, many have become friends. The phones have been hopping and we are back in our summer swing, except nothing is normal anymore.

I've taken the opportunity to make the menu shorter. We have a smaller team, so something has to give. I've fallen out of love with large à la carte menus. To me, they're a relic of the past.

Restaurant food needs to be good first and foremost. The ingredients need to sing on the plate. It's not about the size of the menu, it's about the quality of the food.

It was hard to get mussels during the lockdown but now, hallelujah, they're back. This dish is a little controversial because I put Cidona in my mussels. So should you. It was inspired by Normandy, where they pair mussels with cider so beautifully. I've added crème fraîche to temper the sweetness of the Cidona.

This pie looks like a monster sausage roll. It will only take you minutes to make and it's lovely hot or cold. The filling can be any chutney you like. Occasionally I wedge chorizo in there as well.

A few years ago I was brought over to cook in New York by Kerrygold. We ate in BarButo, a famous and breezy Italian restaurant in the West Village. This kale salad was the highlight. Laden with crunchy, garlicky breadcrumbs, it was a family-style triumph. I've been making it ever since. It's particularly fabulous with steak.

STEAMED MUSSELS WITH CIDONA, CURRY SPICE AND CRÈME FRAÎCHE

SERVES 2

1kg mussels
50g butter
1 small onion, sliced
125g smoked bacon lardons
2 bay leaves (fresh if possible)
½ tsp curry powder
200ml Cidona
2 tbsp crème fraîche
chopped fresh parsley

To prepare the mussels, immerse them in a clean sink of cold water. Agitate. Debeard them one by one into a clean bowl, discarding any that are open and won't close when you gently tap them on the counter. Drain and clean the sink, fill it with cold water again and re-immerse the debearded mussels. Agitate the mussels once more, then lift them from the water, leaving any sediment behind.

Melt the butter in a large saucepan over a medium heat. When the butter starts to foam, add the onion, bacon and bay leaves and cook for 10 minutes, until the onion has softened. Add the curry powder and cook for 1 minute before adding the mussels and Cidona.

Cover the pan and bring to the boil. Cook for 2–3 minutes over a high heat, until all the mussels are open, stirring just once along the way. Do not overcook or the mussels will be tough and rubbery. Discard any that remain closed.

Remove the pan from the heat, then stir in the crème fraîche and parsley.

Serve straightaway with crusty bread.

GOAT CHEESE AND CHUTNEY PIE

SERVES 4

1 x 320g packet of ready-rolled puff pastry, thawed

1 egg beaten with 1 tbsp milk

2 tbsp your favourite relish or chutney

2 x 150g logs of soft rindless goat cheese

a few fresh thyme leaves

Preheat the oven to 185°C.

Unfurl your pastry so the widest part is facing you. Put the parchment from the packet on a flat baking tray.

Working quickly so the pastry stays chilled, brush the egg wash around all four edges to create a 3cm band. Spread the relish or chutney in a line on the bottom third of the pastry without touching the egg wash. Put the goat cheese on top of the chutney, then fleck the thyme on top.

Bring the top half of the pastry over the cheese to meet the bottom half, then press around the edge of the pastry so it all comes together. Seal with a fork.

Deftly transfer the pie onto the parchment-lined tray, then brush the top evenly with the egg wash. Bake in the oven for 20–25 minutes, until crisp and golden. Serve warm or hot.

BARBUTO KALE SALAD

SERVES 4

350g tender young kale
100g Parmesan cheese, grated

FOR THE DRESSING:
1 egg yolk
2 garlic cloves, crushed
6 salted anchovies, chopped
50ml sunflower oil
50ml olive oil
juice of 1 lemon
2 tbsp Dijon mustard
1 tbsp red wine vinegar

FOR THE BREADCRUMBS:
100g panko breadcrumbs
3 tbsp olive oil
1 garlic clove, crushed
½ tsp chilli flakes

Preheat the oven to 180°C.

To make the dressing, whisk everything together until smooth and creamy.

Put the breadcrumbs on a baking tray with the oil, garlic, chilli flakes and some salt and pepper. Cook in the oven for 12–15 minutes, turning once or twice, until golden and crunchy.

Remove the stalks from the kale, wash and pat dry. You can either chop the kale finely or pulse it in a food processor for a short time.

Toss the kale with the dressing, breadcrumbs and Parmesan and serve on a platter for sharing.

I'd do anything to get us all off our phones — including me

18 JULY 2020

Does parenthood automatically come with guilt or is it the fact that I was brought up a Catholic that amplifies it? Either way, the summer has its familial challenges when you have a restaurant in a seaside town. It's busy and that's great after all we've been through, but there's always a worry the girls will be floundering and lonely while we are at work.

They are lucky they have an action woman for a mother, though, who organises the staff, the restaurant and the husband as well. Our summer days are punctuated by zipping home numerous times a day as it was some clever bozo's idea to have a house on a hill away from town for the serenity and the view.

Dungarvan is a haven for little sailors and that keeps them occupied, but I'm afraid I'll be called upon to do some manly dad sailor stuff. However, I'll do anything to get us all off our phones, so if you see nautical photos of me in due course, don't be alarmed. I'll give new meaning to the phrase 'lost at sea'.

These dishes are for busy houses where food can't take over from the business of the day. The risotto is baked — not something I usually do, being a fan of the real thing, but this allows you to have more time to yourself. Eat it with a salad to alleviate the richness, otherwise you'll have to go straight to bed.

The shallot dish is a riff on a dish that was served for years in Le Caprice in London. Was there ever a more glamorous restaurant? I nervously bogtrotted through its doors on a few occasions back in the day, a young and innocent fish out of water. I was a long way from home. I like this with a good old rocket and Parmesan salad. I've left the whole garlic in its skins — prise them open and savour.

This tart is a fabulous little lunch or snack. The hummus, chilli and cumin give it a subtle hint of the Levant.

BAKED LEEK, PEA AND CHEDDAR RISOTTO

SERVES 4

50g butter
1 medium leek, finely chopped
300g Arborio risotto rice, rinsed
150g frozen petits pois
½ tsp smoked paprika
700ml vegetable stock
2 tbsp light cream cheese
100g mature Cheddar cheese, grated

Preheat the oven to 185°C.

Melt the butter in a heavy-based casserole over a medium heat. When the butter starts to foam, add the leek. Cook gently for 5 minutes, then add the rice, peas, smoked paprika and some salt and pepper.

Add the stock and bring to the boil, then cover the casserole and put it in the oven to cook for 25 minutes.

When the rice is cooked, fold in the cream cheese and most of the Cheddar, leaving a little for the top to serve.

STICKY SHALLOTS WITH MOZZARELLA AND PARMA HAM

SERVES 4

80ml olive oil

8 banana (large) shallots, halved (if you can't find large shallots, either double the number of small ones or use 3 red onions, peeled and cut into 6)

1 bulb of garlic, pulled apart and the cloves left whole and unpeeled

1 generous sprig of fresh thyme

3 tbsp balsamic vinegar

2 large balls of mozzarella, torn

8 slices of Parma ham

Preheat the oven to 180°C.

Put the oil, shallots, garlic, thyme and some salt and pepper in a baking dish. Roast in the oven for 15 minutes, turning once or twice, then add the balsamic vinegar. Return to the oven for another 5 minutes or so, until the shallots are soft, sticky and tender. This will all depend on the size of your shallots.

Serve the shallots warm or at room temperature with the torn mozzarella and the Parma ham draped over the top.

SPICED TOMATO TART WITH HUMMUS AND CORIANDER

SERVES 4

1 x 320g sheet of ready-rolled shortcrust pastry, thawed

3 generous tbsp of your favourite flavoured hummus

3 plum tomatoes, thinly sliced

a drizzle of olive oil

a pinch of ground cumin

a pinch of chilli flakes

fresh coriander leaves

Preheat the oven to 185°C.

Unfurl your pastry. Put the parchment from the packet on a flat baking tray. Spread the hummus evenly on top of the pastry, then distribute the tomatoes on top of the hummus. Drizzle with oil, then sprinkle over some cumin, chilli flakes and some salt and pepper. Bake in the oven for 18–20 minutes, until the pastry is crisp.

Eat hot or cold with a scattering of fresh coriander leaves on top and a little salad if you please.

The picnic almost broke me, but hot love made up for it

25 JULY 2020

Silvia was an Austrian au pair that came to help us for a busy summer. We love Austrian au pairs. We've had quite a few over the years and they add a cheerful energy to the house and are natural outdoorsy people.

Silvia settled in quickly. One evening over dinner she told us boldly that she was going to show Máire and I how to make hot love. Hello! She giggled knowingly and informed us that hot love was actually a popular Austrian dessert of microwaved raspberries with a little sugar over vanilla ice cream. We had a lot of hot love that summer.

To recompense, one day I proposed a hike in the Comeraghs and a picnic at the top. I made enough sandwiches to feed an army and packed fruit, crisps, water and two flasks of tea. I would carry the only rucksack. While not exactly K2, I was huffing and puffing even at the lower levels. Silvia looked at me with pity, occasionally offering to carry my load. I wheezed away every offer, eventually reaching the top. My children expressed worry at the sounds emanating from my startled body.

The view was majestic. Calm returned to my lungs and I ate most of the sandwiches, determined to lighten my cursed load. All I had done was transfer the weight to my stomach. On the way down I fell and hit my shoulder off a rock. I still wouldn't relinquish the rucksack. For my pride, I spent the next few months in physiotherapy.

These are picnic suggestions. The salmon brioche rolls are luxurious and the filling has been a starter of mine for years. I love tzatziki. I've added orzo, tomato and almonds to make it a satisfying lunch. The sausage salad is an homage to those lovely Austrians who were part of our home for years. We are still in touch with all of them. They used to bring us sausages from Styria called Käsekrainer, smoked pork sausages stuffed with cheese that oozed, blistered and bubbled as they cooked. They were so good, and so bad. I eyed the defibrillator as I ate them.

SALMON BRIOCHE ROLLS

SERVES 6

150g salmon fillet

75g smoked salmon, finely chopped

3 tbsp crème fraîche

1 tbsp chopped fresh chives

1 tbsp chopped fresh dill

1 tsp horseradish sauce

a squeeze of lemon

6 brioche rolls

Fill a small to medium-sized pot two-thirds full of water. Add some salt and bring to a simmer, then lower the fresh salmon into the water. Poach for no more than 1 minute before removing the pot from the heat and allowing the salmon to cool in the water. Remove the salmon, then pick out any skin and bones.

Flake the poached salmon into a bowl, then add the smoked salmon, crème fraîche, chives, dill, horseradish, lemon and seasoning. Fold everything together gently.

Divide among the brioche rolls and away you go.

ORZO AND ALMOND TZATZIKI

SERVES 4

250g orzo
125g mixed cherry tomatoes, halved
½ cucumber, peeled, deseeded and diced
2 garlic cloves, crushed
200g natural yogurt
50g flaked almonds, toasted
2 tbsp chopped fresh mint
2 tbsp chopped fresh dill
a little orange zest
a drizzle of olive oil

Cook the pasta according to the packet instructions, drain and allow to cool.

Fold the rest of the ingredients into the pasta, including salt and lots of freshly ground black pepper, making sure it's all mixed well.

Serve at room temperature.

POTATO, SHALLOT AND SAUSAGE SALAD

SERVES 6

1kg washed baby potatoes (I'm leaving the skins on)

300g your favourite decent sausages

2 large shallots, finely diced

100ml sunflower oil

2 tbsp red wine vinegar

2 tbsp water

1 tbsp Dijon mustard

1 tbsp wholegrain mustard

a drizzle of maple syrup

1 tbsp chopped fresh tarragon or 2 tbsp chopped fresh parsley

Cut the potatoes in half and cook them in boiling salted water until tender.

Cook the sausages. Allow to cool, then slice thinly.

Meanwhile, put the shallots, oil, vinegar, water, mustards, maple syrup and some salt and pepper in a large bowl and whisk to combine.

Drain the potatoes when cooked. Allow to cool just a little before adding them to the dressing along with the sausages and herbs. The warm potatoes absorb the dressing much more successfully than cold and the shallots mellow in the heat.

Check for seasoning. Serve warm or cold.

A long family lunch

01 AUGUST 2020

Bank holiday weekends beg for long lunches. Some of my fondest memories have been made over lunches, long, lazy affairs with friends that meld into the night. They are often enjoyed while on holiday, where balmy days are assured and eating al fresco cements the leisurely nature of the day.

Dinners can be special too, but my impatience means I have to wait too long before I'm propped at a table and raring to go. I have vivid and warm memories of the best lunches, no matter how far back they go. My addled brain unearths them from time to time when I'm feeling wistful, like a tantalising message from the past.

Lunch should never be complicated or showy. Where possible, I like to serve it on platters. That soothes the cook's nerves and enhances the bonhomie.

I adore ling. We should be championing it more. This dish, however, can be made with any chunky white fish. The sauce is almost an infusion. The spices, chickpeas and oil should get to know each other in a tentative way.

Roasting asparagus intensifies the flavour beautifully. Here, I'm pairing it with shop-bought gnocchi. It's a lovely dish with the lightness of lemon, butter and Parmesan for an easy fix on a nice day.

A true pissaladière is not for the faint-hearted. It should take you straight to Provence. I had the best one of my life at a friend's house recently. A committed Francophile and food lover, his culinary prowess was alluded to over many a pint, but the evidence was slow to come by. Then he cooked an astounding pissaladière. The depth of flavour transported me. The amber of the caramelised onions, potent niçoise olives, abundant anchovies and the crisp base all showed knowledge and commitment to the cause. Washed down with a lovely rosé, we could have been overlooking the Bay of Nice. Fair play to him — it wasn't all talk.

LING WITH CHICKPEAS, ORANGE AND RAS EL HANOUT

SERVES 4

120ml olive oil, plus extra for drizzling

4 x 150g fillets of ling, skinned and boned

2 tbsp crème fraîche

1 garlic clove, crushed

1 tsp ras el hanout (use ground cumin or curry powder if you can't get ras el hanout)

a pinch of golden caster sugar

juice of 1 orange

1 x 400g tin of chickpeas, drained and rinsed

125g mixed cherry tomatoes, halved

a handful of baby spinach

Preheat the oven to 185°C.

Drizzle a little oil in a roasting tin and set your ling on top. Brush the crème fraîche liberally all over the fish. Drizzle with a little more oil, then season with salt and pepper. Bake in the oven for 10–12 minutes, but the time will completely depend on the thickness of your fish. Check it with the tip of a knife after 10 minutes and decide whether it needs a little more time. You are checking for any rawness (translucence) – the fish will become white and flaky the more it cooks.

Warm the 120ml of oil with the garlic, ras el hanout and sugar. Add the orange juice, followed by the chickpeas. (This can be done ahead of time.) When the chickpeas are hot, add the tomatoes and baby spinach, then season. Wilt the spinach for a minute.

Serve in warm bowls with the ling nestled on top.

ROASTED ASPARAGUS WITH BUTTERED GNOCCHI AND PARMESAN

SERVES 4

2 bunches of asparagus
a drizzle of olive oil
a few sprigs of fresh thyme
1 x 500g pack of gnocchi
juice of ½ lemon
50g butter
80g Parmesan cheese, grated

Preheat the oven to 180°C.

Trim the bottom third from each asparagus spear and discard. If the spears are thin, they won't need to be peeled. Put the asparagus in a large roasting tin, then drizzle with the oil. Scatter over the thyme and some salt and pepper, then toss to make sure all the asparagus is coated in oil. Roast in the oven for 6–7 minutes, until tender. Larger asparagus will take a little longer.

Bring a pot of lightly salted water to the boil and add the gnocchi. Once the water returns to a simmer, they will only take 1 more minute to cook.

Lift the gnocchi out of the water with a slotted spoon, then add it to the roasting tin with the asparagus. Add the lemon juice and butter, then season.

Transfer to warm plates, scatter the Parmesan on top and serve.

PISSALADIÈRE

SERVES 4

4 tbsp olive oil, plus extra for drizzling

1 kg onions, thinly sliced

3 sprigs of fresh thyme

2 x 80g tins of salted anchovies, drained and chopped

a handful of good black olives, stoned and roughly chopped

2 tbsp red wine vinegar

1 tbsp golden brown sugar

FOR THE DOUGH:

200g strong white flour

1 x 7g sachet of fast-acting dried yeast

1 tsp salt

150ml warm water

1 tsp olive oil

To make the dough, put the flour, yeast and salt in a large bowl. Slowly add the warm water and oil and mix until it comes together.

Remove the dough to a lightly floured board and knead for 5 minutes (if you have a stand mixer, you can do this with the dough hook). Put the dough back in the bowl, cover with cling film and put it in a warm place to prove for 1 hour.

Meanwhile, heat the oil in a pan over a low heat. Add the onions and thyme, cover the pan with a lid and cook for 20 minutes, stirring once or twice. Uncover and cook for a further 10 minutes over a higher heat until the onions are lightly golden and caramelised.

Preheat the oven to 190°C. Lightly oil a large baking tray.

Towards the end of the onions' cooking time, add the anchovies, olives, vinegar, sugar and some black pepper. Remove the pan from the heat and allow to cool. Remove the thyme.

Turn the dough out of the bowl, knock it back and knead just a little on a floured surface, then roll it out and press it into the tray. Don't let it rise again.

Evenly spread the onion mixture over the dough and drizzle a little oil over the top. Bake in the oven for 25–30 minutes, until crisp. Serve warm or cold, cut into squares.

Take a holiday from your usual fare

08 AUGUST 2020

Summer was never kind to me. As a child we spent weeks on end at Clonea beach while my parents worked in the chemist. The older ones looked after the younger children. I spent my time eating camping stove sausages and peeling the top layer of skin off my body. I was a sun magnet, cursed with permanent sunburn despite being mummified in Ambre Solaire.

I've mentioned before that I'm a butter boy, but summertime demands lighter food. This week's dishes are a spiritual trip to the Mediterranean. Olive oil was sold in our chemist for lubricating the wax out of auld fellas' ears. Warmed, applied and plugged with cotton wool, it worked like a dream. You won't see Elizabeth David writing about that one.

I have a memory of eating souvlaki at dusk on a Greek island a long time ago, the warm, fatty juices of the lamb melding with minted yogurt dripping down my arms. I've never had another one until I made this. It's normally cooked on a skewer over coals. I'm doing it in the oven.

I love using French beans in a salad — not the big, tough, ugly ones, but fine ones that are sweet and yielding. The cooking is of paramount importance. This was drilled into me by Nico Ladenis, a famous and fearsome chef in his day. Beans had to be picked carefully at their root, leaving their ethereal tips, then plunged in a large pot of boiling salted water in batches.

The beans should not be al dente. That was a nonsensical fashion of the time that suppressed their sweetness. Tested constantly while they cooked, getting them wrong was not an option. A little bite remained as they were lifted from the pot and plunged into iced water to set their colour, their chlorophyll popping like emeralds. I've paired them with ripe peaches and soft, creamy goat cheese.

A good gazpacho is a lovely thing on a hot day. This version is a little fruity twist I learned from Josef, a Catalan chef who worked for me years ago.

LAMB SOUVLAKI WITH ROASTED PEPPERS AND MINTED YOGURT

SERVES 4

400g lamb shoulder, cut into large cubes

3 garlic cloves, halved

40ml olive oil, plus extra for drizzling

juice of 1 lemon

1 tsp paprika

1 tsp dried oregano

2 red peppers (or use roasted red peppers from a jar if you wish)

100ml water

4 flatbreads or wraps

FOR THE YOGURT:

250g natural Greek yogurt

2 garlic cloves, crushed

1 tbsp mint sauce

1 tsp honey

Put the lamb in a large ziplock bag with the garlic, oil, lemon juice, paprika, oregano and seasoning. Give it a good squish and put it in the fridge. Marinate for at least 4 hours but preferably overnight.

Preheat the oven to 200°C.

Put your peppers on a tray, drizzle with oil and roast in the oven for 15 minutes or so, until blackened and tender. Allow to cool, then deseed and peel.

Turn the oven temperature down to 165°C.

Drizzle a little oil into a large ovenproof pan set over a medium-high heat and allow it to smoke a little. Carefully tip the lamb into the pan and pick out the garlic. Brown the lamb on all sides. Remove the pan from the heat and add the water. Cover and cook in the oven for 1 hour, until the lamb is soft and tender.

Meanwhile, mix the yogurt with the crushed garlic, mint sauce and honey, then chill until needed.

To serve, warm the flatbread or wraps. Divide the lamb (and its juices), peppers and minted yogurt among them. Roll up tightly and cut in half.

SALAD OF GOAT CHEESE, FRENCH BEANS AND PEACHES

SERVES 4

2 x 200g packets of trimmed French beans
1 red onion, halved and thinly sliced
150g soft rindless goat cheese
2 ripe peaches, halved, stoned and sliced
toasted flaked almonds
a little fresh mint

FOR THE VINAIGRETTE:
100ml olive oil
juice of 1 lemon
½ tsp caster sugar

Cook your beans in a large pot of boiling salted water. Have a bowl of iced water at the ready. After 2 minutes on a rolling boil, lift one out and test it – there should be just a slight crunch. Drain the beans and plunge them into the iced water to cool, then drain again.

Whisk the oil with the lemon juice and sugar, then season.

Dress your beans and onion with the lemon vinaigrette, then divide among four plates or put on a single serving platter.

Cut the goat cheese into rounds and put it around the beans along with the peaches. Scatter the almonds and mint on top and serve.

WATERMELON GAZPACHO

SERVES 8

4 ripe tomatoes, quartered
½ watermelon, roughly chopped
1 red pepper, roughly chopped
1 garlic clove, sliced
1 tbsp finely chopped fresh ginger
50ml olive oil
fresh coriander, roughly chopped
fresh mint leaves, roughly chopped
fresh basil leaves, roughly chopped

Blend everything together really well in batches, season and chill. Serve on a hot day in cold glasses.

What I cook when I'm cooking for another chef

15 AUGUST 2020

I want to tell you about a dinner I cooked a little while back for a man I have a lot of time for. Paddy Lee came to our cookery school eight years ago to do a week-long course. We bonded straightaway. I suppose he was 22 or 23 at the time. He'd been at university in Belfast — twice, it turns out — but it wasn't for him. He had the cooking bug.

He subsequently worked in the Tannery and stayed for three years, solid as a rock. Chefs move about. It's about gathering experience and knowledge in different kitchens before honing your own style. After some illustrious years in Chapter One and the Greenhouse, where he helped the latter to gain two Michelin stars, he and his young family have made the move to France. He has always been quietly ambitious.

Michel Guérard is one of France's iconic chefs. His restaurant, Les Prés d'Eugénie, has held three Michelin stars for over 40 years and he is still in the kitchen in his eighties. This is where Paddy is working now. It's a momentous move for any chef, the highlight of a glittering CV.

I was lucky to get to the English Market the day before. This piece is as much about what you buy as what you cook. As always I went to Toonsbridge Dairy (now open on George's Street in Dublin too), where I bought olives, mozzarella, olive oil, breadsticks and feta and basil dip. This was the starter; no need for fuss. I tore the mozzarella and drizzled it with the oil and a posh gooseberry vinegar, then added flecks of sea salt. Everyone helped themselves.

The main was a yellow pepper spaghetti, as mild mannered as Paddy himself. It's based on a well-loved recipe by Joe Trivelli from *The Modern Italian Cook* that I've tweaked and served with charcuterie. I made anchovy butter to spread on toasted ciabatta for the middle of the table. It was a flavour bomb that was a lovely contrast to the mellow spaghetti.

I'm also giving you a recipe for the dip, as I appreciate that not everyone can get to a Toonsbridge shop. It's fab as a dip or as a sauce with roast lamb.

SPAGHETTI WITH YELLOW PEPPER SAUCE

SERVES 4

50ml olive oil

2 garlic cloves, sliced

1 sprig of fresh rosemary

3 yellow peppers, diced

a pinch of chilli flakes

150ml cream

500g spaghetti

100g Parmesan cheese, grated

Heat the oil in a saucepan over a low heat. Add the garlic and rosemary and cook very gently just until the garlic starts to colour. Remove the rosemary, then add the peppers and chilli flakes. Turn the peppers in the oil, cover the pan with a lid and continue to cook for 20 minutes, until they are soft and melting.

Add the cream and bring up to a simmer, then season and blend straightaway.

Cook the pasta according to the packet instructions. Drain and fold it through the yellow pepper sauce.

Serve with lashings of grated Parmesan.

TOASTED CIABATTA WITH ANCHOVY BUTTER

SERVES 4

100g butter
10 salted anchovies, chopped
a few fresh thyme leaves
juice of 1 mandarin
1 loaf of ciabatta, cut in half lengthways

Melt the butter in a small pan over a low heat. Add the anchovies and thyme and stir for a minute or so, until the anchovies melt into the butter. Add the mandarin juice and remove the pan from the heat.

Toast the halved ciabatta, then smear it with the anchovy butter, cut into chunks and serve. This would be wonderful on its own with charcuterie.

FETA AND BASIL DIP

SERVES 8

200g feta cheese
200g light cream cheese
1 x 140g tub of high-quality basil pesto
zest and juice of 1 lime

Blend everything together in a food processor and chill until needed.

Cooking for one

22 AUGUST 2020

I received a touching email recently that really made me reflect. It was from a widower who loves his food but finds it a little frustrating that most of my recipes are for four. He hates waste but also doesn't want to be eating the same thing over a number of days. His late wife used to say of him, 'He'll eat anything and enjoy it.' She bequeathed all her cookery books to him, hoping that he would do his best to look after himself.

In his letter he asked if I could I give a recipe for one on the odd occasion. Food is obviously important in his house and his late wife was clearly a good cook. She made 'gorgeous lamb neck stews', he wrote. It was evident there was a huge void in his life. He was specific: he likes a lot of fresh fish and his tastes were traditional, like many of his generation.

Motivating yourself to cook when you're by yourself is difficult at the best of times. So today I'm writing these recipes for Bill and everyone who likes to cook who lives alone. Hopefully they will help in some way and give you a little pleasure. They can also be scaled up to feed bigger numbers.

Lamb chops are easy. You can either use the gigot chops or the fancier loin. The mash is a lazily delicious amalgam, packed with flavour. It's an ageing gourmand's joy. I'm referring to myself here! It should be a little sloppy. The chops should be dredged through the mash and slurped unapologetically.

I love hake, and I love asparagus almost as much. It's readily available in supermarkets for many months of the year these days, although the air miles police might protest. I'm choosing thin spears so they cook at the same time as the fish. Use another white fish if you can't find hake. It'll be good with an old-fashioned tartare sauce.

The chicken is a one-pot dish. What lifts it out of the ordinary is the sauce. Blessed with smoked paprika and Parmesan, it will make even the most pedestrian chicken interesting. A little rice would be good with this to soak up the luxurious sauce.

LAMB CHOPS WITH MINTY PEA AND MUSTARD MASH

SERVES 1

2–3 lamb chops
a drizzle of sunflower oil

FOR THE MASH:
2 large potatoes, halved
100g frozen petits pois, thawed
100ml milk
a generous knob of butter
1 tsp prepared English mustard
1 tsp mint jelly

Put your potatoes on to boil with a little salt.

Meanwhile, season the chops. Heat the oil in a pan until it's gently smoking, then carefully add the chops. Cook for 5 minutes on both sides, then if you can, perch them on the fatty side for a couple of minutes to crisp the fat. Remove from the pan and keep warm, then turn your attention to the potatoes.

At almost the last minute, add the peas to the potatoes and continue to cook. Ensure the peas aren't boiling for much longer or they will lose their colour. Drain well, then put everything back into the pot and mash with the milk, butter and some salt and pepper. You may need to use a little more milk to get the required texture. When you're happy, add the mustard and mint jelly.

Serve the mash on a warm plate beside your lamb chops.

HAKE WITH ASPARAGUS, NEW POTATOES AND LEMON

SERVES 1

1 bunch of thin asparagus

4 new potatoes, cooked, peeled and halved

1 garlic clove, sliced

juice of ½ lemon

50ml olive oil

2 tbsp water

1 sprig of fresh thyme or rosemary (optional)

1 x 140g fillet of hake, skinned and boned

Preheat the oven to 185°C.

Trim the bottom third from the asparagus and discard. Put the spears in a roasting tin along with the cooked, halved potatoes, garlic, lemon juice, oil, water and the thyme or rosemary (if using). Put the fish on top and turn it to coat in the oil mixture, then season with salt and pepper.

Bake in the oven for 12 minutes or so — this will depend on the thickness of your fish. If you feel it needs a little more time, just pop it back in the oven for another minute or two.

Transfer the asparagus and potatoes to a plate and serve the fish on top.

CHICKEN WITH RED PEPPER AND SMOKY PARMESAN CREAM

SERVES 1

a drizzle of olive oil

1 red pepper, sliced

1 garlic clove, sliced

150ml cream

1 tbsp grated Parmesan cheese

½ tsp smoked paprika

1 chicken fillet, skin on if possible

Preheat the oven to 180°C.

Heat the oil in a small ovenproof frying pan over a medium heat. Add the red pepper and garlic and cook gently for 5 minutes or so to soften the pepper.

Whisk the cream, Parmesan and smoked paprika together in a small bowl. Set the chicken on top of the peppers in the pan. Pour the creamy mixture over, then season.

Transfer the pan to the oven and bake for 18–20 minutes. Don't be afraid to cut into the chicken to check that it's fully cooked. The sauce should be thick and bubbling and the chicken should be moist and tender. Serve immediately.

These new flavours have inspired me

29 AUGUST 2020

Today I'm giving you recipes for some new flavours I've learned along the way. They are for the curious cook who fancies an adventure. I can be a bit of a cynic. My eyebrows are permanently arched like some over-Botoxed diva. Sometimes I feel like I'm always ploughing the same culinary furrow. I don't scare anyone's horses. It's time this old dog learned new tricks.

I thought fermentation was for sandal-wearing tree-huggers. I still don't know what it's all about, but some chinks of light have started to permeate my stubborn brain. If something tastes nice, though, I'm instantly won over.

Visiting chefs have influenced me, most notably Robin Gill from the Dairy in London. Every year for the Waterford food festival, we get a notable chef from the UK to cook in the Tannery. Originally from Dublin, his food was something completely new to me. I'm a butter, pot, cook, eat kind of guy. His food was an epiphany.

I always try to learn from talented people in my kitchen. Some of them have been around the block, restaurant wise. They give me inspiration and hopefully I give them the freedom to be creative.

This umami dressing was a revelation. Naturally I've heard of umami, but I never understood it. We use this dressing with lots of things these days, from oysters to steak. With this salad, it shines. The depth of flavour is astounding and complex. I've never used nutritional yeast flakes as an ingredient before, but it's available in health food shops. Look for a brand called Red Star.

The cauliflower is cooked in a little brown butter first to give depth. Apologies, it's a little cheffy. The beetroot lends happy sweetness and the sea beet is a bit of showing off, as I live by the sea and I wanted you to see how enlightened I've become. You can use another green.

Wasabi is more familiar. Mixed with sour cream, it makes a punchy alternative to regular horseradish with smoked salmon. This is a refreshing little starter that lets the butterhead be the star.

ROASTED COURGETTES WITH BURRATA, UMAMI DRESSING AND SERRANO HAM

SERVES 4

3 medium courgettes
2 slices of brown bread, crusts removed and torn into small pieces
a good drizzle of olive oil
a few sprigs of fresh thyme
a squeeze of lemon juice
2 balls of burrata or mozzarella
8 slices of Serrano or Parma ham

FOR THE DRESSING:
25g nutritional yeast flakes
1 large garlic clove, crushed
60ml water
30ml apple cider vinegar
30ml tamari or soy sauce
125ml sunflower oil
100ml mayonnaise

To make the dressing, put everything except the sunflower oil and mayonnaise in a blender and mix to combine. With the motor still running, slowly drizzle in the oil until it emulsifies. Add the mayonnaise and blend briefly just until it comes together. Put in the fridge until needed.

Preheat the oven to 185°C.

Top and tail your courgettes, then cut them in quarters lengthways. Put them on a tray with the brown bread, oil, thyme and some salt and pepper, then turn everything in the oil. Bake in the oven for 12–15 minutes, until the courgettes are soft and golden and the bread is crunchy. Squeeze over the lemon juice.

To serve, divide the courgettes among your plates with torn burrata or mozzarella. Spoon over the umami dressing, then drape the ham on top.

BEETROOT WITH NUTTY CAULIFLOWER PURÉE AND BUCKWHEAT

SERVES 6

6 medium beetroot (various colours if possible)
100g buckwheat
a drizzle of rapeseed or olive oil
a handful of greens

FOR THE CAULIFLOWER PURÉE:
100g butter, cut into small cubes
1 small cauliflower, coarsely grated
300ml milk
1 tbsp nutritional yeast
100g crème fraîche

Preheat the oven to 160°C.

Wash the beetroot and wrap each one in foil. Bake in the oven until they are soft to the point of a knife. This could take up to 2 hours depending on the size of the beetroot. When they are cool enough to handle, peel and cut into chunks.

To make the purée, melt the butter in a pan over a medium heat. Cook until it starts to foam, brown and take on a nutty aroma. Be careful, though – don't allow it to go too far.

Add the grated cauliflower and cook, stirring regularly, for 5 minutes or so, until it starts to soften. Add the milk and nutritional yeast and bring to a simmer. When the cauliflower is soft, allow it to cool a little before adding the crème fraîche and some salt and ground white pepper, then blend to a smooth purée. Keep warm.

Toast the buckwheat in a dry pan over a gentle heat for 5 minutes or so.

To serve, spoon the warm cauliflower purée into a pool on a nice platter. Artfully arrange the beetroot on top, then add a drizzle of rapeseed or olive oil. Scatter over the toasted buckwheat, followed by a few pretty greens.

SMOKED SALMON AND BUTTERHEAD WITH WASABI, APPLE AND DILL

SERVES 4

1 butterhead lettuce, carefully washed and dried

150ml sour cream

1 tsp or so wasabi paste, depending on your taste

250g smoked salmon, sliced

1 Granny Smith apple, cored and cut into small batons

a few sprigs of fresh dill

Divide the butterhead among four plates.

Mix the sour cream with the wasabi. To serve, spoon some wasabi cream onto the plates, then top with the smoked salmon, apple and dill.

Dungarvan was like the Klondike during the Gold Rush

05 SEPTEMBER 2020

It was a strange summer. I never want to see its like again. Work was busy. Dungarvan was like the Klondike during the Gold Rush, but I'm keenly aware that wasn't the case for everyone in our business. Due to a freakishly unfortunate set of circumstances, we were drastically short in the kitchen. I now have life-enhancing shares in Johnson's baby powder.

In the Tannery, our summer food is all about seafood and I was on the fish section. When I wasn't being irascible, I enjoyed getting stuck in. There were many moments of self-pity, mostly when getting up for an early breakfast after a long day and late night.

'Thirty-eight years at the stove,' I would moan, 'and all I am is a sausage rustler.' A glare from herself would quieten me and I'd get the head down. It was good for the lads to see I could still do it, leading from the front and all that.

It's autumn now, with its prospect of chilly evenings and a warm fire. I own an inordinate number of coats and jackets. Every eventuality is covered. From the tweedy 'I'm going to a horsey dinner' Paul to music festival 'I can't believe you're in your fifties' Paul, I possess all the appropriate clobber.

I've made this sweet potato dish with feta in the past, but this time I'm going with the smooth creaminess of goat cheese.

I'm using cooked duck leg again, as it's easily available. And barley. It soaks up the flavours from everything around it and fortifies you.

I love a pie but, shocker, I rarely make pastry. What's crucial here is the ham hock. You'll have to order it. Its lip-sticking gelatinousness is like addictive, hammy fudge. The onions are also crucial. They should be melting and sweet. The cheese is grated Cheddar because it was at hand. Use something fancier if you like – Gubbeen, for instance, would give it a marvellous funk.

SWEET POTATO AND SPINACH WITH SPICED PUMPKIN SEEDS AND GOAT CHEESE

SERVES 4

800g small sweet potatoes, peeled and halved

80ml olive oil

1 sprig of fresh rosemary

a knob of butter

80g pumpkin seeds

½ tsp ground cumin

a pinch of chilli flakes

200g baby spinach

150g soft rindless goat cheese

Preheat the oven to 185°C.

Put your sweet potatoes, oil and rosemary on a baking tray, turning everything together to coat in the oil. Put the sweet potatoes cut side down on the tray and cook in the oven for 20–25 minutes, until soft and lightly coloured.

Remove the potatoes to a platter, then drain the remaining oil from the tray into a pot. Add the butter, pumpkin seeds, cumin and chilli flakes and cook over a gentle heat for 2 minutes or so. Add the baby spinach and wilt just for 1 minute. Season.

To serve, drape the wilted spinach mixture over the sweet potatoes, then crumble the goat cheese on top.

BAKED DUCK WITH BARLEY, SHERRY AND FIELD MUSHROOMS

SERVES 4

100g barley

500ml chicken stock

80g butter

3 garlic cloves, thinly sliced

a few sprigs of fresh thyme

2 bay leaves (fresh if possible)

1 cinnamon stick

100ml sweet sherry

4 cooked duck legs

4 thick rashers of smoked bacon

4 field (flat cap) mushrooms, halved

leaves of chard or cabbage, cut into manageable pieces

Soak your barley in plenty of water for 2 hours or more before you use it.

Preheat the oven to 180°C.

Drain and rinse the barley, then transfer to a wide, shallow casserole or baking dish.

Boil the chicken stock and add to the casserole along with the butter, garlic, herbs, cinnamon stick, sherry and some salt and pepper. Bake in the oven for 20 minutes.

Remove the casserole or baking dish from the oven and put the duck legs, bacon, mushrooms, chard or cabbage evenly on top. Make sure the mushrooms and the chard or cabbage are immersed in the remaining stock so they don't dry out. Return to the oven to bake for another 20 minutes, until the duck starts to crisp up and the stock has all been absorbed by the barley.

Serve with a generous amount of Dijon mustard.

HAM HOCK, CHEESE, ONION AND APPLE PIE

SERVES 4

1 ham hock (you can use another small joint of ham if you can't get a hock)
60g butter
2 medium onions, sliced
1 sprig of fresh thyme
100g red Cheddar cheese, grated
1 Granny Smith apple, peeled and grated
1 tsp Dijon mustard
1 x 320g sheet of ready-rolled shortcrust pastry, thawed
1 egg beaten with 1 tbsp milk
a sprinkling of nigella seeds (optional)

Simmer the ham hock for 2½ hours or so, until it starts to fall off the bone. Remove from the pot and allow to cool, then pick off the meat, discarding the abundant fat.

Meanwhile, melt the butter in a saucepan over a medium heat. When the butter starts to foam, add the onions and thyme, cover the pan with a lid and cook very gently for at least 20 minutes, until the onions are soft and melting. Take the pan off the heat and allow to cool.

Add the Cheddar, apple, mustard and some ground black pepper, then fold the ham hock through, making sure it's broken up evenly. Chill the mixture for 30 minutes.

Preheat the oven to 185°C. Line a baking tray with greaseproof paper.

Unfurl your pastry with the wide end towards you. Brush it with the egg wash, then spoon the mixture along the middle, leaving a 3cm edge of pastry clear at each side.

Bring the bottom half of the pastry over the filling to meet the top and press down firmly to expel any air and join the pastry together. Crimp the pastry or press with a fork to get a seal. Brush with more egg wash, then scatter over the nigella seeds (if using). Transfer to the lined tray and bake in the oven for 25 minutes, until golden and crisp.

Serve warm or at room temperature with chutney.

These old dishes make me swoon

12 SEPTEMBER 2020

The sun is beating down as I'm writing this. I'm feeling a bit sheepish as these recipes don't necessarily fit the weather. I'm not going to be too hard on myself, though, as it being Ireland, wintery days are never far away.

The chicken dish is one that I love but hardly have anymore as my people at home are not fans. They've had it one too many times and are never slow to tell me. Such is life when you have a chef at your beck and call.

I have a well-trotted-out story about this dish. We used to have a version of it at home growing up that we would fondly refer to as chicken mush. It tasted lovely but was always a tad overcooked, hence the name. I remember the flesh clung to the bottom of the pot like a disrobed gown, the bird's skeleton peering over the top of the pot as if desperately trying to escape its fate. The inspiration for it comes from that wonderful French classic, poule au pot. These old dishes make me swoon. I'm sure my alter ego is some portly French bon viveur awaiting the onset of gout.

The common theme for all these dishes is the humble turnip. It's like an old flame. I never tire of it. I always look forward to using it abundantly once autumn sets in. Cider is omnipresent when I use turnip. I put some in with the chicken and I'm also glazing the turnip to lend a wonderful sweetness. I don't use fancy cider – there's no need. This dish is soothing. The smoke from the bacon brings the turnip to another level. This, for me, is Irish food.

Simple techniques can transform a dish. These mashed turnips are elevated by the cooking of the butter. It foams and metamorphosises into a nutty, complex creation. I've added a hint of cinnamon and sage for layers. I'd eat these turnips on their own all day long, my stretchy pants at the ready. Hopefully you have the self-discipline that I don't possess.

ONE-POT CHICKEN WITH CIDER

SERVES 4

1 x 1.6kg chicken

4 small onions, peeled

2 carrots, halved

1 large parsnip, cut into chunks

½ turnip, sliced

125g smoked bacon lardons

100g broth mix (widely available in supermarkets in the health food aisle – a mix of barley, lentils and split peas)

a few sprigs of fresh thyme

1 bay leaf (fresh if possible)

1 litre chicken stock

250ml cider

Preheat the oven to 165°C.

Put the chicken in a large heavy-based casserole. Put the veg, bacon, broth mix and herbs around the bird, then pour in your stock and cider. Bring to a gentle simmer, then cover with a lid and cook in the oven for 1 hour.

Remove the lid and turn up the heat to 185°C. Cook for another 20 minutes. Allow to cool a little before prising the chicken from the bone.

Serve in deep bowls with mashed potato. It won't be pretty but it will be delicious.

PORK CHOPS WITH GLAZED TURNIP AND SMOKED BACON

SERVES 4

½ tbsp duck fat

4 thick pork chops, bone in if possible

½ turnip, peeled and cut into 0.5cm-thick slices

150ml cider

50g butter

125g smoked bacon lardons

10 fresh sage leaves

Preheat the oven to 185°C.

Melt the duck fat in a large frying pan or a small roasting tin and allow it to smoke a little. Carefully add the chops. Season and brown on both sides for a couple of minutes, then if you can, perch them on the fatty side for a couple of minutes to crisp the fat.

Remove the chops from the pan and add the turnip. Colour gently on one side, then turn them over. Add the cider, then put your chops on top of the turnip slices. Dot the turnip with butter, scatter the smoked bacon around, then tuck your sage leaves in among the turnip slices.

Bake in the oven for 25–30 minutes, depending on the thickness of your chops. Serve immediately.

MASHED TURNIP WITH SAGE BROWN BUTTER

SERVES 4

1 medium-sized turnip, peeled and cut into small chunks
150g butter
1 small sprig of fresh sage with 4–5 leaves
1 cinnamon stick
a little grated nutmeg (optional)

Boil your turnips until cooked, then strain and mash.

Meanwhile, put your butter in a medium-sized saucepan over a medium heat. It needs to be bigger than you think, otherwise it will overflow. Cook the butter for 3 minutes or so – it should start to foam, then the bubbling and hissing will stop and it will quieten. Turn down the heat and allow it to become nutty around the edges. Add the sage and cinnamon stick and remove the pan from the heat. Allow to infuse for a few minutes.

Strain the butter through a fine mesh sieve on top of the turnips. Season with salt, pepper and a little grated nutmeg (if using).

Mix everything together. You can keep the mashed turnips warm or reheat later.

An easy, logical way to feed your family

19 SEPTEMBER 2020

We managed to get a two-night break in Dublin recently. It was especially lovely to be on the receiving end of a bit of TLC. The city was eerie. I'd expected it, but walking the silent streets felt apocalyptic. Still, I was glad to be there. I've grown to love Dublin more since we moved away from it all those years ago to set up the Tannery. Over time, my enthusiastic forays from Dungarvan revealed aspects of Dublin's character that I'd never appreciated when I lived there.

The girls love breakfast in a hotel. Who doesn't? The Willy Wonka buffets have sadly gone but the thrill of fluffy pancakes and oozing pain au chocolat compensates.

A woman at the next table caught my attention, and not for the better. Her breakfast requests were as complex as the most delicate of corporate mergers. The waiter, who must moonlight as a Buddhist monk, didn't blink through the monologue, a consummate professional.

'One poached egg in the centre of the plate with brown toast and tomatoes. Nothing must touch the egg, that will ruin it.' It sounds simple enough. In fact, it is, but there was more — much more. My face reddened. I am that breakfast chef.

I love people who love food, who treat it as a joy in life. It's not the enemy.

This chicken dish is a family favourite. It's yet another traybake but it's a wonderfully easy and logical way to feed your family.

I don't cook enough Asian dishes. These are comfort noodles with a crunchy topping, just the sort of thing I like to eat anytime but especially when it's a little chilly outside.

For a delicious autumnal dish, I've incorporated little morsels of charcuterie into a robust salad. The dressing is made with sherry vinegar. I'm partial to it but you could use red wine vinegar instead. Leave the poached egg a little runny in the centre. It will ooze into the leaves with a smile.

MALT VINEGAR CHICKEN WITH MUSHROOMS, THYME AND SMOKED BACON

SERVES 4

4 large chicken legs, thighs and drumsticks separated

3 large Rooster potatoes, each cut into 6 wedges

1 tbsp duck fat

3 sprigs of fresh thyme

8 slices of smoked streaky bacon

4 large field (flat cap) mushrooms

2 tbsp malt vinegar

a pinch of chopped fresh parsley

Preheat the oven to 185°C.

Put your chicken, potatoes, duck fat and thyme in a roasting tin. Season and turn everything together until it's all coated in the duck fat. Cook in the oven for 20 minutes.

Remove the tin from the oven and add the bacon and mushrooms. Put the tin back in the oven for a further 15 minutes, until the bacon starts to crisp and the chicken is thoroughly cooked.

Remove the tin from the oven. Season, then add the vinegar and parsley. Fold everything together – the heat from the tin will soften the vinegar.

Serve straightaway.

NOODLES WITH BUTTERNUT SQUASH, SESAME AND COCONUT

SERVES 4

1 butternut squash, peeled and diced into 2cm chunks

3 tbsp toasted sesame oil

1 bunch of spring onions, finely chopped

3 tbsp sesame seeds

300g dried medium egg noodles

a few sprigs of fresh coriander

FOR THE SAUCE:

1 x 400ml tin of coconut milk

2cm knob of ginger, peeled and diced

½ fresh red chilli, deseeded and diced

zest and juice of 1 lime

3 tbsp soy sauce

1 tbsp fish sauce

1 heaped tbsp crunchy peanut butter

Preheat the oven to 185°C.

Put the butternut squash and sesame oil in a roasting tin. Season, mix and cook in the oven for 20 minutes, turning once or twice, until the squash is soft and golden.

Remove the tin from the oven and add the spring onions and sesame seeds. Return to the oven for another 5 minutes.

To make the sauce, put all the ingredients in a small saucepan and whisk together. Bring to a gentle simmer for 5 minutes to let everything get to know each other, then remove the pan from the heat.

Cook the noodles according to the packet instructions. Drain and return to the pot you cooked them in, then add the sauce, tossing to coat.

To serve, divide the noodles among four warm bowls, then scatter your butternut squash mixture evenly on top. Finish with the fresh coriander.

AN AUTUMNAL SALAD

SERVES 4

60g golden raisins

125g smoked bacon lardons

1 x 150g piece of salami, diced

60g hazelnuts, roasted, peeled and lightly crushed

4 eggs

enough interesting salad leaves for 4 people

FOR THE DRESSING:

80g golden brown sugar

100ml sherry vinegar

1 cinnamon stick

1 tsp Dijon mustard

300ml sunflower oil

100ml light olive oil

2 garlic cloves, crushed

Preheat the oven to 185°C.

Soak the raisins in a bowl of just-boiled water for 15 minutes to plump them up, then drain.

To make the dressing, bring the sugar, vinegar and cinnamon to the boil in a small pan, then remove from the heat.

Whisk in the mustard, then slowly incorporate the sunflower oil, followed by the light olive oil, garlic and some salt and pepper. Reserve approximately one-third of the dressing, then refrigerate the rest for another day. It will keep in the fridge for weeks in a Kilner jar.

Put your lardons on a baking tray and cook in the oven for 10–12 minutes, until crisp. Transfer the bacon and its fat to the dressing along with the diced salami, hazelnuts and drained raisins.

Poach the eggs for 5–6 minutes.

To serve, divide the salad leaves among four bowls, then spoon the dressing over the top, taking the charcuterie first as you may not need to use all the dressing. Carefully lift the poached eggs from the pan with a slotted spoon to drain off the water, then sit one on top of each portion of salad.

I'd climb over a mountain of nouveau riche club sandwiches for a nice toastie

26 SEPTEMBER 2020

One of the finest treats in life is the toasted special. It's a uniquely Irish thing, like Tayto. There's nothing fancy in it. You could even ask what gives it the right to be so special. After all, the ingredients are somewhat mundane: ham, Cheddar cheese, tomato and onion. Yet in the right place at the right time, there is nothing nicer. I'd crawl over a mountain of nouveau riche club sandwiches to get to a nice toastie.

I discovered a trencher through Fergus Henderson. He logically plonks a piece of roast beef on a hunk of bread while it rests. The soppy, delicious goo is almost better than the meat itself. I've taken a famous garnish of his also. His roasted bone marrow starter has travelled the world and caused a sensation. He alleviates the marrow's morbid richness with a salad of flat parsley, shallot and capers. Coarse sea salt gives texture. I'm combining the two for a hybrid of deliciousness. I am a magpie.

Bruschetta, Crostoni and Crostini is a book published in 1995 by another food hero of mine, Franco Taruschio from the Walnut Tree in Abergavenny, Wales. It was a seminal restaurant in the UK. It's still there, run by another master, Shaun Hill. Go if you ever can. It will bring tears to your eyes.

Lentils on toast is a surprising delight. I've added cream and salami for a bottom-widening effect. Have it by the fire with a glass of red and think of me. I'm using tinned lentils because they are pretty brilliant. If you can't find them, of course cook your own. Puy lentils are best.

I had a version of the goat cheese on toast in the French House in Soho in January, in another world, another life. They used half a head of roasted new season garlic that loomed over the bread. You prised the golden cloves out and spread then sinfully over the goat cheese-covered sourdough. It was one of the best starters I've ever eaten.

STEAK TRENCHER WITH PARSLEY, CAPERS AND SHALLOTS

SERVES 2

1 tbsp sunflower oil

1 x 250g rib-eye steak

soft butter

2 thick slices of white bread from a good soft loaf

1 tsp Dijon mustard

a drizzle of olive oil

20 leaves of flat-leaf parsley

1 large banana shallot or 2 small shallots, very thinly sliced

½ tbsp small capers

a pinch of coarse sea salt

Heat the oil in a pan over a high heat until it's gently smoking. Season your steak, then carefully put it in the pan. Cook for 3 minutes, then turn it over and cook the other side for another 2 minutes for a medium-rare steak. Cook yours for longer depending on how thickly your steak is cut and how you like it done.

Remove the steak from the pan and put on a plate. Cover with foil and rest in a warm place for 10 minutes.

Meanwhile, butter the bread. Tip the steak juices from the plate into a large bowl. Whisk the mustard into the juices, then add the oil, parsley, shallot and capers.

Slice the steak into strips 1cm thick and add to the bowl, tossing to coat. Divide between the slices of buttered bread.

Top with a sprinkling of coarse sea salt and serve.

BRUSCHETTA OF LENTILS, BALSAMIC CREAM AND SALAMI

SERVES 4

250ml cream
1 x 400g tin of lentils, drained and rinsed
100g sliced salami, shredded
1 sprig of fresh thyme
1 tsp balsamic vinegar
4 thick slices of country loaf
1 garlic clove, cut in half
a drizzle of olive oil

Put the cream in a saucepan and slowly reduce by one-third, taking care that it doesn't boil over. Add the lentils, salami, thyme and balsamic to the reduced cream. Season and keep warm.

Toast the bread, then rub it thoroughly with the garlic.

To serve, put the toast on warm plates, then drizzle over a little oil and spoon the lentil mixture on top.

GOAT CHEESE AND ROASTED GARLIC ON TOASTED SOURDOUGH

SERVES 2

1 head of garlic, peeled (yes, all of it!)
1 sprig of fresh thyme
a small pinch of caster sugar
50ml olive oil
2 slices of sourdough bread
150g soft rindless goat cheese

Preheat the oven to 160°C.

Put the garlic and thyme on a sheet of foil. Season with a pinch of sugar and some salt and pepper. Just before you seal it up into a parcel, drizzle over the oil. Cook in the oven for 20–25 minutes, until soft and golden. Keep warm.

Toast the sourdough, then brush with the garlic oil from the foil parcel.

To serve, smear the goat cheese on the toast and dot the mellow, golden garlic on top.

Get fruity with your dinner and see what happens

03 OCTOBER 2020

Fruit has been commonplace in savoury cooking since medieval times. I had a happy three seasons filming in country houses for *Lords and Ladles* on RTÉ. For those of you who watched, I was the squeamish one never far from a retch when some unsavoury bauble was dangled in front of me.

The cooking was challenging, as you might expect from a sketchy recipe from the 1500s. Our job was to make it palatable — not easy when you only had sheep's ears and testicles to work with. Fruit was always present, however. It's a good idea that continues on to this day. I love a pop of fruit in my cooking. It provides balance and alleviates richness, particularly as the months turn colder and the cooking becomes heavier.

I also love anything with pastry. You might not believe it, but today I'm going to make my own. I don't want you to think I'm a charlatan. I'm using wholemeal flour as it pairs nicely with the figs, but don't worry if you don't have it — just use all plain flour.

A galette is a free-form tart. It's supposed to look rustic and agricultural. It's the gastronomic version of Connell from *Normal People*, resplendent in his GAA shorts, just waiting to be devoured.

The bacon dish is a pleasing traybake. First the bacon, then the apples and leeks, swirling around in the rich, bacony goodness. Wholegrain mustard cuts through it all.

This chutney is a tribute to Gary Rhodes. I still can't believe he's gone. He was an inspiration to a lot of people like me. I remember his debut TV appearance on one of Keith Floyd's programmes. Floyd was clearly annoyed at this upstart hogging his camera time. Rhodes's stardust was evident and he was rarely off our screens for the next two decades. His signature electric hair was tamed over time, but not his enthusiasm. Seedless grapes are the key here. It's an easy reminder of what a unique influence he was on a generation of chefs.

FIG AND GOAT CHEESE GALETTE

SERVES 4

1 egg beaten with 1 tbsp milk
6 ripe figs, halved
150g soft rindless goat cheese, cut into 6 circles
½ tbsp golden brown sugar
1 tsp fresh thyme leaves
a drizzle of olive oil

FOR THE PASTRY:
125g plain flour
125g wholemeal flour
a pinch of salt
125g butter, chilled and diced
1–2 tbsp cold water

To make the pastry, sieve the plain flour into a bowl, then mix in the wholemeal flour and salt. Using your fingers, rub the butter into the flour until it becomes a sandy texture. Add a little cold water until the pastry comes together. Form into a smooth, round disc, wrap in cling film and chill in the fridge for at least half an hour.

Preheat the oven to 185°C. Line a baking sheet with parchment paper.

Roll out the chilled pastry on a lightly floured surface into a thin-ish circle, then transfer to the lined baking sheet.

Brush the pastry lightly with egg wash, then alternate the figs and goat cheese on top, leaving a 3cm lip of pastry all around.

Sprinkle with the sugar and thyme leaves, then bring the pastry back on itself a little to cover the outermost part of the filling.

Brush the exposed pastry with more egg wash, then drizzle the figs and goat cheese with oil and season with a few twists of black pepper. Bake in the oven for 25–30 minutes, until oozing and golden. Serve warm.

MAPLE SMOKED BACON WITH ROASTED APPLES, LEEKS AND WHOLEGRAIN MUSTARD

SERVES 4

1 x 1kg piece of smoked bacon

2 medium leeks, cut at an angle into slices 2cm thick

2 Granny Smith apples, cored and each one cut into 6 wedges

12 new potatoes, cooked and peeled

2 tbsp rapeseed or sunflower oil

2 tbsp melted butter

2 tbsp maple-flavoured golden syrup

250ml cider or water

1 tbsp wholegrain mustard

Put the bacon in a saucepan of cold water and bring to the boil, then reduce the heat and simmer gently for 50 minutes or so, until tender. Drain.

Preheat the oven to 185°C.

Put the leeks, apples and cooked potatoes in a roasting tin, then coat in the oil and melted butter. Put the bacon in the centre of the veg, fat side up. Drizzle the syrup over the bacon. Bake in the oven for 20 minutes, turning once or twice so everything gets nicely golden.

Remove the bacon to rest, leaving the vegetables in the tin. Add the cider and mustard to the tin. Put the tin on the hob and bring to a simmer for 1 minute to make a lovely syrupy glaze.

Slice the bacon and serve with the glazed veg.

A VERY EASY CHUTNEY

MAKES 1 LARGE OR 2 SMALL JARS

500g green or black (or mixed) seedless grapes

1 onion, finely chopped

80g light brown sugar

80ml apple cider vinegar or white wine vinegar

80ml water

½ tsp mixed spice

Put everything in a saucepan and cook over a medium heat for 20 minutes or so, until thick and syrupy. Remove from the heat and allow to cool, then spoon into a Kilner jar. Keep the chutney in the fridge for up to three weeks.

Fussy eaters

10 OCTOBER 2020

I touched on this subject a little during the lockdown, when I threw the toys out of the pram and refused to cook for my children. I'd been at it night and day for weeks and my nerves were jangled with all their terms and conditions. If I could have put them up on eBay, I would have.

Perhaps I shouldn't always expect them to like what we enjoy. Every parent struggles to get their children to eat what we see as the right things. I'm quite fond of the little darlings, though, so I'll persevere and try to feed them what I deem healthy with a little adventure thrown in. Of course there is always the possibility I could be wrong with my choices, but then I think, wrong? Moi?

Always hopeful, I want to introduce new flavours to the more adventurous households. Pasta and cabbage is a lovely combination that I use frequently. I'm adding mortadella. I'm a huge fan — it's like posh luncheon sausage. The fat makes it a bit of a no-go in my house, but I like it in a crisp ciabatta sandwich, its richness cut with a perky chutney. If I can't convince you to use mortadella, use Parma ham or salami, they'll be gorgeous too.

I love root veg. Stump originates in Belgium, a place I spent a very happy weekend this time last year — seems like a lifetime ago. I didn't come across 'stoemp' in Ghent but my love of root vegetables knows no bounds, so I'm happy to include this mash here.

The chicken dish is a tasty mish-mash, designed to use leftover cooked chicken that I deliberately overcook to achieve a pleasingly crisp texture. Chicken crackling is what I'm aiming for with a little Indian twist provided by the garam masala.

RIGATONI WITH CABBAGE, SAGE AND MORTADELLA
SERVES 4

350g rigatoni (penne will work too)
80g butter
10 fresh sage leaves
zest of ½ lemon
½ green cabbage, shredded
6 slices of mortadella (or Parma ham or salami), torn into pieces
lots of grated Parmesan cheese

Cook the pasta in a pot of boiling salted water with a little oil and start to cook it according to the packet instructions.

Meanwhile, melt the butter in a large saucepan and allow it to bubble a little. Tear the sage leaves in half and add them to the butter along with the lemon zest.

When the pasta is nearly cooked, add the cabbage to the pot and cook for 2 more minutes, then drain, reserving 100ml of the cooking water.

Add the pasta with the cabbage and the reserved cooking water to the sage and lemon butter. Season and turn everything together.

To serve, divide among warm bowls, then drape the mortadella on top and serve with lashings of grated Parmesan.

STUMP, SAUSAGES AND APPLE GRAVY
SERVES 4

4 medium potatoes (King Edward or Maris Piper are good)

2 carrots

1 small turnip

80g butter

200ml milk

a pinch of ground nutmeg (optional)

8 of your favourite sausages

FOR THE APPLE GRAVY:

100ml apple juice

200ml beef stock

1 tbsp country relish

1 sprig of fresh thyme or rosemary

Peel the potatoes and carrots and cut into roughly 3cm chunks. Peel and dice the turnip into smaller dice.

Boil the vegetables in a pot of salted water until tender, then drain and return to the pot. Mash with the butter and milk, then season with salt and ground white pepper and a pinch of nutmeg (if using).

Meanwhile, pan-fry the sausages until cooked. This will of course depend on their thickness. Remove the sausages from the pan and keep warm.

Add the apple juice to the pan to deglaze it, then add the stock, relish and thyme or rosemary. Simmer the gravy for 1 minute to bring everything together.

Serve the stump and sausages on warm plates with plenty of the gravy poured over.

BAKED RICE AND SPICED FRIZZLED CHICKEN WITH CHICKPEAS AND MANGO YOGURT

SERVES 4

500ml light chicken stock

250g basmati rice

peel of ½ lemon

2 cooked chicken legs

50g butter

2 tbsp sunflower oil

1 red onion, thinly sliced

2 tsp garam masala

1 x 400g tin of chickpeas, drained and rinsed

FOR THE YOGURT:

2 tbsp mango chutney

150g natural yogurt

Preheat the oven to 180°C.

Bring the chicken stock to a simmer in a casserole, then tip in the rice, add the lemon peel and season. Cover with a lid and bake in the oven for 20 minutes.

Meanwhile, shred the cooked chicken legs and the skin. Put on a small baking tray and bake in the oven for 15–20 minutes, until very crisp.

Melt the butter with the oil in a large pan over a medium heat. Add the onion and cook for 10 minutes, until it's starting to caramelise. Add the garam masala and cook for 2 minutes, then add the chickpeas and the chicken. Season. When it's all heated through, it's ready.

Ripple the chutney through the yogurt, then serve with the rice and spiced chicken. Warm naan would be lovely with this.

Pies that are oozing with joy

17 OCTOBER 2020

A proper pie is an oozing, sticky joy. I am inordinately fond of them. I even on occasion like bad ones. There was a moment in time when a late-night stop at the local 7-Eleven on the way home from a club on Oxford Street was compulsory. A flaccid Scotch egg and a tooth-shattering pasty were often cradled home. There were inescapable ramifications. My corpulent waddle eventually betrayed my late-night secrets.

For those of you interested in how far into the stratosphere pie art can be taken, do an online search for the Pie Room in the Rosewood Hotel, London. You will be gobsmacked. There's a book just out too for those who lust after Calum Franklin's creations. They are as wondrous as a Fabergé egg.

These hand pies are Neanderthal by comparison. They could be made from the leftovers of this very easy Bolognese recipe. Make sure the filling is reasonably dry so it doesn't seep from the pastry. I'm doing mine in the oven as opposed to a fryer.

Baking with filo pastry is easier than you might think. Keep it under a lightly dampened tea towel and you'll be fine. This pie is golden, theatrical and has a very satisfying crunch. Cauliflower and curry are happy companions. I was going to do a straight cauliflower cheese — that would be fab too — but I opted for a little gentle spice. Served in the centre of the table, it's quite a showstopper.

The cock-a-leekie pie in Spitalfields pub in Dublin has become iconic in no time at all and rightly so, as it's utterly fabulous. When I tested the recipe I poached the chicken, intending to use the juices as the binding gravy. But I wasn't happy. The naked bird was underwhelming and bland. I missed the roasting juices and the unctuous skin. So I've done an about turn and am taking some of the work out of the pie by buying a cooked chicken. Choose the best one you can get and keep the juices at the bottom of the bag, they're liquid gold.

BOLOGNESE HAND PIES WITH JALAPEÑO CREAM
SERVES 4

2 tbsp sunflower oil

380g minced beef

2 garlic cloves

1 x 400g tin of chopped tomatoes

1 chicken stock cube

1 tsp smoked paprika

1 tbsp Worcestershire sauce or soy sauce

1 tsp honey

1 x 320g packet of ready-rolled puff pastry, thawed

1 egg beaten with 1 tbsp milk

a sprinkling of sesame seeds (optional)

a few sprigs of fresh coriander

FOR THE JALAPEÑO CREAM:

200ml crème fraîche

10 jalapeño slices, finely chopped

Mix the crème fraîche and jalapeños together and chill.

Heat the oil in a saucepan until it's lightly smoking, then carefully add the beef. Brown for 3–4 minutes, then add the garlic, tomatoes, stock cube and paprika. Reduce the heat and cook gently for 20 minutes, then add the Worcestershire or soy sauce and the honey. Season and cool.

Unfurl the pastry and stamp out 10 circles. Reroll the pastry to get a few more circles. Put a small amount of Bolognese in the centre of each disc. Fold over, crimping to seal, and brush with the egg wash. Sprinkle the sesame seeds on top (if using) then chill in the fridge for 30 minutes.

When you're ready to cook, preheat the oven to 185°C. Bake the pies on a baking tray in the oven for 25 minutes, until golden brown.

Serve hot with the chilled jalapeño cream and fresh coriander on top.

CAULIFLOWER KORMA, RAISIN AND ALMOND PIE
SERVES 4

1 onion, chopped

2 garlic cloves, sliced

a thumb-sized piece of ginger, peeled and chopped

3 tbsp sunflower oil

3 tbsp korma paste

50g ground almonds

2 tbsp raisins

a pinch of caster sugar

1 x 400ml tin of full-fat coconut milk

zest and juice of 1 lime

1 cauliflower, cut into florets

a knob of butter, melted

3 sheets of filo pastry, thawed

50g flaked almonds

Preheat the oven to 185°C.

Put the onion, garlic and ginger in a food processor and whizz to a paste. Tip the paste into a saucepan with the oil and cook over a low heat for 10 minutes. Add the korma paste and cook for a further 2 minutes, until aromatic. Add the ground almonds, raisins, sugar, coconut milk and lime zest and juice. Bring to a simmer for 10 minutes to reduce the liquid by one-third, then set aside.

In a separate pan, boil the cauliflower until soft, then drain thoroughly and add to the sauce, making sure all the cauliflower is coated.

Lightly brush a medium-sized loose-bottomed tart tin with the melted butter.

Lay a sheet of filo pastry on a worktop and brush with butter, then place it in the tin, carefully pressing it into the edges. Repeat with the other two sheets of filo, laying the pastry across each other at angles so it covers the whole tin and is overlapping the sides.

Fill the pastry base with the cauliflower, then fold the pastry back over the top, scrunching the edges together. Scatter the flaked almonds over the top, then bake in the oven for about 25 minutes, until the pastry is golden and crunchy. Serve hot.

COCK-A-LEEKIE PIE

SERVES 4

1 medium leek

80g butter

1 heaped tbsp plain flour

300ml chicken stock plus the roasting juices from the roast chicken

15 leaves of fresh tarragon, chopped

10 ready-to-eat prunes, halved

a pinch of ground nutmeg (optional)

1 roast chicken, free-range if possible

1 x 320g sheet of ready-rolled shortcrust pastry, thawed

1 egg beaten with 1 tbsp milk

Preheat the oven to 185°C.

Trim the leek and cut it in half lengthways. Rinse it under cold running water, making sure there is no grit lurking anywhere. Cut into 1cm-thick slices.

Melt the butter in a saucepan over a low heat. Add the leek, cover the pan and sweat gently until softened. Add the flour and cook for 3 minutes before adding the stock and the roasting juices a little at a time to get a smooth sauce. Cook out for a couple of minutes, then add the tarragon, prunes and nutmeg (if using).

Take the meat and skin from the chicken. Cut the meat into chunks and the skin into a fine hash. Fold through the leek sauce, then season. Put the chicken mix in a tart tin or shallow casserole.

Unfurl the pastry, then cut 3 x 1cm-thick strips from the narrow side of the pastry. Brush the rim of the tin or casserole with the egg wash, then stick the strips to the sides. Brush the strips with more egg wash, then cut out a lid to fit the top of your tin or casserole and put it on top. Crimp the pastry together, then decorate. I use a trellis style but feel free to be artistic.

Brush the top all over with egg wash, then bake in the oven for 40 minutes, until golden and crisp. Serve hot.

I've always been something of a poacher

24 OCTOBER 2020

Does anybody think that poaching food is vaguely parsimonious? Is it like asking a thin-lipped person for their confirmation money? Is it ever done with a sense of luxury as opposed to deprivation?

I've always liked poached food. When I started cheffing, I fell in love with French food. What kept me going was the quest to know more, do more and be more. It was never just a job. There was none of that Nordic foraging nonsense when I was training. It was all butter, cream and bulging arteries. However, when you delve deep, the nuances of French cooking unveil themselves. Poaching is common and ultra-delicious.

With oeufs en meurette, the inky exterior gives way to pristine whiteness and an ochre yolk that oozes into bacon, mushrooms and a red wine sauce. A poule au pot sends my pulse racing. A stuffed poulet de Bresse sits regally astride its subordinate vegetables. The amber broth is served as a first course while the bird awaits.

The south of France gives us bourride, a pungent and delicious fish stew. The broth is thickened by a heady aioli that is sopped up with bread and saffron-poached potatoes. I want to hop on a plane right now.

This poached egg dish is perfect for a bank holiday breakfast. We make a sage and bacon butter that elevates the eggs. The pool of devil-may-care brown butter sets you up for the day.

This mushroom dish is as beige as a pair of Farah slacks but it has a mellow, soothing flavour. I remember having field mushrooms cooked in milk at home, a dim but pleasurable memory. I've added smoked bacon to the milk for interest, barley for agricultural reassurance and Coolea for cheesy comfort.

I often do a cold version of poached salmon with mayonnaise in the summer. I'm adding butter to the stock for warm richness and this fennel jam is just the bomb. I like it with goat cheese as well.

POACHED EGGS WITH BLACK AND WHITE PUDDING AND SAGE BROWN BUTTER

SERVES 4

4 large slices of black pudding

2 large slices of white pudding

a little olive oil

1 tbsp malt vinegar

8 eggs

FOR THE BUTTER:

125g smoked bacon lardons

150g butter

12 fresh sage leaves

Preheat the oven to 185°C.

Put the lardons in a roasting tin and cook in the oven for 10 minutes or so, until golden and crisp.

Brush the puddings with a little oil and bake in the oven for 8–10 minutes, until cooked through.

Meanwhile, melt the butter in a saucepan over a low heat until it begins to gently foam and bubble. Do not stir! This might take 5 minutes or so. Be patient. When the butter turns a nutty colour, add the sage leaves and cook for 30 seconds. Remove from the heat and stir in the crispy bacon, then set aside.

Bring a pot of water to a simmer, then add the vinegar and a pinch of salt. Gently lower the eggs into the water to poach for 3 minutes, then drain with a slotted spoon. A little tip: you can pre-poach the eggs if you like, then plunge them into iced water and reheat them in hot water. This takes the stress out of poaching so many eggs.

To serve, divide the black and white pudding among four warm plates and set two poached eggs on top of each plate. Warm the sage brown butter, then spoon it over the top of the eggs.

FIELD MUSHROOMS AND BARLEY WITH SMOKED BACON MILK
SERVES 2

50g barley

4 large field (flat cap) mushrooms, halved

1 onion, cut into thin rings

2 smoked streaky rashers

2 bay leaves (fresh if possible)

400ml milk

60g Coolea or Cheddar cheese, cut into small cubes

Soak the barley for 2 hours in water, then drain and rinse.

Put the barley, mushrooms, onion, rashers and bay leaves in a saucepan and cover with the milk. Season and drop in the cheese, then cover with a lid and simmer gently for 15 minutes, until the barley is cooked.

To serve, divide between two warm bowls and enjoy the soothing beige.

BUTTER-POACHED SALMON WITH STICKY FENNEL JAM

SERVES 2

30g butter

a few sprigs of fresh dill, stalks and fronds separated

250ml water

a few black peppercorns

2 x 120g salmon fillets, skinned and boned

FOR THE JAM:

1 large fennel bulb

2 strips of orange peel

juice of 1 orange

80g caster sugar

1 star anise

300ml water

1 tbsp olive oil

TO SERVE:

crème fraîche

brown bread

To make the jam, trim the outer leaves and the root from the fennel, then shred it as finely as you can. Put in a pot with the orange peel and juice, sugar, star anise and water. Bring to the boil, then cover the pan with a lid and simmer gently for 15 minutes, until the fennel has softened.

Remove the lid, reduce the heat to low and continue to simmer to allow the liquid to evaporate and become jammy, stirring occasionally. Remove the pan from the heat and stir in the oil. Keep in a jar in the fridge for up to one week.

For the salmon, put the butter, dill stalks, water, a pinch of salt and a few peppercorns in a saucepan that will fit the salmon snugly. Bring to a simmer, then lower in the salmon, making sure it's immersed in the liquid. If not, just top up with a little more water. Poach for 6 minutes, then remove the pan from the heat. Allow to sit for 3 more minutes, uncovered.

Serve the poached salmon on warm plates with the fennel jam, crème fraîche and brown bread. Garnish with the dill fronds.

My take on a famous pork shoulder feast

31 OCTOBER 2020

If you're not familiar with David Chang, that's okay. I can't presume that every nerdy obsession of mine is yours too. In America he is a titan who worked his way up from Korean immigrant beginnings, working his ass off in elite New York restaurants before finding his soul in a broken-down chicken shop in the Lower East Side.

He clad the walls in plywood because that was all he could afford, took on one more cook and started opening late into the night, offering ramen and bao. His first customers were the local exotic dancers who tottered in, bleary and cynical. Then others came. A place with low expectations, banging music, great food and a touch of sleaze is a magnet for chefs. Word got around.

Momofuku quickly became a Mecca. The former chicken shop gave birth to an empire that now has much kudos, Michelin stars and a TV career and cookbooks for David.

I've eaten there twice. The last time we sat by the kitchen, always my favourite spot. A glistening hunk of meat sailed passed me like a burnished Steinway and landed on the next table. It was bo ssam, a wobbly, slow-cooked pork shoulder, served with abundant sauces, pickles and lettuce in which the joyous mixture was wrapped. It was a eureka moment for me, the joy of serving and eating food family-style.

This is a feast for when we can gather again. David Chang uses bone-in pork shoulder, which is always better but a little hard to get. Try your local Polish shop for the pork shoulder — there are always meaty jewels to be found there. I've taken out some salt from the recipe — not something I usually say — and added a touch of soy and garlic. The slaw is a cooling relief from the meat. The spice bag spice is a nifty addition.

Pickles perk things up. When you think you've had enough, just pop a little more cucumber on top and you'll be grand. Lynda Booth gave me this excellent pickled cucumber recipe, which I use all the time.

ROAST PORK SHOULDER WITH HOISIN
SERVES 10

100g coarse salt

100g golden brown sugar

100ml soy sauce

4 garlic cloves, crushed

4kg boneless pork shoulder

400ml water

300ml hoisin sauce

2 heads of butterhead lettuce, leaves separated

1 bunch of fresh coriander

Put the salt, sugar, soy sauce and garlic in a food processor and pulse for 30 seconds. Put half of the mixture on a baking tray and sit the pork on top. Rub the remaining mixture over the pork, then wrap in cling film and marinate overnight in the fridge.

Preheat the oven to 140°C.

Rub off all the mixture from the pork, then transfer it to a roasting tin and pour in the water. Cook in the oven for 4 hours, until a dark crust has formed on the pork and it's completely tender.

Mix any leftover cooking juices into the hoisin sauce.

Serve the pork on a platter, dolloped with some of the hoisin sauce. Add the lettuce and coriander to the platter along with the spice bag slaw and cucumber pickle that follow. The pork will simply pull apart. Use the lettuce to wrap the pork and the accompaniments. Serve the hoisin sauce on the side.

SPICE BAG SLAW

SERVES 10

50g raisins
1 large head of celeriac, grated
2 carrots, grated
1 red onion, very thinly sliced
400ml crème fraîche
juice of 1 lemon
1 tbsp honey
1 tsp spice bag spice

Soak the raisins in a bowl of just-boiled water for 15 minutes to plump them up, then drain.

Put the celeriac, carrots and red onion in a large bowl. Add the drained raisins and the remaining ingredients to the vegetables, stirring to combine. Check for seasoning, then chill until needed.

A FAB AND EASY CUCUMBER PICKLE

SERVES 10

2 cucumbers, lightly peeled (leave a little of the green on for colour)

250g caster sugar

250ml rice wine vinegar

250ml water

2 shallots, thinly sliced

1 fresh red chilli, deseeded and finely diced

a thumb-sized piece of ginger, peeled and finely chopped

Slice the cucumber very thinly — a mandolin is perfect for the job if you have one.

Bring the sugar, rice wine vinegar and water to the boil in a saucepan. Add the shallots, chilli and ginger. Remove the pan from the heat and allow to cool before you add the cucumber.

Chill and use whenever you need it. It will keep for a week in the fridge but the colour will fade.

Coddle with a Waterford twist

07 NOVEMBER 2020

I had a profound encounter in the woods a few days ago while walking my little dog. I was distracted. As always, thoughts swirled round my addled brain. Eventually, the woods enveloped me. Beech trees, russet and golden, arched over the river, like walking through a postcard.

Colligan was one of my father's favourite places. We'd go for a spin on his half-day, when the chemist would close. He would smoke his pipe, absorbing the trees and the sound of the river. I would throw sticks into the water and time them as they eased their way under the bridge to the other side.

I met a lady. We stopped and chatted. It was Clodagh Beresford Hayes, a celebrated poet and hero of mine. I told her of my love of words and how my father would often recite Shakespeare and Latin proverbs at the table at teatime, instilled in him by the monks in Mount Melleray in the 1930s. It was seared onto his beautiful mind but his words thumped off my brutish young brain like missiles.

Words are Clodagh's stock and trade. She tossed the word 'crepuscular' to me like a comforting bone. It means something mythical that appears only in twilight. She recited one of her own poems, under those trees beside that stream. I was rooted. Her poem was 'Ruminant':

> What happens to a heart after death?

> It pounds around the rib cage,
> at last leaps through the sternum
> into the menacing wood.

> Grows a coat of fur, thickening around the neck.
> Becomes crepuscular,
> cannot bear to be seen.

Crumens beneath its beautiful eyes
secrete waxy tears,
its four-chambered stomach barely taking in sustenance.

From spring on its antlers grow an inch each day,
velvety at first as they emerge
but hardening to woody bone for the anger of the autumn rut.

At times the stag tips back his majestic crown;
a Christ with hands nailed up, he bellows to the heavens,
then sheds his antlers and begins again. And again.

My eyes moistened. I hoped she didn't see. The poem was apt. That morning was memorable.

Teatime is still special to me, particularly in winter, hungry after the day. With the fire lighting, the house embraces you. There's nowhere better to be.

These dishes are all simple — do whatever catches your fancy. Eggs, smoked fish and cheese. What's not to like? You can substitute the mackerel for smoked salmon if you're not a fan.

This hash uses chorizo. By now you'll know I'm a devotee. It makes the world a better place.

Coddle is divisive. More than anything I think it's the colour, so I've browned everything and added some bits and pieces to snatch it from Dublin and bring it to Waterford.

BAKED SMOKED MACKEREL OMELETTE WITH MELTED CHEDDAR

SERVES 2

6 eggs

a splash of milk

a good knob of butter

2 fillets of smoked mackerel, flaked

80g Cheddar cheese, grated

3 spring onions, shredded

Preheat the oven to 200°C.

Whisk the eggs with the milk and some salt and pepper.

Melt the butter over a medium heat in an ovenproof non-stick frying pan. When the butter starts to foam, add the beaten eggs and turn them around the pan for a minute or so, scraping the bottom all the while. A spatula is best for this.

Scatter the flaked mackerel over the top of the eggs, followed by the cheese. Transfer the pan to the oven to cook for 12 minutes, until golden and puffy.

Remove the pan from the oven and allow to cool a little, then gently prise the omelette out of the pan using the rubber spatula. Scatter over the spring onions.

If you have difficulty getting the omelette out, simply serve it in the pan.

CHORIZO AND RED ONION HASH

SERVES 4

500g potatoes (Roosters are best), peeled and diced into cubes
3 tbsp olive oil
2 red onions, halved and sliced
2 garlic cloves, sliced
120g sliced chorizo, cut into pieces
4 eggs
chopped fresh parsley
a little sunflower oil

Parboil the potatoes just until they are almost cooked – this should take 12–15 minutes, depending on size. Don't let them break up. Drain and allow to steam dry.

Heat the oil in a large frying pan or wok over a medium heat until the oil is gently smoking, then add the potatoes. Cook until they start to turn golden, then add the onions and garlic. Continue to cook for a further 10 minutes or so, then add the chorizo. Allow the hash to soften and come together while you fry the eggs to your liking in a separate pan.

Season the hash and add the parsley, then divide among warm plates. Season the eggs and put them on top of the hash to serve.

WATERFORD CODDLE

SERVES 4

2 tbsp sunflower oil

8 large sausages

4 rashers of bacon

4 slices of black pudding

4 slices of white pudding

a little butter

1 onion, halved and sliced

2 large Rooster potatoes, peeled and cut into 1 cm dice

1 sprig of fresh thyme

1 tbsp plain flour

600ml chicken stock

2 tbsp soy sauce

Preheat the oven to 185°C.

Heat the oil in a large, wide, ovenproof pan over a medium-high heat until it's gently smoking. Working in batches so that you don't crowd the pan, brown the sausages, bacon and pudding.

Remove all the meat from the pan, tip out any excess oil and carefully give it a wipe with kitchen paper. Put the pan back on the heat, then add the butter. Once it has melted and has started to foam, add the onion, potatoes and thyme. Cook over a medium heat for 10 minutes, until everything softens, then add the flour and cook for 2 minutes.

Add the stock and soy sauce and bring to a simmer. Put the sausages, bacon and pudding back in the pan, making sure everything is submerged in the stock. Transfer the pan to the oven and bake, uncovered, for 20 minutes.

Check that the potatoes are cooked, then season and serve straight to the table.

A chef is taught
and the cooking
is often strained.
A cook is natural,
instinctive,
in harmony with
the food.
I've always
wanted to be
a cook.

20 JUNE 2020

Three of the most delicious comfort food dishes you'll ever eat

14 NOVEMBER 2020

I'm sitting at the kitchen table watching the birds feed. I've no idea what they all are except for one interloping robin. Bird identification is now high on my list of things to learn. It's comforting, watching them. I'm discovering my inner ornithologist. I've taken to buying one of those nuts on a string things once a week to entice them into the garden and they have dutifully obliged.

I bought a clapped-out campervan last year that's parked untidily outside the house. I've wanted one ever since we travelled around New Zealand's South Island, pre-children. I had never felt more carefree. It was sitting in someone's garden, damp and forlorn, but it was love at first sight. I put the call in to the Minister for Finance, only to be met with an interminable silence. But I braved it out. I needed a new toy.

It was for the girls, while they are still young, I reasoned. We'll have adventures that they will remember forever! I got my way in the end. It's a bit of a money pit — that was to be expected — but more worryingly, I've been having recurring nightmares where I wake up spooning Martin Shanahan at Electric Picnic. I might have to get rid of the van or go see a therapist.

Comfort is needed more than ever in our food these days and these dishes offer it in spades. The duck dish uses cooked legs and pre-made Yorkshire puddings for a double cheat, but together they make perfectly gooey sense for a decadent starter for four or as a main for two. I'm serving them with a simple horseradish cream.

I had never heard of sloppy joes until recently, but I've been missing out. An American childhood was rarely without this messy creation, it seems. I got thumbs up from my own two when I made them at home, Halleluiah.

I adore spare ribs. These ones are different. Instead of sticky and unctuous, I'm giving you the more pious bacon ribs. They adorn most butchers' cabinets in County Waterford. I eat them when I need a bacony fix. The sauces are for dipping and slurping without embarrassment.

STICKY DUCK YORKIES

SERVES 4

250ml red wine

1 sprig of fresh thyme

1 heaped tbsp redcurrant jelly

a pinch of mixed spice

2 cooked duck legs (300g)

1 tbsp horseradish sauce

2 tbsp crème fraîche

4 large frozen Yorkshire puddings

Put the wine, thyme, redcurrant jelly, mixed spice and a few twists of black pepper in a saucepan. Bring to the boil and reduce by half.

Remove the skin and any excess fat from the duck legs and discard. Prise the meat from the bone and chop into small chunks.

Remove the thyme from the liquid and discard it, then add the duck meat to the saucepan. Continue to cook over a gentle heat until the mixture is jammy.

Mix the horseradish sauce with the crème fraîche.

To serve, warm the Yorkshire puddings, then divide the sticky duck mixture among them. Serve the sauce on the side.

SMOKED CHIPOTLE SLOPPY JOES

SERVES 6

4 tbsp sunflower oil

1 red pepper, diced

2 garlic cloves, sliced

500g minced beef

1 x 400g tin of chopped tomatoes

2 tbsp golden caster sugar

2 tbsp smoked chipotle Tabasco sauce

1 tbsp tomato purée

1 tbsp yellow mustard

2 onions, sliced into thick rings

6 floury baps or brioche buns

6 slices of Cheddar cheese

a few pickled gherkins (optional)

Gently heat 2 tablespoons of the sunflower oil in a saucepan over a medium heat. Add the red pepper and garlic and cook for a few minutes, until the pepper softens.

Add the beef, breaking it up with the spoon, and cook on a higher heat until it starts to colour. Add the chopped tomatoes, sugar, chipotle Tabasco sauce, tomato purée and mustard. Reduce the heat to very low and cook for 30 minutes, until it's dark and sticky. Season.

Meanwhile, heat the remaining 2 tablespoons of oil in a separate frying pan over a low heat. Add the onions and cook for 20 minutes, until they turn a lovely amber colour.

To serve, cut the baps or buns in half and warm them up. Spoon the sloppy joe mixture on top and top with the onions, cheese and pickles (if using).

MAPLE-DRIZZLED BACON RIBS WITH SOUR CREAM AND APPLE CINNAMON SAUCE

SERVES 4

2kg bacon ribs
maple syrup, for drizzling
150ml sour cream

FOR THE SAUCE:
80g butter
1 tbsp dark brown sugar
½ tsp ground cinnamon
2 cooking apples, peeled, cored and diced

Cut the rib racks in half and put them in a large pot. Cover well with water and bring to the boil, then reduce the heat and simmer until they start to fall off the bone — this might take up to 90 minutes.

Meanwhile, melt the butter in a saucepan over a medium heat until it starts to spit and foam. Watch it carefully. Shortly after, it will quieten and start to change colour. At this point, add the sugar and cinnamon, swiftly followed by the apples. Cook the apples for 10 minutes or so, smushing them as they cook until they become a pulp. Remove the pan from the heat. You can blend the apples with a hand blender or leave them a little lumpy.

When you're ready to serve, take the ribs from the hot water, drain and divide among plates. Drizzle the maple syrup over the ribs and serve with the warm apple sauce and the sour cream on the side.

I like to think of myself as Captain Exciting

21 NOVEMBER 2020

I rarely eat soup. I don't know why, really. If I'm out, perhaps I think there's always something more exciting on a menu and I don't want to miss out. Soups seem somewhat unadventurous and I like to think of myself as Captain Exciting. I'm out of step, of course, as the soup market is huge in Ireland and continues to grow.

One of the reasons I love Ireland is our penchant for giving people nicknames. My friend Crocker (remember *Kojak*?) is a repository of them. He drops juicy monikers without even noticing. His profession as a postman conveniently exposes him to every nickname in the area. There was a fella playing for a local GAA club years ago christened Soup by his teammates as he was deemed to be a thick country vegetable. I laughed quite a lot at that one. The poor fella.

God knows what they called me. I was only ever begrudgingly picked for a team in school. My lack of athletic prowess always relegated me to walking around the pitch with the other unwanted anoraks. I was okay with it, though. All that exertion and smelly changing rooms didn't float my boat. I was nerdy, content with listening to Joni Mitchel in my bedroom, dreaming up future adventures.

I have three very different soups here. Two are broths and the other is a purée. The chicken soup is packed with noodles and would certainly be a meal in itself.

The sweetcorn and coconut soup is a creamy delight. Tinned sweetcorn is one of life's easy pleasures and when blended well, it's like sipping silky ambrosia. The ginger and coconut give it a lift and transport us to a balmier climate.

Slow cooking is second nature to me. With very little effort and just a little patience, a lumpen piece of meat can be transformed into something melting and utterly delicious. Lamb shanks are a favourite. When paired with a broth mix (a blend of barley, split peas and lentils, available in most supermarkets), it becomes something hugely satisfying on a cold winter night.

ROAST CHICKEN NOODLE SOUP

SERVES 4

4 chicken legs

a little sunflower oil

3 tbsp sesame oil

2 red onions, sliced

2 garlic cloves, sliced

3cm piece of ginger, peeled and finely chopped

1 fresh red chilli, deseeded and finely diced

1.5 litres chicken stock

40ml soy sauce

1 tbsp honey

1 tbsp fish sauce

½ Savoy cabbage, cut into pieces

1 x 300g packet of straight-to-wok noodles

4 spring onions, thinly sliced

Preheat the oven to 185°C.

Put the chicken legs on a baking tray, drizzle with the oil, season and cook in the oven for 40 minutes, until the skin is really crisp. I use the crispy skin here, but you can discard it if you don't fancy it.

Heat the sesame oil in a saucepan over a low heat. Add the onions, garlic, ginger and chilli and cook for 5 minutes or so. Add the stock, soy sauce, honey and fish sauce and bring to a simmer. Add the cabbage and cook it for 3 minutes, then add the noodles.

Take the chicken off the bone and chop the meat into chunks. Add it to the broth, followed by the spring onions.

To serve, check the seasoning, then ladle the soup into warm bowls.

CURRIED SWEETCORN AND COCONUT SOUP

SERVES 4

1 tbsp butter

1 onion, finely diced

1 garlic clove, sliced

3cm piece of ginger, peeled and chopped

1 tbsp curry powder

1 small bunch of fresh coriander, leaves and stalks separated

2 x 300g tins of sweetcorn

600ml chicken stock

1 x 400ml tin of coconut milk

1 tbsp chilli oil

a handful of chopped roasted peanuts

Melt the butter in a large saucepan over a low heat. When the butter starts to foam, add the onion, garlic and ginger. Cook for 5–6 minutes, until the onion starts to soften, then add the curry powder and cook for 2 more minutes.

Chop the coriander stalks and leaves roughly, but only add the stalks to the pan at this point. Add the sweetcorn and the stock, bring up to a simmer and cook for 10 minutes. Add the coconut milk and season.

Mix the chilli oil with the coriander leaves and the peanuts.

To serve, ladle the soup into warm bowls, then spoon the peanut chilli oil on top.

LAMB SHANK BROTH

SERVES 6

2 tbsp sunflower oil

2 x 400g lamb shanks

1 tbsp butter

1 large onion, finely diced

3 garlic cloves, sliced

125g smoked bacon lardons

1 tbsp tomato purée

200g broth mix (widely available in supermarkets in the health food aisle – a mix of barley, lentils and split peas)

1.75 litres chicken stock

1 x 500ml can of cider

1 cinnamon stick

1 tsp dried oregano

chopped fresh parsley

Preheat the oven to 160°C.

Heat the oil in a heavy-based casserole over a medium heat until the oil is gently smoking. Season the lamb shanks, then add them to the casserole. Colour the shanks until the meat is dark and crisp. Lift the shanks from the pot, then carefully pour off and discard the oil.

Wipe the pot with kitchen paper and put it back on the hob over a gentle heat. Add the butter. When it starts to foam, add the onion, garlic and bacon lardons and cook for 10–15 minutes, until soft and golden.

Add the tomato purée and cook for a minute or two, then add the broth mix, stock and cider. Bring to a simmer, then return the lamb to the casserole with the cinnamon and oregano. Cover with a lid and transfer to the oven to cook for 90 minutes, until the lamb is falling off the bone.

When cooked, remove the lamb and allow to cool a little, then chop into small chunks. Pop it back in the broth, add the parsley, season and serve. I eat this with a little hot Dijon mustard stirred into my bowl at the last minute.

I cook country food with style and I'm okay with that

28 NOVEMBER 2020

I haven't the discipline or the inclination to do really complicated food. I naturally veer towards bumbusters, as the nail in a country restaurant's coffin is pretty but Lilliputian portions.

There's a fine line between making something look attractive on a plate while also sating the customer's appetite. Some people are put off by hefty, groaning plates literally dripping with excess, me included. However, a sense of generosity in a restaurant is compulsory. You don't want guests complaining they had to stop for chips on the way home. I heard a good expression the other day: country food with style. I'm okay with that.

In saying all this, I marvel at the amazing creations made by some of my fellow chefs. They are true artists and my stubby little fingers couldn't hold a candle to them. Our industry is as diverse as a bag of dolly mixtures and I'm very thankful for it.

Instagram is the source of the ultimate food porn. I gaze in wonder at the posts of the Mickael Viljanens of this world and I'm astonished at their beauty. Back in my world, winter food needs to be a little bit rich. It insulates us against the cold. Sprouts are upon us and I love their farty charm, so much so that I'm putting them in a risotto with lots of cheese and topped with chewy, caramelised roasted parsnips. This unctuous concoction is livened up by a hit of sharp apple. It's a satisfying option for the non-meat eaters in your house at Christmas.

I rarely have gammon, finding it flat in every sense of the word. But here I've given it personality by pairing it with a perky sweet and sour cabbage that's laden with fresh ginger. The nutty sweet potato roasties have a crunchy companion in the form of the sesame seeds and it works well.

I haven't done a mussel dish in a while. Given the time of year, I use clementines whenever possible and they work well together here. Butter and more ginger give them a warm luxury and the parsley breadcrumbs bring texture. This is an easy dish. Once you've prepped the mussels, it can be made in minutes.

Curiosity and appetite are such happy bedfellows. They make life so much richer.

25 JANUARY 2020

BRUSSELS SPROUT RISOTTO WITH TOFFEE PARSNIPS AND APPLE

SERVES 4

80g butter

1 medium onion, finely diced

1 sprig of fresh sage or thyme

400g Arborio risotto rice

200ml cider

1.2 litres hot chicken stock

12 Brussels sprouts, shredded

100g Parmesan cheese, grated

1 red apple, cored and cut into small batons

FOR THE PARSNIPS:

2 parsnips

a drizzle of rapeseed oil

1 tbsp golden brown sugar

a pinch of mixed spice

Preheat the oven to 185°C.

Melt half of the butter in a heavy-based pot. When the butter starts to foam, add the onion and sage or thyme. Cover the pot with a lid, turn down the heat and cook gently for 15 minutes, until the onion is soft and translucent but with no colour.

Meanwhile, peel the parsnips, then cut each into six, lengthways. Put them in a roasting tin with the oil, sugar, mixed spice and seasoning. Turn together until everything is coated, then bake in the oven for 20 minutes, turning once or twice, until they are sticky and golden. Keep warm.

Add the rice to the onion, stirring to coat everything in the butter, then add the cider. Bring to a simmer, then add half of the hot stock and some salt and pepper. Cook over a low heat until the liquid has nearly evaporated, stirring once or twice.

Add the sprouts to the pot along with half of the remaining stock and bring to a careful simmer once more. From this point on you will have to do a little more stirring.

When the stock has evaporated, the sprouts should be almost cooked and so should the rice. You will have to check the texture of the rice. It needs to have a tiny bit of bite. Add more stock to loosen the risotto. It should be a little runny in the pot and not sit in a mound when you stir it.

Dice the remaining butter and add it to the pot along with most of the Parmesan, stirring to combine.

Divide the risotto among warm plates and scatter over the remaining Parmesan, followed by the parsnips and lastly the apple batons. Serve straightaway.

GRILLED GAMMON WITH GINGERY CABBAGE AND SWEET SESAME ROASTIES

SERVES 2

2 gammon steaks

FOR THE CABBAGE:

½ head of Savoy cabbage, shredded

1 garlic clove, sliced

2cm piece of ginger, peeled and finely chopped

100ml water

40ml white wine vinegar

2 tbsp sesame oil

1 tbsp raisins

1 tbsp caster sugar

FOR THE ROASTIES:

1 large sweet potato, peeled and diced into 2cm chunks

a drizzle of sunflower oil, plus extra for the gammon

1 tbsp sesame seeds

Preheat the oven to 185°C.

To make the roasties, put the sweet potato in a small roasting tin. Add the sunflower oil and sesame seeds, then season, making sure everything is coated in the oil. Roast in the oven for 20–25 minutes, turning once or twice, until golden and crisp. Don't worry if some of the sesame seeds get a bit dark, that's okay. Keep warm.

Meanwhile, put all the cabbage ingredients in a pot. Season, cover tightly and cook on full heat until the liquid has evaporated. This will only take about 5 minutes. You want the cabbage to steam but not boil dry. Desist from lifting the lid to look in the pot – you will hear it sizzle as it comes near the end. Turn off the heat, give it a little stir and keep it warm.

Preheat the grill to high.

Oil a tray and brush a little oil on the gammon, then grill for 5–6 minutes.

To serve, arrange the gammon on warm plates with the sweet potato roasties and the cabbage.

MUSSELS WITH CLEMENTINE AND GINGER BUTTER AND PARSLEY CRUNCH

SERVES 2

1kg mussels

1 tbsp butter

2 shallots, halved and thinly sliced

2cm piece of ginger, peeled and finely chopped

juice of 4 clementines

FOR THE PARSLEY CRUNCH:

6 tbsp fresh white breadcrumbs

2 garlic cloves, crushed

a drizzle of olive oil

2 tbsp finely chopped fresh parsley

Preheat the oven to 185°C.

Put the breadcrumbs and garlic on a small baking tray and mix with the oil and some salt and pepper. You need just enough oil to moisten the breadcrumbs. Toast in the oven for 10–12 minutes, turning once or twice, until golden and crunchy. Allow to cool, then mix in the parsley.

Meanwhile, to prepare the mussels, immerse them in a clean sink of cold water. Agitate. Debeard them one by one into a clean bowl, discarding any that are open and won't close when you gently tap them on the counter. Drain and clean the sink, fill it with cold water again and re-immerse the debearded mussels. Agitate the mussels once more, then lift them from the water, leaving any sediment behind.

Put the butter, shallots and ginger in a large pot and cook gently for 2 minutes. Add the clementine juice and the mussels, cover tightly and cook over a high heat, stirring once, for 3–4 minutes, until all the mussels open. This will depend on the size of your mussels. Discard any mussels that are still closed.

To serve, divide between warm bowls and scatter the parsley breadcrumbs on top.

Handy recipes to help and inspire you this Christmas

05 DECEMBER 2020

As you are reading this, I'm very much hoping that the Tannery will be back open. Walking into our restaurant every weekend to our takeaway menu chips away at our souls. It's just a cold, empty building without the people.

That's not to say I didn't enjoy having an easy November. I dutifully trotted after my wife, dreaming of creamy fireside pints as she stormed around Dungarvan on miserable wintery nights.

I cooked a lot, as usual. Sometimes I get confused and think I'm a manservant. Last night, for instance, I had a mini-meltdown as I served tea and bourbon biscuits to the ladies watching *Bake Off*. There was a stray comment about the tea being too milky. If it wasn't raining outside I would have gone for one of my strop walks.

We're now on the countdown so I'm going to give you some handy little numbers to help and hopefully inspire you.

The first is cheffy, but for those who put time aside it will really pay dividends. You can make the terrine in advance — it holds in the fridge for up to four days. You could serve it with your Christmas dinner or it's lovely with pâté or charcuterie too — its built-in fruit serves as a chutney. I serve it just on its own with chilled horseradish cream.

There are very few ingredients in the smoked salmon puff. It's a handy starter, especially when using pre-cooked beetroot. The name comes from my girls when they were small. They loved the colour so much, they christened it princess beetroot.

The dates come by way of Toonsbridge in the English Market. They were handing them out and I was like Oliver Twist asking for more. Make them to accompany drinks. Try to get Medjool dates. I've seen them in the supermarkets. They'll make all the difference.

WARM POTATO TERRINE WITH SMOKED BACON AND DRIED FRUIT

SERVES 8–10

a drizzle of rapeseed oil

125g smoked bacon lardons

1 onion, finely chopped

6 fresh sage leaves, finely chopped

600g Rooster potatoes, peeled

1 parsnip

125g mixed dried fruits (I've used prunes and apricots, cut into small chunks, but cranberries would be lovely too)

50g Parmesan cheese, grated

2 eggs

80ml cream

a little grated nutmeg or mixed spice

a little melted butter, for reheating

Preheat the oven to 170°C.

Heat the oil in a pan over a medium heat. Add the bacon and onion and cook for 10 minutes, until the onion is soft but not coloured. Add the sage and remove the pan from the heat.

Meanwhile, grate the potatoes and parsnip coarsely and put them in a bowl. Squeeze out the excess water, then add to the onion and bacon mixture. Add the dried fruit, Parmesan, eggs and cream and mix well. Season with salt, pepper and the nutmeg or mixed spice.

Double line a 2lb loaf tin with cling film. If you brush the tin with a little oil or spritz it with an oil spray, it will help immeasurably. Pack the tin with the potato mixture, then cover it with foil and cook in the oven for 1½ hours, until it's completely tender when tested with a small knife. Leave to cool completely, then put it in the fridge overnight.

To serve, cut the terrine into 2cm-thick slices. Brush with a little melted butter and put under a hot grill until golden and crisp.

SMOKED SALMON PUFF WITH PRINCESS BEETROOT
SERVES 8

1 x 320g packet of ready-rolled puff pastry, thawed

1 egg beaten with 1 tbsp milk

200g sliced smoked salmon

16 slices of jalapeño peppers

1 x 500g packet of cooked beetroot

1 small bunch of fresh dill

1 x 200ml tub of crème fraîche

Preheat the oven to 185°C. Line a baking tray with parchment paper.

Unfurl the pastry (it will be easier if you leave it out at room temperature for 10 minutes), then cut into eight squares. Brush lightly with the egg wash.

Cut the smoked salmon into smaller pieces, then divide it among the pastry squares, placing it a little off centre. Put two slices of jalapeño on each mound of salmon, then fold over the pastry into a triangle and seal the edges with a fork.

Brush the top of the puffs with more egg wash, then put on the lined baking tray and cook in the oven for 25 minutes, until golden and crisp. You can cook these ahead of time, then just warm them through when you need them.

Meanwhile, grate the beetroot into a bowl, chop the dill stalks and some of the leaves and add them to the bowl followed by the crème fraîche. Season and divide among plates.

Serve the salmon puffs straight out of the oven, garnished with the remaining fronds of dill and the beetroot on the side.

MEDJOOL DATE, GORGONZOLA AND PROSCIUTTO POPPERS
SERVES 8

16 Medjool dates
100g Gorgonzola cheese
1 x 90g packet of prosciutto

Make an incision and remove the stones from the dates. Stuff each date with a little Gorgonzola, then wrap in the prosciutto. Serve on a platter with cocktail sticks for handy consumption.

Perk up this year's turkey with Moroccan spices

12 DECEMBER 2020

This year, for the first time ever, we are taking Christmas Eve off. It's a massively busy day. Traditionally the same families have congregated in the Tannery every year for lunch. For Máire and I, both huge fans of Christmas, it's always quite stressful as we have to get ready for our own home as well. It's a full house all round but we always manage it. Last Christmas Eve was a particular doozie as the breakfast chef decided to go on the razz the night before and had a lie-in. I got the dreaded early morning call, made all the worse as I'd been up late entertaining our visitors the night before. I was definitely the grumpiest chef in Ireland that day.

I always love seeing our customers. Many have become friends over the years, but this year we want to have the time with our children to savour the atmosphere. Who knows, we might even go out for lunch.

It pains me to say it but there might be more people cooking for two this year, depending on the restrictions. The thought of grannies and grandads everywhere being on their own is heart-breaking. Ours are such a fundamental part of our children's lives. We can't even imagine it.

I'm perking up the turkey this year with Moroccan spices. It's for people who want something a little different. Ras el hanout is a gentle spice blend. Be not afraid. I'm also just cooking a crown as many will have fewer people to cook for. The spices give way to the full-on Moroccan flavours underneath the bird as the carrots cook in the dripping turkey juices.

For the non-meat eaters, I have this parsnip cake. You can substitute the parsnips for something else if you like, such as beetroot, though you will need to roast the beetroot beforehand.

This champ is a regular on the Tannery's menu at Christmas and at home. I'm not a fan of 42 types of veg on the plate. Champ allows you to do a two in one. It will also go perfectly with the ham the next day.

ROAST TURKEY CROWN WITH RAS EL HANOUT, CARROTS, DATES AND ALMONDS

SERVES 6

zest of ½ orange

1 tbsp ras el hanout

1 tsp fresh thyme leaves

140g butter, softened

1 x 2kg turkey crown

200ml chicken stock

6 medium carrots

3 tbsp olive oil

2 bay leaves (fresh if possible)

juice of 1 orange

100g whole blanched almonds

8 Medjool dates, stoned and quartered

Preheat the oven to 185°C.

Add the orange zest, ras el hanout, thyme and some salt and pepper to the butter and mix well.

With your fingers or a spatula, gently loosen the skin from the meat of the turkey, taking care not to tear it. Push the butter underneath the skin, making sure all the meat is covered. Leave some butter for the outside of the bird and smear it all over the skin.

Put the turkey on a high trivet in the centre of a deep roasting tin. This will allow the carrots to go underneath later. Pour the chicken stock into the roasting tin, cover the turkey with foil and cook in the oven for 1 hour.

Peel the carrots and cut them at an angle into slices 1cm thick. Remove the foil from the bird, baste it well, then add the carrots, oil and bay leaves to the tin and put it back in the oven. Cook the turkey for 25 minutes, uncovered. It should be golden with a light spicy crust. Remove it from the tin, along with the trivet, then loosely cover with foil and allow to rest.

Add the orange juice and almonds to the carrots in the tin and return to the oven to cook for 20 minutes more, turning the carrots once or twice. When the carrots are soft and the almonds are golden, add the dates and stir through.

Slice the turkey and serve with the glazed carrots and almonds and the sprout champ on page 260.

PARSNIP, SESAME AND RED ONION CAKE WITH MINTED CRANBERRY YOGURT

SERVES 6

1 medium parsnip, chopped into 2cm chunks

1 large red onion, cut into 6 wedges

2 sprigs of fresh thyme

1 tbsp maple syrup, plus more for drizzling

200g plain flour

2 tsp baking powder

1 tsp mixed spice

zest of ½ orange

80g butter, softened, plus extra for greasing

100g Parmesan cheese, finely grated

100ml olive oil, plus more for drizzling

4 medium eggs

2 tbsp sesame seeds

FOR THE YOGURT:

400ml natural yogurt

2 tbsp dried cranberries

a few fresh mint leaves, shredded

Preheat the oven to 180°C. Grease and line a 25cm loose-bottomed cake tin.

Put the parsnip, red onion and thyme on a baking tray. Season, then drizzle over the maple syrup and a little oil, making sure everything is coated nicely. Cook in the oven for 20 minutes, turning once or twice, until lightly golden and nearly cooked.

In a medium bowl, mix together the flour, baking powder, mixed spice and orange zest and set aside.

In a mixer, cream the butter, 2 tablespoons of the yogurt, the Parmesan and the 100ml of olive oil until pale and very fluffy. Add the eggs one at a time and beat until smooth, then fold in the dry ingredients until combined.

Spoon the mixture into the lined cake tin. Put the parsnips and red onion evenly over the top, then scatter over the sesame seeds. Bake the cake in the oven for 40–45 minutes, until the centre is firm to the touch. Drizzle with a little more maple syrup, then let the cake cool before removing from the tin.

To make the minted cranberry yogurt, pour boiling water over the cranberries and let them sit for 15 minutes to plump up. Drain and gently squeeze all the water from them, then mix with the remaining yogurt and the mint. Chill until needed.

To serve, warm the cake, then spoon the yogurt over the top.

BRUSSELS SPROUT AND APPLE CHAMP
SERVES 6

400g Brussels sprouts
1.5kg potatoes, peeled
250ml milk
100ml cream
100g butter
a pinch of ground nutmeg (optional)
1 Gala apple, peeled and finely diced

Trim the sprouts, then cut them in half if they are small or into quarters if they are large.

Bring a medium pot of lightly salted water to boil, add the sprouts and cook for 2–3 minutes, until they start to soften. Drain and refresh under cold running water. Drain off any excess water, then set aside (this can be done in advance).

Cut the peeled potatoes into even pieces, then put on to boil until they are cooked through and soft. Drain and mash.

Heat the milk and cream, then add this to the potatoes along with the butter, nutmeg (if using) and some salt and ground white pepper.

When you're ready to serve, add the sprouts and diced apple to the potatoes, then warm everything together over a low heat until the sprouts are hot. Serve immediately.

Planning what you cook is half the battle.

07 DECEMBER 2019

Useful recipes for the busy days ahead

19 DECEMBER 2020

My wife Máire is a trooper. Before I dragged her into the restaurant business, she had a diverse array of jobs. Her favourite was working at Sherry FitzGerald, a perfect fit for someone who has an insatiable curiosity about other people's houses.

However, prior to that, for a brief number of heady days one Christmas she became a pheasant plucker for a friend who owned a food company. He'd gotten a job lot from the sky and needed urgent help. Feathers and funk clung to her at the end of the day like some medieval punishment, but I admired her grit. I'm not sure I would have done it.

We're lucky to be having some sort of Christmas this year, given the circumstances. There will be visitors but not the massed hungry crowds that some have catered for in their homes in past years. In one way, perhaps it's a relief for the cook.

Burrata is one of my favourite things in the world. Sometimes I quietly sprinkle Maldon salt on it and sinfully slurp it up. I'm pairing it with red cabbage for a Christmassy thrill. I'm not always a fan of red cabbage with the turkey, as its deep tones can dominate. With burrata, though, it's a revelation. Use a decent mozzarella if you can't find burrata. The pomegranate jewels are appropriate and festive.

These crab vol au vents are little blinders — easy, piquant nibbles that can be made in a flash. I'm buying the pre-cooked cases, they're everywhere at the moment. You might not be able to find wasabi, but you could use horseradish instead.

The salad might inspire you to be a little creative with the Christmas leftovers. I'm using ham but you could use turkey, duck or goose. The creamy celeriac soothes and prepares you for the prunes.

I have loved writing for you this year through thick and thin. You got to learn of some of my foibles and let me vent. Next year will be better and I'll keep cooking and telling you the odd story.

Have a totally amazing Christmas. Stay safe.

BURRATA WITH STICKY RED CABBAGE, POMEGRANATE AND ORANGE

SERVES 6

1 medium red cabbage, quartered, cored and finely shredded

a finger-sized piece of ginger, peeled and grated

2 tbsp redcurrant jelly

1 tsp allspice

3 bay leaves (fresh if possible)

75g golden brown sugar

150ml red wine

100ml red wine vinegar

6 small balls of burrata or mozzarella

FOR THE DRESSING:

100ml orange juice

100ml rapeseed oil

100ml olive oil

1 tsp golden brown sugar

1 tsp Dijon mustard

a pinch of chilli flakes

seeds and juice of 1 pomegranate

Put the red cabbage, ginger, redcurrant jelly, allspice, bay leaves, sugar, wine and vinegar in a pot. Stir it all together, bring up to a simmer, then cover the pot with a lid. Cook over a gentle heat for 45 minutes, stirring every now and again, making sure it doesn't go dry.

Remove the lid and cook for a further 10–15 minutes, until the cabbage starts to glaze and all the liquid has evaporated. Season and set aside. This can be done two to three days in advance.

To make the dressing, whisk the orange juice with the rapeseed and olive oils, sugar, mustard, chilli flakes and the pomegranate juice and seeds. Season and chill.

To serve, warm the cabbage and divide it among plates. Put a whole ball of burrata or mozzarella on top of each portion, then spoon over the dressing.

CRAB VOL AU VENTS WITH APPLE AND WASABI

MAKES 18

200ml cream

1 tsp wasabi or horseradish sauce

140g picked crab meat

1 small apple, cored and finely diced

chopped fresh chives

18 mini vol au vents

Put the cream in a saucepan, then bring it up to a simmer and gently reduce by half. Add the wasabi or horseradish followed by the crab, apple and chives and season.

Warm the vol au vents, then fill with the crab cream. Serve while still warm.

WARM CHRISTMAS SALAD

SERVES 6

1 small celeriac

250ml crème fraîche

1 tbsp wholegrain mustard

12 cooked chestnuts, crumbled

a drizzle of honey

leftover ham, pulled into shreds

8 ready-to-eat prunes, halved (substitute raisins if you're scared)

2 handfuls of nice winter salad leaves

FOR THE DRESSING:

100ml sherry vinegar or red wine vinegar

1 tbsp golden brown sugar

1 cinnamon stick

2 cloves

200ml sunflower oil

100ml rapeseed oil

1 tsp Dijon mustard

To make the dressing, put the vinegar, sugar, cinnamon stick and cloves in a small saucepan and bring to the boil, then immediately remove the pan from the heat. Whisk in the sunflower and rapeseed oils and the Dijon mustard, season and set aside. This can be done ahead of time, as it keeps for two weeks in the fridge.

Peel the celeriac with a serrated knife and cut it into the smallest strips that you can — you could use a food processor if you like.

Mix the crème fraîche, wholegrain mustard, one-third of the chestnuts and a drizzle of honey into the celeriac. Season and chill.

When you're ready to serve, put your leftover shredded ham in a saucepan with the dressing, prunes and the remaining chestnuts and warm over a gentle heat.

To serve, divide the leaves among bowls, then add the celeriac to each portion and spoon the dressing over the top.

Looking back on the strangest year

We've just booked our family holiday for 2021 in this sleepy little coastal village on the Costa Brava. There will be 10 of us, two families. I'll cook when the mood takes me. I'll swim, drink wine, listen to music and laugh a lot. There are coastal treks where I'll practise for my next Camino. Every little rocky cove will be a new delight. I'll be carefree again and I'll relish every single bit of it.

I'll look back on 2020 like a bad dream. I have vowed to appreciate any freedom we get in the future and never take anything for granted again. I'll suck in the sweet, salty air, unimpeded by a cursed mask.

My wife was reluctant to book it. She is deemed by our children to be more of a pessimist than I am. I knew this already, though. This is a lady who watches *Air Crash Investigation* before Saturday evening's service because no matter what lies ahead in the restaurant that evening, it can't be as bad as a catastrophic plane crash. A customer's overcooked steak will keep her from her sleep.

However, I need something to look forward to. Otherwise the cold, dark nights will envelop me. Having a holiday booked has given me hope, even if it's somewhat delusional.

The first lockdown passed quickly, but it didn't seem like it at the time. There were lots of long walks and sitting outside in the sun. Utter bliss when I look back on it. School was apparently happening in the girls' bedrooms but they might have been planning a military coup for all I knew. They didn't allow me in as I always go into orbit over the mess.

I get bored quickly, so on May 1st we started doing takeaway in the restaurant. That went well. I liked the fact that we were being productive and there was purpose to the day. It was also something different. That in itself is stimulating.

When we were allowed to reopen, I did it with a stripped-back kitchen team as I didn't think we were going to be so busy. A big mistake. Staycationing was very a real thing and chefs were impossible to get. Let's just say I felt my age at the end of the summer. I was the cliché of the crotchety old chef. There were a few nights I questioned the wisdom of my calling.

I'm keenly aware, though, that being busy was a blessing. Many others were not so fortunate. It stood us in good stead when we entered Level 3 lockdown and the restaurant closed again.

The pandemic has taken its toll on people commercially but more importantly, mentally. It's the unseen toll that's worrying. We all miss things, and the simplest things the most. Meeting friends in the pub. Going to people's houses without having to think about consequences. Planning a weekend away and the nerdy restaurant research that precedes it. I love a good gallivant — a festival here, a city break there. Normal people call it balance.

We all need something to look forward to. When that is taken away, our lives are diminished. For now, the future is suspended.

You'll be relieved to know that I've found my mojo again. The extra time has given me back some space. The realities of living in a seaside town mean we are used to the ebb and flow of the seasons.

I have a little project that has cheered me up no end. At the end of last summer I bought a clapped-out campervan that I've been doing up for the last year (well, somebody else has). I had plans to jaunt around the country with my two girls. We were all looking forward to the adventure. My wife was less convinced, I'm afraid, as the shower had made way for a wine cellar. A very sensible decision, in my view. Negotiations continue.

Next year has to be better, doesn't it? It would be a blessing not to talk about *it*.

There are other distractions, of course. Marauding, machine gun-toting men in the home of the brave. Polar ice caps melting and unsettling global storms that affect the lives of hundreds of thousands of people. Refugees from war-torn countries risking their lives crossing turbulent seas in the hope of a better future. Forest fires raging through California's affluence. Nobody is spared. And then there's Brexit. Oh, for the days when that was all we talked about.

It puts things into perspective when all I do is write recipes. Still, I find food a comfort and I'll keep cooking and writing as long as I can. I want to be a contented, dignified, calm influence on my chefs, like a happy old cat. That will be me next summer. Wait and see.

Starting the year with cauliflower and good intentions

02 JANUARY 2021

Most of us will be feeling a bit more luxuriant after Christmas — the clothes have tightened like an inquisitor's vice. I'm sad that Christmas is over; I love it. January is so flat and dark, it can be hard to do anything other than hunker down.

My cooking demands change — less so in the restaurant than at home, where the resolutions are ganging up on me. We normally have our annual holiday in January. Restauranteurs used to populate the airports like migrating geese. Not so much anymore.

Far-Flung Flynn is my alter ego. That fella gets around. He's a diva, a two-legged version of *Condé Nast Traveler* who will only stay in exotic, Instagrammable dreamscapes. FFF wouldn't be caught dead backpacking lest his reputation and expectations be tarnished. These days, I can only dream.

My dishes this week represent the need to perk up my taste-buds and rein in the calories. They are also a flight of fancy where I swoop and delve into the cooking of different countries. Their food somehow brings me closer to them. Thankfully, there is hope on the horizon.

I love pilafs. This one resonates of gentle spice, contented restraint and humility. I have a rice cooker at home. It's an old friend. I'd have this with shop-bought hummus, mango chutney and warm naan and eat it by the fire. This would also be a magnificent accompaniment to roast lamb or chicken.

I'm a fan of sea trout. This is a one-pan wonder that I cooked at home one night and ate with steamed rice. The soy, ginger and garlic permeate the trout like a whisper. The cabbage gives it a satisfying, healthy crunch.

I'm trying to eat less meat. Don't panic, meat eaters. Inside me lurks the soul of a savage. It won't be long until I'm craving something slow cooked, dark and wobbly. For now, though, I'm starting the year with cauliflower and good intentions, but you know what they say about those.

A GUILT-FREE PILAF

SERVES 4

1 tbsp butter

1 tsp rapeseed oil

1 onion, thinly sliced

1 tbsp garam masala

250g basmati rice

100g dried Puy lentils

50g raisins

2 bay leaves (fresh if possible)

2 strips of orange peel

700ml chicken stock

Preheat the oven to 180°C.

Put the butter and oil in a casserole over a gentle heat. When the butter starts to foam, add the onion and cook for 5 minutes, until it starts to soften. Add the garam masala and cook for a little longer, then add the rice, lentils, raisins, bay leaves and orange peel. Turn everything around in the pan, then add the stock. Season and bring to a simmer.

Cover the casserole and cook in the oven for 20 minutes. Remove from the oven and fluff up the rice with a fork. Serve in warm bowls.

STEAMED SEA TROUT WITH PEPPERED CABBAGE, SOY, GARLIC AND GINGER

SERVES 4

1 small Savoy cabbage, shredded

1 small cauliflower, very thinly sliced

1 x 500g fillet of seat trout, skinned and pin-boned (use salmon if you can't get sea trout)

2 garlic cloves, sliced

a thumb-sized piece of ginger, peeled and finely chopped

60ml dark soy sauce

2 tbsp fish sauce

2 tbsp toasted sesame oil

a drizzle of honey

200ml water

Layer the cabbage, cauliflower and sea trout in a large frying pan or a shallow saucepan. Scatter the garlic and ginger over the trout, then drizzle over the soy sauce, fish sauce, sesame oil and honey. Add the water and season using just a little salt and lots of black pepper.

Cover the pan tightly and cook on the hob on the highest heat for 10–12 minutes. Exactly how long it takes will depend entirely on the thickness of the fish. Don't be tempted to peek. Use a knife to check if the fish is cooked after 10 minutes. The sauce should also be nearly absorbed into the vegetables.

If you find that your fish isn't cooked and your pan is dry, just add a little more water and continue to cook for another minute or two.

WARM COUSCOUS, CAULIFLOWER AND ALMOND SALAD

SERVES 4

200g couscous

320ml almost-boiling water

120ml olive oil

1 red onion, diced

1 red pepper, diced

2 garlic cloves, sliced

½ cauliflower, diced into pieces the same size as the pepper

8 dried apricots, diced the same size as the pepper and cauliflower

2 tbsp ras el hanout or garam masala

a pinch of chilli flakes

zest and juice of 1 orange

1 bunch of fresh coriander, roughly chopped (including the stalks)

2 tbsp flaked almonds, toasted

Put the couscous in a heatproof bowl. Pour over the hot water, then cover the bowl with cling film and let it sit for 10 minutes. Fluff up the couscous with a fork so there are no lumps remaining.

Heat the oil in a wide, shallow pan or wok over a gentle heat. Add the onion, red pepper and garlic. Cook for 15 minutes, then add the cauliflower, apricots and ras el hanout or garam masala and the chilli flakes. Continue to cook for a further 15 minutes, until everything starts to get sticky and begins to caramelise.

Add the orange zest and juice followed by the couscous, coriander and almonds. Season well and fold together gently.

Serve straightaway with hummus or minted yogurt. You can make this in advance and warm it in the microwave or it's delicious at room temperature too.

Big flavour,
very little fuss

09 JANUARY 2021

If you were to ask me this year if I would like to spend half of my time at home chilling, cooking and eating, punctuated with innumerable walks around the countryside in dizzying hoops, I'd say you're grand. I couldn't do it again.

I'm optimistic, though. I've got a family holiday booked for June. I'll swim there if I have to. I've got my eye on a couple of festivals — I'll bring the campervan for the gang. I hanker for the musky tangle of overloaded limbs and flashback laughter the morning after. The post-mortem always occupies the first hours of the next day, supplanted by the anticipation of the upcoming acts. The throb of the music builds and we go again.

Then there's the day job. Keeping creative energy is paramount when you have a restaurant that has been around as long as the Tannery. I'm going to have to figure out how to grow chefs in Petri dishes for the coming year. Without a great team, I can't do any of my globetrotting.

Most of the dishes I write about are made at home. I enjoy the planning and shopping. It takes me out of things. As I shop, I drift into the flavours of the dish. Then I cook them quietly at home.

The eggs are supremely simple. They have texture and bacony depth. Serve them in the centre of the table with a bowl of mash.

I cook lamb chops on the barbecue all year round. They are best with a little char on the outside and a blush in the middle. I diverted to Greece with the accompaniments. I needed the sun.

I'm a root vegetable boy. I make no excuses but I wanted to lighten winter's dark load. A platter of juicy roast chicken, anchovy-scented peppers and cooling aioli did the trick. I'm making the aioli. It's worth it. If you don't fancy making it, add olive oil, lemon and finely crushed garlic to good shop-bought mayo. There is a little challenge here. You will need to spatchcock the chicken, but your butcher will do it for you with no difficulty.

SWIRLED EGGS WITH CRUNCHY BACON CRUMBLE
SERVES 2

125g smoked bacon lardons

80g fresh white breadcrumbs

4 fresh sage leaves, finely shredded

1 tbsp melted butter

1 tbsp olive oil

4 eggs

a pinch of smoked paprika

Preheat the oven to 185°C.

Put the bacon, breadcrumbs, sage and melted butter in a roasting tin. Season and mix together. Bake in the oven for 15–20 minutes, turning once or twice, until they are golden and crispy.

Heat the oil in a non-stick ovenproof frying pan over a medium heat, then crack in the eggs. Season and sprinkle over the smoked paprika. Cook for 2 minutes, then pierce the egg yolks with the tip of a knife and swirl them around the pan.

Sprinkle the bacony breadcrumbs on top of the eggs, then put the pan in the oven for 2 minutes. You want the eggs a little soft – timing is everything with this one. Serve straightaway.

GRILLED LAMB CHOP, CARAMELISED ONION, BUTTER BEAN AND FETA BAKE

SERVES 4

50ml olive oil, plus extra for drizzling

1 red onion, sliced

2 garlic cloves, sliced

1 tsp dried oregano

1 x 400g tin of butter beans, drained and rinsed

12 baby plum tomatoes, halved

12 stoned black olives, roughly chopped

8 lamb chops

200g feta cheese

a jar of mint jelly

Heat the oil in a pan over a medium heat. Add the onion, garlic and oregano and cook slowly for 15 minutes, until the onion is soft and translucent.

Add the butter beans, tomatoes and olives and continue to cook gently for a further 10 minutes, until the tomatoes start to break up just a little and release their juices. Season and set aside until needed.

Heat a ridged griddle pan or large frying pan over a high heat until the pan is gently smoking. Drizzle the chops with a little oil, season and rub it in. Add the chops to the hot pan and cook for 3 minutes on each side and 1 minute on the fatty side of the chops. This is a bit of a balancing act but it will pay dividends when you eat the crispy lamb fat. You may have to cook the chops in batches. Alternatively, you could cook them all in one go under a hot grill.

Let the chops rest for 5 minutes under foil somewhere warm.

To serve, reheat the butter bean mixture and pour any resting juices from the lamb into it. Crumble in the feta and turn gently. Divide among warm plates, then put the chops on top and eat with as much mint jelly as you like.

I love people who love food, who treat it as a joy in life.

CHOPPED ROAST CHICKEN WITH AIOLI AND RED PEPPER AND ANCHOVY DRESSING

SERVES 4

1 x 1.6kg chicken, spatchcocked
(ask your butcher to do this for you)

FOR THE DRESSING:

100ml olive oil, plus extra for drizzling

2 red peppers, thinly sliced

2 garlic cloves, sliced

1 tsp smoked paprika

8 salted anchovies, finely chopped
(I love the Ortiz brand)

juice of 1 orange

2 tbsp balsamic vinegar

a drizzle of honey

1 sprig of fresh rosemary

FOR THE AIOLI:

6 garlic cloves, crushed

2 egg yolks, at room temperature

juice of ½ lemon

1 tbsp Dijon mustard

300ml sunflower oil

50ml olive oil

2 tbsp crème fraîche

Preheat the oven to 190°C.

Put a little oil in a roasting tin and add the spatchcocked chicken, skin side up. Drizzle with oil, season and rub it into the skin. Roast in the oven for 50 minutes, until fully cooked.

Meanwhile, put the 100ml of olive oil in a pot with the peppers, garlic and smoked paprika. Cook gently over a low heat for 20–25 minutes, until the peppers start to shrivel and caramelise. Add the anchovies, orange juice, balsamic vinegar, honey and rosemary and let it bubble gently for a further 10 minutes. Season and remove from the heat. Discard the rosemary.

To make the aioli, put the garlic, egg yolks, lemon juice, mustard, a pinch of salt and some ground white pepper in a blender. Whizz together, then with the motor still running, slowly add the sunflower oil followed by the olive oil in a thin stream until it forms an emulsion. When all the oil has been incorporated, stir in the crème fraîche. Check the seasoning — it may need a little more lemon juice. Put in a bowl on the table so everyone can help themselves. The aioli can be made earlier if you like — it keeps for two weeks in the fridge.

When the chicken is cooked, remove it to a chopping board. Tip any cooking juices into the peppers.

To serve, chop the chicken into 8–10 pieces and put on a platter. Warm the red pepper and anchovy dressing and spoon it over the top of the chicken.

I'm never going to have abs like Joe Wicks

16 JANUARY 2021

I can't resist a good cookbook. I tend to go for the cheffy, nerdy ones as opposed to the glitzy lifestyle ones. I'm never going to have abs like Joe Wicks anyhow. I'd only end up flicking through it while double-jobbing crisps and chocolate in my jim-jams.

These recipes are paying homage to great cookbooks and great cooks. The red cabbage recipe is my take on Stephen Harris's of the Sportsman pub in Kent. Its genius is in its simplicity and is typical of the man. We would call this making a silk purse out of a sow's ear.

To say that what he calls a 'grotty little rundown pub by the sea' punches above its weight is a magnificent understatement. It's won a Michelin star and continually teeters at the top of the top 50 gastropubs in the UK. Chef devotees, me included, make the pilgrimage from far and wide to eat Harris's simple, carefully considered food that sings of the local terroir. I went there a few years back to beg him to come cook in the Tannery for the West Waterford Festival of Food. He came. It was stupendous.

Chez Bruce in Wandsworth is another legendary restaurant. On the site of Marco Pierre White's seminal Harvey's, it is voted London's favourite year after year. It wears its Michelin star easily and has been pampering Londoners with old-school deliciousness for a long time. I am forever ogling the food of the head chef, Matt Christmas, on Twitter and Instagram. Have a look for yourself and drool your way into happy oblivion. As a chef, it's a constant, beautiful barrage of ideas and inspiration.

The plums are something I cook in winter. They are perfect with the wondrous Crozier Blue. The juice from the plums will giddily enhance your favourite sparkling wine, gin or vodka. Do yourself a favour and eat them with these decadent Parmesan biscuits from Chez Bruce. They are a little bit of comforting brilliance.

THE SPORTMAN'S POT ROAST RED CABBAGE (WITH A LITTLE TWIST)
SERVES 6

1 medium red cabbage, tough outer leaves removed
150g butter
1 large sprig of fresh thyme
apple jelly

FOR THE DRESSING:
150g soft rindless goat cheese
100g natural yogurt
a drizzle of rapeseed oil

Preheat the oven to 140°C.

Cut the cabbage in half and put it in a heavy-based casserole with a lid. Add the butter, thyme, salt and lots of black pepper. Cover and cook in the oven for 1½ hours, basting the cabbage once or twice during cooking. When the core of the cabbage is soft, remove the casserole from the oven and set it aside with the lid on.

To make the dressing, blend the goat cheese with the yogurt and rapeseed oil (use a hand blender).

To serve, cut the cabbage into six wedges and put on warm plates. Drizzle the goat cheese dressing around the cabbage along with intermittent blobs of apple jelly.

BAKED PLUMS AND CROZIER BLUE
SERVES 6

6 ripe plums, halved and stoned
200ml cider
2 tbsp light brown sugar
1 sprig of fresh thyme
1 fresh bay leaf
1 cinnamon stick
1 star anise
300g Crozier Blue cheese (or your favourite blue cheese)

Preheat the oven to 185°C.

Put the plums in a small baking dish, cut side up. Add the cider, brown sugar, thyme, bay, cinnamon and star anise, making sure there is an even coating of sugar over the plums.

Bake in the oven for 25–30 minutes, basting the plums once or twice. The length of time entirely depends on the ripeness of the plums – they should be soft and giving to the touch.

When they are cooked, decant them into a bowl and pour the juice over the top.

Serve with the blue cheese and the Parmesan biscuits on the next page.

CHEZ BRUCE PARMESAN BISCUITS
MAKES APPROX. 36

180g Parmesan cheese, grated
165g unsalted butter, softened
½ tsp baking powder
a pinch of smoked paprika
a pinch of cayenne pepper
210g plain flour
1 egg beaten with 1 tbsp milk
a mixture of nigella seeds, caraway seeds, sesame seeds and Maldon sea salt, for rolling

Beat the Parmesan, butter, baking powder, paprika, cayenne and some salt and pepper together, until soft and creamy. Mix in the flour just until it comes together into a dough – don't work the mixture too much at this point.

Roll the biscuit dough into a log about 3cm in diameter. Brush lightly with the egg wash, then roll in the seed mixture. Wrap the log in parchment paper and chill in the fridge for an hour or so.

Preheat the oven to 160°C. Line a baking tray with non-stick baking paper.

Using a serrated knife, slice the log into biscuits about 4mm thick. Place on the lined tray and bake in the oven for 18–20 minutes, until golden. Cool on a wire rack.

Low-cal food has its place, but not here

23 JANUARY 2021

We've settled into a routine at home of daily walks where we plough through podcasts. I'm all art and history, whereas herself loves nothing more than a good murder. I worry about that sometimes.

I'm trying to be reasonably good with the food at home. It's so tempting to go full-on Julia Child every night as we have all this extra time on our hands. Steamed vegetables with misery dressing is the order of the day most days, an unsurprising retribution for Christmas overindulgence.

I won't trouble you with any low-cal recipes this week. In truth, they are the preserve of my wife. She makes zero-fat lentil stews by the bucketful that I dutifully eat while staring wistfully at my skinny jeans.

These dishes were tried and tested over the last few weeks in the dark evenings. I put these three recipes together with the notion that they would be perfect for tea around five o'clock. Then I thought I must be a right old greedy guts if I considered a duck risotto to be a relatively spartan dish.

You might have guessed I'm a sucker for risottos. I hope that in my dotage I'll be given the odd one. I'll suck it in with gummy glee and reflect on past glories. This one has red wine in it, which gives it depth and gravitas. Confit duck legs are another favourite of mine. The salami delivers smoky, Continental heft. I'm using only a few necessary leaves of cabbage — save the rest for another day.

The croissant is a gooey, delicious mess. The creamy goat cheese oozes from the crisp pastry as if trying to escape being ravished by the figs. This compote would be lovey with cheese or perhaps duck another time. Simply double the recipe and it will keep for a week in the fridge.

The pea mash is a firm favourite at home. It's a pretty dish that's simple to make — just the thing for the jaded housebound gourmand. You can substitute the mustard for mint jelly to serve with lamb chops. Delicious and easy.

DUCK RISOTTO WITH CABBAGE, SALAMI AND RED WINE

SERVES 4

100g butter

1 onion, finely diced

2 garlic cloves, sliced

1 large sprig of fresh thyme

300g Arborio risotto rice

a large glass of red wine

600ml chicken stock

4 leaves of Savoy cabbage, shredded

2 confit duck legs, skin and bones removed and the meat shredded

80g Parmesan cheese, grated

50g sliced smoked salami, shredded

1 tbsp horseradish sauce

extra virgin olive oil, for drizzling (optional)

Melt the butter in a heavy-based saucepan over a very low heat. When the butter starts to foam, add the onion, garlic and thyme. Cover and cook for 20 minutes, stirring once or twice.

When the onion is soft and translucent, add the rice, then shortly after that, the red wine. Let the rice absorb the wine for a minute or so, then add two-thirds of the stock. Bring to a simmer, making sure there is no rice around the side of the pot, then cook gently for 10 minutes, until the rice has absorbed all the stock.

Add the cabbage and a little more stock and continue to cook until the stock has all been absorbed once more.

Stirring more frequently now, add the remaining stock. Test the rice — there should still be a tiny bite. In total the rice should take around 20 minutes to cook. Stir in the duck, Parmesan, salami and horseradish.

Season to taste and serve with a little extra Parmesan and a drizzle of good extra virgin olive oil on top if you wish.

STICKY ONION, FIG AND GOAT CHEESE CROISSANTS
SERVES 4

1 tbsp rapeseed oil

1 onion, thinly sliced

1 cinnamon stick

1 sprig of fresh thyme

4 dried figs, thinly sliced

25ml red wine vinegar

1 tbsp redcurrant jelly

4 crisp, freshly cooked croissants

150g soft rindless goat cheese

Preheat the oven to 180°C.

Heat the oil in a small saucepan over a medium heat. Add the onion, cinnamon and thyme, cover and cook gently for 15 minutes, until soft.

Add the figs, red wine vinegar, redcurrant jelly and a twist of black pepper, then let the mixture blip away over a low heat until it becomes jammy.

If you've bought ready-cooked croissants and they are a bit sad, crisp them up in the oven.

To serve, cut open the croissants lengthways and smear with the goat cheese, then spoon in the onion and fig mix. Eat straightaway, while they are still warm.

BLACK AND WHITE PUDDING WITH CRUSHED PEA MASH

SERVES 4

8 medium potatoes, peeled and halved

200g frozen petits pois, defrosted

200ml milk

2 tbsp butter

2 tsp Dijon mustard

a little sunflower oil, for grilling the pudding

sliced black and white puddings, as many as you fancy – I won't judge you

Boil the potatoes in lightly salted water. When they are just cooked, add the peas. After a minute or two, drain well and mash with the milk, butter and mustard. Season and keep warm while you grill the pudding.

Serve on warm plates with the crisp pudding nestling on top of the pea mash.

These veggies will reward a bit of love

30 JANUARY 2021

This week I'm writing about vegetables we don't come across every day. If you're going to try these recipes you might curse me as your search may be frustrating, but I'll try my best to point you in the right direction.

I've been using Jerusalem artichokes for years. I've always been a fan of their sweet nuttiness. An essential part of the Tannery's winter larder, their stout brutishness seduces me. They are an under-loved vegetable but their charm is so much more appealing than their odorous reputation. They are in season from November to March, so you have time to play. Today I'm roasting them with their skin on but I also love to peel them, poach them in milk and bay, then purée them with a little butter. Try this nectar of the gods and you'll be purring like a cat.

Kohlrabi is an understated pleasure. Weird and wonderful, it resembles *Sputnik*, a vegetable satellite orbiting obliviously around us. Its crisp, crunchy texture and mild, sweet flavour lands it somewhere between a turnip and a water chestnut. It makes a wonderful slaw but here I'm roasting it with olive oil, butter, maple syrup and sesame. It's often available in Polish shops if you're fortunate enough to have one nearby. It's available all year but especially during the autumn into spring.

Frivole is a marvel, grown by the pioneering Maria and David Flynn at Ballymakenny Farm in County Louth. They mostly grow a magical array of lesser-known spuds but these little fellows are a curious wonder. They take five months to grow, then are picked in the winter months. A delightful hybrid of purple Brussels sprouts and kale, they are nurtured and hand-picked, then supplied to chefs who await their Ballymakenny delivery like eager young chicks. Theirs is a lovely story of dedication and commitment. I'm serving the frivole here with a gentle barley and mushroom stew that's enhanced with gorgeous Cáis na Tíre cheese (you could use Cheddar). The browned butter adds depth to any vegetable. I'm using malt vinegar this time but normally I use a few drops of lemon. If you can't get frivole, substitute with tenderstem broccoli.

ROASTED JERUSALEM ARTICHOKES WITH BACON AND SPINACH

SERVES 2

6 large Jerusalem artichokes (use more if they're small)
a good drizzle of rapeseed oil
1 tsp butter
2 tbsp buckwheat (optional but lovely)
125g smoked bacon lardons
2 handfuls of baby spinach
a splash of red wine vinegar

Preheat the oven to 185°C.

Scrub the skins of the artichokes to take off the dark outer layer. Cut them in half, then put in a roasting tin with the rapeseed oil. Season and turn everything together. Roast in the oven for 20 minutes.

Meanwhile, melt the butter in a frying pan over a low heat. When the butter starts to foam, add the buckwheat, season and toast for 4–5 minutes, until golden and crisp. Set aside.

After 20 minutes, add the lardons to the artichokes, then return the roasting tin to the oven for another 15 minutes or so, until the artichokes are crisp and golden on the outside but soft and creamy in the middle. The length of time will depend on how big the artichokes are. Remove the tin from the oven and set aside. You can do this ahead of time if you like.

When you're ready to serve, put the roasting tin on the hob over a low heat. I have a gas hob at home, so that's perfect. (If you have an induction hob, just put the tin back in the oven until everything is nice and hot again.) Add the spinach to the tin and start to wilt it for no more than a minute. Add the vinegar, season and serve with the buckwheat scattered over the top.

ROAST KOHLRABI WITH MAPLE SYRUP AND SESAME
SERVES 2

50ml olive oil

2 kohlrabi, peeled and cut into discs 0.5cm thick

1 tbsp butter

1 tsp fresh thyme leaves

2 tbsp maple syrup

2 tbsp sesame seeds

Preheat the oven to 185°C.

Drizzle the oil over the bottom of a shallow casserole or baking dish, then layer the kohlrabi over the base. Dot the butter over the top, then sprinkle over the thyme leaves. Season and drizzle over the maple syrup, then scatter over the sesame seeds.

Bake in the oven for 45–50 minutes, basting once or twice, until the kohlrabi is tender and the sesame seeds are golden and crunchy. Serve immediately.

FRIVOLE, MUSHROOM AND BARLEY STEW WITH CÁIS NA TÍRE

SERVES 4

100g barley	250ml strong vegetable stock (1 cube)
400ml warm water	250ml milk
1 tbsp rapeseed oil	20 frivole or tenderstem broccoli
2 flat cap mushrooms, halved and sliced	100g butter
2 bay leaves (fresh if possible)	1 tbsp malt vinegar
1 cinnamon stick	80g Cáis na Tíre cheese or Cheddar, plus
a little grated nutmeg	a little more to shave on top

Soak the barley in the warm water for 2 hours.

Heat the rapeseed oil in a saucepan over a medium heat. Add the mushrooms, bay leaves, cinnamon and nutmeg. Cook for 5 minutes, until the mushrooms start to soften.

Drain the barley, then add it to the pan followed by the vegetable stock and milk. Bring to a simmer and cook gently for 20 minutes, until the barley is soft and yielding.

Meanwhile, cook the frivole or tenderstem broccoli in boiling salted water for 2 minutes. Drain and refresh under cold running water and pat dry on a clean tea towel.

Put the butter in a separate small pan and begin to cook over a low to medium heat for 3 minutes or so. When it starts to fizz and foam, it's starting to turn into brown butter. Give it 30 more seconds, then remove the pan from the heat and allow to cool a little before adding the vinegar. This can be made ahead of time.

To finish the barley stew, add the grated cheese and season. Add the frivole to the brown butter, season and warm over a low heat.

Serve the barley stew on warm plates with the buttery frivole on top, plus a drizzle of the excess brown butter and cheese shaved on top.

Pasta dishes that will take you right back to Italy ... and France

06 FEBRUARY 2021

I'm looking out on a grey morning here but taking some comfort out of old holiday photos in Umbria that I came across last night. We used to fly into Bergamo to save a few bob on the flight, then the eight-hour ordeal to our destination would begin at the car hire. On one memorable trip, I opened the boot to load the multitude of bags and watched in helpless horror as it rose to meet a concrete column lurking above. It all unfolded in tortuous slow motion. That expensive vision will never leave me. The form wasn't great after that, compounded by nerve-jangling encounters on the Italian motorways.

We stayed in Parma that night. The 40°C heat nearly finished me but Mr Peroni and Manuela Spinelli came to the rescue. She's our Italian queen, a friend to Irish restauranteurs. She booked a table for us in the trattoria of our dreams a short taxi ride from the city. We sat in the garden surrounded by Italian families and twinkly lights. Finally, we were on holiday. It was one of those special nights in a restaurant that can never be repeated or captured again. I ate a lot of pasta.

Béarnaise sauce is one of the great French sauces. I've condensed its flavours into a butter that I'm putting with pasta and leftover chicken. I'm getting you to make more butter than you need and whipping it to make it lighter. Roll it up in parchment, freeze it if you like, then simply cut slices when you need it to drip tantalisingly onto a steak.

We do this spaghetti dish at home all the time without the prawns. It's all about slowly cooking the garlic to deepen the flavour. I added the prawns as I had a handy packet in the freezer but chopped them up as I didn't have a lot. A boy's gotta do what a boy's gotta do.

French onion soup holds a special place in my heart. I've always loved French bistro food. This recipe combines my love of food from two wonderful countries with delicious results.

ROAST CHICKEN RIGATONI WITH BÉARNAISE BUTTER

SERVES 4

500g rigatoni
leftover roast chicken, diced (or 2 cooked chicken breasts)
100g Parmesan cheese, grated

FOR THE BÉARNAISE BUTTER:
3 shallots, finely diced
100ml red wine vinegar
2 tbsp chopped fresh tarragon leaves (reserve the stalks)
450g butter, softened
1 tbsp Dijon mustard

First make the béarnaise butter. Put the shallots, red wine vinegar, tarragon stalks and a few twists of black pepper in a saucepan over a high heat. Reduce the vinegar until it has nearly evaporated, then remove the pan from the heat.

Put the butter in a mixing bowl and beat for 3 minutes, until it becomes light and fluffy. Add the chopped tarragon leaves and mustard. Remove the tarragon stalks from the reduction and discard them, then add the reduction to the butter. Roll the butter in parchment and keep in the fridge.

Cook the pasta as per the packet instructions. Drain, leaving a little of the cooking water in the pot (around half a cup).

Slice off a quarter of the butter and add it to the pasta along with the cooked chicken. Season and serve with the grated Parmesan on top.

SPAGHETTI WITH GARLIC, CHILLI AND CHOPPED PRAWNS

SERVES 2

250g spaghetti

4 tbsp olive oil

3 garlic cloves, sliced very thinly and evenly

a pinch of chilli flakes (more if you like it spicy)

a knob of chilled butter

1 x 150g packet of cooked shelled prawns, roughly chopped

juice of ½ lemon

2 tbsp grated Parmesan cheese

Cook the spaghetti in a pot of boiling salted water as per the packet instructions.

While it's cooking, put the oil and garlic in a large frying pan or wok and cook gently over a low heat for 2–3 minutes, until the garlic is evenly golden. Add the chilli flakes and cold butter, swirl, then remove the pan or wok from the heat. This will prevent the garlic from getting too dark. Add the prawns and lemon juice.

When the spaghetti is cooked, drain it but keep a few tablespoons of the cooking water. Add the spaghetti and cooking water to the prawn and garlic mix, season and toss together well.

Serve in warm bowls with the grated Parmesan on top.

FRENCH ONION PAPPARDELLE WITH GRUYÈRE PANGRATTATO

SERVES 4

80g butter

3 onions, thinly sliced

2 bay leaves (fresh if possible)

100ml cider or apple juice

300ml strong beef stock

a dash of smoked chipotle Tabasco or Worcestershire sauce

500g pappardelle

FOR THE PANGRATTATO:

100g fresh white breadcrumbs

1 large garlic clove, crushed

a drizzle of olive oil

4 tbsp grated Gruyère or Cheddar cheese

2 tbsp chopped fresh parsley

Preheat the oven to 185°C.

Put the breadcrumbs and garlic in a roasting tin, drizzle over some oil, season and mix well. Bake in the oven for 15–20 minutes, until the breadcrumbs are golden and crunchy. Remove from the oven and allow to cool, then add the Gruyère and parsley.

Meanwhile, melt the butter in a large saucepan over a low heat. When it starts to foam, add the onions and bay leaves, cover and cook for 15 minutes, until the onions are soft and translucent.

Remove the lid, turn up the heat and continue to cook the onions for another 5–10 minutes, turning and scraping the bottom of the pan with a wooden spoon every so often, until they have caramelised.

Add the cider or apple juice and the beef stock, bring to a simmer and allow to reduce slowly by one-third. Remove the bay leaves. Add the chipotle Tabasco or Worcestershire, season and set aside.

Cook the pasta as per the packet instructions, drain and put it back in the pot. Pour the onion broth on top, turn everything together and season.

To serve, divide the pappardelle among four warm bowls and scatter the cheesy breadcrumbs on top.

Call me a cantankerous old goat. You might be right.

13 FEBRUARY 2021

I'm a bit of a curmudgeon when it comes to Valentine's Day. It isn't the case that I'm not a romantic. My wife, who corrects my appalling punctuation before my articles wing their way to Dublin, might disagree though. It could be that I'm just on the wrong side of 30 and don't like to be told when I should get all loved up. It's all so, well, forced. Call me a cantankerous old goat. You might be right.

People would always say to us on Valentine's Day, 'You must be so busy tonight.' 'We are, it's great,' we would always reply. In truth, Valentine's night is one of the quietest nights of the year in the literal sense. Furtive, uncomfortable boys bring in their girls. Tables of four and six give way to two tops. The restaurant is hushed because of the diminished capacity and the nervous disposition of the diners. For the most part, the boys just want to be in the pub. This year we will miss them. The glamorous girls brought sparkle to the restaurant. We could all do with more sparkle these days.

For those of you who do want to make the night special, I've come up with a dinner you might like to try. There's a little bit of extra effort to do all three recipes but it's a project well worth doing. Who knows what may come of it? Our own future was bonded through food and my wife is still putting up with me all these years later.

So — baked scallops in the shell with a rim of mash and luxurious smoked paprika butter. How very 1970s. You will have to see if your fishmonger can get scallop shells for you. Otherwise use shallow ramekins.

Luxurious, melting lamb shanks with buttery polenta laden with Parmesan. Who wouldn't succumb? The anchovies are optional and interesting. Be brave. It's a classic combination.

Try my light and airy version of a cheesecake. You can assemble this in advance and put the almonds on at the end. It will finish the night with a twinkle.

That's the thing about food. It allows you to dream.

16 APRIL 2022

COQUILLES ST JACQUES WITH SMOKED PAPRIKA BUTTER SAUCE

SERVES 2

4 large scallops (if they are small, use 8), including their shells – I like the roes on, but remove them if you wish

2 tbsp panko breadcrumbs

FOR THE MASH:

500g potatoes, peeled and halved

50g butter, diced

50ml milk

50ml cream

FOR THE SAUCE:

juice of ½ orange

¼ tsp smoked paprika

1 sprig of fresh rosemary

100g butter, diced

To make the mash, boil the potatoes in salted water until soft, then drain in a colander and set aside until they stop steaming. Put them back in the pot and mash them thoroughly. The more you work them, the lighter the mash will be. If you have a ricer, that would be perfect.

Add the butter, milk and cream to the mash, then season with salt and ground white pepper. Bring everything together as smoothly as you can, then transfer to a piping bag with a medium-sized plain nozzle. If you don't have a piping bag, you can put the mash in a small, sturdy plastic bag and cut the corner off (no nozzle). It works. Pipe the mashed potatoes as neatly as you can around the edge of each scallop shell.

Trim the membrane from the scallops, rinse under cold water and pat them dry. Put the scallops in the centre of the potatoes on the shells, then put them in the fridge until you're ready to cook them.

To make the sauce, bring the orange juice, paprika and rosemary up to a gentle simmer, then whisk in the remaining butter. When it's all incorporated, remove the rosemary. Leave to one side in a warm place.

When ready to serve, heat your grill to high.

Put the scallops on a baking tray. Season and spoon 1 tablespoon of butter over each scallop, followed by a sprinkling of breadcrumbs. Grill the scallops for 4 minutes, then check them. They overcook easily, so err on the side of caution. It's more important to have perfect scallops then golden potatoes. If they are large, the scallops might take a minute more. They should be soft to the touch and have turned from opaque to white.

Serve immediately.

LAMB SHANKS WITH POLENTA, CABBAGE AND ANCHOVIES

SERVES 2

2 tbsp olive oil

2 lamb shanks

1 onion, diced

1 carrot, diced

2 celery sticks, diced

4 garlic cloves, sliced

1 sprig of fresh thyme

1 tbsp tomato purée

a glass of white wine

400ml chicken stock

2 tbsp balsamic vinegar

4 salted anchovies

2 strips of orange peel

1 tbsp golden brown sugar

1 small Savoy cabbage

FOR THE POLENTA:

250ml milk

1 sprig of fresh rosemary

100g instant polenta

80g Parmesan cheese, grated

50g butter

Preheat the oven to 160°C.

Heat the oil in a casserole over a high heat and season the lamb shanks. When the oil is gently smoking, add the shanks and brown them all over for 5 minutes, then add the vegetables, garlic and thyme.

Continue to colour everything for a short while, then add the tomato purée followed by the wine, then the stock, balsamic vinegar, anchovies, orange peel and sugar. Bring to a simmer, then cover and cook in the oven for 2½ hours, until the shanks are soft and meltingly tender.

Trim the stalks from the cabbage leaves and wash. Cook the cabbage in boiling salted water for 3 minutes, until it's just soft. Drain and plunge into iced water to keep its colour. Drain once more, pat dry and set aside.

Remove the lamb shanks carefully onto a plate. Skim off as much fat as you can from the surface of the liquid and pick out the thyme. Season and purée a little with a hand blender – it shouldn't be too smooth, just a little pulpy.

Put the lamb back into the juices and either keep warm or you can reheat it later. Keep in a cool place if the latter – up to this stage can be done the day before. When you're ready to serve, reheat the lamb.

To make the polenta, gently heat the milk with the rosemary for 2 minutes or so, then remove the rosemary. Whisk the polenta into the milk in a steady stream. Cook it out for 5 minutes, then add the Parmesan and butter, season and keep warm.

Add the cabbage to the lamb juices to heat up for a couple of minutes, then you're ready to serve.

Spoon the polenta onto warm plates with a lamb shank on top. Put the cabbage alongside and for the brave add a few more anchovies. Or if you want to make a statement, you can put them on a platter and just help yourselves.

MASCARPONE MOUSSE WITH GRAPE COMPOTE AND FROSTED ALMONDS

SERVES 2

80g mascarpone cheese

100ml cream

1 tsp icing sugar

pinch of orange zest

2 drops of vanilla extract

FOR THE GRAPE COMPOTE:

250g seedless black grapes

juice of 1 orange

1 tbsp caster sugar

FOR THE FROSTED ALMONDS:

1 egg white

1 heaped tbsp icing sugar

3 tbsp flaked almonds

To make the mousse, whip the mascarpone, cream, icing sugar, orange zest and vanilla extract together until it's light and airy. Refrigerate for at least 30 minutes.

Preheat the oven to 170°C. Line a baking tray with non-stick baking paper.

To make the frosted almonds, whisk the egg white, then beat in the icing sugar. Fold in the almonds and spread the mixture on the lined tray. Bake in the oven for 15 minutes exactly. Allow to cool, then break it up into little pieces.

To make the compote, put the grapes, orange juice, sugar and a few twists of black pepper in a small saucepan and cook over a medium heat for 15 minutes or so, until the grapes are soft and jammy. Allow to cool, then refrigerate.

You can assemble your dessert ahead of time. Simply spoon some of the grape compote in the bottom of a nice glass, put twice the amount of mascarpone cream on top, then add the shards of frosted almonds just before you serve.

Balance
is the key.
Learn to trust
your taste-buds.
And remember,
black is never
good in cooking,
unless it's
a truffle.

27 FEBRUARY 2021

So long, packed lunches

20 FEBRUARY 2021

There's only one good thing about the children not being in school and that's not making the lunches. I found that I spent a disproportionate amount of my week thinking about them. I'd turned into your man from *Sleeping with the Enemy*, lining up the contents of their lunchboxes like soldiers every morning to make sure there was enough of the good stuff to fulfil my parental obligations. More fool me, I hear you say. At this stage they should be doing it themselves.

I get excited grocery shopping these days. It's like a day out. Perhaps I linger a little too long but when the highlight of my week is perusing the veg section, I'm reluctant for it to end.

These roti are dead easy. The key is to use the same quantity of flour as sweet potato. If you don't fancy making them, use warm naan or pitta for a shortcut. I love a good shortcut.

The tomato and chickpea stew is a bit of a revelation and can be made in minutes. It's really versatile and also goes particularly well with hummus, rice and couscous for that matter. A handy little number, as we say in the business.

I hadn't eaten tinned corned beef in years. As a boy I used to love it – until I didn't. I bought it recently on a whim. Its fatty familiarity was a comfort all these years later. I also bought brown sauce, something I never eat but I can't have corned beef without it. These flavours are imbued in my childhood memory. I left them behind a while back, when, according to my girls, I became posh.

We're big fans of lettuce wraps. Their healthy, crunchy exterior and devilishly delicious filling pack a satisfying punch. An occasional meat sung from the Chinese takeaway is always a treat at home. Here, I'm cooking chicken thighs in coconut milk, crunchy peanut butter and a hint of chilli. It's a rewarding building project, and one you can eat with immense satisfaction afterwards.

SWEET POTATO ROTI WITH CHICKPEAS, TOMATOES AND CUMIN

SERVES 2

2 tbsp olive oil

2 garlic cloves, sliced

1 tsp ground cumin

1 x 400g tin of chopped tomatoes

1 vegetable stock cube

1 x 400g tin of chickpeas, drained and rinsed

a drizzle of honey

FOR THE ROTI:

2 large sweet potatoes, peeled and diced

plain flour

a little melted butter

TO GARNISH:

2 tbsp natural yogurt

a few sprigs of fresh coriander

Cook the sweet potatoes in boiling salted water until tender, then drain, allow to cool and mash finely with a fork.

Weigh your sweet potato mash, then mix in an equal weight of plain flour. Season with salt and pepper and mix to form a sticky dough. Cover and allow to firm up in the fridge for 30 minutes.

Meanwhile, heat the oil in a saucepan over a low heat. Add the garlic and cumin and cook gently for 2–3 minutes, then add the tomatoes. Bring to a simmer, then crumble in the stock cube and add the chickpeas and honey. Simmer for 15 minutes, season and keep warm.

Divide the sweet potato dough into four even portions, then roll them out on a floured surface – it will take quite a bit of flour.

Heat a dry non-stick pan over a medium-high heat. One by one, cook the roti for 2 minutes on each side, until crisp and golden. Brush with melted butter and keep warm.

To serve, divide the roti between two warm plates. Spoon the chickpeas on top, followed by a squiggle of yogurt and the fresh coriander.

CORNED BEEF AND BUTTER BEAN HASH

SERVES 2

1 tbsp butter
1 tbsp olive oil
1 red onion, diced
1 x 400g tin of butter beans, drained and rinsed
1 x 340g tin of corned beef, roughly chopped
a large handful of baby spinach

FOR THE DRESSING:
100ml cream
1 tsp prepared English mustard
1 tsp brown sauce
a pinch of caster sugar

Heat the butter and oil in a saucepan over a medium heat. When the butter starts to foam, add the onion and cook for 5 minutes, until it starts to colour. Add the butter beans and crush them lightly into the onion with the back of a fork. Let them fry for a few minutes without stirring too much, then add the corned beef and stir it through. Once everything is incorporated and slightly crisp, add the spinach and season.

For the dressing, whisk the cream, mustard, brown sauce and sugar together.

To serve, divide the hash between two bowls and spoon the dressing over the top.

CHICKEN SATAY LETTUCE WRAPS

SERVES 4

6 bone-in chicken thighs (1 kg)

1 x 400ml tin of coconut milk

2 heaped tbsp crunchy peanut butter

2 tbsp soy sauce

4 shakes of fish sauce

½ tsp chilli flakes

1 head of iceberg lettuce

zest and juice of 1 lime

½ cucumber, peeled and cut into thin batons

Preheat the oven to 185°C.

Remove the skin and any excess fat from the chicken, then put the thighs in a snug roasting tin or baking dish, flesh side up.

Whisk the coconut milk, peanut butter, soy sauce, fish sauce and chilli flakes in a pan over a medium heat. Bring to a simmer to amalgamate, then pour the coconut milk mixture over the chicken and transfer to the oven. Cook for 45 minutes, basting twice.

Meanwhile, cut the root off the head of iceberg lettuce, then separate the whole leaves as best you can. Put the leaves in a bowl of iced water for 30 minutes. This will help them get really crisp. Drain and pat dry.

When the chicken is cooked, strain the excess sauce back into the pan and bring up to a simmer. Reduce gently by two-thirds – it needs to be a thick coating consistency. It tends to stick, so stir the bottom of the pan frequently as it reduces. Add the lime zest and juice and remove the pan from the heat.

Take the chicken off the bone (a knife and fork will do it) and tear into shreds. Add the chicken to the reduced sauce, then season. This can all be done ahead of time if you like, then simply reheat.

To serve, spoon the chicken into the lettuce, top with the cucumber batons, wrap it up and enjoy.

Anyone can cook

27 FEBRUARY 2021

Having a cookery school has taught me that most people want simple, tasty food that doesn't take hours to make. That's what I concentrate on: easy techniques that even the most novice cook can master. The most important thing is not to be afraid. Turn down the heat and keep calm.

There are always things you can do to improve your cooking. If something tastes tart, you can counter it with honey, apple or redcurrant jelly, or maple or golden syrup instead of sugar. They add depth of flavour as well as sweetness. If it's too sweet, add a little citrus or vinegar. Balance is the key. Learn to trust your taste-buds. They are a gift, especially these days. And remember, black is never good in cooking, unless it's a truffle.

This week's hake dish was whipped up with fridge leftovers, as I couldn't bear to drive into town that dark, rainy evening. I already had the fish and a few other bits. Sometimes this is how recipes happen – there is no master plan. I'm leaving the fillet whole. I love the rustic haphazardness of it. The sauce will bake into the fish and split a little. It's no beauty but it tastes lovely.

The caldo verde brings back happy memories of a trip to Lisbon with some of my old friends, the 'old' getting more literal by the day. At the end of a very long day, we would gather in a teeming square with young Lisboans to eat steaming bowls of this soup. I can still hear their excited chatter. It was a world away from post-club drunken bumbling in the chipper in Ireland. We were amazed at the civility of it all.

This Caesar dressing is a great tip. There's not an anchovy in sight for those who are wary. Once you add lemon juice to cream, it thickens up enough to coat the leaves, so you can have your Caesar dressing made in minutes. It's important to make the dressing just before you are ready to serve or it will thicken too much.

BAKED HAKE WITH CAULIFLOWER AND HARISSA ORANGE DRESSING

SERVES 4

1 cauliflower
6 tbsp olive oil
800g hake fillet, skinned and boned
2 tbsp flaked almonds
a few sprigs of fresh mint, leaves picked

FOR THE DRESSING:
250ml buttermilk
juice and zest of 1 orange
1 tbsp harissa paste
½ tsp smoked paprika

Preheat the oven to 185°C.

Trim the cauliflower, keeping some of the stalks to roast as well, then cut the head into 2cm-thick steaks. Put the cauliflower flat in a large roasting tin with some of the leaves interspersed. Drizzle with 4 tablespoons of the oil, season and turn to coat. Roast in the oven for 20 minutes.

Meanwhile, whisk together the buttermilk, orange juice and zest, harissa and smoked paprika.

Remove the tin from the oven, then put the fish on top of the cauliflower. Spoon the dressing over the hake along with the remaining 2 tablespoons of olive oil and season. Scatter over the almonds, then put the tin back in the oven for 15 minutes, until the fish is cooked through. It might take a little longer, depending on the thickness of the fish. Don't be afraid to peek into the flesh if you're unsure – it should be white and flaky.

To serve, spoon onto warm plates and scatter torn fresh mint on top.

CALDO VERDE

SERVES 4

4 tbsp olive oil

1 onion, diced

2 garlic cloves, sliced

2 bay leaves (fresh if possible)

450g potatoes, peeled and sliced

1 litre water

200g curly kale (cavolo nero if possible), leaves stripped from the ribs

100g dry-cured chorizo, thinly sliced

Heat the oil in a large saucepan over a low heat. Add the onion, garlic and bay leaves and cook for 15 minutes, until the onion has softened but not coloured.

Add the potatoes and water. Cook until the potatoes are tender, then blitz with a hand blender until smooth.

Shred the kale as thinly as you can, then add it to the soup along with the chorizo. Bring back to a simmer for 5 minutes, season and serve.

CHEAT'S CAESAR SALAD

SERVES 4

2 mini ciabattas
2 garlic cloves, peeled
a drizzle of olive oil
250ml cream
juice of 1 lemon
100g Parmesan cheese, grated
8 heads of Little Gem lettuce or 1 large head of cos lettuce, separated into leaves

Preheat the oven to 185°C.

Cut the ciabattas in half lengthways, put them on a baking tray and toast them in the oven. Cut one garlic clove in half. Rub the cut halves into the toasted side of the bread. Drizzle with oil and keep the toast warm.

Pour the cream into a large bowl. Crush the remaining garlic clove and whisk it into the cream along with the lemon juice and half of the Parmesan. Season, then turn the lettuce leaves in the dressing.

Put a warm piece of toasted ciabatta on each plate. Assemble the dressed lettuce carefully on top, then scatter the remaining Parmesan over the top to serve.

Sunday has always been sacrosanct in our house

06 MARCH 2021

Except for the summer, the restaurant closes after Sunday lunch, when I fly home and start prepping dinner. I love this time. I plan what we might eat days before after much discussion. I find this kind of cooking therapeutic. It's a gentle amble as opposed to the bucking bronco of a restaurant kitchen. These are Sunday dishes, whatever time you choose to eat them. One traditional, one Middle Eastern and one vegetarian.

I recoil at using too many pots and pans when I'm cooking at home. I don't have the luxury of having a washer-upper like we do in the restaurant.

I'm using celeriac with pork steak. There's a risk that the pork will be overcooked and the celeriac undercooked, so the thickness of the celeriac is paramount. I'm adding mushrooms, bacon and sherry. They are all best friends. I'm risking predictability here, so to offset this I'm giving you the recipe for a sort of walnut pesto. It's optional, but it's lovely.

Lamb shoulder is underrated. Why is it always about the leg? This dish bursts with Middle Eastern flavours. You will need to marinate the lamb in the yogurt overnight for best results. Slow cooking is very satisfying. There's so little minding to it. Pour yourself a big gin and tonic and read the Sunday papers.

To some, salt-baking vegetables might seem pointless. At the technique's most complex, the vegetables are enveloped in a salty dough and baked into a succulent revelation, but to be honest it's all a bit too much work. I'm taking a shortcut here by laying vegetables on a bed of salt and baking them. This concentrates their flavour and promotes them to the Premier League. Serve with rice, pasta or couscous as a vegetarian main course.

The wild garlic season has just started. If you know where to find it, gather it enthusiastically and embrace its musky loveliness. I'm making a wild garlic purée that you can use for lots of things, as it keeps well in the fridge. If you can't get wild garlic, the aioli will still be lovely without it.

PORK STEAK AND FRIENDS

SERVES 4

4 tbsp rapeseed oil

1 celeriac, peeled and cut in half

4 field (flat cap) mushrooms

1 x 550g pork steak, trimmed

½ tsp mixed spice

a few sprigs of fresh thyme

6 rashers of smoked streaky bacon

a splash of sweet sherry (optional but fab)

FOR THE PESTO:

1 slice of white bread

a splash of milk

16 roasted walnuts

80g Parmesan cheese, grated

2 garlic cloves, chopped

juice of 1 lemon

50ml olive oil

Preheat the oven to 180°C.

Drizzle a little of the rapeseed oil over the bottom of a roasting tin.

Cut the celeriac halves into slices 0.5cm thick. Slice the mushrooms into the same thickness as the celeriac but at an angle. Put the celeriac and mushrooms in the roasting tin in alternate layers to form a bed for the pork steak.

Put the pork on top of the veg. Drizzle the remaining rapeseed oil over the top, then sprinkle over the mixed spice and thyme and season.

Put the bacon over the top of the pork, allowing it to drape over the vegetables to lubricate them. You want it to crisp and frazzle. Put the tin in the oven and cook for 50 minutes.

When the pork is cooked, splash the sherry over the top (if using) and allow it to mingle with the roasting juices. Rest for 10 minutes under foil.

Meanwhile, to make the walnut pesto, cut the crusts off the bread, splash generously with the milk and allow it to soak for a few minutes. Put in a food processor with the rest of the pesto ingredients, then pulse until everything comes together but is still a little chunky.

Cut the pork into slices and serve with the roasted vegetables and walnut pesto.

SPICED LAMB SHOULDER WITH ROAST VEGETABLE BULGUR WHEAT AND TAHINI DRESSING

SERVES 6

2 tbsp ras el hanout

zest of 1 orange

500g natural yogurt

1 part-boned shoulder of lamb (approx. 1.3kg)

a good drizzle of olive oil

450ml chicken stock

2 tsp ground cumin

1 small bunch of fresh flat-leaf parsley, roughly chopped

1 small bunch of fresh coriander, roughly chopped

FOR THE BULGUR WHEAT:

2 red peppers, each cut into 6 pieces lengthways

1 aubergine, cut into 6 pieces lengthways

1 large red onion, cut into 6 wedges

1 tbsp golden brown sugar

300g bulgur wheat or couscous

FOR THE DRESSING:

2 garlic cloves, sliced

juice of 1 lemon

80ml water

3 tbsp tahini

1 tbsp honey

a pinch of chilli flakes

In a large dish, whisk the ras el hanout and orange zest into the yogurt and season. Immerse the lamb in the mixture, making sure it's thoroughly covered. Cover and marinate in the fridge overnight. This will tenderise the lamb and infuse the meat with the spices.

Preheat the oven to 160°C.

Drizzle some oil on the base of a large roasting tin. Transfer the lamb to one side of the tin but let any excess yogurt drip back into the bowl. You might need to help it along a little with your fingers. It's important that the lamb is coated all over in the yogurt marinade. Drizzle oil over the lamb, then bake in the oven, uncovered, for 90 minutes.

Remove the tin from the oven, then add the vegetables to the side of the lamb. Drizzle with more oil, add the brown sugar, season and mix. Put the tray back in the oven for 1 hour more, turning the vegetables from time to time until they become soft and sticky.

Meanwhile, put the bulgur wheat or couscous in a microwaveable bowl with the chicken stock, cumin and some salt and pepper. Cover with cling film and microwave on high for 4 minutes, then set aside.

Blend all the ingredients for the tahini dressing and set aside.

Remove the lamb from the oven and allow it to rest for 15 minutes under foil.

Mix the bulgur wheat into the vegetables in the tin along with the fresh herbs, incorporating all the juices. Check for seasoning.

Transfer the lamb to a chopping board and carve into slices. Serve with the roast vegetable bulgur and the tahini dressing.

SALT-BAKED ROOT VEGETABLES WITH WILD GARLIC AIOLI

SERVES 4

2 beetroot

2 medium potatoes

1 large carrot

1 kohlrabi

1 parsnip

750g salt

FOR THE WILD GARLIC PURÉE:

2 handfuls of wild garlic leaves, chopped

300ml sunflower oil

a pinch of caster sugar

FOR THE AIOLI:

2 egg yolks, at room temperature

2 garlic cloves, chopped

juice of 1 lemon

½ tbsp Dijon mustard

250ml sunflower oil

50ml olive oil

1 tbsp crème fraîche

Preheat the oven to 130°C.

Trim all the vegetables (you can use any mixture of root vegetables here, not just the ones I've suggetsed), then scrub them really well under cold running water until they are thoroughly clean. It's important that they aren't too big. If necessary, cut them down to an even size.

Pour the salt into a medium-sized roasting tin. Set the vegetables into the salt, pressing them down a little. Bake in the oven for 2 hours, then check. Some of the vegetables will be ready before others; that's just the nature of things. The beetroot and kohlrabi took an extra hour when I made this recipe. When the veg are tender, remove the ones that are cooked, then put the others back in the oven and continue to cook until they, too, are soft.

Meanwhile, to make the wild garlic purée, whizz the wild garlic, oil and sugar in a blender. If it's slow to turn, just drizzle in a little more oil until it blends easily. You only need 2 tablespoons of the purée for the aioli, but this will keep in a sealed jar in the fridge for two weeks. I use it in mash potatoes and pasta when the mood takes me.

For the aioli, put the egg yolks, garlic, lemon juice, mustard and some salt and pepper in a blender or food processor. Blend everything together for 1 minute before starting to drizzle in the sunflower oil in a steady stream so it all becomes incorporated. Drizzle in the olive oil, then fold in the crème fraîche and 2 tablespoons of the wild garlic purée. Check for seasoning. Keep the aioli in the fridge in a sealed container – a Kilner jar is best if you have one – for up to a week.

To serve, brush the excess salt off the vegetables and discard. Cut the veg into manageable pieces and serve warm with the wild garlic aioli.

A touch of green for St Patrick's Day

13 MARCH 2021

I've always regretted not living in New York. London had me in its grasp for many years and when it was time to move, home and elderly parents won the toss.

A few years ago my old pal Donal Crosbie and I were asked to cook a pre-St Patrick's Day dinner for Kerrygold to promote the brand in the US. A snowstorm had enveloped the city. I woke early and trudged through the snow from our hotel in Tribeca the 20 blocks or so to the Hudson Hound, where the dinner was taking place. I stopped for an egg roll and cheap coffee in a convenience store — that's what real New Yorkers do. I was inexplicably happy, head down against the biting flurries, walking towards the West Village. Me, the world's most unlikely explorer.

There was work, then there was play, as there always is with me. We relished those few days in NYC catching up with old and new friends. We stayed in a cool hotel — too cool, as it happens. On the last night they closed the lobby bar to facilitate 'an important private party' in the basement club. The residents could suck it up. I was not happy.

A posse was organised to penetrate the proceedings through the now empty kitchens. There were giggles and anxious hushes as we all squeezed into the service lift for an interminably slow descent. Then the doors opened to a bubble-filled mirage, a tower of champagne coupes worthy of *The Great Gatsby*. We edged towards it, stunned at our own bravado, and grabbed some unattended glasses.

Just as we were getting settled, a group of large men approached us and relieved us of our champagne. It was an after-party for the rock band Green Day and we weren't invited. They escorted us out, all muscles and burly indignation. We laughed a lot that night.

We flew home the next morning, Paddy's Day. One day, when we're allowed to travel again, I'll go see that big parade.

These recipes all have a little bit of green using some of the finest Irish ingredients. Search them out if you can.

ROAST LOIN OF BACON WITH PICKLED RHUBARB AND HIGHBANK ORCHARD SYRUP

SERVES 4

1 x 800g piece of bacon loin

250ml cider

2 bay leaves (fresh if possible)

1 cinnamon stick

250g cavolo nero or regular kale

a knob of butter

a drizzle of sesame oil

2 tbsp Highbank Orchard Syrup or maple syrup

FOR THE PICKLED RHUBARB:

1 tsp mustard seeds

100g caster sugar

100ml rice wine vinegar

100ml water

a small piece of ginger, halved

300g rhubarb, cut into 1cm pieces

To make the pickle, toast the mustard seeds in a hot, dry saucepan for 2 minutes. Add everything except the rhubarb and bring to the boil. Add the rhubarb and cook for 1 minute. Remove from the heat, then transfer to a bowl, making sure the rhubarb is submerged in the liquid. Leave it for a few hours to pickle.

Preheat the oven to 170°C.

Put the bacon in a roasting tin, then pour over the cider and add the bay leaves and cinnamon stick. Roast in the oven, uncovered, for 80 minutes, basting once or twice during the cooking.

When the bacon is cooked, leave it to rest under foil for a few minutes.

Meanwhile, blanch the cavolo nero in boiling salted water for 1 minute (regular kale will need a little longer). Drain well and add it to the tin along with the butter, sesame oil and some black pepper. Turn the kale in the juices.

Slice the bacon and serve on warm plates with the pickled rhubarb, a generous drizzle of Highbank Orchard Syrup and some boiled new potatoes.

FRENCH BEANS AND PARMA HAM WITH GREEN GODDESS DRESSING

SERVES 4

2 x 200g packets of trimmed fine French beans, kept in their packets
8 slices of Parma ham

FOR THE DRESSING:
1 ripe avocado, halved and stoned
1 x 200ml tub of light crème fraîche
2 spring onions, chopped
1 garlic clove, sliced
juice of 1 lemon
1 tbsp chopped fresh tarragon or basil
a little dash of green Tabasco (if you have it) or a few chilli flakes
a drizzle of olive oil

To make the dressing, scoop the avocado flesh into a food processor or blender. Add the remaining ingredients and blitz until smooth.

The next step is a little unorthodox but it works. The time in the microwave will all depend on the thickness of the beans. Put the unopened packets of French beans on a plate in the microwave and cook on high for 3 minutes. Open the bags carefully and allow to cool, then turn the beans in the dressing.

To serve, plate the beans and drape the Parma ham over the top. You may have some dressing left over but it's good with so many things, especially in a roast chicken sandwich.

GLORIOUS GREENS WITH VELVET CLOUD YOGURT, NUTS AND GRAPES

SERVES 4

80ml olive oil

3 garlic cloves, thinly sliced

a pinch of chilli flakes

150ml water

1 x 220g packet of tenderstem broccoli

1 x 200g packet of trimmed fine French beans

1 bunch of asparagus, trimmed

6 tbsp Velvet Cloud sheep milk yogurt (or a good natural yogurt or soft rindless goat cheese)

12 green seedless grapes, halved

2 tbsp pine nuts or almonds, toasted

This dish is all about technique and a little patience, as the garlic subtly perfumes the greens. Heat the oil in a large frying pan or wok over a gentle heat. Add the garlic and cook just until it turns lightly golden. Add the chilli flakes, then carefully pour in the water.

Add the vegetables, season and cover the pan or wok tightly with a lid. Increase the heat to high and cook without lifting the lid for 5—6 minutes, until you hear the pan sizzle. By this time the water will almost have evaporated and the greens will be cooked. Remove from the heat.

Turn everything together in the garlicky emulsion, then put in a warm bowl or platter, family-style. Spoon the yogurt over the top, then scatter over the grapes and the toasted pine nuts or almonds. This is great with rice, pasta or couscous or as a lovely accompaniment to a traditional dinner.

Our healthy-eating plan

20 MARCH 2021

It might sound a bit strange but we've just ordered our dinner from the fabulous Beach House restaurant in Tramore. If you think that's like bringing coal to Newcastle, you'd be right. But the simple fact is that on occasion I want to be cooked for too. The whole world seems to be doing food kits and I want to see what it's all about so I can figure out how I'm supposed to pivot. Now there's an easy word with dramatic consequences.

The summer is looming but things aren't looking good. The Tannery has no outside space and I don't think I'd be allowed to put diners on the roof. There's some figuring out to do yet.

We're living relatively healthily at the moment. The walking is the focal point of the day. Very little carbs and no booze during the week. The trouble with that is by Friday I'm like a fella who's just landed in Ibiza.

This chicken dish is light and bright. The breast is flattened and cooked on a ridged grill pan. It's worth the extra effort. I roast the veg and make a simple lemon and chilli dressing. Eat this with mashed potatoes. It's a nice dish.

I am not a baker but this bread needs no skill and it tastes lovely. It's particularly nice with the leek fondue but that's more coincidence than design.

A few years ago I spent a few days in the kitchen of the Walnut Tree in Abergavenny. Shaun Hill has always been one of my heroes. He's been around even longer than me and remarkably still cooks each service with a vim and vigour that I'm not sure I possess. He radiates intelligence and goodwill. There's a calmness about him that knows his food is good without genuflecting to the many food fashions he's seen. These leeks are now a staple in the Tannery. In the Walnut Tree they were served with lemon sole. The brightness of the finished leeks is of paramount importance and the flour gives them a pleasing, mousse-y texture. They go with practically everything but equally they are happy to just be themselves, old-school and resplendent.

GRILLED CHICKEN WITH ROASTED SPRING VEGETABLES, LEMON AND CHILLI

SERVES 2

2 x 150g chicken fillets

a drizzle of olive oil

1 medium-sized leek

1 bunch of asparagus, trimmed

a few sprigs of fresh thyme

50ml water

a good handful of baby spinach

grated Parmesan cheese

FOR THE DRESSING:

juice of 1 lemon

50ml olive oil

1 small fresh red chilli, deseeded and finely diced

1 level tsp caster sugar

Preheat the oven to 200°C.

Carefully butterfly the chicken fillets – that is to say, cut almost all the way through each one evenly from the side and open the fillet out like a book.

Put the chicken in between greaseproof paper and bat it gently with a rolling pin until it's even and 0.5cm thick. Drizzle with a little oil, season and set aside.

Cut the leek into 1cm-thick ovals, then give them a rinse to make sure they are clean. Put them in a roasting tin with the asparagus, thyme and water. Season and roast in the oven for 15 minutes, until they are soft and a little frazzled.

Remove the tin from the oven and add the spinach to the tin to wilt in the residual heat. Season and keep warm.

While the vegetables are cooking, get a ridged grill pan smoking hot. Turn the chicken in a little olive oil, then add it to the hot pan. Cook it for 4 minutes on one side, then 3 minutes on the other.

For the dressing, whisk the lemon juice with the oil, chilli and sugar, then season. Add a little of it to the vegetables, making sure they are nicely coated.

Serve the chicken on warm plates with the dressed vegetables and a generous scattering of grated Parmesan.

SMOKED BACON, CHEDDAR AND RED ONION BREAD

MAKES 6 MINI LOAVES

125g smoked bacon lardons

2 red onions, thinly sliced

300g plain flour

1 level tsp bread soda

½ tsp salt

100g Cheddar cheese, grated

230ml buttermilk

Preheat the oven to 190°C.

Put the lardons and onions in a cold frying pan, then put the pan on a low to medium heat. The fat from the bacon will eventually render out and make everything nice and juicy. Cook for 20 minutes, until the onions are soft and jammy. Set aside and allow to cool.

Sieve the flour and bread soda into a large bowl. Add the salt, followed by the onion and bacon mixture and then the cheese. Make a well in the centre and add most of the buttermilk. Mix gently with your fingers until it forms a soft mass. If it's too dry, add the rest of the buttermilk. Tip out onto a floured board, then gather it into a cylinder and cut into six even pieces.

Roll into round balls and put on a floured baking tray. Cut a small cross in the middle of each one. Bake in the oven for 25–30 minutes, until the bread sounds hollow when you tap the base. Cool on a wire rack before cutting into slices.

LEEK FONDUE

SERVES 2

1 medium leek
50g butter
½ tbsp plain flour
1 tbsp crème fraîche
1 tsp Dijon mustard

Trim the leek, removing the darkest parts. Slice it in half lengthways, then shred it as thinly as you can. Put the leek slices in a colander, wash them well and give them a gentle shake, leaving a little residual water on them.

Melt the butter in a saucepan over a medium heat. When the butter starts to foam, add the leek and cook for 5 minutes, until it starts to soften. Dust the flour over the top and cook for 2 more minutes, then add the crème fraîche, mustard and seasoning.

Remove from the pan straightaway, then spread out on a tray to cool to keep its colour. This can be kept in the fridge to be gently reheated later.

All about chops

27 MARCH 2021

I brought my baby Weber barbecue for a short spin the other day. It fits into the boot of my car very nicely indeed. When I got it a few years ago I was besotted, lighting it up at every opportunity. I used to perch it in the boot to cook. I only stopped when my eldest observed that the proximity of the petrol tank to the flame might not be the best idea. I cooked lamb chops with salt, then dipped them in aioli. I'm just that kind of guy.

This week is all about chops — easy, familiar and delicious. This lamb chop dish has a hint of Morocco with the almonds, apricots and cumin. The flavours are sweet and subtle. Try to crisp the fat. It's a crime to waste it. I'm serving two chops per person. I used loin chops but you can use any lamb chops you fancy.

I stared at the butcher's counter for a long time before I settled on thick bone-in pork chops. Something cooked on the bone always has more flavour but use what you can find. The juices from the pork and the mushrooms are imperative in the dressing. The length of time that they occupy the pan is determined by the thickness of the chops.

I was looking for a large monkfish tail for this recipe to cut across the bone and make into chops. I may as well have been looking for Eldorado. I settled on hake steaks. They are more easily found. Fillets would be perfect too.

The wild garlic is out. I've just chopped it through a simple butter sauce where normally I would make a purée. This way is lazier but no less delicious. I've added tinned chickpeas, which, by the way, seem to have become somewhat elusive. I'm blaming Brexit.

Incidentally, you could add a few halved baby tomatoes through the sauce as well. They would add a little cheer and would get on very well with the hake. Sometimes you don't realise a dish needs a little something until it's done, but that's the nature of cooking. You can do it differently next time.

LAMB CHOPS WITH SPINACH, CUMIN, ALMONDS AND APRICOTS

SERVES 2

a drizzle of sunflower oil
4 lamb chops
50g butter
50g whole almonds
1 tsp ground cumin
6 dried apricots, sliced
juice of 1 orange
100g baby spinach

Heat a little sunflower oil in a frying pan on a medium-high heat. Season the chops, then add them to the pan and cook for 3 minutes on one side. Turn over and cook for a further 3 minutes, then balance the chops on their fatty sides as best you can. Turn down the heat and let them cook for a further 5 minutes, until the fat is crisp. Transfer the chops to a plate and put in a warm place covered in foil for a little while to rest.

Meanwhile, melt the butter in a frying pan over a medium heat. When the butter starts to foam, add the almonds and cumin. Cook gently for 2–3 minutes, then add the apricots and orange juice. Bring to a simmer, then add the spinach. Remove the pan from the heat, season and let the spinach wilt.

Serve the spinach straightaway with the lamb chops and any of their choppy juices.

WARM PORK CHOP, FIELD MUSHROOM AND GORGONZOLA SALAD

SERVES 4

a drizzle of sunflower oil

2 pork chops, cut from the rack if possible, approx. 3cm thick

3 large field (flat cap) mushrooms, sliced

2 celery sticks

50g butter, melted

a few sprigs of fresh thyme, leaves picked

FOR THE SALAD:

250g salad leaves

12 seedless grapes, halved

100g Gorgonzola cheese

FOR THE DRESSING:

50ml sunflower oil

2 tbsp red wine vinegar

2 tsp Dijon mustard

a pinch of caster sugar

Preheat the oven to 190°C.

Heat the oil in an ovenproof frying pan until it's gently smoking. Season the chops, then add them to the pan and sear them on one side for 5 minutes. Turn over, then transfer the pan to the oven and cook for 15 minutes (less if the chops are thinner).

Meanwhile, put the mushrooms in a roasting tin, bottom side up. Cut the celery at an angle into pieces 3cm thick and put them in the tin with the mushrooms. Drizzle the melted butter over the mushrooms and celery, then scatter over some thyme. Season and cook in the oven for 15 minutes.

To make the dressing, whisk everything together in a large bowl.

When the pork chops are cooked through, remove the pan from the oven and allow them to rest for a few minutes under foil. Remove the mushrooms and celery from the tin, then add them to the dressing along with all the juices from the tin.

Slice the pork thinly, then add it to the bowl with the mushrooms and celery, making sure all the resting juices are added too. Turn the pork, mushrooms and celery together in the dressing and season.

To serve, divide the salad leaves among four plates or put it all on a platter. Scatter the pork mixture on top, then the grapes. Crumble over the Gorgonzola.

HAKE CHOPS WITH CHICKPEAS AND WILD GARLIC BUTTER SAUCE

SERVES 4

2 tbsp olive oil

4 x 200g hake steaks, cut across the bone

FOR THE SAUCE:

juice of 1 lemon

150g butter, diced and chilled

1 x 400g tin of chickpeas, drained and rinsed

a few wild garlic leaves, finely shredded (you can substitute basil)

1 tsp caster sugar

Preheat the grill to 220°C.

Brush a tray with a little of the oil, then sit the hake on the tray. Brush the fish with the rest of the oil, then season. Grill for 12 minutes, then check to see if the hake is cooked through. If not, pop it back under the grill for another couple of minutes — the cooking time will depend on the thickness of the hake steaks. They should be a lovely creamy colour and come away from the bone easily when they are done.

Meanwhile, bring the lemon juice up to the boil in a small saucepan, then whisk in the butter little by little until it has all been amalgamated. Add the chickpeas, wild garlic or basil and the sugar, then keep warm but don't let it boil.

Serve the sauce over or under the fish on warm plates with a few boiled new potatoes on the side.

This Easter menu will allow you to relax and enjoy it

03 APRIL 2021

I'm very good at turning vegetables. Turning them into what, I hear you say. Well, it's the long-lost art of making perfectly even oblong shapes from various types of root vegetables so they can look arty on a plate. It involves hours of practice, patience and mounds of vegetable trimmings. It's like keepy-uppy with a football — impressive but ultimately useless. For the most part it got left behind in the 1990s, when chefs got into a more natural way of cooking. I had a bit of an epiphany myself around that time when I veered towards cooking a more rustic style of food. If I had to turn another carrot, I was going to gouge my own eyes out.

These dishes are for the centre of the table to serve family-style, perfect for Easter. Robust, convivial and easy to serve, they allow you to relax and enjoy the food yourself. I suggest making them all together for one complete meal. Now there's a little project for you.

I'm barbecuing the lamb but you can roast it instead, of course. I mentioned barbecuing last week so you might have deduced that I'm an enthusiast. I managed to locate a pre-marinaded shoulder in one of the supermarkets. It's a fabulous product. Just open the packet and away you go. I'm giving you a simple marinade as I won't presume you found it too.

I originally made this sauce for pasta and it's a blinder. 'Nduja is a soft, spreadable, spicy sausage from Calabria similar to the Spanish sobrassada. Apologies, but it can be hard to find. Use smoked paprika and a little chilli if you can't.

The aubergine and fig is like a warm chutney, lovely with the lamb and lots of other things besides. Think goat cheese or cold meats.

This gratin is inspired by my good friend Eunice. Being invited over to her house for dinner was one of life's great treats and is something to be looked forward to again, I hope. I added courgette and red onion in an effort to make it my own.

Less is more when it comes to many things, including food.

BARBECUED LAMB SHOULDER WITH TOMATO AND 'NDUJA SAUCE

SERVES 6

3 sprigs of fresh rosemary, stalks removed

2 garlic cloves, sliced

100ml olive oil

1 x 1.5kg (approx.) lamb shoulder

FOR THE SAUCE:

2 tbsp olive oil

1 garlic clove, sliced

a small piece of ginger, peeled and finely chopped

1 x 400g tin of chopped tomatoes

100g 'nduja, broken up

2 strips of orange peel

½ chicken stock cube, crumbled

250ml cream

a drizzle of honey

Blend the rosemary, garlic and oil together. Put the lamb in a large plastic bag (a shopping bag is perfect). Add the marinade to the bag and squish it into the lamb so it gets into every nook and cranny. Put in the fridge for at least 6 hours or preferably overnight.

For the sauce, heat the oil in a saucepan over a medium heat. Add the garlic and ginger and cook gently for 2–3 minutes, then add the tomatoes, 'nduja, orange peel and stock cube. Bring to a simmer and cook gently for 10 minutes, then add the cream and honey. Reduce the sauce gently by one-third, scraping the bottom of the pan from time to time to make sure it doesn't stick. Season and whizz with a hand blender until smooth. This can be served warm or at room temperature.

To cook the lamb on the barbecue, it's imperative to use a barbecue with a lid and a thermometer. Gas is easier to control but it can certainly be done over charcoal.

A big piece of meat needs little or no heat underneath it – the heat must come from around it, otherwise the meat will burn.

Preheat your barbecue. If you have gas with two burners, turn off the gas directly underneath the meat once it goes on. You will need a temperature between 140°C and 150°C. If you have charcoal, heat your coals, then push them all around the edges, leaving just a little coal underneath the lamb.

Check the lamb 15 minutes after you put it on to make sure the flame isn't too hot. Continue to cook for 1½ hours, turning once or twice. So 1 hour 45 minutes in total should do it. A meat thermometer is very handy – you need to take the lamb to 165°C. This will be lightly pink. Rest for 20 minutes under foil before slicing.

To roast the lamb, preheat the oven to 180°C. Put the lamb in a roasting tin with a little extra olive oil poured over the top. Roast in the oven for 1½ hours. Remove and allow to rest for 20 minutes under foil before slicing.

Carve the lamb and serve with the sauce, the aubergine agrodolce (on the next page) and the vegetable crumble (on page 333) on the side.

AUBERGINE AGRODOLCE

SERVES 6

75ml olive oil

1 aubergine, diced into 1cm pieces

100g dried figs, roughly chopped

150ml red wine

1 tbsp golden brown sugar

1 tsp five-spice or allspice

1 tbsp balsamic vinegar

Heat the oil in a saucepan over a medium heat. Add the aubergine and cook for 10 minutes, then add the figs, wine, sugar and the five-spice or allspice. Reduce the heat and cook gently for 20–30 minutes, until all the wine has evaporated and it becomes jammy.

Add the balsamic vinegar, then take the pan off the heat. Allow to cool a little, then crush with a potato masher until it all comes together.

PROVENÇAL VEGETABLE CRUMBLE
SERVES 6

2 fennel bulbs
1 courgette, thinly sliced
1 red onion, sliced
2 garlic cloves, thinly sliced
1 tsp fresh thyme leaves
250ml cream
250g vine-ripened cherry tomatoes, halved

FOR THE PARMESAN CRUMBLE:
70g plain flour
60g butter, diced into small cubes
1 tsp caster sugar
100g Parmesan cheese, grated

Preheat the oven to 190°C.

Put the flour, butter and sugar in a food processor or mixing bowl and mix until it has the texture of breadcrumbs. Add the Parmesan and keep in the fridge while you roast the veg.

Trim the fennel stalks off the bulbs, then cut the fennel in half and then into 1cm-thick slices. Put the fennel in a bowl along with the courgette, onion, garlic, thyme and some salt and pepper. Turn everything together and transfer to an ovenproof dish. Roast in the oven for about 20 minutes, turning once or twice, until soft.

Pour the cream over the vegetables, then add the tomatoes and top with the Parmesan crumble. Return to the oven for another 15 minutes, until bubbling and golden.

Leave to cool a little before serving.

Eggs are at the heart of so much that is good about food

10 APRIL 2021

Eggs are our No. 1 purchase at home by far. Wait, sorry, that's a lie. Eggs are our No. 1 *food* purchase. I'm not really privy to the others. All I know is that the DPD man will probably be having Christmas dinner with us this year as the ladies in our house have got to know him so well. They treat me like a mushroom and I'm happier that way. There's less fluctuation of my blood pressure. Sometimes I think if we had more children, we'd have to call them Zara and Asos and the DPD man would be their godfather.

I revere eggs. They are the foundation of so many things that are good. They can be functional but they can also be an integral part of so many things that give us pleasure.

This smoked mackerel tart is simpler than you might think. People are getting more ambitious with their cooking and are trying things they may never have done before. A lot of it is about having the time, I suppose, but I find that a little bit of success gives you confidence. The flavours are lightly smoky and familiar to the people who love this sort of thing. You can buy the pastry and pre-cooked beetroot if you prefer. Personally, I always like a kick from horseradish but you can add yours to taste.

The last time I had piperade was on my one and only trip to San Sebastián a couple of years back. It was mighty. I don't know why it took me so long to get there but it will be one of my first ports of call when we get out of this mess. It was the last night and the soft, eggy delight of this classic was on a tapas tour a few hours before we met the rugby team from Perpignan. The rest I wouldn't even tell to a guard.

The asparagus relies on precisely boiled eggs. When crushed with a fork, the yolk becomes an unctuous dressing that I just help along with some cream. It's a lovely, simple pairing that shows that when done correctly, things don't need to be complicated.

SMOKED MACKEREL, BEETROOT AND DILL TART

SERVES 6

2 fillets of smoked mackerel (150g), skin and bones removed

2 cooked beetroot, cut into slices 0.5cm thick

250g crème fraîche

3 egg yolks

1 tbsp chopped fresh dill

1 tbsp horseradish sauce

FOR THE PASTRY:

200g plain flour

a pinch of salt

100g butter, chilled, plus extra for greasing

1½–2 tbsp cold water

Grease a 23cm wide, fairly deep tart tin.

To make the pastry, put the flour in a mixing bowl with a pinch of salt, then grate in the cold butter. Rub it in with your fingertips until it resembles breadcrumbs, then stir in enough cold water to bring it all together into a smooth but not sticky dough.

Roll the dough out on a lightly floured surface until it's big enough to line the tin. Chill the pastry case in the fridge for 20 minutes.

Preheat the oven to 180°C.

Trim the edges of the pastry and prick the base several times with a fork. Line with greaseproof paper and baking beans. Bake in the oven for 15 minutes, then remove the beans and paper and bake for another 5 minutes, until golden.

Turn the oven down to 160°C. Lay pieces of mackerel and beetroot alternately over the base of the tart.

Put the crème fraîche in a bowl and whisk in the egg yolks, dill, horseradish and some salt and pepper. Scrape this into the tart, making sure it's nice and even and that the mackerel and beetroot are submerged. Bake for 25 minutes.

Allow to cool and eat at room temperature.

SMOKY PIPERADE WITH CHORIZO

SERVES 4

50ml olive oil

1 medium onion, halved and thinly sliced

1 red pepper, thinly sliced

1 yellow pepper, thinly sliced

2 garlic cloves, sliced

6 slices of chorizo, shredded

½ tsp smoked paprika

6 vine-ripened cherry tomatoes, quartered

4 salted anchovies, roughly chopped (optional)

1 tbsp red wine vinegar

½ tbsp caster sugar

50g butter

6 eggs, beaten

a few sprigs of fresh basil (optional)

Heat the oil in a saucepan over a medium heat. Add the onion, peppers and garlic and cook for 15 minutes. Add the chorizo and smoked paprika, then reduce the heat to low and cook gently for a few more minutes before adding the tomatoes, anchovies, vinegar and sugar. Keep cooking on a low heat until the mixture is soft and jammy, then season and remove the pan from the heat. This will last for a couple of days in the fridge if you want to make it ahead of time.

Melt the butter in a large frying pan or wok over a low heat. When the butter starts to foam, add the eggs. With a spatula, fold the eggs from the bottom to the top to cook evenly. This will take no more than a couple of minutes.

When the eggs start to set, add the pepper mixture. Warm everything through gently — the eggs must be soft and creamy.

Season and serve immediately garnished with a little torn basil if you have it.

BUTTERED ASPARAGUS WITH CRUSHED EGG AND CHIVE DRESSING

SERVES 2

1 bunch of asparagus
a good knob of butter
100ml water

FOR THE DRESSING:

3 eggs
2 tbsp cream
1 tbsp finely chopped fresh chives
1 tsp malt or white wine vinegar

To make the dressing, put the eggs in a pot of boiling water and cook for precisely 6 minutes. Remove them from the pot and run under cold water to cool them down as quickly as possible. Peel, then crush with a fork. Add the cream, chives, vinegar and seasoning.

Put the asparagus in a pan and add the butter and water. Season, cover tightly and turn the heat on full. Cook the asparagus for 3 minutes or so, until the water has evaporated and you start to hear sizzling. They are ready.

Serve straightaway with the egg dressing and brown bread soldiers.

I have a soft for a spice bag

17 APRIL 2021

I have a soft spot for a spice bag. That might be shocking news for those of you who think I live on quinoa and freshly pressed fennel juice. Underneath this youthful exterior and unblemished skin lies a dark, greedy heart.

Fridays are takeaway night. It's often Chinese and there is always a spice bag. I trawl through the menu in the hope of finding something new that excites me. I could go to the Indian when I crave spice, but that would involve two stops and unnecessary complication.

I made this gently spiced effort at home. As I sometimes do, I've designed these three to go together. They're all fairly easy. Coconut rice is nothing new but it was my first time making it. I've mentioned my 25-year-old rice cooker before. It's my type of gadget, with two settings: on and warm. Even I, Mr TOT (Terrified of Technology), can't get it wrong.

However, you don't need to have a rice cooker — this recipe is one for the oven. I'm cooking the rice in light coconut milk and a few spices, then embedding the spiced ling and spring onions in it to finish cooking. Ling is a revelation. If you can't find it, use hake or well-trimmed monkfish. I'm giving two options for spice — a madras is a little more assertive than its gentle korma cousin.

These fritters have to be deep-fried. I tried shallow frying them like patties but they weren't nearly as nice. I suppose that makes them bhajis, doesn't it? If you don't have a fryer, be careful. Use a deep pan and drop a little of the mixture in to see if the oil sizzles. Leave the heat on medium-high and cook them in batches. They are delicious.

Tarka is a method of flavouring with whole spices using oil or ghee. It brings a fresh, spicy crunch to everything. I've made a simple mango and cucumber chutney with yogurt, coriander and mint sauce, a little trick from home when I don't have any fresh mint handy.

Altogether this is a lovely, refreshing, fragrant dinner. I hope you give it a go.

SPICED LING WITH FRAGRANT COCONUT RICE AND SPRING ONIONS

SERVES 4

1 x 400g ling fillet

1 tsp madras or korma spice blend

a little butter to dot on top of the fish

4 whole spring onions, trimmed

a few sprigs of fresh coriander

FOR THE COCONUT RICE:

250g basmati rice, rinsed

1 x 400ml tin of light coconut milk

300ml water

10 green cardamon pods, lightly crushed

3cm piece of ginger, unpeeled and roughly sliced

1 cinnamon stick

2 slivers of lemon peel

1 tsp salt

Preheat the oven to 175°C.

Put the rice, coconut milk, water, cardamon, ginger, cinnamon, lemon peel and salt in an ovenproof pot. Mix well and bring to a simmer, then cover and cook in the oven for 15 minutes.

Cut the ling into 3cm chunks, then coat it lightly in your spices and a little salt.

After the 15 minutes are up, sit the ling on top of the rice. Push it down gently to semi-submerge it, then dot the top of the fish with butter. Intersperse the spring onions, cover and return to the oven for another 10 minutes or so, until the fish is done.

Serve with a scattering of coriander.

CURRIED CARROT, APRICOT AND GREEN CHILLI FRITTERS

SERVES 4

400g grated carrot

½ tsp salt

125g gram flour (chickpea flour)

6 dried apricots, thinly sliced

1 medium fresh green chilli, deseeded and finely diced

2 tbsp chopped fresh coriander (including the stalks)

1 tsp garam masala

1 tsp curry powder

½ tsp baking powder

½ tsp nigella seeds (optional)

vegetable oil, for deep-frying

Put the carrot in a colander, add the salt and mix well. Leave to stand for 30 minutes to draw the water out of the carrot, then squeeze it to wring out any last drops of water and transfer to a large bowl with the rest of the ingredients except the oil. It's best to work all the ingredients together by hand. It's good to do a bit of squishing. If it seems dry, add a splash or two of cold water to bring it together so there is no excess flour.

Heat the oil in your deep-fryer to 180°C.

Working in batches, deep-fry tablespoon-sized nuggets until they are golden brown. Keep warm in the oven while you fry the rest. Eat hot.

MANGO AND CUCUMBER TARKA

SERVES 4

1 ripe mango (it must be ripe!)
½ cucumber
1 small fresh red chilli, deseeded and finely diced
1 tbsp vegetable oil
1 tsp cumin seeds
1 tsp coriander seeds
4 tbsp natural yogurt
1 tsp mint sauce
a drizzle of honey
freshly chopped coriander

Peel and dice the mango into 2cm chunks. Peel the cucumber, halve it lengthways and thinly slice. Put the mango and cucumber in a bowl, then add the chilli.

Heat the vegetable oil in a small saucepan until it starts to smoke, then add the cumin and coriander seeds. The seeds should crackle. Remove the pan from the heat immediately and give the seeds a careful swirl, then drain on a piece of kitchen paper and add them to the mango and cucumber.

Add the remaining ingredients and mix everything together. This will keep in the fridge for up to three days.

Three great culinary traditions: Italy, Greece and Grogans

24 APRIL 2021

I'm a bit of an over-planner, to say the least. Many years ago, when there used to be holidays, I'd spend weeks researching a trip. Every day was meticulously planned with happening areas, restaurants, bars and some culture. I'd hide under the duvet at night on my phone until the wife inevitably found me. It was all a bit much, really. I promise the new me is going to be sizzlingly spontaneous. But first, I'm going to kiss the ground of whatever country I'm blessed to land in.

I'm the same with cooking. This comes from years of making mise en place lists in the kitchen. Restaurant cooking can be complicated so I tend to keep it simple at home, but even then there has to be a list.

I'm a sucker for a sausage. They don't even have to be posh for me to love them. Italian sausages are chunky and firm, not at all like the ones we grew up with. They usually have a hint of fennel seed and perhaps a little chilli. They have a natural affinity with polenta and the charred, silky cabbage here. A little cinnamon in the braising liquid adds musk and mystery to the pot. Use good, large, chunky sausages if you can't get Italian ones. I'm using one per person but use more if you feel you need to.

I love a Greek salad. Here I'm sitting a dainty concoction on top of an open omelette. It's a lovely thing that will be ready in no time at all. Be sure to have all the components prepped before you make the omelette just to help you get it right. A non-stick pan is essential for this.

I'm obsessed with cheese toasties and food trucks. When I came across Griolladh, a tiny operation in Malahide, I was smitten. Loose Canon on Drury Street in Dublin makes a blinding toastie too, but the place that has my heart is my beloved Grogans, unabashedly plain and simple — just a pot of English mustard, a pint of Guinness and lashings of sentiment. I'm nearly welling up here. This is my somewhat fancier homage to a great Irish tradition.

POT ROAST ITALIAN SAUSAGES WITH SPRING CABBAGE AND POLENTA

SERVES 4

50ml olive oil

4 large Italian sausages (350g)

1 York cabbage, cut into quarters with stem left intact

1 onion, quartered

½ garlic bulb (cut it across the equator)

100ml chicken stock

100ml white wine

2 tbsp balsamic vinegar

1 tbsp golden brown sugar

1 cinnamon stick

1 sprig of fresh sage

a few dots of butter

FOR THE POLENTA:

200ml milk

100ml water

1 sprig of fresh thyme

100g instant polenta

80g Parmesan cheese, grated

60g butter

Preheat the oven to 180°C.

Heat the oil in a wide ovenproof pan over a medium-high heat. Add the sausages and the cabbage, cut side down. Add the onion and garlic and colour everything lightly for 5 minutes or so. Add the chicken stock, white wine, balsamic vinegar, sugar, cinnamon, sage and butter. Season, then cover and cook in the oven for 30 minutes.

When the sausages are nearly ready, put the milk, water and thyme in a saucepan and bring up to a simmer. Whisk in the polenta in a continuous stream. Cook over a gentle heat for 3—4 minutes, whisking frequently. Remove the thyme, then add the Parmesan, butter and some salt and ground white pepper and keep warm.

To serve, dollop the polenta onto warm plates with the sausage, cabbage and a drizzle of the balsamic juice on top.

GREEK SALAD OMELETTE

SERVES 2

8 large mixed olives, stoned and torn in half (it just looks better)

6 baby plum tomatoes or cherry tomatoes, halved

½ red onion, thinly sliced

¹/₃ cucumber, peeled and diced

1 tsp honey

a pinch of smoked paprika

2 tbsp olive oil

1 tbsp butter

5 eggs, beaten

100g feta cheese

a few sprigs of fresh mint

Preheat the oven to 180°C.

Prepare all the vegetables and have them ready to go.

Stir the honey and smoked paprika into the oil and set aside.

Melt the butter in an ovenproof non-stick pan over a medium-high heat. Season the eggs. When the butter starts to foam, add the eggs to the pan. Stir and scrape the eggs around the pan with a spatula for 2 minutes, then pat them down and allow the bottom to set while you put the veg on top.

Working quickly, crumble over the feta cheese, then drizzle over the smoked paprika oil. Put the pan in the oven for 1 minute to warm everything through — you want to keep the eggs soft and silky.

Serve in the pan with a scattering of fresh mint leaves on top.

MY FAVOURITE GRILLED CHEESE SANDWICH

MAKES 2

8 slices of tinned peach, roughly chopped

a few drops of smoked chipotle Tabasco sauce

250g mature Cheddar cheese, grated

a generous spreading of soft butter

4 slices of good wheaten bread

2 hefty smears of English mustard

I assemble the sandwich in a non-stick frying pan – there's less mess.

Mix the peaches and Tabasco sauce into the cheese.

Butter the bread generously, then put two slices in a non-stick frying pan, buttered side down, over a low heat. Smear the mustard on the bread. Divide the cheese mixture on top of the two slices of bread. Put the other slices of bread on top, buttered side up, and press together. Cook for 3 minutes or so, until golden and crunchy. Turn over carefully and cook on the other side for 2 more minutes.

Serve immediately. If you want to make it even more special, you could pimp it up with crushed avocado for a fancy brunch.

Barbecue escapades

01 MAY 2021

The May bank holiday weekend has come as a shock. January and February trudged along. We spent a lot of it in front of the fire. There was comfort in that. March and April gathered tempo. Plans were hatched. We are looking forward to having the bit between our teeth again, in one way or another. I have butterflies.

The cooking at home continued throughout. I give my 15-year-old a stipend to manage my Instagram account so I stay can stay hip. She takes the money but eyes me with pity. I even made my first TikTok but I won't be going there.

I've written about my barbecue escapades already this year so you'll know it brings me much joy. I was going to cook a pork shoulder — it's wondrous and not often tried. Larger joints of meat are revelatory on the barbecue. Their charred, smoky succulence will make you a devotee as soon as you try them. However, when I went to my local Polish shop, my source for lesser-found pork cuts, I found a hefty, beckoning pork neck, one of my favourites. A shoulder will work too, of course, but if you find one of these, I urge you to try it.

These dishes are meant to go together like old pals. Spain has my heart so I'm keeping faithful until I see her again.

The pork has a simple marinade. Just keep it low and slow and you'll be grand.

At one point I had two Catalan chefs working in our kitchen. That was a fiery but happy time. They showed me how to make escalivada. The vegetables are cooked over the flames until charred, then peeled, chopped and seasoned, like a reverse ratatouille in a way. They wouldn't be happy with that description. Their chests would proudly puff while they admonished me for my ignorance of Catalan cuisine. Escalivada was created first, of course.

I'm using ajo blanco, that lovely chilled almond soup, as a dressing for Little Gems. God only knows what they would say about that. It would have caused a full-blown kitchen revolució.

BARBECUED PORK NECK WITH SHERRY, GARLIC AND ROSEMARY

SERVES 8

1 x 2kg piece of boneless pork neck or shoulder

1 large sprig of fresh rosemary

1 garlic bulb

4 strips of orange peel

100ml cream sherry

4 tbsp olive oil

2 tbsp rock salt

For best results for this recipe you will need a barbecue with a lid and preferably a built-in thermometer. Mine is gas. I just find it much easier to use, although the purists might disagree.

Put the pork in a plastic shopping bag, then tear the rosemary into pieces on top of it. Cut the garlic in half through the equator, then break it into the bag. Add the orange peel, sherry, oil, salt and lots of freshly ground black pepper. Scrunch everything together really well, making sure the ingredients are broken up and crushed. This will open up their flavours. Wrap the pork up tightly in the bag and marinate it in the fridge overnight.

The next day, bring the temperature of the barbecue up to 170°C with the lid down. If you have a machine with two burners, turn the centre one off at this point. There should be no flame directly under the meat.

Scrape the marinade off the pork, then put it on the grill and close the lid. Turn the heat down. The temperature should be no more than 150°C at all times.

Turn the pork every 20 minutes or so. It will take at least 1 hour 45 minutes if it's a boneless shoulder and perhaps up to 2 hours 15 minutes if it's neck. The core temperature on a meat thermometer needs to be between 70°C and 75°C.

For charcoal grills, light the coals as usual, then move them to the edge of the barbecue so there is very little direct heat underneath. Otherwise the same rules apply: low and slow.

Allow the meat to rest for 20 minutes before carving and serving with the escalivada and Little Gems on the following two pages.

ESCALIVADA

SERVES 8

2 aubergines

2 medium onions, unpeeled

2 red peppers

6 vine-ripened cherry tomatoes, quartered

50ml red wine vinegar

½ tsp smoked paprika

2 garlic cloves, crushed

50ml olive oil

1 tbsp honey

The barbecue should be set at no more than 150°C if you're doing this dish separately from the pork on the previous page. I put the vegetables on to cook along with the pork after an hour or so.

Put the whole aubergines, onions and peppers on the grill and close the lid. Cook everything for 30–40 minutes, turning once or twice, until the vegetables are charred and completely soft. Remove from the grill and put in a bowl until they are all cool enough to peel and roughly chop. Make sure to keep any juices to add back into the chopped vegetables along with the tomatoes.

Meanwhile, warm the red wine vinegar with the smoked paprika and garlic for 3 minutes. This will soften the vinegar and cook the garlic and paprika a little. Add this to the vegetables, followed by the oil and honey. Season and mix well.

You could add basil to this if you wish for another dish, but I'm not fond of basil and pork together so this time I'll leave it out.

This will keep in the fridge for three days or so. Leftovers, if any, would be lovely with goat cheese.

LITTLE GEMS WITH AJO BLANCO, GRAPES AND TOASTED SOURDOUGH

SERVES 8

1 thick slice of sourdough bread, chopped up finely

6 heads of Little Gem lettuce, leaves separated

16 mixed seedless grapes, halved

FOR THE AJO BLANCO:

200g blanched whole almonds

1 garlic clove, crushed

300ml water

50ml extra virgin olive oil, plus a little more for the breadcrumbs

1 tbsp red wine vinegar

a splash of your favourite sherry (optional)

To make the ajo blanco, blend the almonds, garlic, water, oil, red wine vinegar, sherry (if using) and some salt and ground white pepper together until smooth, then put in the fridge to chill.

Heat a little more oil in a frying pan over a medium heat. Add the sourdough crumbs and some salt and pepper and cook until golden.

When ready to serve, put the Little Gem leaves on a platter, then spoon over the dressing followed by the breadcrumbs and grapes.

Crowd pleasers

08 MAY 2021

I'm very excited today as I've just got hold of my new baby by a very kind and fortuitous route. He's 41 inches in length, the same in width and a stout 58 inches high. He gleams in the sunlight and if he could talk he'd sound like Tony Soprano, badda-bing badda-bang, know what I mean?

Enough already. I'll put you out of your misery but not like Tony would. I am the new owner of my very own NYC hot dog cart. I've got goosebumps just thinking about it. He already has a name courtesy of a friend who is good at these things: Diamond Dogs. ⚡ How cool is that! Some of you right now might be having visions of me all kitted out as Ziggy Stardust, doling out hot dogs on the Greenway, 'Rebel Rebel' pumping through the air. Bowie sighted in Dungarvan. It would be like the moving statues all over again. Stay tuned.

The dishes this week have no connection other than they are simple and could be used for different circumstances.

The lahmacun is a Turkish spice-laden meat pizza that's usually made with lamb but I'm using beef as I haven't featured it in a while and it's equally delicious. Normally it's considered to be a flatbread more than a pizza and is usually eaten rolled up, so the dough needs to be as thin as possible. I need to explore Turkish cuisine more, it's one of the world's most underrated. Another thing for an ever-expanding bucket list.

These little pots are so rich I was tempted to call them Cheddar Collisons in honour of the two clever brothers from Limerick who founded Stripe but they are totally delicious and perfect for an eventual dinner party. Buy good mature Cheddar — I'm using the Little Milk Company, it's lovely and local to me. The spiced raisins are somewhat different and easy to make but you could use your favourite chutney if you like.

Fresh mackerel is in season now. This is an easy bake that can bring the best out of the fish for a simple lunch or dinner. This can all be done ahead of time if you like and kept in the fridge until you are ready to cook.

What kept
me going
was the
quest to
know more,
do more and
be more.
It was
never just
a job.

LAHMACUN

MAKES 4

300g lean minced beef

1 small red pepper, finely chopped

1 red onion, thinly sliced

2 garlic cloves, sliced

1 small bunch of fresh flat-leaf parsley, stems finely chopped (keep the leaves for garnish)

2 tbsp tomato purée

½ tsp mixed spice

½ tsp ground cumin

½ tsp smoked paprika

½ tsp ground cinnamon

½ tsp chilli flakes

2 tbsp pine nuts, toasted

4 tbsp natural yogurt

1 tsp sumac, for dusting (optional)

FOR THE DOUGH:

450g strong white flour

1 tsp caster sugar

½ tsp salt

1 x 7g sachet of fast-acting dried yeast

a drizzle of olive oil

300ml warm water (use 1 part boiling to 2 parts cold)

To make the dough, put the flour, sugar and salt in a mixing bowl. Add the yeast and oil to the warm water. Mix well and gradually add to the dry ingredients to form a dough.

Tip the dough out onto a floured surface and knead for 5–6 minutes. Or if you have a stand mixer fitted with a dough hook, this can be done in half the time.

When the dough is smooth and elastic, put it back in the bowl, cover the bowl with cling film and leave to rise in a warm place for 45 minutes or so, until doubled in size.

Meanwhile, for the topping, put the minced beef, pepper, half of the red onion, garlic, parsley stalks, tomato purée, spices and some salt and pepper in a food processor and pulse until smooth. If you don't have a food processor, just mix it well by hand.

Remove the dough from the bowl onto a lightly floured surface and knock it back.

I'm making two pizzas for four people, so divide the dough into two balls, cover with cling film and put back in the fridge to chill for 30 minutes. This will make the dough easier to work with.

Preheat the oven to 220°C. Grease two baking trays with oil.

Roll out the dough as thinly as you can, then put them on the trays. Spread the beef mixture thinly on top of the dough, then bake in the oven for 15 minutes or so, until the dough is golden and crisp.

To serve, scatter over the remaining red onions and the toasted pine nuts with artistic dollops of yogurt, torn parsley leaves and a dusting of sumac (if using).

CHEDDAR CUSTARD POTS WITH SPICED RAISINS

MAKES 6

250ml cream
250ml milk
a pinch of grated nutmeg
150g mature Cheddar cheese, grated
3 large egg yolks (4 if they are small)

FOR THE RAISINS:
50g raisins
20g golden brown sugar
2 tbsp sherry or red wine vinegar
2 tbsp water
2 cloves

Preheat the oven to 150°C.

Put the cream, milk and nutmeg in a saucepan and bring carefully to a simmer, then remove from the heat. Whisk in the cheese until it's melted and smooth, then leave to cool for 15 minutes.

Put the egg yolks in a bowl and whisk in the cheesy cream. Season and pour into a jug.

Put six ramekins in a deep roasting tin, then fill them evenly with the custard. You may have some left over depending on the size of your ramekins. Add boiling water to the tin until it comes one-third of the way up the ramekins.

Bake in the oven for 25–30 minutes, until just set (it may take a little longer). There will still be a gentle wobble in the centre when cooked. Remove the ramekins from the tin and allow to cool – these are best eaten at room temperature.

Meanwhile, put the raisins, brown sugar, vinegar, water and cloves in a saucepan and bring to a simmer. Cook over a gentle heat until the liquid is syrupy, then remove the pan from the heat and allow to cool.

Divide the raisins evenly on top of the custards. Serve with toast.

FRESH MACKEREL WITH NEW POTATOES, SAGE AND BACON

SERVES 2

4 fillets of the freshest mackerel

4 rashers of rindless streaky bacon

8 fresh sage leaves

a drizzle of sunflower oil

8 new potatoes, cooked in their skins

a few knobs of butter

2 tbsp malt or white wine vinegar

First make sure the mackerel has no bones. The best way to ensure this is to run your forefinger down the length of the flesh. If you feel some, cut them out making a V-shaped incision with your knife.

Wrap each fillet with a rasher of bacon, incorporating one sage leaf in each.

Drizzle sunflower oil on the bottom of a baking tray and lay the mackerel fillets on the tray. Break the cooked new potatoes around the fish, then dot with the butter and the remaining sage leaves. Drizzle over the vinegar and season.

When you're ready to eat, preheat the grill.

Pop the tray under the grill and cook for 10–12 minutes, until the bacon crisps a little and the fish is cooked. Serve straightaway.

Early summer days

15 MAY 2021

We're ramping up here in Dungarvan. Next Friday we're opening the Castle Green Market. There are three stalls and we've got one. It's a tiny little thing but it helps the restaurants that don't have any outside dining. We're lucky to have a supportive local authority.

There will be benches, festoon lighting and a festival vibe. My long list of dishes has been shortened to fit on a blackboard and the equipment has been squished in. I'm doing toasties, sausage rolls and seafood sandwiches. I'm hatching plans for savoury doughnuts that will include my crab crème brûlée, chicken liver parfait and bacon jam. There will be chowder, something sweet and drinks. That's a lot to get into a small hut. The hot dog cart will be tucked in by the side, protected from the wind by the castle walls.

I'll have my eldest helping — the lure of her own money at last was too much to resist. It will be open at the weekends at first, then we'll open up more when people can travel. This will get us into the swing of things until the restaurant opens. I have a good feeling about it.

This week's dishes are bright and perfect for early summer days. The classic coq au Riesling is given texture by a filo pastry crown that shatters into the chickeny juices. This is one of my favourite recent dishes. It's lighter than its wintery brother, perfect for the longer evenings or a satisfying lunch.

Smoked salmon and new potatoes are of course lovely together. The peas and broad beans imbue the dish with vibrancy, while the apple and dill butter bring it all together. It's a lovely bowl of food.

The coriander oil really elevates this carrot dish and gives it verdancy and zing. The toasted almond yogurt is a perfect foil for the rich, buttery carrots. These are so much more than the sum of their parts. You can make a fab main course by serving this with couscous, no meat necessary. Or have them as a side to make your Sunday lunch a bit funky.

COQ AU RIESLING PIE

SERVES 4

150g butter

2 tbsp sunflower oil

1 large onion, cut into 2cm dice

125g smoked bacon lardons

250g chestnut mushrooms, halved

3 garlic cloves, sliced

2 bay leaves (fresh if possible)

1 sprig of fresh thyme

8 boneless chicken thighs

2 tbsp plain flour

250ml dry Riesling

250ml chicken stock

150ml cream

1 tbsp Dijon mustard

3 sheets of filo pastry, thawed

Melt half of the butter with the sunflower oil in a saucepan over a medium heat. Add the onion and bacon lardons and cook for 10 minutes, until the onions soften a little. Add the mushrooms, garlic and herbs and let them cook while you prepare the chicken.

Cut each chicken thigh into two pieces, then add them to the pan along with the flour. Cook for 3 minutes or so but be careful that the flour doesn't burn.

Add the wine and bring to a simmer while stirring to ensure the flour cooks out evenly. Add the stock and cream and cook gently for 15 minutes, stirring occasionally. Add the mustard, season and allow to cool. This can all be done a few hours or even a day ahead.

Preheat the oven to 180°C.

Transfer the chicken mixture to a shallow casserole or baking dish. Lightly scrunch the three sheets of filo pastry over the top of the dish. Melt the remaining butter and brush the pastry nice and evenly with it.

Bake the pie in the oven for 25 minutes, until crisp and golden. Serve with a green salad on the side.

WARM SALAD OF BABY POTATOES, SMOKED SALMON, APPLE AND BROAD BEANS

SERVES 2

100g broad beans or frozen petits pois

8 baby potatoes, cooked, peeled and halved

1 tbsp roughly chopped fresh dill

½ Granny Smith apple, peeled and diced (eat the other half)

100g sliced smoked salmon

FOR THE BUTTER:

200ml apple juice

80g butter, diced and chilled

1 tsp horseradish sauce

Bring the apple juice up to a simmer in a small saucepan, then whisk in the butter, followed by the horseradish. Keep warm.

Pod the broad beans and cook them (or the frozen petits pois if that's what you're using) for 2 minutes in boiling salted water. Drain, then plunge into iced water to keep their colour. Drain once more when cold.

When you're ready to serve, warm the cooked potatoes gently in the apple and horseradish butter, then add the broad beans and dill. Season.

To serve, divide the potato mixture between warm bowls, then scatter with the apple and lay slices of smoked salmon over the warm salad.

GLAZED CARROTS WITH CORIANDER OIL AND TOASTED ALMOND YOGURT

SERVES 4

120g butter

100g caster sugar

1 sprig of fresh thyme

1 star anise

400ml water

8 medium carrots, scrubbed

FOR THE YOGURT:

120g flaked almonds

1 tsp cumin seeds

6 tbsp natural yogurt

FOR THE CORIANDER OIL:

1 large bunch of fresh coriander, roughly chopped (including the stalks)

1 small fresh green chilli, deseeded and finely chopped

a small piece of ginger, peeled and finely grated

110ml sunflower oil

50ml olive oil

Bring the butter, sugar, thyme, star anise and water to a simmer in a large pot. Season, then add the carrots. Cook for 30–40 minutes, until the carrots are tender.

Remove the carrots, then put them in a shallow casserole or baking dish. Reduce the cooking liquid until it starts to thicken, then pour it over the carrots to be warmed through later.

For the toasted almond yogurt, put the almonds and cumin seeds in a dry pan over a medium heat. Toast carefully for 2–3 minutes, until the almonds are golden. Add a pinch of salt, then tip out onto a plate to cool. When cool, fold them through the yogurt and chill until ready to serve.

For the coriander oil, put all the ingredients in a blender with a pinch of salt and pulse until smooth.

To serve, warm the carrots through, then put artful dollops of the yogurt and coriander oil on top.

Sure-fire winners for family dinners

22 MAY 2021

All parents worry about their children; it's part of our job. In the greater scheme of things, is fretting about what they eat really important as long as they're happy and healthy? That depends on how you look at the world, I suppose. For me, there's nothing more satisfying than seeing your child relishing their dinner.

I've written extensively about the food we eat at home. Indeed, some might say they know as much about what's going on in our house as I do. I think a lot about what I'm going to feed our girls. It bothers me that one of them doesn't eat vegetables. For 14 years I've tried to change this, with very little success. I'm hoping something will click eventually. It's important for young adults to have enthusiasm for and a worldliness with food.

These dishes, however, are sure-fire winners with my family. You'd be entitled to question, as I did, whether a pasta cake is any better than a traditional bowl of pasta. I'm not sure that it is. What this *does* have is a sense of theatre – that and the fact that you can get it ready ahead of time. It's abundant in 'don't scare the horses' flavours. I add a Parmesan cream for luxury and rocket leaves for freshness and a bit of hope.

I'm a demon for sausage rolls. I make these with pork mince, which is now readily available. It's an easy recipe that could be handy as a dinner or to put in a lunchbox. I use the fabulous Irish-produced Roll-It pastry. It's head and shoulders above the rest but a little more work, hence the name. You can use ready-rolled puff but you'll have to stretch it out just a little more to accommodate the meat.

The meatball dish is an amalgam. It's also a big cheat made with ready-made meatballs and baked beans. If Nigella can chop up fish fingers and magic them up into her fish finger bhorta, surely I can take a few shortcuts too.

BAKED PASTA CAKE WITH ROCKET AND PARMESAN CREAM

SERVES 4

300g penne, farfalle or conchiglie
2 tbsp olive oil
2 garlic cloves, thinly sliced
1 x 400g tin of chopped tomatoes
1 tbsp tomato purée
1 tsp paprika
½ tsp chilli flakes
100ml chicken stock
100g Parmesan cheese
2 balls of mozzarella, cut into 2cm chunks
3 tbsp fresh white or panko breadcrumbs

FOR THE PARMESAN CREAM:
150ml cream
100ml chicken stock
80g Parmesan cheese, grated

FOR THE ROCKET:
100g rocket
2 tbsp olive oil
1 tbsp balsamic vinegar

Preheat the oven to 180°C. Brush a 20cm springform tin with oil, then line the base with parchment.

Cook your pasta as per the packet instructions, then drain and set aside.

Meanwhile, heat the oil in a large saucepan over a low heat. Add the garlic and cook gently for 2 minutes, until lightly coloured. Add the tomatoes, tomato purée, paprika, chilli flakes and stock and season generously. Bring to a gentle blip, then cook for 10 minutes. Mix the cooked pasta, tomato sauce and Parmesan together.

Spoon half of the pasta mixture into the prepared springform tin, then scatter the mozzarella on top. Cover with the remaining pasta. Pat down well, scatter the breadcrumbs over the top and drizzle with oil. (You can do this ahead of time and finish when you need it.) Bake in the oven for 25 minutes, until crisp and golden.

To make the sauce, bring the cream to a simmer with the stock. Reduce gently for 2–3 minutes, then whisk in the Parmesan. Season and keep warm.

Run a knife around the edge of the cake tin before releasing the sides of the tin and transferring the cake to a platter. Turn the rocket in the oil and balsamic vinegar, season and bunch it on top of the cake. Serve with a jug of warm Parmesan cream.

CHEESY PORK AND APPLE ROLLS
SERVES 6

450g pork mince

100g fresh white breadcrumbs

100g mature Cheddar cheese, grated

2 Granny Smith apples, peeled and grated

1 egg, beaten

2 tbsp country relish or chutney

1 tbsp prepared English mustard

1 tbsp thyme leaves (reserve a few for garnish)

1 tsp salt

½ tsp ground white pepper

a good pinch of ground nutmeg

a dusting of plain flour

1 x 400g packet of Roll-It puff pastry, thawed

1 egg beaten with 1 tbsp milk

Put the pork in a large bowl with the breadcrumbs, cheese, apples, egg, relish or chutney, mustard, thyme, salt, pepper and nutmeg. Scrunch it up using your hands.

On a floured surface, roll out the chilled pastry as evenly as you can into a neat rectangle. Cut the pastry in half lengthways — a pizza cutter is excellent for this.

Brush the pastry lightly with the egg wash, then form two lengths of filling along the middle of both pieces of pastry. Fold the pastry over the filling and seal it.

Transfer the rolls to a baking tray lined with parchment or foil and brush with the remaining egg wash. Make a few incisions in the pastry along its length with a knife.

Scatter a few extra leaves of thyme on top for decoration, then put in the fridge to rest for 30 minutes.

Preheat the oven to 185°C.

You can cook the rolls whole or cut them before baking. Bake in the oven for 30 minutes, until puffy and golden. Serve warm.

BAKED MEATBALL CASSEROLE WITH SWEET PAPRIKA BEANS

SERVES 4

1 tbsp sunflower oil

12 ready-made meatballs

125g smoked bacon lardons

2 garlic cloves, thinly sliced

1 x 400g tin of chopped tomatoes

150ml concentrated chicken stock

1 tsp paprika

1 x 400g tin of baked beans

1 tbsp maple syrup

1 tbsp Worcestershire sauce

a few dashes of Tabasco (the smoked chipotle version if possible)

Preheat the oven to 185°C.

Heat the oil in a wide, shallow, heavy-based casserole over a high heat. When it's gently smoking, add the meatballs and bacon and colour for 5 minutes or so. Add the garlic and give it a gentle swish around the casserole, then add the tomatoes, stock and paprika. Bring to a simmer and cook for 5 minutes or so.

Add the beans, maple syrup, Worcestershire sauce and Tabasco. Season and bring to a simmer again, then pop in the oven to cook for 25 minutes, until a light crust starts to form.

Serve with rice, mash or even toast.

Comfort food that's perfect after a long day

29 MAY 2021

There's a palpable tension in the office as I'm finalising this week's column. My wife, who I sometimes fondly refer to as Chairman Mao, is not a happy camper. She is my in-house editor. The content of this column doesn't usually bother her. Today, however, there is a seething silence.

You might remember a Tom Hanks film called *The Money Pit*? It turns out that I'm the owner of a four-wheeled version of that house: my 1994 campervan. To be fair, I didn't pay a lot for it.

So far it has been seen by four mechanics, but when I brought it to a specialist a number of weeks ago for a little exterior sprucing up, there was a lot of sighing and groaning. It was not a good prognosis. Words like 'cut your losses' are not what a fella wants to hear when he's only spent one night in 20 months in his lifelong dream.

My thoughts turn to food once more for a bit of comfort. The first recipe is a bit of a dinner. The chop is big. On the bone is always best, but this one is a whopper. It doesn't necessarily sing of summer, but it will satisfy you after a long day with a glass of red.

The fennel risotto, on the other hand, will instantly transport you to the Mediterranean. I'm a massive fan of fennel, having been converted while making soupe de poisson in Chez Nico in London all those years ago. These days I pair it with all manner of fish but also with lamb or creamy goat cheese. At its best it is a thing of beauty that zings of freshness, but beware — its particular green gives way to a sad tell-tale brown in no time at all.

These spuds are handy little fellas. The flavour works with the crispy bacon, butterhead lettuce and chive-laden sour cream. This salad would also be a good accompaniment to steak.

PORK RACK CHOPS WITH STICKY SHALLOTS AND SAGE AND CHEDDAR MASH

SERVES 2

2 tbsp rapeseed oil
2 x 250g thick pork rack chops
4 banana shallots, halved lengthways
1 sprig of fresh thyme
2 tbsp balsamic vinegar

FOR THE MASH:
500g floury potatoes, such as Maris Piper, peeled and halved
150ml milk
60g butter
60g mature Cheddar cheese, grated
6 fresh sage leaves, finely shredded

Put the potatoes on to boil. When they're cooked, drain and mash with the milk and butter. Add the Cheddar and sage, then season with salt and ground white pepper and keep warm.

Meanwhile, heat the oil in a frying pan over a medium-high heat. When the oil is gently smoking, add the chops carefully to the pan. Cook for 5 minutes on one side, then turn the chops over and turn down the heat a little.

Add the shallots and thyme, then season. Continue to cook for a further 10 minutes or so, taking care that the shallots are turned every so often as they soften.

For the last part of the cooking time, hold the chops one by one on their side to crisp the fat for a minute. When this is done, lay them down once more, then add the balsamic vinegar to the pan. Turn off the heat and swirl everything around to coat. Cover the pan and allow the chops to rest for a few minutes, then serve with the mash.

FENNEL RISOTTO WITH ROASTED VEGETABLE SALSA VERDE

SERVES 4

a generous knob of butter

2 tbsp olive oil

1 small onion, finely diced

½ fennel bulb, finely diced

2 garlic cloves, sliced

2cm piece of ginger, peeled and finely diced

1 star anise

400g Arborio risotto rice

150ml white wine

1.1 litres chicken or vegetable stock

100g Parmesan cheese, grated

FOR THE SALSA VERDE:

1 courgette, halved lengthways and thinly sliced

½ fennel bulb, thinly sliced

1 small fresh red chilli, deseeded and sliced

3 tbsp olive oil

250g vine-ripened cherry tomatoes, halved

2 tbsp capers

2 tbsp roughly chopped fresh dill

2 tbsp roughly chopped fresh basil

2 tbsp roughly chopped fresh mint

Preheat the oven to 185°C.

For the risotto, melt the butter with the oil in a heavy-based pan over a low heat. When the butter starts to foam, add the onion, fennel, garlic, ginger and star anise. Cover and cook gently for 15 minutes, stirring once or twice, until the onion softens but doesn't brown.

Add the rice and turn it in the juices for a minute or two. Add the wine followed by one-third of the stock and bring to a gentle simmer.

Meanwhile, put the courgette, fennel and chilli in a roasting tin. Season and drizzle over the oil, turning to coat. Roast in the oven for 15 minutes before adding the tomatoes and capers, then put the tin back in the oven for another 10 minutes.

To finish, add the remaining stock to the rice bit by bit over a low heat, stirring until it's all absorbed. Add the Parmesan at the end and more butter if you like. Season and allow to rest while you add the herbs to the roasted vegetables.

Serve the vegetables on top of the risotto, either family-style in a large bowl or in individual bowls.

JERK POTATOES WITH BUTTERHEAD LETTUCE, CRISPY BACON, SOUR CREAM AND CHIVES

SERVES 4

250g rindless smoked streaky bacon

16 baby potatoes, cooked

2 tsp jerk seasoning (if you can't find jerk seasoning, use Cajun or taco seasoning)

1 large or 2 small heads of butterhead lettuce, leaves separated

FOR THE SOUR CREAM:

1 x 200g tub of light sour cream

2 tbsp chopped fresh chives

1 tsp horseradish sauce

Preheat the oven to 190°C.

Lay the bacon out in a roasting tin and cook in the oven until it's crisp, then transfer to a piece of kitchen paper to drain.

Put the cooked potatoes in the roasting tin and turn them in the residual bacon fat, then crush with a fork until they are flat and even. The flatter they are, the crispier they will be. Dust the potatoes with the jerk seasoning and bake in the oven for 20–25 minutes, until crisp.

Meanwhile, mix the sour cream with the chives and horseradish, then put it in a nice presentation bowl.

To serve, put the lettuce leaves on the base of a serving platter or bowl and put the dish of sour cream in the middle, then arrange the warm potatoes and bacon on top.

For when we entertain again

05 JUNE 2021

So we're back, with a small new team feeding our overnight guests. I know we are luckier than a lot of restauranteurs who don't have rooms to offer people.

I welcome a fresh perspective in the kitchen. Keeping current is so important. It's all too easy to get bored of your own ideas, especially when you've been knocking round a kitchen as long as I have. I greedily soak up something new at every opportunity.

I never quite got round to mastering all the foam business, though. It's too technical for me. Any attempt always ended up with sauce in my hair or splattering the ceiling like a gory John Carpenter movie. That and the fact that my cooking veered more towards Fergus Henderson than Ferran Adrià left me distinctly uninterested.

These dishes are designed for entertaining on this bank holiday weekend. Hallelujah. I've missed having people at home. We've modified a shed into a funky outside space. The joys of country living really kick in when the music gets turned up. The sheep don't complain.

I adore hake's fleshy goodness. The garlic cream takes it to another level without overpowering it. Orzo's slippery subtlety is a perfect coupling. With anything rich I balance it with vibrancy, this time in the guise of a roasted pepper dressing. I'm using a packet of multicoloured mini peppers for a pop of colour and serving it family-style, as we need all the conviviality we can get these days.

I've been a bit obsessed with tenderstem broccoli for a few years now. I need a break. I also need to embrace the humble and maligned old-fashioned stuff. I leave the stems on to provide solid and flavourful contrast. This crab butter is fancy because of the saffron but it's worth a pinch to elevate the crab for this elegant starter.

The steak plays second fiddle to the onions in this dish. I'll never get to the stage where I eat no meat but I'm certainly eating less of it. These onions are sweet and unctuous. The Boursin and rocket bring just the right amount of kick to liven up proceedings. Use goat cheese if you're not a fan of Boursin.

When done correctly, things don't need to be complicated.

10 APRIL 2021

BAKED HAKE WITH ORZO, GARLIC CREAM AND ROASTED PEPPER AND OLIVE DRESSING

SERVES 4

250g orzo

a drizzle of olive oil

1 x 500g hake fillet, skin on and bones removed

FOR THE GARLIC CREAM:

2 tbsp olive oil

3 garlic cloves, sliced thinly and evenly

100ml concentrated chicken stock

250ml cream

1 sprig of fresh rosemary

a squeeze of lemon

FOR THE DRESSING:

4 tbsp olive oil

1 packet of mini mixed peppers, cut in half

½ tsp smoked paprika

juice of ½ orange

80g olives, stoned and halved

a few sprigs of fresh basil, leaves torn

Cook the orzo as per the packet instructions. Drain in a colander and cool under cold running water. Make sure any excess water is removed. Turn it in a little oil and season, then spread it out in a large baking dish and set aside.

For the garlic cream, put the oil and garlic in a saucepan and turn it to a low to medium heat. It's important that the garlic cooks slowly and evenly until it turns light golden. Add the chicken stock and reduce by half, then add the cream and rosemary. Bring the cream up to a gentle blip, then cook for 10 minutes, until it reduces a little and starts to thicken. Take the pan off the heat and remove the rosemary, then add the lemon juice and season.

For the dressing, put the oil and peppers in a pan and cook on a medium-high heat for 10 minutes or so, until the peppers soften and char. Add the smoked paprika, followed a little later by the orange juice. Season and remove the pan from the heat. When cool, add the olives and torn basil.

Preheat the oven to 185°C.

Season the hake fillet on the flesh side, then lay it on top of the orzo in the baking dish, skin side up. Press the fish down into the pasta a little, then spoon the garlic cream all around the fish, making sure it soaks into the pasta. Drizzle a little oil over the skin, then season.

Bake the hake in the oven for 20—25 minutes. The cooking time will entirely depend on the thickness of the fish — you will have to check that it's white, not translucent, and flaky.

When the fish is cooked, spoon the dressing on top and serve in the middle of the table. You could peel the skin off the hake before you put the dressing on — it's worth a try. Sometimes it comes off really easily, other times it doesn't.

OLD-FASHIONED BROCCOLI WITH PINE NUTS AND CRAB AND SAFFRON BUTTER

SERVES 2

250g broccoli

juice of 1 orange

a small pinch of saffron (strands or powder) – less is more!

100g butter, diced and chilled

½ tsp Dijon mustard

100g crab meat

1 tbsp toasted pine nuts

Trim the broccoli evenly, making sure you keep as much of the stalk as possible. Cook for 3 minutes or so in boiling salted water, until tender but not falling apart. Drain and set aside.

Meanwhile, bring the orange juice and saffron to a gentle simmer in a saucepan. Mix in the butter bit by bit with a wooden spoon until it has all been amalgamated (a whisk will only tangle and trap the saffron strands). Add the mustard, followed by the crab, then season.

To serve, divide the broccoli between two warm bowls. Spoon the crab sauce on top and scatter over the pine nuts.

SLOW-ROASTED ONIONS WITH STEAK, BOURSIN AND ROCKET

SERVES 2

3 medium onions

2 tbsp sunflower oil

100ml apple juice

2 tbsp raisins

1 tbsp apple cider vinegar

1 sprig of fresh thyme

1 tsp golden brown sugar

1 tbsp butter

200g of your favourite steak

1 x 80g packet of Boursin cheese

a handful of rocket leaves

Preheat the oven to 165°C.

Peel the onions and cut them in half along their circumference.

Heat the oil in an ovenproof pan over a medium heat until it's gently smoking, then carefully put the onions in the pan, cut side down. Colour the onions for 5 minutes without moving them, until they char and turn dark brown.

Turn off the heat, then turn the onions over and add the apple juice, raisins, vinegar and thyme. Dust the onions with the sugar and dot each onion with a little of the butter. Season, cover the pan and put it in the oven to cook for 30 minutes.

Meanwhile, cook the steak as you like it and allow it to rest in a warm place.

When the onions are soft and tender, divide them between two warm bowls.

Add any steak resting juices to the pan you cooked the onions in.

To serve, cut the steak into strips and intersperse them among the onions. Spoon over the raisins and pan dressing, then add a smear of Boursin to each onion before topping with the rocket.

Our fighting spirit has returned

12 JUNE 2021

It's almost embarrassing to say that the Christmas decorations were still up 10 days before we reopened the restaurant for our townhouse guests. Closing all those months ago on Christmas Eve was upsetting. Those three weeks open in December were not worth the subsequent trauma. I'd been in the restaurant a few times over the months to check on things but I hated every minute and couldn't wait to leave. It was like entering the *Mary Celeste*. The warmth and life had gone out of it. The decorations could wait. Who was going to see them?

A lot of people have re-evaluated their lives. In truth, our time at home was cherished but as the evenings lengthened, reality gnawed away and our fighting spirit had to return for our 25th summer in the Tannery.

All our key staff are back, thankfully. There's a combined service of 77 years in our front-of-house team. Máire and Una have been here from Day One. Valerie came to help when Ruth was born and Daniel came from Poland when Anna was born, famously calling a few hours after her delivery to say he, too, had arrived. 'Can I call you back tomorrow, Daniel? I just had a baby.' He didn't understand at the time that Máire was speaking literally.

These are three simple summer fish dishes. I'm pairing a niçoise salad with smoked mackerel and a punchy butter bean aioli. The eggs should be just set. These details are important. Then you have a dish that's perfect for a sunny day.

The mussels are my version of a mouclade, the lesser-known cousin of moules marinière. The peas bring life to the gentle spices and make you long to eat these beside the sea with a lovely cider or crisp white wine.

Slow-cooking calamari in olive oil is a subtle revelation shown to me by a Catalan chef many years ago. Frozen works best, as it becomes as tender as a whisper. The vegetables give it a lovely crunch. I love to eat this as a light lunch or tapa with a roasted garlic mayonnaise and good bread.

SMOKED MACKEREL NIÇOISE WITH BUTTER BEAN AIOLI

SERVES 4

4 eggs

1 x 200g packet of trimmed fine French beans

8 new potatoes, cooked and halved

1 small red onion, halved and thinly sliced

4 ripe plum tomatoes, quartered

16 stoned olives

1 x 200g packet of smoked mackerel

a few sprigs of fresh basil

FOR THE AIOLI:

1 x 400g tin of butter beans, drained and rinsed

2 garlic cloves, sliced

150ml cream

juice of ½ lemon

FOR THE DRESSING:

100ml olive oil

3 tbsp red wine vinegar

2 tbsp chopped fresh chives

a squeeze of honey

For the best results, make the butter bean aioli in a food processor. Simply blend all the ingredients until smooth, then season with salt and ground white pepper and chill.

For the dressing, just whisk everything together.

Lower the eggs into a pan of boiling water. Cook for 7 minutes, then refresh them under cold running water and peel carefully.

Cook the French beans in boiling salted water for 2 minutes, then refresh under cold running water. (Or for a quick cheat you can cook the packet of beans in the microwave for 2–3 minutes, depending on how thick they are.)

Put the French beans, cooked potatoes, red onion, tomatoes and olives in a large bowl. Season, then add the dressing and turn so everything is coated.

To serve, spoon a pool of butter bean aioli on the centre of the plates, then divide the dressed salad mixture nicely on top. Flake the mackerel over the salad and garnish with fresh basil leaves.

MUSSELS WITH CURRIED PEA CREAM AND CRUNCHY BREADCRUMBS

SERVES 4

1.5kg mussels

1 tbsp butter

1 small onion, diced

2 garlic cloves, sliced

200ml dry cider

200g frozen petits pois, defrosted

150ml cream

1 tsp curry powder

a few sprigs of fresh coriander

FOR THE BREADCRUMBS:

3 tbsp olive oil

100g panko breadcrumbs

1 garlic clove, sliced

To prepare the mussels, immerse them in a clean sink of cold water. Agitate. Debeard them one by one into a clean bowl, discarding any that are open and won't close when you gently tap them on the counter. Drain and clean the sink, fill it with cold water again and re-immerse the debearded mussels. Agitate the mussels once more, then lift them from the water, leaving any sediment behind.

Melt the butter in a pot over a medium heat. When the butter starts to foam, add the onion and garlic and cook for 5 minutes. Add the cider, followed by the mussels. Cover the pot and increase the heat to high, shaking the pot now and then until the mussels all open. This will take only 2–3 minutes, depending on the size of the mussels.

Put a colander over a large bowl and drain the mussels into it, allowing the juices to flow into the bowl. Remove the colander with the mussels and set aside. Discard any mussels that are still closed.

Let the mussel juices sit for a few minutes — this will allow any sediment to sink to the bottom of the bowl — then decant the liquor back into the pot. Add the petits pois, cream, curry powder and coriander to the juices. Bring to a simmer and cook for 5 minutes, then season and blend with a hand blender (much less messy). This can be done ahead of time and reheated.

Meanwhile, heat the oil in a small frying pan over a medium heat. Add the breadcrumbs, garlic and seasoning, then cook the breadcrumbs until they are golden and crunchy.

Take the top shells off the mussels and discard.

When you're ready to serve, warm the pea cream and drop in the mussels to heat, but be careful not to cook them any further.

To serve, divide the mussels among warm bowls and top with the crunchy breadcrumbs.

CONFIT CALAMARI WITH CHEAT'S AIOLI, PEPPERS, ORANGE AND SAFFRON

SERVES 4

2 tubes of squid (250g approx.), cleaned and cut into thin strips

1 red pepper, thinly sliced

1 yellow pepper, thinly sliced

2 garlic cloves, halved

120ml light olive oil

100ml sunflower oil

juice of 1 orange

1 sprig of fresh rosemary

a small pinch of saffron

a small pinch of chilli flakes

FOR THE CHEAT'S AIOLI:

6 tbsp good mayonnaise

2 garlic cloves, crushed

a squeeze of lemon juice

Put the squid, peppers, garlic, oils, orange juice, rosemary, saffron and chilli flakes in a saucepan. Turn together so everything is coated in the oil. Cover and bring to a bare simmer, then cook for 15–20 minutes, until the squid is soft and tender and the peppers are melting.

Meanwhile, to make the aioli, remove 2 tablespoons of the cooking liquid from the pan and allow to cool. Whisk this into the mayonnaise along with the garlic and lemon juice.

I like to serve this warm, along with the oil, in those lovely tapas dishes that we so fondly remember from our holidays.

Becoming a better cook is all about adventure.

13 AUGUST 2022

Dreaming of travel

19 JUNE 2021

I don't profess to be an expert of any country's food in particular but if there was a league table, I'd say French, Italian and Spanish are the cuisines I'm most comfortable cooking, with a bit of Middle Eastern bringing up the rear. I love Indian food but don't cook it nearly enough. Chinese food intimidates me. I feel underequipped and hopeless, very much like every maths exam I ever did.

I have a long list of countries and their food that I need to embrace as soon as I can take to the skies. Vietnam, Turkey, Malaysia. I'm so desperate to travel, I'd even relish discovering the lesser-known charms of the Isle of Man.

These recipes travel the world. Like disparate children, they all have their qualities but you couldn't possibly choose between them.

I'm very fond of this pork meatball dish. You'll need to pull out the food processor and get stuck in. The flavours are big and bold, and the creamy goodness of the coconut sauce adds to the pleasure. A plain and simple rice is the only other thing you will need.

This calzone is utter madness and all the more delicious for it, a chilli con carne wrapped in a pizza's embrace. The smoke comes from the smoked chipotle Tabasco and the jalapeños deliver some necessary fire to the affair.

I'm giving you a great recipe for pizza dough but there are very good frozen dough balls out there now or even ready-rolled dough to make it noticeably easier for you. I would never judge. The mixture will be easier to work with if it's chilled, so if you wanted to make it the day before, so much the better.

I've noticed that a few of the supermarkets have started doing boneless chicken thighs. This makes me very happy as it's my favourite part of the bird. Chermoula is a Middle Eastern revelation. It's perky and warm at the same time due to the lemon, herbs and spices. Normally served with fish, it gives life to the sticky, unctuous chicken.

FRAGRANT PORK MEATBALLS WITH COCONUT, CUCUMBER AND CASHEWS

SERVES 4

500g pork mince

100g fresh breadcrumbs

1 egg, beaten

4 spring onions, finely chopped

2 garlic cloves, chopped

2cm piece of ginger, peeled and grated

1 small fresh red chilli, deseeded and finely chopped

1 bunch of fresh coriander

1 x 400ml tin of coconut milk

100ml chicken stock (made from ½ cube)

3 tbsp dark soy sauce

a drizzle of toasted sesame oil

80g cashew nuts

½ cucumber, cut into ribbons with a peeler

Preheat the oven to 180°C.

Put the pork, breadcrumbs, egg, spring onions, garlic, ginger, chilli, half of the coriander (including the stalks) and some salt and pepper in a food processor. Pulse a few times until everything comes together. Don't overblend the mix, otherwise it will become pasty.

Mix the coconut milk, stock and soy sauce together and pour into a shallow casserole or baking dish.

Divide the pork mix into 12 and roll into meatballs. (If the mixture is too soft, just put it in the fridge for a little while to firm up.) Put them in the coconut milk mixture, all in one layer if possible. Drizzle a little sesame oil over each one. Cook in the oven for 25 minutes, until the meatballs are cooked through.

Serve over jasmine rice with the cashew nuts, strips of cucumber and the remaining coriander picked over the top.

CHILLI CALZONES WITH SMOKED JALAPEÑO SOUR CREAM

MAKES 6

FOR THE CHILLI:

3 tbsp sunflower oil

500g lean beef mince

1 large onion, finely diced

3 garlic cloves, sliced

2 tsp plain flour

2 tsp ground cumin

1 tsp ground coriander

½ tsp chilli powder

300ml concentrated beef stock

1 x 400g tin of chopped tomatoes

1 x 400g tin of kidney beans, drained and rinsed

1 tbsp tomato purée

2 tbsp Worcestershire sauce

2 tbsp maple syrup

1 tsp dried oregano

FOR THE DOUGH:

300ml cold water

1 x 7g sachet of fast-acting dried yeast

500g '00' or strong white flour, plus extra for dusting

1 tsp salt

FOR THE EGG WASH:

1 egg beaten with 1 tbsp milk

FOR THE SOUR CREAM:

200g sour cream

50g jalapeño peppers, finely chopped

a dash of smoked chipotle Tabasco sauce

To make the dough, put 200ml of the cold water in a jug. Boil the kettle and add another 100ml. This will give the perfect temperature for the yeast. Stir in the yeast and let it activate for 5 minutes, until frothy.

Put the flour and salt in a large bowl (or the bowl of a stand mixer fitted with the dough hook), then slowly add the liquid, kneading until it all forms a dough. Continue to knead for 5–6 minutes more, then cover the bowl with cling film. Allow to prove in a warm place for 1 hour, until the dough has doubled in size.

Dust a surface with flour. Knock back the dough, then divide it evenly into six balls. Put the balls on a floured baking tray, cover and put in the fridge.

To make the chilli, heat the oil in a large saucepan over a high heat. Add the mince and onion and cook for 10 minutes or so, squishing the meat against the sides of the pan to break it up.

Reduce the heat, then add the garlic, flour and spices and continue to cook for another 5 minutes before adding the stock, tomatoes, kidney beans, tomato purée, Worcestershire sauce, maple syrup and oregano. Cook, uncovered, over a gentle heat for 45 minutes, until it's thick and glossy. Season and allow to cool. It needs to be cold to work with.

Preheat the oven to 200°C. Line a baking tray with parchment paper.

Take the dough balls out of the fridge. Allow them to sit at room temperature and prove a little more, then roll them out one by one on a floured surface.

Put an even amount of chilli on the top third of the dough. Brush the edge with a little egg wash, then fold over the dough to seal the calzone, making sure there is no air trapped inside.

Transfer to the lined tray, leaving space between the calzones. Repeat with the remaining dough and chilli filling. Brush the tops of the calzones with egg wash, then bake in the oven for 25–30 minutes, until puffed and crisp.

Mix the sour cream with the jalapeño peppers and Tabasco and chill in the fridge.

Serve the chilled jalapeño sour cream alongside the calzones.

CHICKEN THIGHS WITH HONEY AND CHERMOULA

SERVES 4

2 tbsp sunflower oil

12 boneless, skinless chicken thighs

2 tbsp honey

FOR THE CHERMOULA:

50g fresh coriander

50g fresh parsley

2 garlic cloves, sliced

1 small fresh green chilli, deseeded and sliced

80ml olive oil, plus extra for drizzling

zest of 1 lemon

1 tbsp mint sauce

½ tsp ground cumin

½ tsp ground coriander

Put all the ingredients for the chermoula in a liquidizer and blend until smooth.

Heat the sunflower oil in a pan over a medium heat until it's gently smoking. Add the chicken thighs and colour for 6–7 minutes before adding the honey. Continue to cook over a medium heat for another 6–7 minutes, until the chicken is cooked through (this will depend on the thickness of the chicken).

Season and serve with the chermoula.

The best cooks have the confidence to adapt.

16 MAY 2020

Back in the game

26 JUNE 2021

It's all taken off like a rocket, from zero to me running around like a headless chicken as if the last six months had never happened. I was rusty but snapped back into it.

We are very busy so I'm not complaining. People are clamouring to be looked after and are generally good-humoured.

The intersection just outside our restaurant resembles the Shibuya Crossing in Tokyo. It can take an inordinate amount of time to get to our guest rooms, which normally can be reached in less than 60 seconds. What a transformation from when we first opened up all those years ago.

I've done my first cookery class in over a year in the school. It felt strange but good. The people had waited a long time, interminably patient due to all the unavoidable cancellations. The course was seafood and sauces, possibly my favourite course to teach.

Summertime by the sea is all about fish. I simply can't get my head around people who don't love it — look at all they're missing! I love bold flavours. Not over the top like a boorish alpha male, just assertive and true. You have to be in no doubt what you're eating. But pleasure is the goal, of course.

I have to watch my use of chorizo, as I would put it in everything. But here there seemed to be no better partner for the robust monkfish. It's an easy dish. A little dollop of mashed potato would be perfect or rice to keep it lighter.

I've brushed bacon ribs with mustard, then dusted them with breadcrumbs and enhanced them with a drizzle of maple syrup, another favourite of mine. The sweetcorn is pilfered. I saw a mouth-watering Instagram photo from Chicc, an amazing food truck in Dublin. I spent what seemed like hours trying to figure out what was on it. In the end, I guessed. I'll have to pay them a visit.

The last dish is a hybrid tapenade. The hot spiced chickpeas elevate it to something much more than a dip. It's fun to play around with your spices. I'm using za'atar for a floral touch and cayenne for heat.

BAKED MONKFISH WITH SMOKY TOMATOES, ROSEMARY AND CHORIZO

SERVES 4

3 tbsp olive oil

3 garlic cloves, sliced

2 x 400g tins of chopped tomatoes

100ml concentrated chicken stock

2 strips of orange peel

juice of 1 orange

1 tbsp tomato purée

1 tbsp honey

1 tsp smoked paprika

a splash of sherry if you have it

500g trimmed monkfish tail

200g dry-cured chorizo

1 x 125g packet of mixed baby tomatoes

2 sprigs of fresh rosemary

Preheat the oven to 185°C.

Heat the oil in a saucepan over a low heat. Add the sliced garlic and cook until evenly light golden. Add the tomatoes, stock, orange peel and juice, tomato purée, honey, smoked paprika and sherry (if using), then cook until the sauce is reduced by one-third. Season.

Put the sauce in a shallow casserole or baking dish. Cut the monkfish into 3cm chunks. Remove the skin from the chorizo as best you can and cut into 2cm chunks at an angle.

Alternate the monkfish and chorizo in the casserole or dish, then intersperse the tomatoes and rosemary. Bake in the oven for 25 minutes or so, until the monkfish is cooked. Serve straight to the table.

CRISP RACK OF BACON RIBS WITH MESSY AND DELICIOUS SWEETCORN

SERVES 4

2 x 500g racks of bacon ribs
2 tbsp Dijon mustard
a generous drizzle of maple syrup
120g dried breadcrumbs
a drizzle of rapeseed oil

FOR THE SWEETCORN:
4 fresh or cooked corn on the cob
4 tbsp ready-cooked crispy fried onions
2 tbsp chopped fresh chives
1 tsp smoked paprika
4 tbsp sour cream
coarse sea salt

Simmer the bacon racks in a large pot of water for 90 minutes or so, until tender. You may have to cut them in half to fit in your pot.

Preheat the oven to 200°C.

Remove the ribs from the pot and drain, then transfer to a foil-lined baking tray. Brush with the mustard and drizzle with maple syrup, then dust generously with the breadcrumbs. Drizzle rapeseed oil over the top of the breadcrumbs. Cook in the oven for 15–20 minutes, until crisp and golden.

Meanwhile, cook the corn in lightly salted boiling water for 10 minutes. (Ready-cooked corn just needs reheating for a couple of minutes.)

Mix the crispy onions, chives, smoked paprika and some coarse sea salt and pepper together on a plate.

Drain the corn on kitchen paper. Smear with the sour cream, then roll it in the coating. Serve straightaway with the bacon ribs.

GOAT CHEESE AND TAPENADE WITH HOT SPICED CHICKPEAS

SERVES 8

200g stoned green olives

150g soft rindless goat cheese

1 garlic clove, sliced

2 tbsp olive oil

a drizzle of honey

100ml sunflower oil

1 x 400g tin of chickpeas, drained, rinsed and patted dry

1 tbsp za'atar or ground cumin

½ tsp cayenne pepper

Blend the olives, goat cheese, garlic, oil, honey and a few twists of black pepper in a food processor until smooth.

Heat the sunflower oil in a pan over a high heat until it's gently smoking. Carefully add the chickpeas to the oil and cook for 10 minutes or so, until golden and crispy.

Drain the chickpeas through a sieve and put on kitchen paper. Season with the za'atar, cayenne and a little salt, then serve as soon as you can with the tapenade.

This is the way I love to cook in summer

03 JULY 2021

The full return of hospitality is only days away. Reopening this time was particularly challenging.

Innovation has been important. A successful business cannot stand still. The things we want now are not what we wanted 20 years ago. Who would have guessed that I would be moonlighting as maître d' of a hot dog cart?

Talking to some of my contemporaries, many feel the same. We're all getting older and the bones aren't so forgiving. The hangovers are less frequent but more assertive. There has been a lot of reflection.

We carry on because we still take pride in our business but also because we have to. Being self-employed has many benefits but it also has many downsides. The buck always stops with you. So we've resolved to mind ourselves and our staff. The decision to only open the restaurant five days a week in what will be a massively busy summer has been huge. The rooms remain open for seven. It just means that it's one team, days off together, so they — we — can wind down and get to the other side intact.

I'm mostly on an Italian vegetable vibe this week. This is the way I love to cook in summer. It's lighter, the colours pop and dazzle and the flavours transport you.

This peperonata dish is vibrant and tasty. I've added puff pastry (any excuse) and some tangy creaminess with the feta. Let the peppers cook slowly, it makes all the difference.

I've got a bit of a crush on polenta at the moment. It's the ease of it and the fact that it takes on other flavours so well. It's a beautiful blank canvas. There's a bit of knife work in the caponata. Take your time to get it right. I'm using the lovely Knockalara sheep cheese from just down the road. A creamy goat cheese will do to complement the rocket. How very 1990s of me.

Ottolenghi turned me on to quinoa. I've added 'nduja into the mix but you can leave it out, of course. For those of you who are curious, it brings a delicious porky heat to the affair without bullying the quinoa.

PEPERONATA PUFF PIE WITH FETA AND OLIVES

SERVES 6

50ml olive oil

2 onions, sliced

2 red peppers, sliced

2 yellow peppers, sliced

2 garlic cloves, sliced

1 tsp ground cumin

1 tsp ground coriander

1 x 400g tin of chopped tomatoes

1 tbsp honey

a pinch of chilli flakes

200g feta cheese

16 large olives, stoned and roughly chopped

1 x 320g packet of ready-rolled puff pastry, thawed

1 egg beaten with 1 tbsp milk

Heat the oil in a saucepan over a medium heat. Add the onions, peppers and garlic, cover and cook gently for 20 minutes, until everything softens.

Add the cumin and coriander and continue to cook for a further 10 minutes, uncovered.

Add the tomatoes, honey and chilli flakes. Cook a little longer, until the mixture gets sticky. Season and transfer to a baking dish. Crumble the feta over the top, followed by the olives. Allow to cool.

Preheat the oven to 185°C.

Unfold the pastry (it will be easier if you let it come up to room temperature), then lay it over the top of the baking dish. Brush with the beaten egg and score the pastry lightly to make an attractive pattern. Scatter a few more chilli flakes over the top for effect. Bake in the oven for 30 minutes, until golden.

Serve with a crisp green salad.

SOFT SMOKY POLENTA WITH EASY CAPONATA AND KNOCKALARA CHEESE

SERVES 4

FOR THE CAPONATA:

50g raisins

4 tbsp olive oil

1 red onion, cut into 1cm dice

2 garlic cloves, sliced

1 aubergine, finely diced

1 sprig of fresh thyme

1 tsp ground cumin

2 tbsp small capers

2 tbsp red wine vinegar

a drizzle of honey

FOR THE POLENTA:

150ml milk

100ml water

1 tsp smoked paprika

100g instant polenta

50g Parmesan cheese, grated

1 tsp butter

TO FINISH:

150g Knockalara sheep cheese or another creamy cheese

a handful of rocket

Soak the raisins in a bowl of just-boiled water for 15 minutes to plump them up, then drain.

While the raisins are soaking, heat the oil in a saucepan over a low heat. Add the onion and garlic and cook for 5 minutes. Turn the heat up to medium and add the aubergine, thyme and cumin. Cook for 15–20 minutes, until the aubergine completely softens. Add the drained raisins along with the capers, vinegar, honey and some salt and pepper. Cook for 5 more minutes to allow the flavours to come together, then set aside.

Meanwhile, bring the milk, water and smoked paprika to a simmer in a large saucepan. Add the polenta in a thin drizzle and cook, stirring occasionally, for 3–4 minutes before adding the Parmesan, butter and seasoning. It shouldn't be too stiff but if it is, add a little more milk.

Serve on warm plates with the caponata, sheep cheese and rocket on top.

STUFFED AUBERGINES WITH FENNEL, QUINOA AND 'NDUJA

SERVES 4

2 aubergines

1 fennel bulb

50ml olive oil, plus extra for drizzling

2 garlic cloves

1 sprig of fresh rosemary, finely chopped

100g 'nduja, chopped

6 dried apricots, chopped

150g tricolour quinoa

450ml lightly salted water

a squeeze of lemon

Cut the aubergines in half lengthways, then carefully cut out the flesh as best you can with a vegetable knife, leaving a 1cm-thick shell.

Chop the flesh into fine dice, then trim and dice the fennel the same size.

Heat the oil in a saucepan over a medium heat. Add the garlic and rosemary and cook for 2 minutes, then add the diced aubergine and fennel. Cover and cook for about 15 minutes, until everything starts to soften, stirring occasionally and taking care that it doesn't colour.

Add the 'nduja and apricots, cook for a further 10 minutes, season and set aside. It should all be melting and glossy.

Meanwhile, bring the salted water to a boil. Add the quinoa and cook for 12–15 minutes, until just soft. Drain off any excess water, then add the quinoa to the aubergine mixture in the pan and season.

Drizzle a little oil over the raw aubergine shells and season. Spoon the filling into the shells. You can put the stuffed shells in the fridge at this point until needed.

Preheat the oven to 185°C.

Put the stuffed aubergines on a baking tray. Bake in the oven for 30 minutes, until the tops get a little crispy and the skins are cooked.

Serve with a squeeze of lemon and a little salad on the side.

Cuisine paysanne has my heart

10 JULY 2021

It's almost Bastille Day. Some time back I wrote about a joyous restaurant experience I had in the South of France pre-pandemic (see pages 24–25). Auberge de la Môle delivered on my ridiculously high expectations. The friends had been talking about it for years and I was crippled with jealously. I finally got there and ate in a bistro straight out of central casting. Abundant terrines, perfect confit de canard with sauté potatoes and persillade, mousse au chocolate and the most ethereal of creme caramels. What I wouldn't give to be there now.

I crave French country cooking like this. It is the mothership. It's not the overworked food of a hushed, intimidating, three-star restaurant that I want, but the crackle of Brasserie Lipp or the exquisite intimacy of Bistro Paul Bert. I prefer the haute left out of my cuisine. Cuisine paysanne – the food of the people, rustic, delicious and world famous – has my heart.

These dishes are only a flicker of what French food can offer. I sometimes imagine I'm Rick Stein in the bucolic depths of *Secret France* or on that barge put-putting on the Canal du Midi eating all the way down to Sète. What a dream.

The first two are from the South of France. Socca is a street food from Nice made from chickpea flour. I've added piment d'espelette to give it a little fire and roasted peppers, anchovies and crème fraîche to make it a dish. If you can't get piment d'espelette, you can use smoked paprika.

The brandade is a perfect example of how to elevate simple ingredients. Salt cod, potatoes, onions, olive oil and garlic are blended together to make one of my favourite French dishes. I'm using fresh cod and salting it myself as salted cod is hard to get here, then pairing it with roasted fennel, a classic combination. O'Connells in the English Market has the real deal if you're anywhere nearby.

I never tire of duck confit. This tart isn't light but it's very special. A green salad will do with it, otherwise you might have to go straight to bed afterwards.

SOCCA WITH PIMENT D'ESPELETTE, PEPPERS AND ANCHOVIES

SERVES 6

100ml olive oil

2 red peppers, thinly sliced

2 garlic cloves, thinly sliced

1 sprig of fresh rosemary

juice of 1 small orange

250g chickpea flour (gram flour)

500ml water

1 tsp piment d'espelette or smoked paprika

200g crème fraîche

as many anchovies as you like

Preheat the oven to 220°C.

Put half of the oil in a saucepan with the peppers, garlic and rosemary. Cover and cook over a gentle heat for 15 minutes, until soft. Add the orange juice, uncover the pan and allow to reduce, then season and set aside.

In a large bowl, combine the chickpea flour, water and piment d'espelette or smoked paprika, season generously and stir to blend.

Brush a non-stick 30cm pizza pan (or a non-stick ovenproof frying pan will do) with some of the remaining oil. Put it in the oven until the oil starts to sizzle, then pour a quarter of the batter into the pan. Bake in the oven for 4–5 minutes, until the batter is set and a little brown around the edges. Keep the pancake warm and repeat with the rest of the batter.

Cut the socca into slices and serve with the peppers, a dollop of crème fraîche and a few anchovies.

COD BRANDADE WITH ROASTED FENNEL AND OLIVES

SERVES 4

1 x 250g piece of skinless cod fillet

1 tsp salt

150ml olive oil

1 garlic clove, thinly sliced

1 small onion, thinly sliced

1 bay leaf (fresh if possible)

250g potatoes, peeled and very thinly sliced

300ml milk

a squeeze of lemon

1 large fennel bulb, quartered (reserve the fronds for garnish)

1 strip of orange peel

1 star anise

50ml water

a few olives

Sprinkle the cod with the salt, cover with cling film and put it in the fridge for 3 hours, then rinse under cold water and cut into chunks.

Preheat the oven to 185°C.

Warm 50ml of the oil in a large saucepan over a gentle heat. Add the garlic, followed by the onion and bay leaf. Cover and cook until the onion is soft and translucent but not coloured.

Add the potatoes and milk, making sure the potatoes are just covered by the milk. Cover with the lid again and simmer over a low heat until the potatoes are thoroughly cooked.

Add the cod and cook for 5 minutes, until it starts to flake. The mixture needs to be sloppy but not too wet.

Remove the bay leaf and season with salt and ground white pepper. Add a little of the remaining oil and the lemon juice and purée with a hand blender.

Meanwhile, put the fennel on a small tray with the orange peel, star anise, water and the remaining oil. Season. Cover and bake in the oven for 20–25 minutes, until the fennel is soft and sweet.

To serve, spread the brandade onto plates. Top with the fennel, olives and a few fennel fronds and pan juices. Serve warm or at room temperature.

DUCK CONFIT TART

SERVES 6

4 confit duck legs

4 eggs

2 garlic cloves, chopped

75ml milk

75ml cream

1 tbsp fresh thyme leaves

a little ground nutmeg

butter, for greasing

1 x 320g sheet of ready-rolled shortcrust pastry, thawed

4 shallots, diced

500g baby potatoes, cooked and sliced

Preheat the oven to 185°C.

Remove the skin and meat from the duck. Discard the skin and chop the meat into rough chunks.

Beat the eggs with the garlic, milk, cream, thyme, nutmeg and some salt and pepper.

Lightly butter a 20–25cm pie dish, then line it with the pastry. You will have to do a little surgery to make it fit but you won't see it in the end.

Add the duck and shallots to the base of the dish, then layer the potatoes over the duck. Pour the egg mix over the top and bake in the oven for 50 minutes, until set. Serve immediately.

Entertaining at home

17 JULY 2021

We have converted a shed into an outside dining area. There was a bit of investment but in the end we have another space to use in which to have people over. We've always been a good house for that. The kitchen has nearly seen as much dancing as eating over the years, although perhaps that's on the wane a bit now as we hurtle towards our dotage.

I was never blessed with the going-to-bed gene, always wanting to squeeze the last few drops out of the night. I'm usually treading the fine line between staying up as late as I possibly can without being found out doing so. The agitated thump of footsteps on the stairs signals an abrupt end to the music.

I get great satisfaction cooking for friends. It's never fancy, always practical. The cooking has to be soothing and part of the enjoyment of the evening. I prefer to cook alone so I can immerse myself in it. It's always family-style, a big pot of something or other that looks impressive and generous. I don't do small portions but I also hate waste – another fine line.

These dishes are meant to go together although they don't have to. The rigatoni is rich. I rarely put cream in my pasta but this really calls for it. Get good sausages and roll them into balls. It won't take long and is worth the effort.

Elderflower and tomato are lovely together. It elevates the simple salad that is all about the best ingredients. Heirloom tomatoes are wonderful, flavourful and craggy. The most important thing is the flavour. There's nothing worse than a disappointing tomato.

I first came across this French bean salad many years ago in dear old Chapter One. Chef Ross Lewis would separate the bean lengthways to make for finer eating but I won't do that to you. It's difficult to find ripe peaches. If you can't find them, use tinned. It will be better. I've added a little coriander seed crumble to the affair to make it my own.

RIGATONI WITH SAUSAGE MEATBALLS, PEPPER CREAM AND THYME

SERVES 4

400g good-quality sausages

4 tsp olive oil

1 red pepper, sliced

1 yellow pepper, sliced

2 garlic cloves, sliced

150ml cream

100ml chicken stock

1 large sprig of fresh thyme

500g rigatoni or penne

a squeeze of lemon

80g Parmesan cheese, grated

Squeeze the meat from the sausages and roll into balls the size of a €2 coin, then put in the fridge to set.

Heat the oil in a large saucepan over a gentle heat. Add the peppers and garlic and cook for 15 minutes, until soft and sticky.

Lift all the peppers and garlic from the pan, leaving the peppery oil. Turn up the heat a little, then add the meatballs. Fry the meatballs for 5 minutes or so, until golden all over, then reintroduce the peppers and garlic to the pan.

Add the cream, stock and thyme and bring to a simmer. Cook for 5 minutes, until the cream has reduced a little and the meatballs are cooked through.

Meanwhile, cook the pasta as per the packet instructions. Drain and add to the sauce, then season and add a little lemon juice.

Serve in warm bowls with lashings of grated Parmesan.

HEIRLOOM TOMATOES WITH BUFFALO MOZZARELLA AND ELDERFLOWER VINAIGRETTE

SERVES 4

600g heirloom tomatoes

4 small or 2 large balls of buffalo mozzarella

1 tbsp capers

a few sprigs of fresh mint

FOR THE VINAIGRETTE:

50ml olive oil

juice of 1 orange

3 tbsp elderflower cordial

3 tbsp white wine vinegar

To make the vinaigrette, whisk the oil, orange juice, cordial and vinegar together.

Slice the tomatoes in an interesting and haphazard way, they will always look better. Tear the mozzarella and divide it among four plates, then arrange the tomatoes alongside. Scatter over the capers, season everything, including the mozzarella, with coarse sea salt and black pepper, then spoon the dressing on top.

Add a few mint leaves for perk, then serve. This would also be lovely on a platter to serve family-style.

FRENCH BEAN, PEACH AND TOASTED ALMOND CRUMBLE

SERVES 4

2 x 200g packets of trimmed French beans
3 ripe peaches

FOR THE DRESSING:
1 shallot, very finely diced
5 tbsp olive oil
2 tbsp red wine vinegar

FOR THE CRUMBLE:
2 tbsp butter
80g dried breadcrumbs
50g flaked almonds
1 tsp coriander seeds

Cook the French beans in boiling salted water for 3–4 minutes, until just tender. Drain and refresh under cold water to cool them down as quickly as possible to keep their colour. Pat dry on a clean tea towel.

Put the shallot in a bowl with the oil, vinegar and some salt and pepper and whisk to combine. Add the beans and turn them in the dressing.

Melt the butter in a pan over a medium heat. When the butter starts to foam, add the breadcrumbs, almonds and coriander seeds. Cook for a few minutes, until golden and crunchy. Remove the pan from the heat and season.

Cut the peaches into large chunks and divide among four plates or put them all on one serving platter. Position the beans on top, then spoon over the crumble.

My favourite pairing for food has always been music

There are many things I've missed during all this. It's not just the hopping on a plane to go on holiday. It's the everyday, almost mundane, stuff that I've missed the most. The hustle and bustle on the streets, the chance encounters with friends, the midweek man gatherings in Downey's.

I'm looking forward to going to a gig in Dublin like a man waiting to get out of prison. I'll meet a likeminded gang in Grogans for pints and toasties just to warm up. We'll head to the Olympia, do a bit of age-inappropriate jumping around. A hardy one or two will head up to Whelan's with me for a shimmy. On the way home I might pop into the Globe just to suspend the reality of a night that's nearly over or head straight to Charlie's on George's Street for pork belly before I go around the corner to bed down for a few hours in the Central Hotel.

The next morning in reception, Isobel will give me a wry eye. 'Well, Mr Flynn, how late were you?'

'Late enough, Isobel,' I'll smile, not giving anything away. 'See you next time.'

Food and music have always been intertwined for me. In my London days, after-service forays to Borderline off Oxford Street or Powerhouse in the Angel were essential to keep my head straight. The madness of the Mean Fiddler was left until the weekend. The beautiful, sweaty chaos of a Sunday lunch gig there is engraved in me. You'd meet half of Ireland. The last song was always 'Loaded' by Primal Scream. Then we were spewed out, blinking into the afternoon Harlesden sunlight and the reality of the oncoming week.

The Central Hotel became my Dublin base on my mostly solo trips (I have a patient wife). It was rough around the edges, like a dear old friend who's lost his way. I loved going through its doors almost as much as I looked forward to leaving them behind, exiting onto Exchequer Street right into the middle of everything. The morning after always followed the same routine: a browse round Fallon and Byrne and a coffee, then I'd eventually make my way home.

During my trips, I might venture up to Eatyard behind the old Bernard Shaw on Richmond Street, where wall-to-wall hipsters nested. There was a lot of beard gazing but the vibe was cool and relaxed. I knew I'd landed in Dublin.

There would be eager chats with friends beforehand. Would we go to Etto for mussels? Or Uno Mas for tortilla and flan de queso? Before Hall & Oates a few years ago, we went to San Lorenzo on George's Street just around the corner from the Olympia, all of us 1980s kids. The pasta fortified us. Mrs Flynn sang along and stared up at Daryl Hall all doe-eyed. I'm fully convinced she would have run off with him in a heartbeat. It was 'So Close' but in fairness he's a very cool man. I understood.

I couldn't really go all Henry VIII with the restaurants unless she was with me, though. That would be like poking the dragon. The envy could quickly morph into resentment and my wings might be clipped. It was always a delicate balance worthy of the negotiating skills of Boutros Boutros-Ghali.

A visit to Dax before U2 was special. Perhaps it's a sign of our age that this is what we want before a gig, but I was all over those lobster-stuffed courgette flowers. Margarita Mondays in 777 after Sigrid was memorable for tacos and the many, many margaritas, but surely it's the case that you have to drink twice the amount if they are half the price. There were even a couple of post-gig trips to the George, where the pretty boys always got served before me. I understood, eventually.

Our favourite pre-gig venue is Locks for Sunday lunch. They made us feel special. We'd walk through Portobello half-wishing we lived there. Relatives and friends flew in to see the Cure and the National on different occasions. We started with the dinkiest oysters with brunoise of apple and elderflower vinegar. Their ethereal whipped chicken livers and the memory of those days, with the sun streaming in the window, are still with me.

Upon reflection, my last night in the Central, just before the first lockdown, was rather special. I was supposed to go to China Crisis (the most aptly named band ever), which was cancelled on the way up, but that didn't deter me. Three of us ate all kinds of delicious in Clanbrassil House. I walked back to the hotel. The streets were quiet. Then on Camden Street I saw a fox on the other side of the road, just sauntering home, like me. Maybe he knew. We walked for a while together, eyeing each other up. I took a photo, then we parted ways.

The next morning, I showed Isobel. 'Ah, Mr Flynn, there's a pair of you in it,' she said.

That was my last night in the Central. It closed shortly afterwards, unannounced. It will be given a glitzy makeover and become a Hoxton, but for me, my adventures in Dublin will never be the same.

Dublin lunch set my mind to pairing fish and meat as I had a few creamy pints

24 JULY 2021

I was in Dublin yesterday. It felt good to be walking around my old stomping ground of the South William Street area again. The sun was out and thankfully there wasn't a single marauding youth to be seen. Change was evident from the last time I was there – more outside tables and a sense of cautious joy.

It was a family day out, allowing everyone a bit of time to shop. My clothing needs were put at the top of the list, as unlike others I never had the luxury of my own DPD man during the pandemic. This is a frightening prospect as I've never been comfortable when my wife takes over my styling. That, for me, is a capitulation of one's masculinity. On the other hand, if it were left up to me I'd happily shop in symphony with the odd eclipse. I was becoming ragged.

We went for lunch. I had my eye on the scallops with corn cream and crispy chicken skin. They were lovely but it got me thinking. I've never been entirely sure of the idea of surf and turf. I needed to go to Grogans to settle the nerves and think it through over a couple of creamy pints.

I associate lobster with summertime and trips down to Boatstrand on the Copper Coast. I'm pairing it simply with Ibérico ham and butter. Its flavour is deep and intense and its heavenly fat melts on your tongue. If you can't get it, use Serrano or Parma ham – just look for a deep colour as that reflects the intensity. Sea beet is a favourite of mine but use asparagus if you're not feeling forage-y.

Korean gochujang paste is a revelation. Sweet and hot, it goes with clams like a dream. I was looking for chicken wings but they were scrawny and miserable so I settled for drumsticks. Apologies if a few ingredients are hard to get. If you can't find the paste, use 2 tablespoons of harissa and white wine will work instead of the mirin.

This frittata is a handy, satisfying number. The crab cream elevates it but it would also be good on brown bread on its own.

GRILLED LOBSTER WITH IBÉRICO BUTTER AND SEA BEET
SERVES 2

1 x 1kg lobster
100g Ibérico ham, finely chopped
200g butter, softened
sea beet or asparagus
a squeeze of lemon

I'm using a large lobster so half is plenty for one person, especially when there is a generous coating of butter. It's important to treat the lobster humanely, so put it in the freezer for 30 minutes to render it insensible. Dispatch the lobster as quickly as possible by piercing its head with a large knife at the cross in the centre of its head. This is not an easy business but you have to be determined.

Plunge the lobster into a large pot of boiling salted water, cover and cook for 16 minutes. I'm slightly undercooking the lobster to allow me to grill it with the butter later. Remove from the water (keep the water in the pot) and allow to cool on a tray.

Mix the finely chopped ham through the butter.

Blanch the sea beet or asparagus in the lobster water for 30 seconds, then refresh under cold water to keep its colour.

Split the lobster down the middle with a heavy knife and crack the claws with a hammer. Remove any unwanted material from the meat, then smear the butter generously over the lobster. At this point you can put it in the fridge until you're ready to eat.

Preheat the grill.

Cook the lobster under the grill for 5–6 minutes, until the butter is bubbling.

Dredge the sea beet through the butter, then serve with whatever accompaniments you fancy and a squeeze of lemon.

GOCHUJANG CHICKEN DRUMSTICKS WITH SWEET AND SOUR CLAMS

SERVES 4

1kg chicken drumsticks

3 tbsp gochujang Korean chilli paste

a drizzle of sunflower oil

1kg clams, washed

50ml mirin

30ml rice wine vinegar

1 tsp caster sugar

1 tsp grated fresh ginger

1 tsp toasted sesame oil

a few sprigs of fresh coriander

Trim the knuckles off the drumsticks with a heavy knife (this is optional but it does make them daintier), then put the drumsticks in a large ziplock bag with the gochujang and a little sunflower oil. Squish everything together and marinate in the fridge for 3–4 hours.

Preheat the oven to 185°C.

Put the drumsticks in a roasting tin and cook in the oven for 30 minutes, turning once during cooking.

When the chicken is done, put the rest of the ingredients in a large pot, cover and cook for 2–3 minutes over a very high heat, until the clams open.

Serve immediately over the drumsticks, making sure you get every bit of juice from the pot.

PEA AND BACON FRITTATA WITH CRAB CRÈME FRAÎCHE
SERVES 6

1 tbsp butter

a drizzle of sunflower oil

125g smoked bacon lardons

1 bunch of spring onions, chopped

500g baby potatoes, cooked, left unpeeled and sliced

100g frozen petits pois, defrosted

8 eggs beaten with a little milk

3 tbsp grated Parmesan cheese

100g crab meat

200ml crème fraîche

1 tbsp horseradish sauce

Preheat the oven to 190°C.

Heat the butter and oil in an ovenproof non-stick frying pan over a medium heat. When the butter starts to foam, add the lardons and cook for 5 minutes or so, then add half of the spring onions along with the sliced cooked potatoes and the peas. Cook for another 2 minutes, then add the eggs beaten with a little milk and some salt and pepper, keeping the pan over the heat while you mix everything together. Scatter the Parmesan over the top, then put the pan in the oven to cook for 20 minutes.

Meanwhile, pick through the crab to make sure there is no shell, then mix the meat with the crème fraîche, horseradish and the remaining spring onions. Season.

You can serve this straight out of the pan with the crab cream melting over the top or allow it to cool, turn it out and cut it into wedges. Either way is delicious.

Raw revolution

31 JULY 2021

It took me years to come around to raw food. My generation of Irish was not conditioned for it. In most of our houses the mantra would have been the opposite, the recipes mostly taken from *Boiled to Bejaysus: The Cookbook*.

I first had carpaccio of beef in London's swanky Le Caprice in the 1980s while trying to impress an even swankier girlfriend. It reluctantly slipped down my gullet as if it knew it was wasted on me. I came around shortly after as my more urbane sensibilities came to the fore.

A cooked oyster with blue cheese put me off oysters for years. The notion of those two together should have made the chef hang up his whites in shame. I only became a convert when a surprise platter of them appeared in front of us in Bentley's one evening, accompanied by a looming Richard Corrigan. You don't say no to Richard so I necked them like a pro. They were a revelation and I've been a convert ever since.

While I was a budding chef I found myself working for the wonderful Rowley Leigh in Le Poulbot, a Roux Brothers restaurant in the city of London. He had a tuna tataki on the menu and it was my job to prepare it. I tentatively tasted morsels to check the seasoning and gradually turned a corner, as if my brain finally acquiesced and gave me permission to enjoy it.

This is a delicious gazpacho. The verdancy of it is important, hence the name. Eat it on a rare hot day and count your blessings.

The freshest mackerel is a brilliant substitute for tuna. It's a delicate affair, give it a go. Let the fishmonger do the filleting but still check for bones and you'll love it. The seasonings are subtle. The pickled ginger and soy cure the mackerel, alleviating any worries you might have about its raw state.

My love for carpaccio long outlasted the girlfriend. The beef should be gossamer thin. This recipe is different from the ubiquitous rocket and Parmesan accompaniment. The texture of the vegetables along with the dressing is a crisp and creamy foil.

A GREEN AND GOOD GAZPACHO

SERVES 6

2 ripe avocados, stoned and flesh removed

1 cucumber, peeled and sliced

3 spring onions, chopped

150g frozen petits pois, broken up (helps keep the colour)

10 fresh mint leaves, plus extra torn leaves to garnish

zest and juice of 1 lime

400ml apple juice

50ml olive oil

a swirl of natural yogurt

a drizzle of extra virgin olive oil

Blend the avocados, cucumber, spring onions, peas, mint, lime zest and juice, apple juice and oil together and chill.

When you're ready to eat, serve the gazpacho in pretty bowls or china cups with a swirl of natural yogurt and a drizzle of good extra virgin olive oil on top.

MACKEREL TATAKI

SERVES 2

350g mackerel fillets (200g when all the skin and bones have been removed)

½ tsp finely diced fresh red chilli

1 tsp toasted sesame oil

½ tbsp finely chopped pickled ginger

2 tbsp light soy sauce

1 spring onion, finely chopped

a little black pepper

1 tsp toasted sesame seeds

Mix all the ingredients except for the sesame seeds together (I haven't added salt as the soy sauce will season it). Chill for 1 hour.

Serve with the sesame seeds sprinkled on top and some brown toast on the side.

BEEF CARPACCIO WITH RAW VEGETABLES AND HERBED CRÈME FRAÎCHE

SERVES 2

1 fillet steak, trimmed of all sinew

3 tbsp light crème fraîche

1 small shallot, finely diced

1 tbsp chopped fresh chives or chervil, plus extra to garnish

½ tbsp chopped fresh tarragon, plus extra to garnish

1 tsp red wine vinegar

1 x 200g packet of snack (baby) carrots

4 radishes, sliced

a drizzle of rapeseed oil

Put the steak in the freezer for 15 minutes. This firms it up and makes it easier to slice. Cut the steak into six slices across its circumference.

Put three slices on parchment, slightly overlapping the slices. Cover with another piece of parchment, then bat gently with a rolling pin until the beef is thin and even. Repeat for the other slices, then chill.

Mix the crème fraîche with the shallot, herbs and vinegar in a large bowl, then season. Add the vegetables to the dressing, then turn everything together to coat.

To serve, overturn the beef onto two plates and peel off the parchment. Divide the vegetables between the two plates, drizzle over a little rapeseed oil and garnish with a few extra herbs.

Food trucks have come a long way from the greasy burger van of old

07 AUGUST 2021

I've started filming a new television series due to be released next spring. Every Monday and Tuesday for the foreseeable I'll be going around the country filming *Paul Flynn's Food Truck Favourites*, capturing the best of this new Irish phenomenon. I even get to play in my very own food truck for a while so I can drag out my cooler, more casual alter ego, Paulie.

I've long being fascinated with food trucks. After all, I started out in a chip van when I was 15. That certainly wasn't a vocation but it did give me a sense of freedom and the money to bulk up my record collection. That nomadic feeling was never available in a Michelin-starred kitchen. The greasy burgers that were being dispensed back then are a million miles from the fabulous inventiveness of today's cool food trucks. I'm looking forward to the adventure.

Today's dishes are all about the height of summer. I hadn't come across Bomba rice in an Irish supermarket until recently. Since then it's been like a Bomba festival in our house. Use Arborio if you can't get it. The method is to let it boil, spit and bubble like a paella. It's not the silky smooth amalgamation of a risotto. I'm serving this with a simple aioli. They are a compelling combination.

The last time I ate devilled eggs was in the brilliant Spitalfields in Dublin As an egg fan I had high hopes when I ordered them but theirs were stratospheric. It just goes to show that in skilled hands, even the simplest ingredients can be sublime. I'm going off-piste here and making a devilled egg dressing to go with Little Gem lettuce, baby potatoes and spring onion – a feisty partnership.

The salmon dish is a warm salad. I'm baking the fish then breaking it up in the tray and mixing it with courgettes, butter beans, lemon and dill. It's all a bit rugged but very tasty. Served on a large platter, it makes for the perfect summer lunch.

CHICKEN AND CHORIZO BOMBA

SERVES 6

4 tbsp olive oil, plus a little extra for drizzling

2 red onions, diced

2 garlic cloves, sliced

100g dry-cured chorizo, sliced

8 skinless, boneless chicken thighs, diced into 3cm pieces

300g Bomba or Arborio risotto rice

1 x 400g tin of chopped tomatoes

900ml chicken stock

1 sprig of fresh thyme

½ tbsp smoked paprika

2 strips of orange peel

juice of 1 orange

1 large or 2 medium courgettes, thinly sliced

FOR THE AIOLI:

2 egg yolks, at room temperature

1 large garlic clove, finely grated

juice of ½ lemon

1 tsp Dijon mustard

250ml sunflower oil

50ml olive oil

Heat the oil in a large saucepan over a gentle heat. Add the onions and garlic and cook for 5 minutes, then add the chorizo and chicken. Cook for a little longer to allow the oil to render out from the chorizo, then add the rice, tomatoes, stock, thyme, paprika, orange peel and juice and some salt and pepper. Bring up to a bubble and simmer for 18–20 minutes, until all the liquid has nearly evaporated.

Overlap the sliced courgette evenly across the top of the rice. Drizzle over a little oil, cover and turn off the heat to allow the courgette to steam for 5 minutes.

For the aioli, put the egg yolks in a bowl with the garlic, lemon juice, mustard and some salt and ground white pepper. Put the bowl on top of a folded tea towel and slowly whisk in the sunflower oil in a thin stream, little by little, until it is all emulsified, then whisk in the olive oil. Add a little more lemon juice to taste. Keep in the fridge until needed – it will happily last for a few days.

I love to serve this straight to the table with the aioli on the side to dollop on top.

LITTLE GEMS WITH BABY POTATOES AND DEVILLED EGG AND SPRING ONION DRESSING
SERVES 4

12 baby potatoes, boiled, peeled and halved
4 heads of Little Gem lettuce, leaves separated
½ tsp paprika

FOR THE DRESSING:
6 eggs
3 spring onions, thinly sliced
100ml cream
2 tbsp olive oil
1 tsp prepared English mustard
a few drops of Tabasco sauce

Cook the eggs in boiling water for 6 minutes precisely. Refresh under cold water, then peel and mash with a fork. Whisk in the spring onions, cream, oil, mustard, Tabasco and some salt and pepper.

Arrange the cooked potatoes on a small platter and top with the Little Gem lettuce leaves. Season and spoon the dressing over the top with a few pinches of paprika to finish.

ROAST SALMON WITH COURGETTE AND BUTTER BEAN SALAD

SERVES 4

80ml olive oil

4 x 100g darnes of salmon, skin removed

a pinch of chilli flakes

2 courgettes

1 x 400g tin of butter beans, drained and rinsed

juice of 1 lemon

2 tbsp chopped fresh dill

a pinch of caster sugar

Preheat the oven to 200°C.

Drizzle a little of the oil on the bottom of a roasting tin and put the salmon on top. Pour over the rest of the oil, season and add the chilli flakes. Roast the salmon in the oven for 12 minutes. I like the salmon to be a little pink in the centre but you can leave it in a little longer if you prefer.

Meanwhile, wash the courgettes and pat them dry, then peel off strips lengthways with a vegetable peeler, leaving the central core.

When the salmon is done, add the courgette ribbons to the hot tin and turn them in the oily juices so they wilt a little. Add the butter beans, lemon, dill and sugar and season with salt and pepper.

Break the salmon up gently with a fork and mix it in. Serve at room temperature.

I still love a rough-and-ready picnic but today I'm going posh

14 AUGUST 2021

My memories of day trips with my family when I was younger are of a number of us squeezed into the back of my father's VW Beetle, coughing all the way to our destination through my father's pipe smoke that toxically married with my mother's cigarette smoke. We'd emerge from the car spluttering and relieved, as if we had been immersed in a Dickensian fug for the duration of the journey. It cured me of any desire to smoke, so in a way they were doing me a great favour.

We never ventured too far. Having their own business meant my parents were wedded to it. Sundays and half-day Thursdays were the only times they could take us away to visit cousins at the homeplace, Fallagh, the farm outside Kilmacthomas or visit my father's friend who happened to be a monk in Mount Melleray Abbey. Despite being religiously indifferent, I still have a great fondness for that unique place.

We spent endless summer days camping and getting sunburned on Clonea beach, eating soggy tomato sandwiches and grilling sausages. I still love a rough-and-ready picnic. Sandwiches pulled out of a rucksack after a hike always taste like heaven, especially if there's a view. Egg sandwiches predominate in our house. We never tire of them. Coupled with a packet of crisps, a few biscuits and tea out of a flask, it's a taste of summer.

Today I'm going posh. I possess a very nice picnic basket, full of nice glasses, cutlery and china. It's a once-in-a-blue-moon sort of thing but the food needs to complement it.

The noodle salad is full of flavour. It's a world away from soggy tomato sandwiches.

I'm mixing dainty, everyday frozen prawns with avocado, herbs and crème fraîche. Paired with a brioche roll, it's luxuriously delicious. I'm also giving you a recipe for soft white rolls if you fancy a bit of an extra challenge.

The next salad is a pared-down panzanella. The bread soaks up the roasting juices of the peppers. It's an upmarket version of the tomato sandwiches of my youth.

CHICKEN NOODLE SALAD WITH PEANUT AND CUCUMBER SAUCE

SERVES 4

1 tbsp sesame oil

4 boneless chicken thighs

300g thin Chinese egg noodles

FOR THE SAUCE:

100ml soy sauce

2 tbsp caster sugar

2 tbsp Thai fish sauce

2 tbsp water

½ cucumber, peeled and cut into 0.5cm dice

2cm piece of ginger, peeled and grated

1 fresh red chilli, deseeded and finely diced

1 bunch of fresh coriander, roughly chopped (including the stalks)

zest and juice of 1 lime

4 tbsp salted roasted peanuts, chopped

2 tbsp sweet chilli sauce

1 tsp mint sauce

Put the sesame oil in a hot frying pan over a medium-high heat. Add the chicken thighs, season and cook for 12–15 minutes, until cooked through. Remove the pan from the heat. When cool, chop the chicken.

Add the soy sauce, sugar, fish sauce and water to the pan while it's still warm to ensure the sugar dissolves, then add the cucumber, ginger, chilli, coriander, lime zest and juice, peanuts, sweet chilli sauce and mint sauce. Set aside.

Cook the noodles in a pot of boiling water according to the packet instructions. When the noodles are al dente, drain in a colander and refresh under cold water to make sure they don't stick together.

Put the noodles in a bowl, add the sauce and toss everything together. Chill for an hour or so and it's ready for your picnic.

PRAWN AND AVOCADO ROLLS

SERVES 4

250g frozen small prawns, thawed

200g light crème fraîche

1 ripe avocado, diced

½ Granny Smith apple, peeled and finely diced (eat the rest)

juice of ½ lemon

2 tbsp chopped fresh dill

2 tbsp chopped fresh chives

4 brioche rolls

FOR THE ROLLS:

450g strong white flour

50g butter, diced

1 tsp salt

150ml warm water

150ml warm milk (38°C is perfect)

2 x 7g sachets of fast-acting dried yeast

1 tsp caster sugar

If using shop-bought brioche rolls, simply mix all the ingredients together and fill the rolls.

If you want to make your own soft white rolls, sieve the flour into the bowl of a stand mixer, then add the butter and salt and mix together.

Put the water, milk, yeast and sugar in a jug and whisk together. Let it sit for 10 minutes, until frothy.

Fix the dough hook to the stand mixer and turn it on to low. Slowly add the liquid and knead for 5 minutes, until the dough comes cleanly away from the sides of the bowl and is silky and elastic. Cover with cling film and leave in a warm place for about 1 hour to double in size.

Grease and flour two baking sheets. Lightly flour a surface and turn the dough out onto it. Knead for a minute or two, then divide into 12 equal pieces. Shape into fat lengths as evenly as you can. Put six onto each baking sheet. Brush with a little extra milk and dust lightly with more flour. Cover with cling film and allow to prove again for 20–25 minutes.

Preheat the oven to 230°C.

Bake in the oven for 15 minutes, until golden. Transfer to a wire rack to cool. Eat what you need that day and freeze the rest.

ROASTED PEPPER, BREAD AND ORANGE SALAD

SERVES 4

2 red peppers

2 yellow peppers

1 mini ciabatta loaf, torn into pieces

6 tbsp olive oil

1 orange, peeled and cut into segments

12 mixed stoned olives

1 tbsp capers

a few sprigs of fresh basil

Preheat the oven to 200°C.

Put the whole peppers and torn-up ciabatta in a roasting tin, then drizzle the oil over the top. Turn everything in the oil and season generously.

Put the tin in the oven and roast for 15 minutes or so. Remove all the bread when it's golden and crisp but continue to cook the peppers for another few minutes, until they start to char and soften.

Put the peppers in a bowl and cover it with cling film to make them easier to peel and deseed. Retain all the juices.

Cut the peppers into chunks and put in a bowl with the toasted bread, roasted pepper juices, orange segments, olives, capers and basil leaves. It's now ready to be packed for your picnic.

Food doesn't have to be complicated to be sublime

21 AUGUST 2021

Sometimes you might be lucky enough to find yourself in a place that surpasses all expectations with friends who, like me, consider food to be the centre of their world. I was recently asked to be part of Mark Moriarty's show, *Beyond the Menu*. Jess and Dave Murphy from the wonderful Kai in Galway were deservedly being featured.

There was a Big Green Egg positioned on a heavenly pier in Oughterard that hovers over Lough Corrib, a finger pointing to the lake's beauty. It was a perfect evening. My friend Mickael Viljanen, who in many people's opinion is the best chef in Ireland, was there too. A table at the tip of the pier was ours. There will never be a better table.

We prepared the food and had the craic. We immersed ourselves in the cooking. It came as naturally as breathing.

There was Connemara rack of lamb brushed with American mustard and rosemary. A deep glaze appeared as it cooked. Potatoes in their skins were pre-boiled and flung beside the lamb like craggy rocks. The smoke from the fire underneath sweetly penetrated them as they sat there blistering.

Whole monkfish was dismembered unsteadily by me. I blamed the knife, but it was the royal company that made me taut.

Mikey said to cover the fish liberally with Hellman's mayonnaise, like a mother would cover her child in factor 50. It won't stick to the grill and come off it a broken mess. It was a revelation. Best of all was a crab salad. The meat was bound with (more) Hellman's, lemon juice and zest, chives and salt, finished with fennel fronds and olive oil. It was so good because the crab itself was magnificent and also subliminally because the setting was so perfect. I'll write about it next week. Today, I'll focus on those smoky spuds instead. This smoked mackerel butter is lovely with them.

The lamb dish is something I have made at home recently, but at its heart it was inspired by that night on that pier in Lough Corrib.

LAMB CHOPS WITH RAS EL HANOUT TOMATOES, COUSCOUS AND ELDERFLOWER YOGURT

SERVES 4

8 lamb chops

FOR THE COUSCOUS:
200g couscous
300ml hot chicken stock
2 pieces of lemon peel
1 cinnamon stick or a pinch of ground cinnamon

FOR THE TOMATOES:
4 tbsp olive oil
250g mixed baby tomatoes
juice of 1 orange
1 tsp ras el hanout or ground cumin

FOR THE YOGURT:
200ml natural yogurt
2 tbsp elderflower cordial

Heat the barbecue.

Put the couscous in a bowl with the hot chicken stock, lemon, cinnamon and seasoning — be generous with the pepper. Cover with cling film and allow to steam for 10 minutes before forking through.

Season the chops, then cook them on the hot barbecue for 6–7 minutes on each side, until they become charred and crispy.

Meanwhile, heat the oil in a pan over a medium heat. Add the tomatoes, orange juice and ras el hanout or cumin. Season and warm through until the tomatoes start to soften.

Mix the yogurt with the elderflower.

To serve, spoon the couscous onto a platter. Put the chops and tomatoes alongside. The juices from the tomatoes should season and moisten the couscous. Serve the elderflower yogurt on the side.

WHOLE MONKFISH WITH ROSEMARY SALT AND CHARRED LEMONS

SERVES 4

1 x 800g piece of whole monkfish, bone in, skin and sinew removed (get the fishmonger to do this for you)

4 tbsp mayonnaise

2 lemons, halved

a glug of good olive oil

FOR THE SALT:

1 packed egg cup of fresh rosemary leaves

1 egg cup of coarse sea salt

2 egg cups of fine sea salt

Put the rosemary leaves in a food processor or blender with the coarse salt and pulse six or seven times, until the rosemary breaks down but you still have the crunch of the coarse salt. Mix with the fine salt by hand. Spread it out on a tray and allow to dry for a few hours in your kitchen, then put in a sealed jar — it will keep for weeks.

Heat the barbecue.

Brush the monkfish liberally with the mayonnaise, then add a few twists of black pepper. Put the fish on the barbecue, bring the lid down and turn down the heat to medium. If you are using a charcoal barbecue, make sure there is no direct heat or flame underneath the fish.

Cook for 10 minutes, then turn over. Cook for another 5 minutes, then add the lemons to the grill, cut side down. They will caramelise in a short while and add a lovely deep note to the finished dish.

The monkfish is ready when the bone at the thicker part starts to separate from the flesh. Be careful not to overcook it. Another tell-tale sign is if the meat at the thinner end of the tail starts to look dry and starts to break off the bone. Don't be afraid to use a knife at this point to see if it's done.

Remove the monkfish to a serving platter, drizzle over the oil and simply serve with the rosemary salt on the side. Add the charred lemons on the side to squeeze over the top. The smoked potatoes on the next page are the perfect accompaniment. A little aioli or homemade mayo on the side wouldn't go astray if you have it to hand (see the recipe in the simple crab salad on page 427).

SMOKED POTATOES WITH SMOKED MACKEREL BUTTER AND CORNICHONS

SERVES 4

12 new potatoes, scrubbed, steamed and cooled

cornichons

FOR THE BUTTER:

150g butter, softened

200g smoked mackerel fillets

4 spring onions, roughly chopped

zest of 1 lemon

1 tsp horseradish sauce

Put the butter in a bowl. Break up the mackerel, removing the bones and skin, but leave the flesh in reasonably large chunks. Add the spring onions, lemon zest, horseradish and a few twists of black pepper, then fold it all together. This can all be done ahead of time, then rolled into a log in cling film or parchment and put in the fridge.

When you're ready to eat, put the cooked potatoes on a low heat on the barbecue. Cover and cook for 10 minutes or so, turning once or twice.

Serve the smoked potatoes with the mackerel butter and cornichons on the side.

I spend half of my life in the shop

28 AUGUST 2021

The home cooking has abated. The restaurant takes precedence now. Our two chicks have been left floundering, having been pampered for all those months while we were closed. I'm not feeling especially guilty as they are old enough to fend for themselves. Inexplicably, they get stellar results in home ec despite being chronically saucepan-shy at home.

They went vegetarian for a week in support of their visiting cousins from Switzerland, two of whom have gone to the other side. Hangry texts were sent our way: 'There's nothing in the fridge. This is ridiculous.' There was plenty there. I spend half of my life in the shop.

To be fair, the same one has turned out to be a super worker, helping me at Diamond Dogs. She's clued in and will work away without complaint. The money supports her clothes addiction, almost. A 15-year-old needs her style.

The cod is a one-pot dish. The fish nestles in the lightly spiced rice. It's all about timing, as a thin piece of cod will only take 10 minutes or so, a thicker piece a little longer. This saffron dressing is a bit posh. It's inspired by the wonderful Simon Hopkinson from my favourite cookbook, *Roast Chicken and Other Stories*.

I'm a big cavolo nero fan. It's more tender than curly kale, which can be as tough as old boots. I served the salami on the side to keep all the vegetarians happy. The sourdough gives a lovely texture (double carbing!). I'm using Coolea cheese but use Parmesan if you can't get it.

I wrote about this crab salad last week. In truth it's all about the crab meat. It stays reasonably faithful to Mark Moriarty's version but I'm going to make my own mayonnaise.

I'm doing all my dishes for two this week just to mix things up but they can all be scaled up.

BAKED COD WITH SPICED PEPPER RICE AND SAFFRON CREAM DRESSING

SERVES 2

a glug of olive oil

2 pointed red peppers, sliced

1 garlic clove, sliced

1 tsp tomato purée

200g Arborio risotto rice

2 pieces of orange peel

450ml light chicken or vegetable stock

1 sprig of fresh rosemary

1 x 350g cod fillet, bones removed, skin on

FOR THE DRESSING:

juice of 1 orange

150ml cream

1 tsp Dijon mustard

a small pinch of saffron strands

Preheat the oven to 185°C.

Heat the oil in a large ovenproof saucepan over a gentle heat. Add the peppers and garlic and cook for 10 minutes, then add the tomato purée and rice. Turn everything together, then add the orange peel, stock and seasoning. Bring to a simmer and cook for 5 minutes to begin to cook the rice.

Add the rosemary and sit the cod beside it, skin side up. Drizzle a little more oil on the skin and cover the pan tightly with a lid, then bake in the oven for 15 minutes. When the rice is cooked, carefully peel the skin from the fish.

Meanwhile, for the dressing, bring the orange juice to a gentle simmer, then whisk in the cream and mustard. Season, then add the saffron, remove from the heat and allow to cool.

Dig in, breaking apart the fish and spooning the saffron dressing liberally over the top.

SPAGHETTI WITH CAVOLO NERO, TOMATOES, COOLEA AND SALAMI

SERVES 2

a few wafer-thin slices of sourdough bread

3 tbsp olive oil, plus an extra drizzle for the bread

2 garlic cloves, thinly sliced

a knob of cold butter

1 sprig of fresh rosemary

a pinch of chilli flakes

a handful of cavolo nero

10 vine-ripened cherry tomatoes, halved

200g spaghetti

80g Coolea or Parmesan cheese, grated

good salami, sliced or diced

Preheat the oven to 185°C.

Put the sourdough on a baking tray, drizzle over some oil, season and bake in the oven for 10–12 minutes, until golden and crunchy.

Heat the 3 tablespoons of oil in a large saucepan pan (I like to use a wok) over a gentle heat. Add the garlic and cook until it slowly starts to become evenly and lightly golden. Add the butter, rosemary and chilli flakes, then remove from the heat.

Pick, wash and shred the kale, then add it to the pan along with the tomatoes. The heat of the spaghetti will cook it just enough when you add it later.

Cook the spaghetti as per the packet instructions, then drain, saving half a cup of cooking water. Add the spaghetti and water to the pan and turn everything together. Season and add the roasted bread and half of the cheese.

Serve in warm bowls with the remaining cheese and the salami on top.

A SIMPLE CRAB SALAD

SERVES 2

200g the best possible crab meat

1 tsp chopped fresh chives

a little squeeze of lemon

really good olive oil for drizzling

fennel fronds or dill and edible flowers to make it pretty

FOR THE MAYONNAISE:

2 egg yolks, at room temperature

juice of ½ lemon

1 tsp Dijon mustard

250ml sunflower oil

50ml olive oil

To make the mayonnaise, put the egg yolks in a bowl with the lemon juice, mustard, salt and ground white pepper. Put the bowl on top of a folded tea towel — this will keep it in place while you slowly whisk in the sunflower oil in a thin stream, little by little, until it's all emulsified.

Once this is done, whisk in the olive oil. You may need a little more lemon juice to taste. Keep in the fridge until needed — it will happily last for a few days.

Pick through the crab, making sure there is no shell. Put it in a bowl with 2 tablespoons of the mayonnaise, the chives, lemon juice and seasoning. Spoon into a bowl and smooth down the sides.

Drizzle with your best olive oil and arrange the herbs and flowers appealingly on top.

It's time to put the cardigan back on

04 SEPTEMBER 2021

I can't believe it's September already. It's as if the summer went past in a surreal blur and here we are with the evenings creeping in on us again.

I look forward to the seasons changing, though. There's a chill in the air and the sticks are ordered for the winter. It's important to get them when they are dry, otherwise I'll be cursing through the winter when we need the solace of a comforting fire.

I begin to cook in a different way. The bright reds of tomatoes and peppers are filtered out as we gradually wave goodbye to the Mediterranean. In come autumnal colours and flavours. It's time to put the cardigan back on. I've become a fan, a sure sign of the years passing.

I think plaice is wholly underrated. It's mostly condemned to be swaddled in batter, its soft, sweet luxury ignored for the rough and tumble of the chipper. I'm making a piquant, creamy crust for it to lie under. The jalapeño and lime give it a jolt so it doesn't get too comfortable under its warm duvet. I eat the skin underneath — it melts into a gelatinous goo that I adore. I'd serve this with boiled potatoes and perhaps tenderstem broccoli or a frisky green salad. Less is more when it comes to many things, including food.

Amazing puddings are available to us on this island. Black and white keeps everyone happy but you can mix and match according to your preference, as they both go with the mushrooms. Kale pesto is full of gravitas. I'm using the wonderful Coolea cheese to give it an Irish lilt. You could use another Irish hard cheese or Parmesan, of course.

I'm a sucker for a chunky broth. I'm doubling up on the pulses for extra heft and adding allspice for a bit of character. Two smoked rashers will get on famously with the cabbage to make for a satisfying autumn soup.

GRILLED PLAICE WITH JALAPEÑO, LIME AND PARSLEY CRUST

SERVES 4

150g fresh white breadcrumbs

6 slices of jarred jalapeño pepper, roughly chopped

1 garlic clove, roughly chopped

zest of 1 lime

4 tbsp roughly chopped fresh flat-leaf parsley

2 tbsp mayonnaise

4 x 225g double fillets of plaice

a drizzle of olive oil

Preheat the grill.

Put the breadcrumbs, jalapeños, garlic, lime zest, parsley, mayonnaise and seasoning in a food processor and pulse until blended but not pasty.

Put the plaice fillets on an oiled tray, skin side down. Lightly season, then spread the breadcrumb mixture evenly over the fish. Drizzle with a little oil, then grill for 6–8 minutes, depending on the thickness of the fish.

Lift carefully off the tray, transfer to warm plates and serve.

FIELD MUSHROOMS AND BLACK AND WHITE PUDDING WITH COOLEA AND KALE PESTO

SERVES 4

4 large field (flat cap) mushrooms, trimmed

a little melted butter

a few fresh thyme leaves

280g white pudding, sliced

280g black pudding, sliced

FOR THE PESTO:

100g cavolo nero, shredded

80g Coolea or Parmesan cheese, grated

1 garlic clove, sliced

100ml sunflower oil, plus extra for the baking tray

50ml rapeseed oil

2 tbsp flaked almonds, toasted

2 tbsp red wine vinegar

1 tbsp honey

Preheat the oven to 180°C.

Put all the ingredients for the pesto in a food processor and pulse until it's almost smooth. Don't overwork it, though, or it will lose its colour.

Brush a baking tray with a little sunflower oil and put the mushrooms on top, the underside facing up. Drizzle with the melted butter, then add the thyme and season. Arrange the puddings around the mushrooms, then bake in the oven for 15 minutes.

Serve with the kale pesto and some crusty bread.

SPICED CABBAGE, BORLOTTI BEAN AND LENTIL SOUP
SERVES 6

150g dried borlotti or butter beans (or you can use tinned beans and add them later)

100g dried Puy lentils

2 bay leaves (fresh if possible)

50ml olive oil

4 large shallots, thinly sliced

2 garlic cloves, sliced

2 rashers of smoked bacon

6 fresh sage leaves, roughly chopped

1 head of York cabbage, shredded

½ tsp allspice

1.5 litres chicken stock

1 x 330ml bottle of cider

Soak the dried beans and lentils separately in plenty of cold water for a few hours before you start the soup. Drain.

Put the beans in a pot and cover with water, about 10cm above the beans. Add the bay leaves and bring to a simmer. Skim off any scum and cook gently for 20 minutes before adding the lentils. Cook for about 20 more minutes, until just soft. Drain and allow to cool.

Put the oil, shallots, garlic, bacon and sage in a separate pot over a medium heat. Cook for a few minutes, until the shallots are soft and translucent. Add the shredded cabbage and allspice and continue to cook the cabbage gently until it starts to soften.

Add the stock and cider and bring to the boil, then add the cooked beans and lentils. Continue to cook for a few more minutes, season and serve.

Nothing makes me happier than a big tasty stew

11 SEPTEMBER 2021

Nothing makes me happier than a big tasty stew. Well, almost nothing. A plate piled high with seafood in a Spanish beach bar accompanied by jugs of cool, cheap wine would make me happier. That might be attainable very soon, as tomorrow I go on my third Camino. This is where I turn to prayer and hope it all doesn't turn to muck again. As usual I'm not as prepared as I should be but I will prevail.

I'm looking forward to the day when my hardworking wife will come with me. God knows she likes to walk. 'Next year,' she always says, 'when the girls are older.' She would love it. It's good for the head and the soul but maybe not the feet. I've been breaking in my new walking boots by walking to the pub in them. That's practice of a kind.

I leave you with these stews, all very different but each satisfying in its own way.

The first is a take on the classic bouillabaisse. I've been making it for as long as I've been cooking but haven't made it recently. There are more ingredients than I would normally use but it's a smooth, gentle, creamy feast for the seafood lover, as fragrant as a tropical breeze. Serve over steamed jasmine rice for full effect.

I ate beef stroganoff for the first time in 30 years at an 80th birthday party recently. There was buckets of the stuff as they are very generous people. It was a retro sensation. I *might* have gone back for three plates before I was ushered home. This pork stroganoff is an homage. I haven't used parsnip in months so I was chomping at the bit to include it.

I imagined the colour of this beetroot stew before I cooked it. The Beaujolais is a tantalising alliteration — it just sounded good. In truth, any red wine will do. The Gorgonzola will seductively melt into it all the same and the walnuts give an earthy crunch. This can be made a day ahead. It will be even better once the flavours spend some time together.

POACHED SEAFOOD IN GINGER AND COCONUT BROTH

SERVES 4

300g mussels

3 tbsp sunflower oil

1 onion, finely chopped

2 garlic cloves, sliced

3cm piece of ginger, peeled and finely chopped

10 green cardamon pods, lightly crushed

1 tsp mild curry powder

½ tsp ground cumin

½ tsp ground coriander

750ml chicken or vegetable stock

1 x 400ml tin of full-fat coconut milk

50ml lime cordial (or the juice of 2 limes and a pinch of sugar)

1 x 300g salmon fillet, cut into chunks

1 x 300g monkfish fillet, trimmed and cut into 1cm-thick slices

8 langoustines

4 spring onions, cut into chunks

1 punnet of vine-ripened cherry tomatoes, halved

1 tbsp toasted sesame oil

roughly chopped fresh coriander

roughly chopped fresh basil

To prepare the mussels, immerse them in a clean sink of cold water. Agitate. Debeard them one by one into a clean bowl, discarding any that are open and won't close when you gently tap them on the counter. Drain and clean the sink, fill it with cold water again and re-immerse the debearded mussels. Agitate the mussels once more, then lift them from the water, leaving any sediment behind.

Heat the oil in a large, deep pot over a medium heat. Add the onion, garlic and ginger and cook gently for 5 minutes or so, then add the spices. Cook these carefully for a couple of minutes, until they release their aroma, then add the stock. Reduce by one-third, then add the coconut milk, lime cordial or juice and season. This can be done a couple of hours ahead if you wish.

Bring the broth to a gentle simmer, then drop in the mussels, salmon and monkfish. Cook gently for 5 minutes, uncovered, then add the langoustines, spring onions, tomatoes and sesame oil. After 2 minutes, add the fresh herbs.

Discard any mussels that are still closed. Check for seasoning and serve over rice.

PORK, PARSNIP AND APPLE STROGANOFF

SERVES 4

1 pork fillet

1 medium parsnip, peeled

3 tbsp rapeseed oil

225g button mushrooms, halved

2 tsp paprika

150ml sour cream

100ml chicken stock

6 gherkins, thinly sliced

juice of ½ lemon

chopped fresh flat-leaf parsley

1 Granny Smith apple, thinly sliced and cut into batons

Trim the pork fillet of its sinew, then cut into 1cm-thick slices at an angle. Cut each slice into a 1cm strip. Cut the parsnip to replicate the size of the pork as best you can.

Heat the oil in a large pan or wok over a high heat, until gently smoking. Add the pork and parsnip and cook for 5 minutes, until everything is golden brown.

Add the mushrooms and paprika and cook for 1 more minute before adding the sour cream, stock and gherkins. Add the lemon, parsley and seasoning, then bring to a simmer and you're done.

To serve, spoon onto warm plates with some rice, then top artfully with the fresh apple.

BEETROOT, BEAUJOLAIS AND RED ONION STEW WITH GORGONZOLA AND WALNUTS

SERVES 4

1kg raw beetroot (4–5 large beetroot)
4 large red onions
500ml Beaujolais red wine
250ml vegetable stock
2 tbsp redcurrant jelly
2 strips of orange peel
2 star anise
1 cinnamon stick
1 sprig of fresh thyme
200g Gorgonzola cheese
80g walnuts, toasted

Peel the beetroot (it's advisable to wear rubber gloves), then cut into large, even wedges. Peel the red onions and cut into similar-sized wedges as the beetroot.

Put the veg in a pot and pour in the wine and stock. Add the redcurrant jelly, orange peel, star anise, cinnamon stick, thyme and some salt and pepper. Bring to a simmer. Cover but leave the lid askew to let out some steam so the liquid can reduce while the beetroot cooks. Simmer gently for 1 hour or so, until the beetroot is tender.

Check the seasoning, then serve warm with the Gorgonzola and walnuts on top.

Eating all around us on the Camino

The first thing to come was the wine – two groaning jugs, one white, one red – and three small bowls to drink it in. We all laughed in unison. I had been telling the boys about these mythical bowls but they didn't believe me. Here they were at last. I was vindicated.

We were in O Gato Negro, a Formica-coated gem in Santiago de Compostela. Having been given a tip on social media, I was determined to get there but the secret was well and truly out, and possibly has been since the 1950s. As spartan as a monk's cell, it was as packed as a restaurant can be in these times. It took two nights to get in, as the patriarch who came to the door told us that we could only reserve for the following evening. He was as brusque as only the chronically busy can be. It was unintended as he was just trying to deal with my non-existent Spanish while serving, cleaning and pouring as fast as his wiry, ageing frame would let him.

We walked just short of 100 kilometres over four days on the Vía de la Plata route that starts in Seville, almost 1,000 kilometres from Santiago. Us part-time pilgrims started from the delicious little city of Ourense. It nestles in a considerable valley, so, setting off before dawn, I wheezed up to the top, my face alternating through the colours of the Spanish flag as I puffed and spluttered.

There was a granny at the top. There always is with me. She addressed us in Spanish then switched to English when she saw our blank faces, but underneath I detected a French accent. She had walked from Salamanca with her backpack, some 350 kilometres to the south. With a wave of her hand and a smile, she dismissed us disdainfully as tourists. We went on our way, emasculated. Our bags, save for water, lotions and potions, were being ferried from hotel to hotel by our tour company.

It's essential to travel with a curious mind. Pat, a farmer of my vintage, ploughed on like a tough old goat, never flagging for a minute. Dof, more than 10 years younger and a triathlete, glided over the distance like a ghost. I continued to puff but I'm stubborn and the lads were patient.

We ate everything. Hunger is the best sauce. Acorn-fed lomo with piquillo peppers. Garbanzos (chickpeas) stewed with tripe. Lentils with unidentifiable porky bits. We greedily sucked the heads of langoustinos, their juices a jolt of bisque-like pleasure, because that's what Anthony Bourdain would have done.

We had grizzled chicharrón (fried pork rinds). Bacon stewed with chestnuts and pulpo, octopus as warm and tender as a baby's bottom. We washed it all down with buckets of Albariño, Ribera and cool, crisp Estrella beer. We ate and drank like kings.

We made our way through the tracks and dreamy roads, crunching on thousands of hazelnuts. Occasionally a fig plopped alongside them for company. What a tart that would make, I always thought. We were mostly lucky with the weather, with only one bad day. 'Buon Camino' would be our spirit-lifting greeting from the always friendly locals. Do they ever tire of it?

Our first night in Santiago was a joy. People, mostly Spanish, danced in the streets to two guitarists, all singing along to well-worn Spanish songs. You could sense the elation — they were getting a glimpse of their old lives once again.

When you walk the Camino for however long, you will end up in Plaza del Obradorio. It's a special place. The joy on people's faces, the relief and the emotion are all palpable. Some hug, some cheer. Some lie down to take it all in. I could watch it all day. Each and every one has their own reason for walking.

I want to go twice next year if I can find the time. To my huge frustration, we only found the market on the last hour of the last day. It burst and bustled with people sheltering from the downpour outside. Tiny restaurants proliferated. Wonderful smells wafted through the building alongside the freshest fish imaginable. We looked at each other with disbelief and regret. How on earth had we missed this?

We'll have to come again. The Camino de Santiago has been there a long time before us and will be there a long time after we are gone. We're just specks on a well-worn road.

Spice up your life

Menu writing is a mysterious art. A glimpse at one person's menu might make you salivate, hop into the car and pound on their door, insisting on being served immediately, whereas another might make you roll your eyes at the self-indulgence.

Long ago, when I was a young chef, the best restaurants had long, flowery descriptions, almost always in French. It was often intimidating for the customers. The pretension of it all. It was all crisp shirts, asphyxiating ties and arse-clenching bills. Thankfully things chilled out over the years and now you don't have to go to the Sorbonne to get your dinner.

Then came the opposite. Clipped precision. No extraneous information. 'Sole, barley, hogweed' or something like that. It would nearly put a fella off.

Some menus leap out at me, like Kai in Galway and Chez Bruce in London to name just two wildly different but captivating and unique examples. Kai's menu starts with the font, a replica of Jess Murphy's handwriting. It's as singular as the food. Chez Bruce is full of old-school French classicism, my first love. Unfashionably long, I spend an inordinate amount of time poring over it.

A single word on a menu can put people off, e.g. 'spiced'. Often when I put it on my menu, some people think immolation is imminent and that they will have to be hosed down by the fire brigade. Surprisingly, it can mean the death of a dish on a menu.

These dishes showcase some of the myriad spices — few of them with heat, all with different characteristics. The chicken is gentle and easy, with soft, sweet flavours that are at the same time complex but simple. The aubergine adds a sticky depth of flavour.

The cauliflower is warm and luxurious. You could make the roti if you are so inclined or you could buy wholemeal wraps to cradle everything inside.

I can use cinnamon again now we are in autumn. This is a family-pleasing traybake. The maple syrup complements the sausages admirably. The croissants add texture and sop up any wayward juices. There's no scaring the horses here.

CHICKEN WITH YOGURT, MILD SPICES AND STICKY AUBERGINE

SERVES 4

250g natural yogurt

2 garlic cloves, crushed

2cm piece of ginger, peeled and grated

1 tsp curry powder

4 chicken fillets

1 tsp cumin seeds

1 tsp coriander seeds

1 tsp garam masala

zest of ½ orange and juice of 1 orange

1 tbsp tomato purée

1 tbsp honey

FOR THE AUBERGINE:

3 tbsp butter, plus extra melted butter for drizzling

2 aubergines, diced into 1cm pieces

TO SERVE:

poppadoms

a few sprigs of fresh coriander

Mix the yogurt, garlic, ginger, curry powder and some salt and pepper together. Sit the chicken fillets in the yogurt, making sure they are completely immersed. Leave to marinate for a minimum of 4 hours, but the longer, the better – the yogurt will both tenderise and flavour the chicken.

Melt the butter in a saucepan over a medium heat. When the butter starts to foam, add the aubergines, cumin and coriander seeds and garam masala. Cover and cook for 15 minutes, until the aubergines soften.

Add the orange zest and juice, tomato purée and honey. Turn up the heat a little and continue to cook for another 10 minutes, until the aubergines start to caramelise. Keep an eye on the bottom of the pan, as once the honey is in it can burn. Season and remove from the heat. The aubergines should be soft and squidgy with a deep, balanced flavour.

Preheat the oven to 190°C.

Lightly oil a roasting tin. Lift the chicken from the marinade, retaining a thick coating of yogurt around the meat. Put it in the oiled tin and drizzle the melted butter over the top. Cook in the oven for 20–25 minutes, until the chicken is cooked through.

Serve the sticky aubergine with the chicken, poppadoms and fresh coriander, with boiled rice on the side.

CAULIFLOWER AND CHICKPEA KORMA WITH ROTI

SERVES 6

1 small head of cauliflower, broken into small florets

1 onion, chopped

1 garlic clove, chopped

3cm piece of ginger, peeled and chopped

50ml sunflower oil

2 tbsp ready-made korma paste or powder (look for the Green Saffron brand)

1 x 400g tin of chopped tomatoes

1 x 400g tin of chickpeas, drained and rinsed

1 x 400ml tin of coconut milk

200g vine-ripened cherry tomatoes, halved

zest and juice of 1 lime

1 tsp caster sugar

a few sprigs of fresh coriander

FOR THE YOGURT:

6 tbsp natural yogurt

chopped fresh mint

FOR THE ROTI:

225g self-raising flour

½ tsp salt

2 tbsp melted butter

150ml water

sunflower oil and butter, for frying

For the roti, put the flour, salt and melted butter in a bowl (or the bowl of a stand mixer if you have one). Slowly add the water and mix until everything comes together. You may not need all the water, so add it little by little towards the end. If the dough is too wet, just add a little more flour. Knead for 5 minutes, then cover with cling film and allow to rest for 30 minutes.

Turn the dough out onto a floured surface, then roll into a thick sausage and cut into six even pieces. With floured hands, shape into balls and roll each one out as thinly as you can. It's best to cook them as you roll as they stick to parchment paper unless it is well oiled.

To cook, put ½ tablespoon of sunflower oil and ½ tablespoon of butter in a pan over a medium high-heat (the oil raises the burning point of the butter). When the butter starts to foam, add a roti and cook for 2–3 minutes on each side, making sure the roti is golden and speckled before you take it from the pan. Transfer to a clean tea towel and continue with the rest of the roti.

While the dough is resting, make the korma. Boil the cauliflower florets in salted water just until soft, then drain and set aside.

Put the onion, garlic, ginger and oil in a food processor and pulse until evenly chopped (or just chop everything as finely as you can by hand). Put the mixture in a large saucepan set over a medium heat and cook for 10 minutes. Add the korma paste or powder and continue to cook for 3 more minutes or so, then add the chopped tomatoes, chickpeas and coconut milk. Bring to a simmer and reduce gently for 10 minutes.

Add the cooked cauliflower along with the tomatoes, lime zest and juice, sugar and some salt and pepper. Bring to a simmer for 1–2 minutes, then it's ready to serve.

Mix the yogurt with the mint and serve on the side of the korma with the warm roti and fresh coriander leaves scattered over.

BAKED SAUSAGES WITH CINNAMON ONIONS AND CRISPY CROISSANTS

SERVES 4

50g butter

4 large onions, sliced

1 large sprig of fresh thyme

$1/3$ tsp ground cinnamon

a splash of water

1 tsp golden brown sugar

1 tbsp maple syrup

a splash of red wine vinegar

8 large sausages

4 croissants

Preheat the oven to 200°C.

Put the butter, onions, thyme, cinnamon and a splash of water in a saucepan set over a low to medium heat. Cover and cook gently for 15 minutes, until the onions soften.

Remove the lid and turn up the heat so the liquid starts to evaporate and the onions start to caramelise. Scrape the bottom of the pan periodically, making sure you dislodge any sticky brown bits as they appear.

Add the sugar. This will speed up the caramelisation process, so keep a good eye on it so the onions don't start to burn. After a few minutes, when the onions are lightly golden, add the maple syrup, vinegar and some salt and pepper, then transfer the onions to a baking tray. Smooth the onions out a little, then put the sausages on top and bake in the oven for 15 minutes.

Tear the croissants into rough chunks, then nestle them in among the sausages. Bake for another 5 minutes, then eat with mustard.

I prefer
the haute left
out of my
cuisine.
Cuisine paysanne
— the food of
the people,
rustic, delicious
and world famous
— has my heart.

10 JULY 2021

Evocative, old-school recipes

25 SEPTEMBER 2021

I came to love quail many years ago during my time at Chez Nico in London, where they were always on the menu. The occasional surplus one was given to me. I would savage it like a hungry terrier.

A quail pie nearly always features on our winter menu in the Tannery, the lithe meat encased in puff pastry along with smoked ham, foie gras and brioche. It is a thing to behold even if I do say so myself, a committed non-trumpet-blower.

Kidneys were also on Nico's menu but these were more often veal, surgically trimmed and sliced, quickly sautéed with innumerable bay leaves, then coated in a shimmering veal and blackcurrant jus. Nico was justly famous for his sauces. My job was to pass the many stocks through pristine layers of muslin and woe betide if I got it wrong.

Unbeknownst to myself, I'm writing an homage to that famous restaurant, as my first taste of prune and Armagnac ice cream was there. It was never the most popular in Dungarvan, as Irish people associate prunes with their bottoms. But I defy anyone not to be mesmerised by Nico's warm tarte Bourdaloue with prune and Armagnac-laden ice cream and a transcendental custard. I'm inhaling its wobbly beauty now, but only in my memory.

Quail features prominently in Middle Eastern cooking. It's a world away from the haute cuisine of those rigid times. Things have loosened up and so have I. I know they are difficult to get — your best bet is if you have a good relationship with your local restaurant, as they can order them for you. This dish is warm, musky and evocative. We need that these days.

This kidney dish is unashamedly rich. I've left the bay in it, mostly for show. If you can lay your hands on fresh bay it will make all the difference.

I'm all about Jerusalem artichokes right now. Their knobbly skins hold much delight. Here I'm doing a version of a cocktail party classic (if you move in those circles) and have worked it into a pleasing starter. It's a little bit retro, but then, so am I.

QUAIL WITH BULGUR WHEAT, ALMONDS AND GRAPES

SERVES 4

8 whole quail

juice of ½ lemon

2 tbsp olive oil, plus more for the dressing

2 tsp sumac

a pinch of chilli flakes

a drizzle of honey

FOR THE BULGUR WHEAT:

300g bulgur wheat

500ml chicken stock

zest and juice of 1 orange

1 tbsp ras el hanout

2 tbsp almonds, toasted

mixed seedless grapes, halved

chopped fresh flat-leaf parsley

chopped fresh mint

Marinate the quail with the lemon juice, oil, sumac, chilli flakes, honey and some salt and pepper. An hour will do to let the flavours permeate.

Preheat the oven to 190°C.

Put the quail in a roasting tin along with any residual juices in the bowl. Roast in the oven for 20 minutes, until lightly golden.

Put the bulgur, chicken stock, orange zest and juice, ras el hanout and some salt and pepper in a microwaveable bowl. Mix together, cover with cling film and cook for 3 minutes on high. Remove the cling film and allow the bulgur to cool, then fluff it up with a fork. Add the almonds, grapes, parsley, mint and a little more oil to dress. Check the seasoning and it's ready.

Serve the quail on top on the bulgur salad, then drizzle the cooking juices over the top.

SAUTÉ OF LAMB KIDNEYS, BAY LEAVES AND BLACKBERRIES

SERVES 2

6 lamb kidneys

2 tbsp rapeseed oil

6 bay leaves (fresh if possible)

50ml chicken stock

50g butter, diced and chilled

1 tsp wholegrain mustard

a few drops of lemon juice

10 wild blackberries (fewer if shop-bought, as they are bigger)

Cut the kidneys in half lengthways and trim off as much of the sinew as you can, then season.

Heat the oil in a pan over a high heat, until gently smoking. Put the kidneys in the pan, cut side down, and cook for 2 minutes, gently pressing on the rounded side as they curl. Turn over and add the bay leaves to the pan. Cook for 1 more minute. I want them lightly pink on the inside.

Deftly remove the kidneys and bay from the pan with a slotted spoon, leaving any juices in the pan. Turn down the heat to a flicker. Add the chicken stock and let it bubble a little, then whisk in the butter one cube at a time. When it's all been amalgamated, add the mustard and lemon juice, then add the kidneys and bay leaves back to the pan. Check the seasoning.

Serve in warm bowls with the blackberries punctuating the top.

JERUSALEM ARTICHOKE DEVILS ON HORSEBACK

SERVES 4

12 or so medium Jerusalem artichokes (they vary greatly in size)

juice of 1 lemon (keep a few drops for the dressing)

1 tsp salt

2 tbsp olive oil

2 sprigs of fresh thyme

12 soft, ready-to-eat prunes, halved

1 packet of Parma ham

FOR THE KALE:

2 tbsp walnut or olive oil

4 tbsp cream

leaves of cavolo nero or baby spinach

Peel the artichokes and put them in a pot. Cover with water, add the lemon juice and salt and simmer for about 20 minutes or so, until soft. Drain.

Heat the oil in a pan over a medium heat. Add the artichokes with the thyme and cook until they are glazed and golden, then season.

Cut the artichokes in half. Sandwich them with half a prune, then wrap them in torn Parma ham. It's optional whether you skewer them or not.

Mix the walnut or olive oil with the cream and a few drops of lemon juice, then season. Turn the kale in the dressing.

Serve the artichokes with the dressed kale on the side.

Inspired by
a Roman holiday

02 OCTOBER 2021

We were lucky to get to Rome a few weeks ago for a much-appreciated weekend. I always consult Katie Parla's website whenever I'm there. She pointed me towards Armando del Pantheon some years ago, the trattoria of my dreams. This time, unfortunately, it was closed for the summer holidays, so we went to Roscioli on the Saturday. Sunday was difficult, as most places are shut. We had been to the lovely Antico Arco on the last trip and I really wanted somewhere more rustic and cacophonous. After much deliberation I settled on Caesare al Casaletto, a raved-about simple restaurant in the suburbs. It was out – very far out, end of the tramline out – but it was exactly what we wanted. We heard it before we saw it. The chatter drifted into the night and drew us in. We sat in a twinkly courtyard full of boisterous Italian families.

The menu was cavernous. I could have got lost in it. I meekly asked for an English version. We seemed to be the only people who weren't Italian. A good sign.

I spotted a coratella, a dish of lamb offal. Heart, lungs, spleen and liver. I'd leave that for another time but it did reassure me I was in for a true taste of Rome. We ordered more than we needed, more out of curiosity than hunger. Among the delicious fritti there came a deep-fried gnocchi in a cacio e pepe sauce. I had seen this dish online and was consumed by lust.

I couldn't find a recipe so I'm making a stab at it here. It's pretty good but I don't think I can replicate it, as half of what makes it special is the atmosphere of that restaurant. It works with shop-bought gnocchi but it's better if you go the extra mile and make your own.

The butternut squash dish is seasonal, gentle and pleasing, perfect for a chilly autumn day.

The gooey onion filling of these tarts and the sweet and sour dressing evoke the flavours of Sicily for me. The ricotta is a creamy and appropriate foil to provide a little of that special comfort that only Italian food can give.

PAUL FLYNN

FRIED GNOCCHI WITH CACIO E PEPE SAUCE

SERVES 4

500g peeled Maris Piper potatoes

1 large egg, beaten

125g plain flour

100ml olive oil

a little ground nutmeg

fresh sage leaves

FOR THE SAUCE:

50g butter

30g plain flour

250ml chicken stock

250ml milk

1 tsp ground black pepper

100g Parmesan cheese, grated

Cut the potatoes into even-sized pieces and steam until tender, then drain. Mash as finely as you can — a ricer is best for fluffy gnocchi. Put the mashed potato in a bowl and add the egg, then sieve in the flour little by little. Add the tablespoon of oil, nutmeg and a pinch of salt, then bring everything together into a dough.

Turn out onto a floured surface and knead a few times to break down the gluten in the flour. If it's a bit wet you can add a little more flour to firm it up. Divide the dough into four balls, then roll each ball into lengths the size of a thick sausage. Cut into 3cm pillows, then press down gently with the back of a fork to flatten just a little so they cook evenly. Put in the fridge on a floured tray until you need them.

To make the sauce, melt the butter in a saucepan over a gentle heat, then add the flour. Cook for 3 minutes, then add the stock little by little, whisking all the time to ensure there are no lumps. Add the milk, then whisk in the black pepper, half of the Parmesan and a little salt. Cook for a couple of minutes, then set aside.

Heat some of the oil in a frying pan over a medium-high heat. Working in batches, fry the gnocchi for approximately 2 minutes on each side, slipping a few sage leaves into the pan to flavour the oil. Keep warm while you cook the rest.

Serve the gnocchi on a pool of the sauce. Garnish with the sage leaves and scatter the remaining Parmesan on top.

PENNE WITH ROASTED BUTTERNUT SQUASH, GOAT CHEESE AND HAZELNUTS

SERVES 4

1 butternut squash, peeled, halved, deseeded and cut into 1cm-thick slices

a generous drizzle of olive oil

a few sprigs of fresh thyme

400g penne or your favourite pasta

150g soft rindless goat cheese

juice of 1 orange

3 tbsp natural yogurt

100g hazelnuts, roasted, peeled and crushed a little

80g Parmesan cheese, grated

Preheat the oven to 185°C.

Put the butternut squash in a roasting tin and add the oil, thyme and some salt and pepper. Roast in the oven for 25 minutes or so, until golden and soft.

Cook the pasta as per the packet instructions.

Meanwhile, blend the goat cheese, orange juice and yogurt together.

Drain the pasta, saving half a cup of the cooking water, then put the pasta and the cooking water back in the pot.

Add the roasted squash to the pasta, making sure to scrape all the juices from the tin into the pot. Turn everything together carefully and season.

Serve with a dollop of the goat cheese cream with the hazelnuts and Parmesan scattered over the top.

SWEET AND SOUR ONION AND RICOTTA TARTS
SERVES 6

6 large onions, thinly sliced

60g butter

1 sprig of fresh thyme, plus extra leaves

1 cinnamon stick

1 x 320g packet of ready-rolled puff pastry, thawed

1 egg beaten with 1 tbsp milk

200g ricotta cheese

FOR THE DRESSING:

100ml red wine vinegar

50ml water

50g raisins

1 tbsp golden brown sugar

100ml olive oil

50g pine nuts, toasted

Put the onions, butter, thyme, cinnamon and some salt and pepper in a large saucepan. Add a splash of water, cover and cook for 15 minutes over a medium heat.

Remove the cover and turn the heat up a little. Cook for a further 10 minutes, scraping the bottom of the pan periodically, until the onions are soft and golden. Check the seasoning and allow to cool.

Unfurl the pastry and cut it into six squares. Divide the onions among the pastry squares, taking care to leave plenty of pastry clear around the edges. Brush the pastry lightly with the egg wash, then bring each corner up to meet each other in the middle and pinch the sides together.

Brush the tarts with more egg wash, scatter a few thyme leaves over the top and pop them in the fridge for a while to set.

Preheat the oven to 190°C. Line a baking tray with parchment paper.

Put the tarts on the lined tray and bake in the oven for 20–25 minutes, until crisp and golden.

Meanwhile, put the vinegar, water, raisins and sugar in a small saucepan and bring to the boil, then remove from the heat straightaway. Whisk in the oil, then add the pine nuts to the dressing.

To serve, spoon the ricotta on top of the tarts, then anoint with the dressing.

Making the most of precious duck fat

09 OCTOBER 2021

I first came across confit in the form of a crisp, unctuous duck leg many moons ago. I was smitten and my passion has endured over the years without dimming for an instant. The process — a form of preservation — is ancient, a Gascon tradition that symbolises all that is good about French cooking. The meat was salted, poached in its own fat, then placed in a crock. The fat should completely cover the meat; this acts as a seal and a preservative. Before the days of refrigeration, the crock was buried in the ground to keep it at a constant temperature through the winter. The meat could last for months. These days, duck legs are frequently canned and are a commonplace feature in the traiteurs of France. Lucky them.

The fat from duck or goose is precious. Rendered down, it makes for the most wonderful roast potatoes. There is a tub of duck fat in my fridge at all times. I tip the excess fat from the occasional smoked streaky rasher into it to add another layer of flavour to my roasties.

The confit process normally requires fully immersing the meat in the fat, but in fairness that requires an inordinate amount of fat. I'm paring back here, using less fat and also cutting out the salting process as we don't need to be digging up our dinner from the ground.

Today I'm making all these dishes for two for a little change but you can scale them up as needed.

You will need two hefty pork chops, cut from a rack. The fennel is tart and crisp, perfect to cut through the richness of the chops. The secret with all these dishes is to pack the fat with flavour. You can use the fat multiple times — it gets better as it goes along.

I'm using chicken legs as the lesser cuts of meat always work better for confit. The potatoes will go in as well and will accept the process gratefully. The leeks bring colour and the dill and crème fraîche a bit of welcome perk.

I'm serving celeriac here with two amiable friends. It's a lovely, comforting dish for a winter evening.

CONFIT PORK CHOPS WITH GARLIC, FENNEL AND LEMON

SERVES 2

2 x 300g pork chops on the bone

1 x 180g jar of Silverhill duck fat

1 large sprig of fresh thyme

1 bay leaf (fresh if possible)

1 lemon

1 cinnamon stick

2 cloves

1 large garlic bulb

FOR THE SALAD:

1 fennel bulb

2 tbsp olive oil

a splash of red wine vinegar

a pinch of caster sugar

Preheat the oven to 140°C.

Put the chops in a small, deep roasting tin. Add the duck fat, thyme, bay leaf, lemon peel, cinnamon, cloves and plenty of salt and pepper.

Cut the bulb of garlic in half along the equator, then put it in the bottom of the tin, cut side down. Cover tightly with foil and cook in the oven for 2 hours. The pork should be completely tender. This can be done a day or two in advance if you wish — the pork will taste even better.

Meanwhile, trim and shred the fennel — a mandolin is perfect for this. Chop any fronds and mix them with the fennel, then add the oil, vinegar, sugar and seasoning and toss gently to coat.

To finish the dish, remove the pork from the fat and scrape any excess from the chops. Put the pork on a plate. Carefully lift out the garlic and remove the fat from it too. Cut two wide strips of peel from the lemon, then cut the lemon in half and you're ready.

Heat a large, dry frying pan over a high heat. Add the chops and cook for 3 minutes on each side, until brown and crisp. Remove the chops from the pan and put on kitchen paper to drain. Keep warm. Drain any excess oil from the pan, then add the garlic and the lemon halves, cut side down. Cook for 3 minutes, until golden.

Serve the chops with the fennel salad and the caramelised lemon and garlic.

CRISPY CHICKEN LEGS AND POTATOES WITH LEEK FONDUE

SERVES 2

4 chicken legs

1 x 180g jar of Silverhill duck fat

3 garlic cloves, roughly chopped

peel of ½ orange

1 sprig of fresh rosemary

2cm piece of ginger, peeled and roughly chopped

1 star anise

½ tsp smoked paprika

6–8 baby potatoes

FOR THE FONDUE:

1 leek

a knob of butter

1 heaped tsp plain flour

2 tbsp crème fraîche

1 tbsp chopped fresh dill

1 tsp Dijon mustard

Preheat the oven to 140°C.

Put the chicken in a small, deep roasting tin or casserole. Add the duck fat, garlic, orange peel, rosemary, ginger, star anise and smoked paprika. Pop in the whole baby potatoes and season generously. Cover tightly with foil or a lid, then cook in the oven for 2 hours. The chicken needs to be completely tender and ready to fall off the bone.

When cooked, remove the chicken and the potatoes from the tin or casserole, draining off all the excess fat.

Cut the leek in half lengthways and shred it as finely as you can. Wash it to make sure there is no dirt present but leave a little excess water on the leek.

Melt the butter in a small pan over a medium heat. When the butter starts to foam, add the shredded leek. The water in the leek will help it steam. Add the flour and cook for 2–3 minutes, until the leek is soft, then add the crème fraîche, chopped dill and mustard. Season and set aside.

Turn the oven up to 200°C.

Put the chicken and potatoes in a roasting tin, skin side up, and cook for 20 minutes or so, until crisp. Serve with the warm leek fondue.

CELERIAC WITH SOUSED MUSHROOMS, SMOKED BACON, CREAM CHEESE AND APPLE

SERVES 2

1 small celeriac

1 x 180g jar of Silverhill duck fat

2 garlic cloves, crushed

peel of 1 lemon

1 sprig of fresh thyme

4 cloves

1 tsp whole black peppercorns

4 field (flat cap) mushrooms, trimmed

a drizzle of malt vinegar

a few fresh sage leaves

4 smoked streaky rashers

1 brioche bun, halved

1 tbsp light cream cheese

1 apple, thinly sliced

Preheat the oven to 160°C.

Trim the skin from the celeriac with a serrated knife, then cut it in half. Cut the celeriac into 2cm-thick slices, then put in a casserole along with the duck fat, garlic, lemon peel, thyme, cloves, peppercorns and a pinch of salt. Cover and cook in the oven for 1 hour, until the celeriac is soft and tender.

Turn the oven up to 200°C.

Remove the celeriac from the casserole, then put it in a roasting tin, draining off the excess fat. Put the mushrooms beside the celeriac, then sprinkle the malt vinegar over the top and season. Put the sage on next, then drape the bacon over the top of the mushrooms. Put the tin back in the oven to cook for 10 minutes or so, using the last couple of minutes to toast the brioche.

Smear the cream cheese on the brioche, then assemble everything nicely as an open-face sandwich with the apple on top. The celeriac would be a lovely accompaniment to a Sunday roast.

Championing root vegetables

16 OCTOBER 2021

I like the soil, graft and tradition of root vegetables. Carrots, parsnips and turnips from Ardmore. Spuds from Ballinacourty. Beetroot from Bohadoon. All sitting proudly in our local veg shop, Country Store. Conor, the owner, chats about his twin passions, horses and GAA, as he loads bags of spuds into the boots of people's cars. This is connection. It's hard to get that with vegetables that spend more time in an airport than I do.

This chicken and root vegetable stew is all that I love about one-pot cooking. The flavours combine and enhance each other as the stew blips along. A little barley supports the dish. Ginger, cider and cream are the other main ingredients, while a hint of cardamon lends a bit of sultriness to the affair. Eat with rice or boiled potatoes for a bit of comfort.

The turnip and Cheddar parcels are showstoppers, perfect for a vegetarian main course. The mashed turnip is infused with a nutmeg-scented brown butter and good Cheddar cheese, then enveloped in crisp filo pastry sprinkled with almonds to become ultra-crisp and gooey.

I love gratins of any kind, but this method allows you to prepare the gratin one or two days before, then colour it when you need it – a handy tip for (cough) Christmas. Here I'm using potato and parsnip and combining it with mortadella and a little pear. It's something I'm very fond of. It holds great memories for me of a chefs' trip to the Dolomites. A perfect little bar had a porcine hunk of mortadella resting alluringly behind the counter. There was lots of snow, a wayward Egyptian, a jealous Italian, some Russians, plenty of crisp little beers and even more craic. The lady behind the bar would hack off pieces of mortadella when she thought we were waning. It did the trick. We ate it like giddy gannets. By the end of the night we were half mortadella, half beer and wholly shook, but what a memory! What more could a man on a ski holiday ask for?

CHICKEN, ROOT VEGETABLE AND BARLEY STEW WITH CIDER AND GINGER CREAM

SERVES 4

50g barley

1 carrot

1 parsnip

1 turnip

1 red onion

100g butter

2 rashers of smoked streaky bacon

2cm piece of ginger, peeled and finely chopped

1 large sprig of fresh thyme

2 bay leaves (fresh if possible)

10 green cardamon pods, lightly crushed

8 boneless, skinless chicken thighs, cut in half

1 litre chicken stock

1 x 330ml bottle of cider

250ml cream

Soak the barley in a bowl with plenty of cold water for an hour or so.

Peel and dice the carrot, parsnip, turnip and onion into 1cm pieces, then put them in a pot along with the butter, bacon, ginger, herbs and cardamon pods. Cover and cook over a medium heat for 20 minutes, until the vegetables are softened but not coloured.

Drain the barley and add it to the vegetables along with the chicken, stock and cider and bring to a simmer. Cook gently for 30 minutes, then add the cream. Let the cream settle into the stew for a few minutes, season and it's ready to serve.

TURNIP, BROWN BUTTER AND CHEDDAR TARTS
SERVES 4

1 large sprig of fresh thyme

80g butter, plus extra for brushing

1 turnip, diced

a little ground nutmeg

80g mature Cheddar cheese, grated

4 sheets of filo pastry, thawed

a pinch of flaked almonds

Preheat the oven to 185°C.

Cook the turnip in lightly salted boiling water until completely tender. Drain thoroughly, then mash.

Melt the butter in a pot over a low to medium heat. After a minute or two it will start to foam, spit and fizzle but will then settle down and start to change colour to a nutty golden brown. This will take a little bit of time but you have to be patient while the butter transforms. Check by inserting a dry spoon to nudge away the top layer of foam to peek underneath. There should be little brown particles and the butter should smell nutty. If in any doubt, just turn down the heat. The whole process should take no more than 5 minutes. It seems like an eternity but don't take your eyes off the pot.

When you have your amber colour, remove the pan from the heat. Add the thyme and nutmeg and allow to infuse for a couple of minutes before adding the brown butter to the mashed turnip along with some salt and pepper. Allow to cool, then fold in the cheese.

Lightly brush a sheet of filo pastry with melted butter, then fold it in half into a rough square. Spoon a quarter of the mix into the centre of the pastry, lightly brush with melted butter, then bring the four corners up to meet each other. Pinch the pastry together just above the turnip so there is a substantial collar of loose filo. This will make the tarts look very attractive. Brush the top of the pastry with more melted butter and sprinkle over the almonds. Repeat for the other tarts.

Put the tarts on a parchment-lined baking sheet. Cook in the oven for 25 minutes, until crisp and golden. Serve as a main course with a winter salad.

GRATIN OF PARSNIP, PEAR AND MORTADELLA
SERVES 6

8 large potatoes

2 large parsnips

500ml milk

250ml cream

3 garlic cloves, crushed

1 large sprig of fresh thyme

a little grated nutmeg

2 tinned pear halves, roughly chopped

80g Parmesan cheese, grated

4 slices of mortadella or salami

Peel the potatoes and parsnips, then slice them very thinly – a mandolin is best for this. Put the potatoes and parsnips in a heavy-bottomed pot. Add the milk, cream, garlic, thyme and nutmeg. Mix everything together, cover and cook over a low heat, stirring from time to time, being very careful that it doesn't catch on the bottom.

When the potatoes are completely tender, stir in the pears, Parmesan and some salt and ground white pepper.

Transfer half of the mixture to a casserole, then layer over the mortadella or salami slices. Cover with the remaining mixture. Add a little residual liquid over the potatoes to form a protective coating. This will turn into an attractive glaze when the dish is cooked. At this point, you can put it in the fridge to cook within the next couple of days.

When you're ready to cook, preheat the oven to 180°C.

Bake in the oven for 45 minutes, until burnished, bubbling and golden. Serve hot.

Leave nothing to waste

23 OCTOBER 2021

This week is all about pork belly. It's a universally popular cut with everyone except, perhaps, the fat police. What makes it so delicious, though, is that very fat.

It's enjoyable to cook — you can literally see the meat becoming a wobbly wonder before your eyes. It succumbs to slow cooking, gradually morphing from something dense and unpromising into a sticky delight.

I've always had an attraction to the lesser cuts. They require just that little bit more imagination. That doesn't necessarily translate to being difficult to cook. In fact, just leaving those cuts alone in a pot or tray to blip away on their own with some herbs or spices is all you need to do to transform them into something sublime.

Today I'm taking one pork belly and showing you three different dishes. The best cooks are the ones who can take leftovers and make something special with them. There should be zero waste. The trimmings are simply fodder for a fertile imagination.

The softly spiced pork belly will work with half a belly with no difference to the cooking time. Spices work wonders. I'm settling for the comfort of winter spice. As a result I'm eschewing the skin, so no crackling, I'm afraid. The borani adds freshness and a bit of welcome colour. It's also lovely as a dip or as part of a mezze platter.

This cassoulet is a simple store cupboard recipe made with the lovely Polish kielbasa sausage. To my shame I only came across it for the first time on my upcoming food truck TV programme. You can get various types in Polish shops. If you don't have access to a Polish shop, just use a good chunky sausage and some smoked paprika instead. This can also be a stand-alone dish without the pork belly — you can make the cassoulet with just the sausage and perhaps confit duck instead.

The rillette takes me straight to a little French bistro. It's important to pulse the meat just a couple of times as you don't want it turning into cat food — a bit of texture is necessary. Eat with toast and cornichons.

The best cooks are the ones who can take leftovers and make something special with them. There should be zero waste. The trimmings are simply fodder for a fertile imagination.

23 OCTOBER 2021

SOFTLY SPICED PORK BELLY WITH BEETROOT BORANI

SERVES 10

3 onions, unpeeled and cut into 1cm-thick circles

1 garlic bulb, unpeeled and halved

a large piece of ginger, roughly cut

a few sprigs of fresh thyme

4 bay leaves (fresh if possible)

1 x 2.5kg piece of pork belly, skin off, bone in

a drizzle of rapeseed oil

1 tbsp mixed spice

300ml water

4 tbsp golden brown sugar

FOR THE BORANI:

2 x 500g packets of cooked beetroot

100g walnuts

2 tbsp rapeseed oil

1 tsp coriander seeds

1 tsp golden brown sugar

½ tsp mixed spice

3 tbsp natural yogurt

2 tbsp chopped fresh dill

1 tbsp red wine vinegar

1 tbsp honey

Preheat the oven to 165°C.

Put the onions flat in a roasting tin to form a trivet, then add the garlic, ginger, thyme and bay. Put the pork belly on top of the onions, skin side up. Drizzle over the rapeseed oil to help the spices stick. Scatter the mixed spice evenly over the pork, then season generously with coarse salt and black pepper. Add the water to the tin, cover tightly with foil and cook in the oven for 2 hours.

Turn the oven up to 185°C.

Remove the foil, then sprinkle the brown sugar evenly over the pork. Return the pork to the oven to cook for a further 30 minutes, until completely tender and burnished.

For the borani, put the beetroot in a food processor along with any residual juices. Without turning the machine on (leave it unplugged to be on the safe side), cut the beetroot into smaller chunks with a knife. This helps with the processing and is a lot less messy than cutting it on a chopping board.

Put the walnuts in a frying pan with the oil, coriander seeds, sugar and mixed spice and cook over a medium heat for 2–3 minutes, until the walnuts are toasted and caramelised.

Add the walnuts to the beetroot, then add the yogurt, dill, vinegar and honey. Season and blend to a purée, leaving a little texture in the beetroot.

Slice the pork and serve with the beetroot borani and something green. Roast potatoes would be delicious too. Save any remaining pork — it will keep for up to three days in the fridge and can be used in the cassoulet or rillette on the following two pages.

KIELBASA CASSOULET WITH PARMENTIER POTATOES AND SOUR CREAM

SERVES 6

1½ tbsp duck fat

1 large onion, finely chopped

3 garlic cloves, sliced

2 x 400g tins of chopped tomatoes

2 x 400g tins of butter beans, drained and rinsed

200ml strong chicken stock

1 tsp paprika

1 tsp dried oregano

300g kielbasa sausage, cut into 2cm chunks

150g leftover cooked pork belly, cut into chunks (optional)

FOR THE POTATOES:

½ tbsp duck fat

4 large Rooster potatoes, peeled and diced into 1cm cubes

3 garlic cloves, unpeeled and lightly crushed

TO SERVE:

1 x 200g tub of sour cream

a few sprigs of fresh dill

Preheat the oven to 185°C.

Put the duck fat in a casserole with the onion and garlic and cook gently for 15 minutes, until the onion is soft and translucent. Add the tomatoes, beans, stock, paprika and oregano and bring to a simmer. Add the sausage and the pork belly (if you have it). Season and cook in the oven, uncovered, for 30 minutes.

Meanwhile, for the potatoes, heat the duck fat in an ovenproof frying pan until it's gently smoking. Dry the potatoes in a clean tea towel and carefully add them to the duck fat along with the garlic. Season and give them a little time on the hob, then put them in the oven and cook for about 20 minutes, until golden and crisp. Drain on kitchen paper.

Serve the parmentier potatoes on top of the cassoulet along with the sour cream and dill.

A SIMPLE RILLETTE OF PORK

SERVES 4

300g leftover cooked pork belly
½ tbsp Dijon mustard
½ tbsp wholegrain mustard
1 large shallot, finely chopped
1 tbsp red wine vinegar
1 tsp honey
a few sprigs of fresh flat-leaf parsley

TO SERVE:
cornichons
1 baguette

Cut the pork belly into chunks. It's important to have a decent amount of fat on the pork, so don't be tempted to trim it off.

Warm the pork belly slightly for 1 minute in the microwave, then put it in a food processor with the mustards, shallot, vinegar, honey, parsley and some salt and pepper. Pulse three or four times but no more. It's important to have some texture in the mixture. Taste for balance and seasoning, then put in a sealed jar in the fridge.

Eat within a couple of days with cornichons and a sealed good baguette.

I have one piece of advice for all cooks

30 OCTOBER 2021

Kitchen disasters are bad enough when they happen in your own kitchen but they turn into a catastrophe when they happen in someone else's.

We were invited to dinner in a friend's house recently. Beef Wellington was on the menu — tricky to make and also to cook. There was a fat treasure waiting in the Aga for my opinion. I had given an Aga course that day, so apparently I was doubly qualified to give my tuppence worth.

The pastry was still pale and flaccid. I inserted the tip of a knife into the meat. It was firm and alarmingly, there was no blush in the juices. I should have followed my instinct and pulled it out there and then, but it went back in for 5 more fatal minutes then out to rest for 20 minutes before carving.

I knew as soon as the first slice came off. What pink there had been had evaporated. It was delicious all the same, but I still felt responsible. Only the candlelight spared my blushes.

I have one piece of advice from all of this: every kitchen needs a meat thermometer! I got one for our friend's house as a small recompense for Wellygate.

So hopefully no kitchen disasters here. This is an elegant duck tart that's not difficult to make. We are buying the pastry and the cooked duck legs that I love so much. Apples, redcurrant and sesame make up the rest of it along with a hint of spice for interest.

I really wanted to make this salad with beef short rib but while it would have been stupendous, it would also have been a bit of a palaver. Instead, I'm making it with rib-eye steak. There's not a salad leaf in sight but all the ingredients resonate of autumnal cooking. It's hearty but not heavy with a gorgeous, sturdy dressing.

The roasted figs and plums are delicious with blue cheese and the oaty crumble. I've made extra syrup to use with cava or prosecco. It perks things up and adds a bit of glamour.

DUCK AND SPICED APPLE GALETTE

SERVES 4

2 tbsp malt vinegar

1 tbsp golden brown sugar

1 tbsp butter

1 tsp wholegrain mustard

½ tsp mixed spice

2 cooking apples, peeled and cored

2 confit duck legs (300g), skin removed and the meat shredded

1 x 320g sheet of ready-rolled shortcrust pastry, thawed

1 egg beaten with 1 tbsp milk

1 tbsp redcurrant jelly, melted

1 tbsp sesame seeds, toasted

redcurrants, for scattering (optional)

Preheat the oven to 185°C.

Put the vinegar, brown sugar, butter, mustard and mixed spice in a saucepan. Quarter and slice the apples into 1cm-thick pieces, then add to the pan. Cook on a high heat for 5 minutes, until the apples soften but don't let them get mushy. Fold the shredded duck meat through the apples, season and allow to cool.

Unfold the pastry, then put the parchment from the packet on a baking tray and lay the pastry on top. Brush the pastry with egg wash, then spread the mixture on the base, leaving a 3cm border all around. Turn the edge of the pastry in on itself to form a lip, then brush the edge with egg wash again.

Bake in the oven for 20 minutes, then remove from the oven, brush the tart with the melted redcurrant jelly and scatter over the sesame seeds and redcurrants (if using). Return to the oven to bake for 5 minutes more.

Eat warm with a watercress salad dressed with a little nut oil as a perfect accompaniment to the galette.

A SPECIAL AUTUMN SALAD

SERVES 4

1 x 250g rib-eye steak

½ celeriac

½ Savoy cabbage

2 ripe pears

1 packet of radishes

80g walnuts, toasted

FOR THE DRESSING:

150ml sherry or red wine vinegar

3 tbsp raisins (blonde if possible)

2 tbsp golden brown sugar

1 cinnamon stick

1 sprig of fresh thyme

2 tbsp Dijon mustard

200ml sunflower oil, plus extra to cook the steak

100ml olive oil

To make the dressing, put the vinegar, raisins, brown sugar, cinnamon stick and thyme in a small pan. Bring to the boil, then immediately take off the heat. Whisk in the mustard, then drizzle in the sunflower and olive oils. Season and set aside. This will make more than you need but it will keep for two weeks or more in the fridge.

Heat a little sunflower oil in a pan over a high heat, until it's gently smoking. Season the steak and carefully put it in the pan. Cook for 3 minutes on each side for medium-rare. The cooking time will depend on how you like your steak and how thick it is, so you will have to use your judgement. Remove the steak from the pan and allow to rest, covered, in a warm place.

Peel and thinly slice the celeriac into a bowl (a mandolin is perfect for this). Trim and shred the cabbage, then wash and dry it and add to the celeriac. Slice the pears and radishes, then add them to the bowl along with the toasted walnuts.

Thinly slice the steak and add it to the vegetables along with any juices from the plate. Spoon over some of the dressing, season, mix and it's ready to eat.

I like to serve this with a little horseradish crème fraîche. Just mix 1 tablespoon of horseradish sauce into a 200ml tub of crème fraîche and there you have it.

CROZIER BLUE, ROASTED PLUM, FIG AND OAT CRUMBLE

SERVES 4

4 ripe figs, halved
4 ripe plums, halved and stoned
200ml apple juice
1 tbsp dark brown sugar
1 star anise
1 cinnamon stick
1 bay leaf (fresh if possible)
1 sprig of fresh thyme
150g Crozier Blue cheese (or another blue cheese if Crozier is unavailable)

FOR THE CRUMBLE:
110g butter, softened
100g jumbo oats
55g plain flour
25g caster sugar
a pinch of salt

Preheat the oven to 185°C.

Put the figs and plums in an ovenproof dish, then add the apple juice and scatter the sugar over the fruit. Add the spices and herbs, then bake in the oven for 20 minutes, until the fruit is soft and tender. Allow to cool.

For the crumble, put the butter, oats, flour, sugar and a pinch of salt in a bowl and rub together until combined into a crumble mixture – it should have a sandy texture. Spread out on a baking tray and bake in the oven for 12–15 minutes, until golden.

Serve the cheese with the fruit, the crumble and a little residual syrup.

I'm a massive fan of a good curry

06 NOVEMBER 2021

I'm a massive fan of a good curry although it's not something I cook on a regular basis at home. There are some excellent and ambitious restaurants opening up around the country that show just how fabulous and diverse Indian food is.

Having said that, I'll happily dig into a chicken tikka masala as keenly as the next man. I sop up the remnants from the foil container with my Peshwari naan, the sauce inevitably dripping onto my shirt.

I've even relished the leftovers for breakfast — the flavour hit is the perfect foil for a seedy head. My fingers this time greedily curl around the remnants of sauce and I slurp it in before anyone catches me. It's not unusual for another shirt to bite the dust. I'm as messy as a toddler.

These recipes are entirely different. The chicken dish is adapted from Pat Chapman, a chef and author who founded the Curry Club in the UK. I have a book of his dating from the 1990s. This is a gem of a recipe. It resembles a korma, so it's a crowd pleaser. The saffron is optional but lovely. There's a bit of spice action going on but if you don't have them all, don't worry, it'll be good all the same.

The lamb vindaloo comes courtesy of our friends Jane and James. Jane did our flowers when we opened the restaurant 25 years ago. They invited us to dinner when everybody else was afraid to have a chef to the house. Over the years we've had lots of good times together. This is one of the dishes from many years ago; I still remember it. It's not as hot as you might think but if you are worried, just omit the chilli. It's a bit of a hybrid but it works. Eat with naan and mango yogurt to cool it down. You can buy frozen cubes of mango in the supermarket — I'm never without them.

While not a curry, this egg dish is easy and delicious. The tarka refers to a method of cooking the whole spices. Leave the egg runny so it lubricates the potatoes.

BENGALI CHICKEN REZALA

SERVES 4

4 tbsp sunflower oil

1 tsp coriander seeds, crushed

1 tsp cumin seeds

½ tsp black mustard seeds

½ tsp fennel seeds

½ tsp sesame seeds

½ tsp fenugreek seeds

2 onions, finely diced

3 garlic cloves, finely chopped

4 boneless, skinless chicken fillets, cubed

2 fresh green chillies, sliced lengthways

1 x 400ml tin of coconut milk

2 tbsp sultanas

2 tbsp ground almonds

2 tsp garam masala

1 tsp caster sugar

20 saffron strands (optional)

juice of 1 lime

chopped fresh mint

chopped fresh coriander

Heat the sunflower oil in a saucepan over a medium heat. Add the spices and cook for 30 seconds, then add the onions and garlic. Turn down the heat and cook for 15 minutes, until the onions start to caramelise.

Add the chicken and chillies and turn them around in the pan until the chicken starts to take on a little colour.

Add the coconut milk, sultanas, ground almonds, garam masala, sugar and saffron (if using) and bring to a simmer. Cook for 6–7 minutes, until the sauce thickens and starts to coat the chicken, then add the lime juice and some salt and pepper. Finally, stir in the mint and coriander.

Serve with basmati rice and warm naan.

PULLED LAMB VINDALOO WITH MANGO YOGURT

SERVES 6

4 onions, cut into 1cm-thick rings

1 x 2kg lamb shoulder, bone in

4 garlic cloves, crushed

2 tbsp vindaloo curry paste

1 tbsp golden brown sugar

1 tbsp finely chopped fresh rosemary

1 tsp chilli flakes

250ml red wine

100ml red wine vinegar

FOR THE YOGURT:

150g mango flesh, thawed if frozen

150g natural yogurt

TO SERVE:

warm naan

Preheat the oven to 170°C.

Arrange the onions on the base of a roasting tin to form a trivet and sit the lamb shoulder on top.

Blend the garlic, curry paste, sugar, rosemary, chilli flakes, red wine, vinegar and some salt and pepper. Pour on top of the lamb and massage it in. Cover tightly with foil and cook in the oven for 3 hours.

Remove the foil and cook for 1 more hour, until the lamb is crusty on the outside and meltingly tender inside and can be pulled apart.

To make the mango yogurt, simply blend the mango and yogurt together.

Serve the pulled lamb with warm naan to roll the meat up in and drizzle the yogurt on top.

SPICED POTATOES WITH CHILLI-FRIED EGGS

SERVES 2

3 tbsp sunflower oil

2 large Rooster potatoes, peeled and cut into 1cm cubes

2 garlic cloves, skin on and lightly crushed

½ tsp cumin seeds

½ tsp coriander seeds

a knob of butter

4 eggs

1 small fresh red chilli, deseeded and sliced

a pinch of nigella seeds (optional)

Heat the oil in a large frying pan over a medium-high heat. When the oil is gently smoking, carefully add the potatoes and mix them into the oil. Cover and cook for 10 minutes or so to let the potatoes steam. Remove the lid and add the garlic, cumin and coriander seeds and a pinch of salt, then keep cooking to allow the potatoes to crisp up. Drain on kitchen paper and keep warm.

Wipe out the pan and put it on a high heat, then add the butter. When the butter starts to foam, crack the eggs into the pan and cook for 1 minute, then add the chilli and nigella seeds (if using). Season.

Serve the fried eggs on top of the potatoes.

A whiff of wintry smoke

13 NOVEMBER 2021

I love food imbued with a gentle smoke. It always makes winter more tolerable. I avoid anything over-smoked, though. It just gives off unpleasant soccer hooligan vibes, the smoke so dominating it can ruin my day.

I have quite a few food heroes. Some are chefs and some are food writers. The common thread with them all is a love of simple food. They are also great communicators. One notable lady is Diana Henry. I have all of her many books. For a fella who's been around for a long time, she always brings something new and makes me realise how much more I still have to learn about food.

Her book *Salt Sugar Smoke* is a particular favourite. Diana takes the reader on a journey around the extremities of Europe with her recipes, places I've never been to in the curtailed mind of a classically French-trained chef. I relish those journeys. The atmospheric photos are transportive. In my mind I'm devouring a belly-warming stew while snatching glimpses of an icy landscape through the frostbitten windows of a winter cabin.

The first dish is a riff on a kedgeree. I've just substituted the rice for sheets of pasta and layer the whole thing up like a lasagne. I'm not using a lot of fish; it's a flavouring for the rest of the dish. This can be made ahead of time then baked when you need it. It's perfect for the freezer if you want to get ahead of yourself.

The next dish is a version of baked cheese. It's for a niche market of cheese and turnip lovers and is deliciously off-piste. I'm using Cavanbert from Corleggy. Use a ripe Brie or Camembert if you can't find it. Be brave, try it. They go together like a dream.

The cabbage might seem like an unusual addition to this frittata, but to be honest I'd stick cabbage into anything given a chance. A little more horseradish mixed with crème fraîche would be a wonderful accompaniment. The dish will have a sweet, gentle smoke, just how I like it.

LEEK AND SMOKED HADDOCK LASAGNE WITH CURRY SPICES

SERVES 6

600ml milk

250ml cream

2 tsp curry powder

2 bay leaves (fresh if possible)

2cm piece of ginger, peeled and finely chopped

2 leeks, cut into 0.5cm-thick rounds

250g smoked haddock fillet, bones removed

2 tbsp raisins

50g butter

40g plain flour

9 dried lasagne sheets

120g mature Cheddar cheese, grated

50g Parmesan cheese, grated

Put the milk, cream, curry powder, bay leaves, ginger and some salt and pepper in a pot and whisk together. Add the leeks, smoked haddock and raisins, cover and gently bring to a simmer. Cook for 3 minutes, then allow to cool off the heat.

Stir the leeks and smoked haddock to break up the fish into smaller pieces. Strain all the liquid from the pot into a bowl and set aside the leek and haddock mix.

Melt the butter in a separate saucepan, then add the flour. Whisk together over a gentle heat, then slowly add the cooking liquid until you get a smooth cream sauce. Continue to cook over a very low heat for 10 minutes, whisking frequently to make sure there are no lumps in the sauce. It will gradually thicken up. Check the seasoning.

Pour a layer of curry cream over the base of a deep casserole or baking dish, then add three sheets of pasta on top. Scatter half of the leek and haddock mix over the pasta, then enough of the sauce to cover, followed by some of the cheese.

Put another layer of pasta sheets on top, followed by the remaining leek and haddock mix, some more sauce and more cheese.

Cover with the final layer of pasta, then top with the remaining sauce and cheese. At this point, when it's cool you can put it in the freezer if you like.

Preheat the oven to 185°C.

Bake in the oven for 40 minutes, until golden and bubbling. Allow to stand for 10 minutes before cutting into slices to serve.

BAKED CAVANBERT WITH CIDER-ROASTED TURNIP AND BLACK FOREST HAM

SERVES 2

1 small turnip

200ml cider

1 tbsp butter

½ tbsp golden brown sugar

1 cinnamon stick

1 sprig of fresh thyme

1 x 200g wheel of Cavanbert cheese (if it's a little larger, it doesn't matter – or use a ripe Brie or Camembert)

a drizzle of maple syrup

4 slices of Black Forest smoked ham

Preheat the oven to 180°C.

Peel and chop the turnip into 1cm dice as best you can. It will be a little tricky but use your best knife and take your time.

Put the turnip in a shallow casserole or baking dish. Add the cider, butter, brown sugar, cinnamon, thyme and some salt and pepper. Bake in the oven for 40 minutes, turning once or twice, until the turnip is tender (leave it in longer if it's still hard).

Unwrap the cheese and put it in the centre of the turnip. Drizzle everything with a little maple syrup and put the casserole back in the oven for a further 10 minutes to warm through.

To serve, artfully drape the ham over the cheese. Put in the centre of the table and help yourself.

SMOKED MACKEREL AND CABBAGE FRITTATA
SERVES 6

1 tbsp butter

a little olive oil

1 red onion, sliced

3 leaves of Savoy cabbage, shredded

8 unpeeled baby potatoes, cooked and thickly sliced

1 tbsp horseradish sauce

6 eggs

2 fillets of smoked mackerel, skin and bones removed

a good pinch of grated Cheddar cheese

Preheat the oven to 200°C.

Melt the butter with the oil in a non-stick ovenproof frying pan over a gentle heat. When the butter starts to foam, add the onion and cabbage and cook for 5 minutes. Add the cooked potato slices and continue to cook for a minute or so.

Put the horseradish sauce in a bowl, crack the eggs on top and beat with some salt and pepper. Turn the heat up in the pan, then add the eggs. Mix everything carefully together with a spatula, scraping the bottom of the pan in a gentle motion for a minute or two as the egg sets.

Scatter pieces of mackerel evenly over the top of the eggs and scatter over the cheese. Transfer the pan to the oven and bake in the oven for 12 minutes or so, until the eggs are set and the top is golden.

To serve, you can turn this out onto a chopping board or slice it directly from the pan. Best eaten warm.

Three pies ... okay, one's a crumble

20 NOVEMBER 2021

In my childhood home, we were the guinea pigs for every 1970s food fad going: dried Potato Smash (just add water), Angel Delight, Findus Crispy Pancakes and my lingering memory, Fray Bentos steak and kidney pies. I never minded them, really, although the wet blanket that passed for a crust resembled something that was discarded from an operating theatre more than a crisp golden topping. Despite this, I am still a massive fan of pies in all their shapes and sizes.

Some years ago, Máire and I flew over to Heston Blumenthal's Fat Duck for lunch. I know! *eye roll* How very Celtic Tiger of us. So after 'snail porridge', 'sound of the sea' and innumerable other courses, including the final and most impressive one, 'the wallet buster', we exited onto the street, sweating, with a few hours to kill before the flight home.

We passed the Hinds Head, Heston's other premises in Bray, Berkshire, a Michelin-star pub with a legendary reputation for pioneering British food. I had to go in. I ate the steak and kidney pudding and since I was there I also tucked into a Scotch egg followed by a treacle tart to keep it company. My wife ate nothing but looked on with a combination of wonder and disgust. It was a long flight home for all sorts of reasons.

This chicken pie is fab. I've adapted it from a Greek recipe by buying a pre-roasted chicken. It cuts out a lot of faff. The eggs in the pie are a revelation and the humble, well-softened onion supports the chicken admirably.

I had to stop myself putting chorizo into the peperonata pie. It would work brilliantly but I wanted to keep it vegetarian. But don't let me stop you. A little bit in with the peppers would be lovely. I'm also making the mash with olive oil and Parmesan. It's a nice change.

Okay, perhaps the sausage crumble isn't technically a pie but I wanted to make every recipe different today. Use the largest sausages you can find and that will keep the cooking times accurate.

GREEK-STYLE CHICKEN PIE

SERVES 6

100g butter, plus extra melted butter for brushing

6 onions, diced

2 bay leaves (fresh if possible)

1 x 1.2kg shop-bought freshly cooked chicken

3 eggs, beaten

5 sheets of filo pastry, thawed

Preheat the oven to 200°C.

Put the butter in a saucepan with the onions and bay leaves. Cover and cook over a gentle heat for 20 minutes, until the onions become soft and translucent.

Take the chicken from its bag and pour all the chicken juices into the onions to reduce and become jammy, then take the pan off the heat.

Remove the skin from the chicken. Discard half and chop the rest of the skin finely. Chop the chicken into chunks. Add the skin and meat to the onions, followed by the eggs. Mix everything together and season.

Brush a deep springform cake tin (mine is 25cm wide x 5cm deep) with melted butter. Line the tin with four of the filo pastry sheets at alternate angles along the base and sides of the tin. The pastry should overhang the sides and each sheet should be brushed with a little melted butter.

Put the chicken mixture in the tin. Fold the last sheet of filo in half and put it on top of the chicken mixture. Bring the overhanging filo back over the top to seal and brush the top with a little more melted butter.

Bake in the oven for 30 minutes, until golden and crisp. Serve with a green salad.

PEPERONATA PIE

SERVES 4

4 tbsp olive oil

2 garlic cloves, sliced

2 red peppers, cut into chunks

1 sprig of fresh rosemary

1 tsp smoked paprika

1 x 400g tin of chopped tomatoes

1 x 400g tin of kidney beans, drained
and rinsed

1 vegetable or chicken stock cube,
crumbled

1 tbsp honey

FOR THE MASH:

1.5kg potatoes, peeled

100g Parmesan cheese, grated

150ml milk

50ml olive oil

Put the oil in a pot with the garlic, peppers and rosemary. Cover and cook for 15 minutes over a gentle heat, turning once or twice.

Remove the rosemary and add the smoked paprika (and some diced chorizo if you want) and continue to cook for a little while longer over a higher heat.

Add the tomatoes, kidney beans, crumbled stock cube and honey. Let everything blip and reduce for 15 minutes or so, until the mixture becomes thick and unctuous. Season and put in a casserole.

Meanwhile, boil the potatoes until soft, then drain. Mash them with the Parmesan, milk, oil and some salt and ground white pepper.

Spoon the mashed potatoes on top of the peperonata in the dish. This can all be done the day before if necessary or frozen if required.

Preheat the oven to 185°C.

Cook the peperonata pie in the oven for 25 minutes, until the mash is golden. Serve warm.

SAUSAGE, SWEET POTATO AND RED ONION CRUMBLE
SERVES 4

1 sweet potato, peeled, halved and cut into 1cm-thick slices

3 red onions, quartered

8 large sausages

a few sprigs of fresh thyme

2 bay leaves (fresh if possible)

3 tbsp olive oil

100ml chicken stock

FOR THE CRUMBLE:

175g plain flour

100g butter, diced

50g Parmesan cheese, grated

Preheat the oven to 190°C.

Put the sweet potato, onions, sausages and herbs in a medium-sized roasting tin. Drizzle over the oil and turn everything together, then pour over the chicken stock.

To make the crumble, put all the ingredients in a bowl and rub together until you get a sandy texture, then scatter it over the sausage mixture.

Bake in the oven for 30–40 minutes (depending on the size of your sausages), until the crumble topping is crunchy and golden. Serve straightaway.

A memorable winter dinner

27 NOVEMBER 2021

I love cooking at home for people who love food. There's pleasure in the planning and the preparation and even in the shopping. It's a process.

The number of people you have coming will determine the menu. That, and the time of year. If it's the depths of winter you're not going to be giving them a tomato salad. If it's a hot summer day you won't be cooking stew. It's logic, really.

There are other considerations too. Age, gender — this all matters. Unless Grandad is hip and enlightened, you might not give him couscous. Indeed, no teeth, no steak! Something soft and melting will keep him sweet. There's always the will to consider.

A gang of ladies might not be into Fergus Henderson's roasted bone marrow. Okay, that's an extreme, but you get my drift. The lads are diverse too. We have the metrosexuals or the country boys. I am friends with both. There's a menu for all. Food is kaleidoscopic in its options.

I realise all these generalisations are extremely risqué these days. Sometimes I wonder have we lost our sense of humour along with a couple of years of our lives.

The soup is old-fashioned and delicious. The sherry lifts the mushrooms to new heights but it's optional. It will still be lovely without it.

The duck cake is a showstopper. It's a two-part process. The sticky duck filling resonates of gentle Moroccan flavours and the potato mixture holds everything together. Once they are prepared, the rest is easy. It's just a question of assembly. It can even be made the day before, then baked the next day. I like to eat this with simply done cabbage, tenderstem broccoli or a green salad.

I'm a fan of roasted winter fruit. Syrupy cooked figs and plums are an almost Christmassy joy when they come out of the oven. I've included spice and herbs to add to the complexity. They nestle on a silky cushion of a brown sugar panna cotta. The whole thing is as delightful as a Wibbly Wobbly Wonder.

CHESTNUT MUSHROOM, PARSNIP AND SHERRY SOUP
SERVES 6

80g butter

a splash of olive oil

1 onion, finely diced

1 large parsnip, finely diced

1 garlic clove, sliced

1 sprig of fresh sage

500g chestnut mushrooms, chopped

1.4 litres chicken stock

150ml cream

a little ground nutmeg

75ml cream sherry (optional)

a nice Irish hard cheese like Coolea or a good Cheddar, grated

Melt the butter with the oil in a pot over a gentle heat. When the butter starts to foam, add the onion, parsnip, garlic and sage. Cook for 15 minutes or so, until the vegetables really soften. Add the mushrooms, turn up the heat and cook for a further 10 minutes.

Add the stock and bring to a simmer. Add the cream and nutmeg and cook gently for a little while. Add some salt and pepper and finally the sherry (if using). Remove the sage and blend the soup thoroughly with a hand blender or liquidizer.

Serve with a dusting of grated cheese on top.

STICKY DUCK, DATE AND POTATO CAKE

SERVES 6

50g butter

a little residual fat from the duck legs

4 onions, sliced

1 sprig of fresh thyme

1 tbsp golden brown sugar

1 tsp ras el hanout

½ tsp ground cinnamon

4 confit duck legs, skin removed and the meat shredded

8 dates, stoned and chopped

FOR THE POTATO MIXTURE:

1.2kg floury potatoes, peeled

100g butter, plus extra melted butter for brushing

150ml milk

a pinch of ground nutmeg

4 eggs, beaten

1 egg yolk, beaten

100g panko breadcrumbs or stale breadcrumbs

Put the butter, duck fat, onions and thyme in a large pan. Cover and cook for 10 minutes over a gentle heat. When the onions soften, add the sugar and spices and continue to cook, uncovered, for another 10 minutes, until the onions start to get sticky.

Add the duck and the dates and let it all come together over a gentle heat for another 5 minutes, until the mixture becomes almost jammy. Season, remove the thyme and set aside.

Meanwhile, boil and strain the potatoes, then mash them with the butter, milk, nutmeg, salt and ground white pepper. Beat the four eggs with the one yolk and fold it in – it should resemble a thick, lumpy batter.

Brush a large springform cake tin all around with melted butter, then dust with the breadcrumbs. Put half of the potato mixture in the tin, then top with the duck mixture but do not take it right to the edge – leave a 2cm border.

Cover the duck with the remaining potato, smooth the top and dust with more breadcrumbs. Drizzle a little melted butter over the top of the cake.

Preheat the oven to 190°C.

Cook the cake in the oven for 45 minutes, until golden and bubbling. Let it stand for 15 minutes before running a knife around the edges and releasing from the tin to serve.

ORANGE PANNA COTTA WITH ROASTED FIGS, PLUMS AND THYME

SERVES 6

350ml cream
80g golden brown sugar
peel of 1 orange
2 drops of vanilla extract
2½ leaves of gelatine
350ml milk

FOR THE FRUIT:
6 ripe figs, halved
4 ripe plums, halved, stoned and quartered
100ml apple juice
50g golden brown sugar
2 cinnamon sticks
1 sprig of fresh thyme

Put the cream, sugar, orange and vanilla in a larger pot than you think you need and bring gently to a simmer, then set aside and keep warm.

Meanwhile, soak the gelatine in cold water until it softens.

Remove the orange peel from the cream. Squeeze out the gelatine, then whisk it into the warm cream. When you're sure it's melted, whisk in the milk. Divide the mixture among six nice serving dishes or china cups. Put in the fridge to set for at least 4 hours.

Preheat the oven to 185°C.

Put the fruit in a baking dish, cut side up. Pour in the apple juice and sprinkle over the sugar. Tuck in the cinnamon and thyme and bake in the oven for 20–30 minutes, until melting and tender. This will all depend on how ripe your fruit is.

Allow to cool and serve on top of the panna cotta.

Get your festive feast off to a stunning start

04 DECEMBER 2021

The big day is approaching rapidly. Annoyingly, it now starts at the end of the summer when the Christmas shops open, then really kicks into gear when the TV ads and festive cookery programmes pummel us from the beginning of November. I'm almost burnt out from it all by December. I always have a massive grumblefest around this time. The dragging-out of Christmas almost takes the good out of it. Almost!

My spare thoughts are dominated by twinkly lights, baubles and glitter. It's almost unbecoming for a man of my age. I constantly think of menus, recipes, parties and people. My lists give birth to more lists. The social butterfly in me has been curtailed these last couple of years. I need to go to parties to flit again and get back to normal before I become a recluse. Like Howard Hughes but without the money.

Over the next few weeks I'm going to be concentrating on all things Christmas, beginning today with a few nifty starters. Not everybody has starters on Christmas Day. Lots are content with a few nibbles as they steel themselves for the onslaught of calories. These easy dishes can of course be served anytime you wish. They are elegant but not complicated — who needs any more complication when your oven is stuffed to the gills and the stress levels are stratospheric?

Goatsbridge Trout is a heart-warming Irish producer success story. Its subtlety and gentle smoke have enamoured me. Trout roe adds the glamour that is required at this time of year. Be not afraid, it's just a little salty pop that can quickly become addictive. The trout is available in specialist shops. Use smoked salmon if you can't find it.

These little goat cheese pots are perfect if you're having a few people over. You can make them the day before to make life easy. Serve with toasted baguette on the side.

The prawns are a bit of a riff on the Spanish dish pil pil, but gentler and more nuanced. I'm serving this with toasted brioche on the side to mop up the precious juices once the prawns are gone.

GOATSBRIDGE TROUT, CUCUMBER AND BUTTERHEAD WITH CLEMENTINE DRESSING

SERVES 6

2 heads of butterhead lettuce, leaves separated

1 cucumber

200g Goatsbridge smoked trout or smoked salmon

FOR THE DRESSING:

juice of 2 clementines

100ml sunflower oil

100ml rapeseed oil

2 tbsp chopped fresh dill

1 tbsp baby capers

1 tsp wholegrain mustard

a pinch of caster sugar

2 tsp trout roe (optional but lovely)

Put the clementine juice, oils, dill, capers, mustard, sugar and some salt and pepper in a bowl and whisk together. Stir in the trout roe (if using) and refrigerate. This can be done the day before.

When ready to serve, put the lettuce leaves on a festive platter. Take ribbons off the cucumber with a vegetable peeler until you reach the core of the cucumber (you can discard this).

Cut the smoked trout or salmon into strips, then scatter it over the lettuce and cucumber.

Whisk the dressing to amalgamate, then spoon it over the salad to serve.

WHIPPED GOAT CHEESE AND CRANBERRY POTS
SERVES 8

1 large cooking apple, peeled, cored and sliced

1 tbsp water

1 tsp golden brown sugar

a pinch of ground cinnamon

2 x 150g logs of soft rindless goat cheese

1 x 180g tub of light cream cheese

1 tsp honey

roughly chopped salted almonds

dried cranberries

Put the apple in a small pot with the water, sugar and cinnamon. Cook over a medium heat for 4–5 minutes, until the apple breaks down and gets mushy. Help it along with a wooden spoon so it's relatively smooth.

Break up the goat cheese into a bowl and add the cream cheese and honey. Whisk with an electric hand whisk, starting slowly at first, until it's light and fluffy.

Using nice ramekins or old-fashioned china cups, put a layer of apple on the bottom of each cup, followed by the whipped goat cheese. Put in the fridge until needed, then scatter with some almonds and dried cranberries.

Allow to come to room temperature before serving.

PRAWNS WITH SMOKED PAPRIKA AND ROSEMARY BUTTER

SERVES 6

150g butter

50ml good olive oil

1 garlic clove, thinly sliced

½ tsp smoked paprika

a pinch of chilli flakes

1 sprig of fresh rosemary

30 large Dublin Bay, king or tiger prawns, shells removed

juice of ½ orange

Put the butter, oil, garlic, smoked paprika, chilli flakes and rosemary in a shallow pan and heat until the butter melts. Let it bubble gently for a minute or two. You can do this ahead of time if you like and set aside.

Add the prawns to the butter and poach over a low heat for 2–3 minutes, depending on the size and type of prawn. When cooked, add the orange juice and some salt and pepper.

Serve in warm dishes with toasted brioche. You could even serve it on top of the brioche.

I'm putting stuffing on the side for the first time ever this year

11 DECEMBER 2021

I've decided to pare back this year and not cook a whole turkey. The crown will do. I'm not a mad fan of the legs anyhow but I will miss the visuals of the whole bird. Another minus is that there is nowhere to put the stuffing. I have to come up with another plan.

Often during a Christmassy cookery class someone will ask if I stuff my bird. I always quip that it's called stuffing for a reason. A stuffing that's baked on the side is a rude impostor! I have always argued that to make a stuffing properly delicious, it needs those juices from the turkey as it roasts. It's a missed opportunity otherwise. Hopefully I'll be happily eating these recipes and not miserably chewing on my own words, as for the first time ever I am putting the stuffing on the side. I'm calling it a pudding to spare my blushes.

I'm cooking the crown over slices of celeriac with smoked bacon and optional but delicious porcini. The stock is there to help steam the bird for the first part of cooking, then I'll leave it uncovered to colour and strain the mushroom juices for this somewhat decadent sauce. (I'm abandoning gravy this year.) I then crush the celeriac for another flavour-imbued vegetable and to make life easy.

The stuffing recipe is a bit of a hybrid: half stuffing, half pudding. In case you're not having ham, I've put bacon in it. I personally couldn't live without a ham at Christmas, whatever about the turkey. You can cook this pudding the day before if you like, then cut slices off it and warm them according to your needs or simply cook and serve on the day. I've made extra for the obligatory sandwiches later.

I'm giving you a couple of options for vegetable dishes although I would suggest that if you have the celeriac you might not need the parsnips. Sometimes more is more just for the sake of it, plus it's another thing to wash. All you need, then, are a few roasties to complete the picture and everything should be perfect. I'll have my fingers crossed.

TURKEY CROWN WITH SHERRY CREAM

SERVES 8

1 celeriac

4 slices of smoked streaky bacon

20g dried porcini mushrooms (optional)

1 large sprig of fresh thyme

2 bay leaves (fresh if possible)

300ml chicken stock

1 x 1.8kg turkey crown

100g butter, softened

a squeeze of lemon

FOR THE SHERRY CREAM:

150ml cream

100ml cream sherry

10 cooked chestnuts, roughly chopped (optional)

a squeeze of lemon

Preheat the oven to 185°C.

Trim the celeriac with a large serrated knife and cut into five even slices. Put these in the bottom of a medium-sized roasting tin, then add the bacon, porcini (if using), thyme, bay and stock.

Sit the turkey on top of the celeriac, brush the skin with most of the butter using the back of a spoon and season. Cover with foil and roast in the oven for 1 hour.

Remove the tin from the oven and baste the skin with any remaining butter, then put it back in the oven for 45 minutes to finish cooking and turn golden.

Set the turkey aside on another tray to rest, covered with foil. Take the bacon, porcini, thyme and bay out of the tin, then strain off the juices into a saucepan.

Leave the celeriac in the tin. Run a knife through it to make it easier to work with, then crush and check for seasoning. Add a little lemon juice and transfer to a bowl to keep warm.

For the sauce, put the turkey juices from the resting tray in the saucepan with the strained cooking juices, then bring to a simmer. Add the cream and sherry and reduce for a couple of minutes, until the sauce starts to thicken. Add the chestnuts (if using) and a little lemon juice.

Slice the turkey and serve with the crushed celeriac, the pudding on page 492 and the sprouts and parsnips on page 493. Delicately spoon the sauce over the top like a professional.

SAGE, ONION AND CRANBERRY PUDDING

SERVES 10

100g mixed raisins and dried cranberries

120g butter, plus extra melted butter for brushing

2 onions, finely chopped

125g smoked bacon lardons

10 fresh sage leaves, shredded

500g fresh white breadcrumbs

zest and juice of 2 clementines

½ tsp mixed spice

a good pinch of ground nutmeg

350ml warm milk

2 eggs, beaten

Preheat the oven to 185°C.

Soak the raisins and cranberries in a bowl of just-boiled water for 15 minutes to plump them up, then drain.

Melt the butter in a saucepan over a low heat. When the butter starts to foam, add the onions, bacon lardons and sage. Cook for about 15 minutes, until everything is soft, jammy and without colour. Remove the pan from the heat.

Add the drained raisins and cranberries to the onions. Fold in the breadcrumbs along with the zest and juice of the clementines. Add the spices and season, then add the milk and eggs. Bring everything together.

Take two sheets of foil and brush the shiny side with melted butter. Roll the stuffing in the foil to form two large sausage-shaped puddings. This can be done a day or two before.

Bake the puddings in the oven for 45 minutes, then cut into steamy wedges to serve.

CRUSHED SPROUTS WITH NUTMEG BROWN BUTTER

SERVES 8

100g butter
$^1\!/_3$ nutmeg, freshly grated
500g Brussels sprouts, halved

Put the butter in a saucepan over a low to medium heat. Without stirring, allow it to melt and bubble. A foam will appear after a short time. When it does, turn the heat down. After a minute or so, the foam will settle and start to turn an amber colour around the edges. Remove the pan from the heat, add the nutmeg and set aside. Cook the sprouts in a pot of boiling salted water. They will need to be soft all the way through while still keeping their colour. Drain and crush with the nutmeg brown butter and some salt and pepper.

PARSNIPS WITH CINNAMON AND GINGER ALE

SERVES 8

1kg parsnips
80g butter, diced
150ml ginger ale
150ml chicken stock
2 cinnamon sticks
a few sprigs of fresh thyme

Preheat the oven to 185°C. Take the root off the parsnips, then peel and cut them into quarters lengthways. Put them in a roasting tin with all the remaining ingredients. Cover with foil and bake in the oven for 30 minutes. Remove the foil and turn the parsnips in the juices, then put the tin back in the oven for a further 15 minutes, until the parsnips get sticky. Keep warm until needed.

Walk-away-and-let-them-cook recipes

18 DECEMBER 2021

As I write, we still hope to have family home from Zurich for Christmas. The house will be full to the brim. We couldn't have them last year, so this year we intend to make the most of it. I'll have to get my own bottle bank.

These are special occasion dishes. Feeding a gang can get to you if you let it. There are lots of permutations. Vegetable dodgers, shellfish allergies, pescatarians and vegetarians. None of this will deter me.

Everyone has their role. My sister-in-law is the organiser. Her husband is the dishwasher Jedi. He spends most of his time hunched over the thing at Christmas. I always suspect he might have wine stashed in there.

The kitchen will be humming. Hordes of teenagers will make an appearance only when they are hungry. The shopping and chopping will be never-ending but the food will comfort us as we do our best to block out the grim reality of the last two years.

Our OCD Westie (think Jack Nicholson in *As Good As It Gets*) will be reversing through people's legs in the kitchen as she's got some bizarre issue with the floorboards. Throw in hard-of-hearing Granny and Grandad and it will be long-awaited, glorious mayhem.

Baked cheese should be compulsory at Christmas. This is really easy and also a little bit different. You can find filo pastry in the freezer section of major supermarkets and this chutney is a doddle to make.

The osso buco is a meat lover's dream. Your butcher should be able to get the beef shin for you. The figs and spices make it festive. I would eat it with mash but creamy polenta would be lovely too.

The salmon is a great dish for a crowd. There's no messing with pots and pans. The idea is to spoon the salmon apart and mix through the cabbage. The Pernod adds a nice touch but in fairness I don't expect you to buy a bottle just for the quantity you need here. Sambuca would also work. It's nice to have a bit of fish at Christmas to mix things up a little.

BAKED COOLEENEY CAMEMBERT WITH CRIMSON GRAPE CHUTNEY

SERVES 6

4 sheets of filo pastry, thawed
80g butter, melted
2 x 200g rounds of Cooleeney Camembert cheese
a few sprigs of fresh thyme, leaves picked

FOR THE CHUTNEY:
500g seedless red grapes
200ml red wine
1 cinnamon stick
2 cloves
1 heaped tbsp redcurrant jelly

Preheat the oven to 185°C.

For the chutney, put all the ingredients in a saucepan. Bring to a simmer and cook for 15–20 minutes, until thick and syrupy. Allow to cool and store in the fridge.

Meanwhile, take two sheets of filo pastry, one on top of the other, and brush the top lightly with melted butter. Put the cheese in the centre and sprinkle some thyme over it, then bring the filo up and around the cheese. Scrunch it around the Camembert to seal. The rougher it is, the better it will look.

Transfer to a buttered baking tray and repeat the process with the other round of cheese. This can be done ahead of time and kept in the fridge.

Bake in the oven for 25 minutes, until golden and crunchy.

Serve with the chutney, either heated or at room temperature.

OSSO BUCO OF BEEF, RED WINE AND FIGS

SERVES 6

4 pieces of beef shin, cut 3cm thick across the bone (1.5kg in total)

3 tbsp plain flour

4 tbsp sunflower oil

2 red onions, quartered

125g smoked bacon lardons

120g dried figs, halved

2 garlic cloves, halved

3 star anise

300ml beef stock

200ml red wine

1 tbsp redcurrant jelly

3 bay leaves (fresh if possible)

Preheat the oven to 165°C.

Cut the outside sinew of each piece of beef two or three times so it doesn't curl while cooking. Turn the beef in the flour and some seasoning, then pat off any excess flour.

Heat the oil in a wide casserole over a medium-high heat until it's gently smoking. Add the beef and brown on both sides. Add the red onions in the gaps, then scatter over the bacon, figs, garlic and star anise.

Add the beef stock, red wine, redcurrant jelly and bay leaves. Cover and cook in the oven for 2½ hours, until completely tender. Serve hot.

BAKED SALMON WITH WARM RED CABBAGE, FENNEL AND PERNOD CRÈME FRAÎCHE

SERVES 8

1 small red cabbage, very finely shredded

2 fennel bulbs, finely shredded (keep the fronds for garnish)

1 x 125g packet of radishes, quartered

200ml olive oil

juice of 1 orange

juice of 1 lemon

1 tbsp golden brown sugar

1 tbsp coriander seeds

1 x 1.5kg side of salmon, skinned, boned and trimmed

200ml crème fraîche

a drizzle of Pernod (optional)

Preheat the oven to 185°C.

Put the cabbage, fennel and radishes in a roasting tin. Add most of the oil along with the orange juice, lemon juice, brown sugar, coriander seeds and some salt and pepper. Mix everything together and put the salmon on top, pour over the remaining oil and season the fish (this can be done beforehand). Bake in the oven for 25 minutes.

Mix the crème fraîche with the Pernod (if using), then drizzle it over the salmon. Garnish with the reserved fennel fronds.

To serve, flake the salmon apart roughly, then gently mix through the vegetables. Serve a little extra crème fraîche on the side.

Christmas leftovers

24 DECEMBER 2021

We started a new tradition last year. A few families gathered on Christmas morning in the park for mulled wine and bubbles. Dungarvan Bay sparkled in the winter cold. It was great fun but we all had to go after an hour or so, as everyone's dinner was in the oven.

I always prefer Christmas dinner on Stephen's Day. The second day is more relaxed. There's very little to do as it's already cooked. The hours can ebb and flow. It's a liberating feeling after the hectic week that came before.

I'm a great man for the leftovers but I want to see the back of the turkey after two days. In the end I never know who's consuming who, but I always feel the turkey wins the battle.

Hopefully these no-fuss dishes might come in handy when you're in a leftovers quandary. There's not a turkey curry in sight. There's one common thread here and that's the use of the cooking juices of the turkey and especially the ham, with its sticky, powerful glaze. It's pure gold.

The casserole is a tasty little affair. It's light and the saltiness of the ham permeates the butter beans so they become little hammy bon bons floating in a sweet cidery lake. I used baby spinach but you can use leftover sprouts, either cooked or uncooked, but raw will have to be sliced and put in with the ham to cook. Either way, this recipe will still be a fitting end to your lovely Christmas ham.

I'm buying the Yorkshire puddings and the filling is easy. The horseradish gives pep and the salad lightness to the heft of the last few days. The amount you make is entirely up to you, but a bag of frozen Yorkshire puddings typically has eight. If you want to make more filling, just increase the stock to heat up the meat.

I'm staying light with this quirky version of a Caesar salad. You could argue that if it doesn't follow a classic recipe, then it isn't a Caesar salad. I wouldn't disagree but it tastes great all the same.

Have a lovely Christmas.

CHRISTMAS HAM CASSEROLE WITH WINTER GREENS AND CIDER

SERVES 6

1 tbsp butter

2 red onions, diced into chunks

1 sprig of fresh thyme

2 x 400g tins of butter beans, drained and rinsed

150ml cider

150ml chicken stock

2 star anise

300g leftover cooked ham chunks (including all the sticky bits and glaze)

1 tbsp Dijon mustard

1 tsp golden brown sugar

a handful of baby spinach or sprouts (as many as you like)

Melt the butter in a saucepan over a gentle heat. When the butter starts to foam, add the onions and thyme and cook for 10 minutes or so, until soft.

Add the butter beans, cider, stock and star anise. Bring to a gentle simmer for a few minutes, then add the ham, mustard and sugar. After a further 10 minutes of gentle cooking, add the spinach or sprouts, a little salt and plenty of pepper.

Serve immediately in warm bowls.

TURKEY AND HAM YORKIES WITH CRANBERRY AND HORSERADISH CREAM

SERVES 8

200ml chicken stock

300g diced cooked turkey and ham (including any sticky bits)

a pinch of mixed spice

200ml sour cream

1 tbsp cranberry sauce

1 tsp horseradish sauce

1 packet of frozen Yorkshire puddings

a few handfuls of salad leaves

FOR THE DRESSING:

juice of 1 mandarin or ½ orange

50ml olive oil

a pinch of caster sugar

Preheat the oven to 150°C.

Warm the stock in a saucepan, then add the turkey, ham and mixed spice. Set aside and keep warm.

Mix the sour cream, cranberry and horseradish together.

Cook the puddings in the oven for 10 minutes to defrost and crisp up.

Meanwhile, whisk the mandarin or orange juice, oil, sugar and some salt and pepper together, then use this to dress the salad leaves.

Drain off any excess stock from the meat, then remove the pan from the heat and fold in the sour cream mix. Use this to fill the Yorkshire puddings and serve with the dressed salad on the side.

TURKEY AND HAM CRUNCH WITH CHRISTMAS CAESAR SALAD

SERVES 4

a drizzle of olive oil

thinly sliced cooked turkey and ham

a scattering of breadcrumbs (panko if possible)

100ml cream

juice of ½ lemon

juice of 1 mandarin

juice or jelly from the turkey or ham

80g Parmesan cheese, grated

4 heads of Little Gem lettuce

Preheat the oven to 180°C.

Brush a little oil on the bottom of an ovenproof dish, then cover the base with the turkey and ham slices. Scatter over the breadcrumbs and drizzle with a little more oil. Bake in the oven for 20 minutes, until golden and crunchy.

Meanwhile, mix the cream with the lemon and mandarin juice, meat juices or jelly, most of the grated Parmesan and some salt and pepper. Dredge the leaves through the dressing and put in a bowl, then dust with the remaining Parmesan.

Serve the two dishes side by side and let everyone help themselves.

Enjoy one last blowout this weekend

01 JANUARY 2022

There's a blackboard outside our neighbour's pub that says, '2021: written by Stephen King, directed by Quentin Tarantino.' I couldn't agree more. Every chink of light had a ball of muck on the other side. This year has to be better.

On a personal note, the hair loss and weight gain have stopped me from dressing like a 30-something. My wife remains mute. I suspect she's being kind but in 2022 I have to regain my mojo so I can wear my yellow going-out shoes again.

Cooking is about the only gift I've been given. It comes naturally to me. I'm not sure where it came from but I'm glad I have it. I would be a terrible electrician.

There's one more blowout before we all go on a diet. As ever, these are dishes I mostly cook at home. I write a rough description as I cook, then finesse the recipe as we photograph them for the *Irish Times*. Harry Weir, the photographer, puts a bit of twinkle into my food as sometimes it can look a bit, well … agricultural. We work well together.

The idea for the mushroom carbonara was given to me by my friend Ivan Whelan, a scion of the Ballymaloe Allens. He has cooking in his blood. He used chanterelles but it's the wrong time of year for those, so I had to use chestnut mushrooms.

I adore Puy lentils. When served with fish they bring a meatiness to the affair. I'm using hake but any white fish will do. The ginger lifts and the spinach lightens. The chilli is there for warmth, not heat. Restraint is my new byword.

Call me Shortcut Sam but I've been a fan of shop-bought gnocchi for some time. This has a Mediterranean vibe. I needed a bit of a change.

'Nduja is fab. A little in any dish will perk it up like a jolt of lightning, especially potentially drab chicken.

Thank you for reading my little vignettes throughout the year. At the end of it I hope you have found new favourite recipes for you and your families to enjoy. Happy New Year.

CHESTNUT MUSHROOM CARBONARA

SERVES 4

1 tbsp olive oil

a good knob of butter

250g chestnut mushrooms, thinly sliced

2 garlic cloves, sliced

2 tbsp roughly chopped fresh flat-leaf parsley

400g spaghetti

100g Parmesan cheese, grated

3 eggs, beaten

Heat the oil and butter in a large frying pan or wok. When the butter starts to foam, add the mushrooms and garlic, then turn the heat to high for a couple of minutes to cook the mushrooms. Add the parsley and season generously, then remove the pan from the heat.

Cook the pasta as per the packet instructions in a pot of boiling salted water.

Meanwhile, add most of the Parmesan into the eggs and mix.

When the spaghetti is ready, lift it out with tongs or a pasta fork and add it to the mushrooms, quickly followed by the egg and Parmesan mixture. Lift up the spaghetti so the egg mixes and thickens but doesn't scramble. Mix the mushrooms through.

Season and add a few tablespoons of the pasta cooking water so the mixture is moist but not wet. Serve immediately with the remaining Parmesan sprinkled on top.

HAKE WITH LENTILS, BABY SPINACH, GINGER AND CHILLI

SERVES 4

250g dried Puy lentils

3 tbsp olive oil, plus a little more for drizzling

1 garlic clove, sliced

3cm piece of ginger, peeled and finely chopped

1 fresh red chilli, deseeded and diced

600ml chicken stock

50g butter, diced

4 x 180g hake fillets, skin on, bones removed

2 handfuls of baby spinach

a squeeze of lemon

Soak the Puy lentils for at least 30 minutes, then drain.

Heat the oil in a wide pan over a low heat. Add the garlic, ginger and chilli and cook gently for 2 minutes. Add the drained lentils and stock. Bring up to a gentle simmer and cook for 15–20 minutes, until the lentils are soft and the liquid has mostly evaporated.

Dot the butter over the lentils and sit the hake on top. Drizzle with a little oil and season. Cover the pan and put it on a low heat to allow the hake to steam for 10 minutes or so, depending on the thickness of the fish.

Lift the fish carefully from the pan and keep warm for a minute while you add the spinach to the lentils. Fold it through along with the lemon juice to wilt for just a minute.

Serve straightaway with the hake on top and mashed potatoes on the side.

GNOCCHI WITH CRISPY CHICKEN, PEPPERS AND 'NDUJA

SERVES 4

400g boneless, skinless chicken thighs, cut into 1cm-thick strips

3 tbsp olive oil

1 x 250g packet of small mixed sweet peppers, halved

2 garlic cloves, sliced

150g 'nduja (chorizo is a good substitute)

1 x 500g packet of gnocchi

2 tbsp balsamic vinegar

fresh basil leaves or pesto

Preheat the oven to 200°C.

Put the chicken in a roasting tin and drizzle over the oil, then roast in the oven for 10 minutes. Add the peppers, garlic and 'nduja, broken up into 2cm chunks. Put the tin back in the oven for a further 15 minutes.

Meanwhile, cook the gnocchi as per the packet instructions. Drain and add to the tin. Fold everything together gently so you don't break up the gnocchi, then stir in the balsamic vinegar.

Serve with some fresh basil leaves or pesto on top.

I'm a late convert to halloumi

08 JANUARY 2022

Right, that's it! Time to rein things in for a while. I'm not really a New Year's resolution guy. There's no point, really, as I always cave in. It's just a matter of time before I succumb to one temptation or another, but this time, at least for this week, it'll be different. These dishes are on the lighter side. I also kept them vegetarian to regain some wholesomeness after living like Henry VIII for the last month.

I need a burst of colour to lift me. The last few weeks have been tough. Normally I'm pedantic about using tomatoes only in their proper season. Indeed, I've been known to be a bit judgemental about the whole thing. Now, however, I'm going to let it slide because let's face it, there are bigger fish to fry and there is also a good selection of them all year round in most supermarkets.

These are all one-pot dishes, which will be a relief for the cook in your home after the effort of Christmas.

The cauliflower is gently spiced to bring a touch of the Levant to the dish. These flavours are always a welcome change to the meat and two veg of the previous weeks. Za'atar is a deliciously floral spice blend if you can get your hands on it. If you can't, don't worry, just leave it out. This dish is lovely with hummus to bring all the flavours together.

I was never a big fan of halloumi. Its rubbery texture left me bewildered. The sandal-wearers could have it with my blessing. The flavour also eluded me until one day I ate it freshly fried at a friend's house and was immediately converted. I suddenly got it. The crisp exterior and squeaky saltiness had me hooked. I have been its champion ever since.

I'm craving rice after all the spuds. This pilaf is good on its own but its warmth would go brilliantly with roast lamb or chicken.

CARAMELISED CAULIFLOWER, CHICKPEA AND SESAME BAKE

SERVES 4

1 x 400g tin of chopped tomatoes

2 garlic cloves, crushed

2cm piece of ginger, peeled and grated

200ml strong vegetable stock

1 tsp za'atar (optional)

1 tsp sesame seeds, toasted

1 tsp honey

½ tsp ground cumin

½ tsp ground cinnamon

1 x 400g tin of chickpeas, drained and rinsed

1 cauliflower, quartered

4 tbsp toasted sesame oil

Preheat the oven to 180°C.

Put the tomatoes, garlic, ginger, stock, za'atar (if using), toasted sesame seeds, honey, cumin and cinnamon in a medium-sized roasting tin and bring to a gentle simmer on the hob. Cook for 5 minutes to let all the flavours get to know one another. Add the chickpeas, then nestle the cauliflower in among them. Drizzle the sesame oil over the cauliflower and season.

Bake in the oven, uncovered, for 1 hour, until the cauliflower is tender. Serve straight to the table.

HALLOUMI WITH OLIVES, TOMATOES AND CARDAMON
SERVES 4

3 tbsp olive oil, plus more for drizzling

2 x 225g packets of halloumi cheese, cut into 0.5cm-thick slices

250g mixed cherry tomatoes

80g mixed stoned olives

8 green cardamon pods, crushed and husks dispensed with as much as possible

a pinch of chilli flakes

juice of ½ orange

a drizzle of honey

a few sprigs of fresh mint

Heat the oil in a frying pan over a high heat until it's gently smoking. Working in batches, add the cheese and fry it on one side – this will only take a minute or so.

Carefully turn the slices over to colour them on the other side too, then add the tomatoes, olives, cardamon and chilli flakes. Warm these through, then add more oil and the orange juice. There should be enough to make a light dressing. Add the honey and season.

To serve, transfer to a serving dish and tear over some fresh mint leaves.

CARAMELISED ONION AND AUBERGINE PILAF

SERVES 4

3 tbsp olive oil

1 tbsp butter

2 red onions, sliced

2 garlic cloves, sliced

1 tsp cumin seeds

1 tsp coriander seeds

1 aubergine, cut into 0.5cm dice

200g basmati rice

2 pieces of orange peel

2 tbsp raisins

1 tsp harissa

450ml vegetable or chicken stock

natural yogurt

a few sprigs of fresh coriander

Preheat the oven to 180°C.

Melt the oil and butter in an ovenproof saucepan or casserole over a medium heat. When the butter starts to foam, add the onions, garlic and the cumin and coriander seeds. Cook for 10 minutes.

Add the aubergine and continue to cook for a further 15 minutes, until the aubergine has completely collapsed and has changed colour. Add the rice, orange peel, raisins and harissa, then add the stock and some salt and pepper. Bring to a gentle simmer, cover and cook in the oven for 25 minutes.

Serve with the some yogurt on the side and garnish with fresh coriander leaves.

Ask not how you can save your bacon, ask how your bacon can save you

15 JANUARY 2022

There are some ingredients that I just can't help myself using on a frequent basis. This week I'm featuring one of them: smoked bacon lardons.

I naturally gravitate towards bacon. It's such a prominent part of our food culture that's it's almost part of me. I cannot imagine cooking without it. I was elated some years ago when I first spotted those nifty little packets of lardons on the shelves. No more slicing rashers, one less thing to wash up. It's the little things.

I adore a traditional cassoulet, a delicious beany concoction packed with duck confit, pork and Toulouse sausage and a bubbling breadcrumb crust. Eaten with plenty of Dijon mustard and red wine to wash it down, it is French country cooking at its best. My wife discourages any engagement as there are windy consequences but that doesn't stop me. I'm using shop-bought confit duck, black or white pudding and ordinary breakfast sausages to make it handy.

This hot potato and bacon salad is perfect for a cold day and ranch dressing adds a new dimension that lifts everything. You can leave the skins on the potatoes if you like. The ranch dressing has quite a few permutations. It's delicious with the addition of spring onions and dill but perfectly nice without them.

I was worried that this soup was too simple but it's Ireland in a pot. I was in the mood for something light and soothing on a cold day. Let the vegetables slowly cook before you add the stock. This will ensure that every bit of sweetness and character are accentuated and it becomes more than the sum of its parts. If you want to make it more luxurious, I've added an optional chive and horseradish cream. It will float on the broth like a decadent cloud. Either way, it's the essence of simplicity. Use a mixture of your favourite root vegetables so it becomes your own. I bought an assorted veg mix from a supermarket, a brilliant idea with no waste. The barley will give it substance and soak up the smoky flavours of the bacon. All hail the bacon.

A FAMILY CASSOULET

SERVES 4

2 cooked confit duck legs

1 onion, diced

1 carrot, diced

125g smoked bacon lardons

1 tbsp tomato purée

½ tsp smoked paprika

1 x 400g tin of butter beans, drained and rinsed

300ml chicken stock

1 sprig of fresh thyme

4 chunks of white or black pudding

4 sausages

a scattering of fresh white breadcrumbs

Preheat the oven to 185°C.

Remove the residual fat from the duck legs, then put the fat in a shallow casserole with the onion, carrot and bacon. Cook over a medium heat for 10 minutes, until the vegetables soften.

Add the tomato purée and smoked paprika. Continue to cook for 2 minutes or so, then add the butter beans, stock and thyme. Bring to a simmer and allow to reduce and thicken a little.

Cut the duck legs in half at the joint and sit them on top of the beans. Intersperse the pudding and sausages and scatter over the breadcrumbs. Bake in the oven for 30 minutes, until golden and bubbling.

Serve straight to the table.

HOT POTATO AND BACON SALAD WITH RANCH DRESSING

SERVES 2

2 tbsp sunflower oil

2 large Rooster potatoes, peeled or unpeeled and cut into 1 cm dice

125g smoked bacon lardons

2 heads of Little Gem lettuce, leaves separated

2 tbsp grated Parmesan cheese

FOR THE DRESSING:

2 tbsp mayonnaise

2 tbsp natural yogurt

2 tbsp buttermilk

1 small garlic clove, crushed

2 spring onions, finely chopped (optional)

a little chopped fresh dill (optional)

Heat the oil in a pan or a wok over a medium heat. Add the potatoes and cook for 10 minutes or so, until they start to soften. Add the bacon and continue to cook, turning the mixture intermittently, until the potatoes are cooked and the bacon is crisp.

Meanwhile, make the ranch dressing by mixing everything together.

Drain the potatoes and bacon on kitchen paper. Arrange on a plate with the Little Gem leaves and the dressing and Parmesan on top to serve.

A WINTER SOUP WITH HORSERADISH CREAM

SERVES 6

80g butter

1 onion, sliced

1 small leek, sliced

125g smoked bacon lardons

3cm piece of ginger, peeled and finely chopped

a few sprigs of fresh thyme

1 bay leaf (fresh if possible)

800g mixed root vegetables: carrot, parsnip, turnip, celeriac, Jerusalem artichokes and/or potatoes

50g barley

1 litre chicken or vegetable stock

FOR THE HORSERADISH CREAM:

150ml cream

1 tbsp chopped fresh chives

1 tsp horseradish sauce

Melt the butter in a pot over a gentle heat. When the butter starts to foam, add the onion, leek, bacon, ginger, thyme and bay. Cover and cook for 15 minutes.

Meanwhile, peel and cut your vegetables into even bite-sized pieces, then add to the pot along with the barley. Cover and cook gently for 15 minutes, until everything starts to soften.

Add the stock and bring to a simmer. Cook for 15 minutes or so but don't let the vegetables go mushy. Season.

Whip the cream to soft peaks, then fold in the chives and horseradish.

Serve the soup in warm bowls with a spoonful of the horseradish cream floating on top.

Fill your kitchen with nice smells and happy children

21 JANUARY 2022

It can be frustrating trying to feed a family. Some days I feel like throwing the toys out of the pram and telling them to cook for themselves. But we all tend to be softer these days and give in to our little darlings' every whim. I, too, am guilty of being a helicopter parent.

I'm constantly trying new things at home as they are often the foundation of my recipes here. That's not to say that they always get eaten! But these are three dishes that will hopefully become new family favourites.

Pasta is big in our house. After all these years of eating my cooking, an ordinary bowl of spaghetti Bolognese remains my girls' favourite. I roll my eyes in frustration at the mundaneness of it all. Then I join in and finish the lot.

Orzo is easier to get now than it used to be. It's a dinky little rice-like pasta that makes for a delicate dish. You could use any small pasta but I urge you to try it. The field mushrooms, spinach, lemon and Parmesan are easily familiar so it's a good crowd pleaser.

Betty's hotpot was a feature in our house growing up, not so much on the table as on the telly. I pricked my ears when it was mentioned in the Rovers Return. I imagined a steamy bowl of Lancashire lamb nestling under juice-drenched but crispy potatoes. I wanted to visit Coronation Street just to eat it. This version uses beef with a hint of chorizo. It's given depth and stickiness by the abundant chutney. The layered spuds on top give it a delicious texture that's just a little bit different from your average pie.

I'm a sucker for a spice bag. I almost wish I never discovered that addictive blend of spices. This simple traybake will fill your kitchen with the most delicious smells imaginable. The chicken thighs and sweet potatoes soak up the oily juices like a magical sponge. If I was bold I would say to eat it with sour cream on the side but I won't as I'm trying to be good. But you don't have to listen to me.

ORZO WITH MUSHROOMS, SPINACH, LEMON AND PARMESAN
SERVES 4

a good knob of butter
4 field (flat cap) mushrooms, sliced
2 garlic cloves, sliced
a few fresh sage leaves, chopped
400g orzo
a handful of baby spinach
zest and juice of 1 lemon
100g Parmesan cheese, grated
a pinch of ground nutmeg (optional)
a drizzle of olive oil

Melt the butter in a large saucepan over a medium heat. When the butter starts to foam, add the mushrooms, garlic and sage. Cook for 3–4 minutes and keep warm.

Cook the orzo as per the packet instructions. Drain but reserve half a cup of the cooking water. Add the cooked orzo and the water to the mushrooms along with the spinach, lemon zest and juice, most of the Parmesan, the nutmeg (if using) and some salt and pepper. Fold everything together off the heat – you want to just barely wilt the spinach.

Serve in warm bowls with a drizzle of olive oil and the remaining Parmesan scattered on top.

CRUNCHY POTATO, BEEF AND CHORIZO HOTPOT
SERVES 4

2 tbsp olive oil

2 onions, finely diced

2 garlic cloves, chopped

400g minced beef

150g dry-cured chorizo, peeled and finely diced

1 x 400g tin of chopped tomatoes

300ml chicken stock

4 tbsp tomato chutney or country relish

1 tbsp honey

1 tsp smoked paprika

3 large Rooster potatoes, peeled or unpeeled and very thinly sliced

melted butter, for brushing

Heat the oil in a shallow casserole over a medium heat (if you don't have a casserole, use a large heavy-based frying pan). Add the onions and garlic and cook for 5 minutes, until the onions start to soften. Add the beef and chorizo, turn the heat up and cook for 5 minutes more, until the beef has coloured a little.

Add the tomatoes, chicken stock, chutney or relish, honey, smoked paprika and some salt and pepper. Reduce the heat to low and cook for 30–40 minutes, stirring occasionally, until it becomes thick and glossy.

Preheat the oven to 185°C.

If you're using a baking dish, transfer the hotpot mixture to it now. Either way, layer the potatoes over the top, brush with the melted butter and season. Cook in the oven for 30–40 minutes, until the potatoes are cooked and golden.

Serve straight to the table.

STICKY SPICE BAG CHICKEN TRAYBAKE

SERVES 4

8 chicken thighs, skin on

2 sweet potatoes, peeled and cut into long, thick wedges

4 tbsp olive oil

4 onions, peeled and quartered with the root left on to hold them together

4 fresh red chillies, deseeded and sliced lengthways

2 tbsp balsamic vinegar

1 tbsp spice bag spice

1 tbsp honey

a few sprigs of fresh coriander

Preheat the oven to 185°C.

Trim the chicken thighs of excess fat but leave the skin on. Put the chicken and sweet potatoes in a roasting tin, drizzle over the oil and mix everything together. Roast in the oven for 20 minutes.

Add the onions, chillies, balsamic vinegar, spice bag mix, honey and some salt and pepper to the tin. Return to the oven to cook for a further 20 minutes or so, until the chicken thighs are cooked through and everything is melting and sticky.

Serve with fresh coriander leaves scattered over.

Tasty one-pot dinners that won't get you in a stew

28 JANUARY 2022

I'm taking some poetic licence when it comes to these stews as I want to open the mind a little. We know they are good for us but they seem to be mundane. Some of you no doubt make wonderfully delicious stews but unfortunately my first introduction to them growing up was in the form of a brown soup with floating carrots and stringy beef that you excavated from your teeth as the day went along.

In fairness, some of the packet mixes are amazing. I've arrived home on the odd occasion to discover a tasty concoction lurking in a pot. When I express amazement, I'm reluctantly told a packet has been used to arrive at this deliciousness. What magic.

Before I talk myself out of a job, I'll tell you about today's dishes. The first one probably isn't a stew. It's more of a pot roast, I suppose, but I'm putting it in because there's meat, liquid and vegetables. You'll know by now that I'm attracted to one-pot dishes and simple techniques but the fact is that if you put harmonious ingredients in a pot and give some consideration to how you cook them, the inevitable result is that it will be lovely.

This tagine is perfect if you want to introduce gentle spices into your dinner. It can be made with beef, lamb or chicken thighs. Or substitute the meat altogether for chunky butternut squash. I'm using beef this time. If you're using chicken you will need to cut the cooking time down to 1 hour. With something like this the timing can fluctuate depending on the size of the meat but the general rule is it's ready when it's tender.

I have fallen head over heels for Galicia. This lentil recipe is an approximation of a dish I had in O Gato Negro, an ancient and unpretentious gem of a restaurant in Santiago de Compostela. God only knows what porky bits lurked in its murky depths but they were wobbly and delectable. We drank bowls of red wine to wash it down and absorbed the clamour of a very special restaurant. I was in heaven.

POT ROAST LAMB WITH BALSAMIC AND PORCINI MUSHROOMS

SERVES 4

½ leg of lamb (approx. 1.5kg) on the bone
a drizzle of olive oil
2 red onions, quartered
4 garlic cloves, sliced
a few leaves of fresh sage
1 tbsp dried porcini mushrooms
400ml chicken stock
2 tbsp balsamic vinegar
1 x 400g tin of butter beans, drained and rinsed
chopped fresh flat-leaf parsley

Preheat the oven to 165°C.

Put the lamb in a casserole, drizzle with oil and season. Add the red onions, garlic, sage and porcini followed by the chicken stock and balsamic vinegar. Cover and cook in the oven for 1½ hours.

Uncover, add the butter beans and put the casserole back in the oven to cook for a further 30 minutes.

Remove the lamb, cover with foil and allow to rest for 20 minutes.

Add the parsley to the sauce, carve the lamb and serve with mashed potatoes.

A SIMPLE TAGINE

SERVES 4

2 tbsp olive oil

400g beef chuck, cut into 2cm dice

1 onion, diced

1 large carrot, diced

2 garlic cloves, sliced

1 tsp tomato purée

1 tsp ground cumin

½ tsp ground cinnamon

1 x 400g tin of chickpeas, drained and rinsed

8 dried apricots, sliced

300ml chicken stock

a squeeze of honey

Preheat the oven to 160°C.

Heat the oil in an ovenproof pan over a medium-high heat until it's gently smoking. Add the beef, season and brown for a couple of minutes. Add the onion, carrot and garlic and continue to colour for another minute or two.

Turn down the heat, then add the tomato purée and spices followed a minute later by the chickpeas, apricots, stock and honey. Bring to a simmer, cover and cook in the oven for 1½ hours, until the beef is tender. Check the seasoning.

Serve with couscous, hummus and warm flatbread.

GALICIAN PORKY BITS AND LENTILS

SERVES 2

4 tbsp olive oil

1 pork loin chop (140g approx.), cut into thin strips

125g smoked bacon lardons

100g black pudding, diced

1 x 400g tin of brown or Puy lentils

2 garlic cloves, sliced

a few leaves of fresh sage or thyme

½ tsp smoked paprika

a splash of cream sherry (optional)

juice of 1 medium lemon

a pinch of golden brown sugar (optional)

Heat half of the oil in a frying pan over a high heat until it's gently smoking. Add the pork, bacon and pudding and cook for 3–4 minutes, until crisp.

Turn down the heat, then add the lentils (including the juices from the tin), garlic, herbs and smoked paprika. Add the sherry (if using) and bring to a gentle simmer.

Drizzle in the remaining oil and the lemon juice, then season. If you think the lemon is a little sharp, you could add a pinch of sugar.

Perfect with boiled potatoes and aioli.

The death of a campervan dream

05 FEBRUARY 2022

You know those smug people who say they never regret a thing? I'm not one of them. I have a habit of making rash decisions that come back to haunt me. The latest episode represents an end to an aspiration of mine, at least for a while: my campervan.

You get what you pay for and my 1994 lady proved that point. Where I was hoping I had discovered a diamond in the mud, all I found was more mud.

Of course I had it checked out before I bought it. It got the blessing of a mechanic who professed it had a fine engine before I committed. The interiors were perfect but a little tired so I spent a large wedge on reupholstery and general pimping to make my adventures as plush as possible.

I stuck garish flowers all over the exterior. My teenage daughters declared it too much, called me an attention-seeker and jumped ship but I was determined to channel my inner hippy. If I couldn't get to Electric Picnic, then at least I would get on a few excursions with the lads. The Flower Power Express was ready to roll. Father Ted, eat your heart out.

Rust was the problem. It crept in and stole my dream. My camper needs the attention of someone who's handy with such things, whereas I'm so useless I even have to get my wife to change a plug. I have to sell it and I'm very sad. I need a bit of comfort.

These dishes all have comfort in spades. They are all for two but can be scaled up as needed. I'm concentrating on fish as that's my mood. If anyone fancies a campervan, the stove is in pristine order. I'd nearly come over and cook for you.

The bubble and squeak is all about using leftover veg. It's a moveable feast depending on what you have.

For the stew I'm using salmon as it's easily available and goes perfectly with the leek and potatoes.

This satay is satisfying when you want something different. Needless to say, try to get the best prawns you can. Frozen are fine, just make sure they're large and plump.

SMOKED MACKEREL BUBBLE AND SQUEAK WITH SWEET MUSTARD DRESSING

SERVES 2

leftover potatoes, mashed or boiled – enough for two

leftover cooked vegetables, e.g. carrots, peas, turnip, cauliflower, cabbage

a good knob of butter

2 fillets of smoked mackerel, skin and bones removed

FOR THE DRESSING:

100ml sunflower oil

2 tbsp chopped fresh dill

1 tbsp golden brown sugar

1 tbsp white wine vinegar

1 tbsp wholegrain mustard

½ tbsp Dijon mustard

Crush the leftover cooked potatoes and vegetables together (it needs to be 50% potato) with a fork into a rough mash.

Melt the butter in a non-stick frying pan over a medium-high heat. When the butter starts to foam, add the mash to the pan and spread it out. When it starts to turn golden, bring it together and mash it down again. Repeat the process until it's crispy. You will see it bubble and hear it squeak. Season and keep hot.

Meanwhile, whisk all the ingredients for the mustard dressing together until it forms an emulsion.

Flake the smoked mackerel on top of the bubble and squeak. Drizzle the dressing over and serve straightaway.

A VERY SIMPLE SEAFOOD STEW

SERVES 2

50g butter
1 leek, cut lengthways, sliced and washed
1 bay leaf (fresh if possible)
300ml chicken or vegetable stock
150ml cream
1 tsp horseradish sauce
8 baby potatoes, cooked, peeled and sliced
250g salmon fillet, skinned and diced into 2cm chunks
a squeeze of lemon
chopped fresh dill

Melt the butter in a pan over a medium heat. When the butter starts to foam, add the leek. It will help if there's a little residual water on the slices so they will steam in the buttery juices. Add the bay leaf, cover and cook over a gentle heat for 10 minutes.

Add the stock, pour in the cream and bring to a simmer. Stir in the horseradish, then add the cooked potatoes and the salmon. Poach the salmon for 3–4 minutes, then add the lemon, seasoning and finally the dill.

Serve immediately.

PRAWN SATAY WITH PICKLED CUCUMBER

SERVES 2

1 x 400ml tin of full-fat coconut milk

2 heaped tbsp crunchy peanut butter

1 medium fresh red chilli, deseeded and sliced

juice of 1 lime

2 tbsp dark soy sauce

1 tbsp fish sauce

1 tsp golden brown sugar

200g raw, shelled large prawns

FOR THE PICKLED CUCUMBER:

2 tbsp rice wine vinegar or 1 tbsp white wine vinegar

2 tbsp water

1 tbsp caster sugar

½ cucumber, peeled into strips

Put the coconut milk in a saucepan with the peanut butter and chilli and reduce by one-third over a low heat. Add the lime juice, soy sauce, fish sauce and sugar, then blend lightly with a hand blender. You can make this ahead of time.

Return the pan to the heat, then add the prawns and poach gently for 2–3 minutes, depending on their size.

Meanwhile, put the vinegar, water and sugar in a small saucepan and bring to the boil, then immediately remove from the heat. Allow to cool, then add the cucumber. This can also be done ahead of time and kept in the fridge if you like.

Serve the prawn satay with basmati rice and the pickled cucumber on the side.

Let's make hot love

12 FEBRUARY 2022

When our children were younger, we had a series of Austrian girls who helped us out at home during our hectic summers. They all came from a teacher training college in Graz and as one left she promised to find a replacement for the following year. We had five in all and they became part of the family — we are still in touch. They were outdoorsy and frequently dragged us up mountains, hiking with militaristic vigour. They were good for us.

Some years back we decided to visit one of them in January, when we take our restaurant holidays. We stayed in Vienna, where there were still remnants of Christmas, the shopfronts sparkling like jewel boxes. We took a train journey over the snow-capped mountains to Graz. It was magical. I'll never forget the beauty.

The girls were all proudly Styrian. When I expressed my admiration of Vienna with its history, opulent Habsburg palaces, cafés, art and of course music, they sniffed and dismissed the Viennese as arrogant. I quietened myself, sensing the tension.

We ate schnitzel and Sachertorte and explored twinkly lit villages under blankets of snow. We visited Sylvia's grandparents on their farm, drank schnapps and ate cheese-laden Käsekrainer sausage. We dipped bread in grassy pumpkin oil from their own mill and visited the Zotter chocolate factory. It put Willy Wonka in the shade.

In Vienna we huddled over a classic Tafelspitz: boiled beef in broth with vegetables, strong horseradish, apple sauce and a flurry of chives. It cosseted us from the cold and I loved it. For Valentines, I'm paying homage to that romantic city with steak for two, Tafelspitz style.

The beetroot rösti complements the steak perfectly. Make this first, the sauces second and lastly the steak.

In summer 2012 a newly arrived Sylvia announced that she'd like to show us how to make hot love. Crikey, I thought to myself, slightly alarmed. It turns out it's a ubiquitous dish of ice cream and hot berries that is popular all over Austria and is now my own family's favourite. I've added a little optional strudel flourish as a salute to a memorable time in a spectacular country.

TAFELSPITZ STEAK

SERVES 2

2 x 250g striploin steaks

1 tbsp sunflower oil

a knob of butter

1 sprig of fresh thyme

FOR THE SOUR CREAM:

200ml sour cream

2 tbsp chopped fresh chives

1 tbsp horseradish sauce

FOR THE APPLE SAUCE:

1 large cooking apple, peeled, cored and sliced

3 tbsp water

1 tbsp golden brown sugar

a pinch of ground cinnamon

To make the apple sauce, put the apple, water, sugar and cinnamon in a small saucepan and cook over a medium heat for 10 minutes, until the apple breaks up and turns into a sweet compote. You can help it along by breaking up the apple a little with a wooden spoon halfway through cooking.

Mix the sour cream, chives and horseradish together and put in a nice bowl.

Season the steak, drizzle over the oil and rub it in. Heat a heavy-based grill pan, or even better, a ridged chargrill pan, over a high heat. When the pan is smoking gently, add the steaks.

For medium rare they will need 2 minutes on each side. For medium, 2½ minutes. They should feel a little soft and springy. Just leave them on a little longer if you prefer them more cooked.

When they are nearly ready, add the butter and thyme. Baste the steaks, then put them on a warm plate along with any residual butter. Cover in foil to rest for 5 minutes or so.

When serving, pour any residual juices over the steaks as a delicate little gravy. Serve with the apple sauce and horseradish and chive sour cream on the side.

SMOKED BACON AND BEETROOT RÖSTI

SERVES 2

3 large Rooster potatoes (approx. 400g), peeled

1 red onion, thinly sliced

1 large raw beetroot, washed and grated

125g smoked bacon lardons

2 tbsp duck fat, melted

a few sprigs of fresh thyme, leaves picked

Preheat the oven to 185°C.

Grate the potatoes with a coarse grater. Squeeze the excess water from the potatoes and discard.

Put the grated potato in a bowl with the onion, beetroot, bacon lardons, melted duck fat, thyme and some salt and pepper. Mix well.

Heat a medium-sized ovenproof non-stick frying pan over a medium heat. When the pan is gently smoking, add the potato mixture and flatten it evenly around the pan with the back of a spoon.

Cook for 5 minutes or so, until the potatoes start to colour. Put the pan in the oven to cook for 20–25 minutes (depending on how thick the rösti is), until golden and crisp.

Remove the pan from the oven and allow to cool a little. Loosen the sides and bottom as best you can with a spatula. Cover the pan with an upturned plate and carefully flip the rösti onto the plate. This can be made ahead of time and warmed up when you need it.

HOT LOVE

SERVES 2

250g frozen raspberries
1 tbsp caster sugar
a little melted butter
1 sheet of filo pastry, thawed
1 tbsp icing sugar
good-quality vanilla ice cream

Preheat the oven to 185°C.

Put the frozen raspberries and sugar in a small pan and cook over a medium heat for a short while, until the mixture bubbles and thickens. Remove from the heat and leave in the pan to warm later.

Brush a little melted butter on a baking tray, then unfold the filo pastry flat on top. Brush the top with butter, then scrunch the pastry lightly with your hands so it turns into craggy folds. Sieve the icing sugar evenly on top, then bake in the oven for 8 minutes or so, until golden and caramelised. Remove from the oven and allow to cool.

To serve, scoop as much ice cream as you like into a pretty bowl. Heat the sauce and spoon it over the top. Break the filo in two and perch it on the side of the bowl. Sometimes this is served with whipped cream as well. But I'm a man of restraint so I'll leave it up to you.

I'm obsessed with my chest freezer

19 FEBRUARY 2022

I've developed an obsession: my freezer. All my family seems to see these days is me upended, my head buried in its depths, muttering like a deranged man.

Every so often I make it my business to get to the bottom of it. Our 'freezer week' of eating can throw up a mad jumble of half dinners like the aftermath of an ecstasy-fuelled supermarket sweep. Bits and bobs are cobbled together, sometimes with dubious results. I don't always get it right, although I shouldn't really be saying that.

It's a chest freezer; that's part of the problem. Anything could be lurking in its chilly depths. My mother-in-law has a fabled goose in hers that we reckon has been there for at least seven years. In her mind, frozen is frozen. She's just waiting for the appropriate occasion. That, or I think she might be waiting for me to volunteer to cook it. Frankly, I'm terrified at the prospect.

Today I wanted to do new versions of old classics. A Spanish-inspired roast chicken is something a little different. Its burnished, buttery skin glistens while perched above a crusty baked rice that's infused with the perfume of chicken juice, smoked paprika, orange and rosemary. It's a one-tray affair that would be lovely eaten with aioli and a simple green salad.

This baked potato is a riff on tartiflette, that formidable potato dish from the French Alps that groans with Reblochon cheese, cream, bacon and onions. Just what a fella needs after a hard day skiing in Les Trois Vallées. I'm caramelising the onions a little with just a hint of cinnamon. I've chosen Gubbeen cheese but you could change it, by all means. As long as the cheese melts, that's the main thing.

The next, very simple dish is the love child of chowder and haddock smokies. It's rich so you don't need a lot of it. The cream carries the sweet smoke of the haddock perfectly. I'm using a pre-prepared chowder mix that's easily available. Some brown bread is all you need to accompany it.

ROAST HONEY PIMENTON CHICKEN AND RICE
SERVES 6

1 x 1.6kg chicken (free-range if possible)
300g basmati rice
600ml chicken stock
1 x 400g tin of chopped tomatoes
juice of 1 orange
a pinch of chilli flakes
1 tbsp honey
200g cherry tomatoes on the vine

FOR THE BUTTER:
120g butter, softened
2 garlic cloves, crushed
zest of 1 orange
1 tbsp chopped fresh rosemary
1 tsp smoked paprika

Preheat the oven to 185°C.

Make the flavoured butter by mixing it with the garlic, orange zest, rosemary, paprika and some salt and pepper.

Massage the butter into the chicken thoroughly, put the chicken in a large roasting tin and roast in the oven for 45 minutes, basting the chicken once or twice.

Remove the tin from the oven and scatter the rice around the bird, then add the chicken stock, chopped tomatoes, orange juice, chilli flakes and some salt and pepper. Mix everything together, then put the tin back in the oven to cook for a further 20 minutes.

Remove from the oven once more. Drizzle the honey over the chicken, then put the vine tomatoes on the rice and return to the oven to cook for a further 15 minutes, until the rice is crusty and the chicken is fully cooked and golden.

Allow to rest under foil before carving the chicken and serving with the rice.

A GROWN-UP BAKED POTATO
SERVES 2

2 large baking potatoes
a knob of butter
2 onions, thinly sliced
125g smoked bacon lardons
1 sprig of fresh thyme
a pinch of ground cinnamon
1 tsp golden brown sugar
1 tbsp red wine vinegar
100g Gubbeen cheese, grated

Preheat the oven to 180°C.

Wash the potatoes and wrap each one in foil. Bake in the oven for 1½ hours, until soft and tender.

Meanwhile, melt the butter in a saucepan over a gentle heat. When the butter starts to foam, add the onions along with the bacon, thyme and cinnamon. Cover and cook for 10 minutes to allow the fat to render from the bacon.

Remove the lid, turn up the heat a little and cook until the onions start to caramelise. After 5 minutes or so, add the sugar and continue to cook until the onions are golden and sticky, then add the red wine vinegar, salt and pepper and remove from the heat.

Peel back the foil from the potatoes and make an incision so the potato opens up. Stuff first with the onions, followed by the cheese. This can be done ahead of time if you like.

Put the potatoes back in the oven and cook for 15 minutes or so, until the cheese is melting and the potatoes crisp up. If you're feeling bold, eat with a drizzle of sour cream.

CHOWDER SMOKIES
MAKES 4

a little soft butter, for greasing the ramekins

250g chowder mix (e.g. smoked haddock, salmon, cod)

2 spring onions, thinly sliced

1 tbsp raisins

100g mature Cheddar cheese, grated

250ml cream

Preheat the oven to 190°C. Grease four large ovenproof ramekins with butter.

Divide the chowder mix, spring onions and raisins among the ramekins, followed by the cheese and cream. Season and bake in the oven for 20 minutes, until golden and bubbling.

Serve with brown bread.

Are these three veggie dishes too simple?

25 FEBRUARY 2022

The restaurant reopened at the beginning of February after a longer than usual holiday. It seems ages ago now but when we closed, the 8 p.m. restrictions were still in place. Another hurdle to get over in a world full of them. All the staff needed a break. After two years of, er, 'pivoting', where we tried everything — takeaways, picnics, hot dogs, Christmas starters and duck pies — our brains were rattled.

On reopening, we made changes to the way we operate, vowing to remove some of the stress from all our lives. None of us are getting any younger. We reviewed the menu with a critical eye, as we always do. I wanted to make it more vegetable centric. It's impossible for me to remove meat and fish — I love them too much and so do our guests. However, I was determined to put vegetables a little more centre stage. I feel it's the right thing to do.

These dishes are not for the Tannery. As ever, they are for the home cook and are as simple as I can make them. Sometimes I look at the method, not so much the ingredients, and wonder if the recipes are *too* simple, but I think it's my job to demystify cooking and make it easier for people. They work, that's the thing.

The success of the roasted root vegetables lies in cutting them evenly so they cook uniformly. You can cut down on the harissa if you don't want it too spicy. I added baby peppers towards the end simply because I thought they were cute. The butter bean hummus has a light lemony touch that adds a cooling creaminess to the affair.

I initially got this beetroot bake wrong. I used pre-cooked beetroot but it looked pallid and tasted of disappointment. The fresh beetroot really makes a difference. It's sprightly and promising. The baharat is a subtly complex spice blend. You can use mixed spice if you can't find it.

This spiced carrot and chickpea stew happens to be vegan. It makes a lovely side dish or can really shine as part of a mezze platter with couscous.

ROOT VEGETABLE FEAST WITH HARISSA AND BUTTER BEAN HUMMUS
SERVES 4

1 cauliflower, cut into even-sized florets

2 red onions, quartered, with the roots left intact

4 small carrots, cut into chunks

100ml olive oil

250g baby peppers or 1 large red pepper

10 dried apricots, halved

2 tbsp harissa

1 tsp cumin seeds

1 tsp coriander seeds

FOR THE HUMMUS:

1 x 400g tin of butter beans, drained and rinsed

200ml light crème fraîche

2 garlic cloves, crushed

juice of ½ lemon

2 tbsp olive oil

1 tsp honey

Preheat the oven to 180°C.

Put the cauliflower, red onions and carrots in a roasting tin. Add the olive oil, season and roast in the oven for 20 minutes, turning once while cooking.

Remove the tin from the oven and add the baby peppers, apricots, harissa and the cumin and coriander seeds. Cook for a further 20 minutes, until all the vegetables are tender and the mixture is sticky.

For the hummus, put everything in a food processor, season with salt and ground white pepper and whizz until smooth.

Serve the roasted vegetables with the hummus and some warm flatbread.

BAKED BEETROOT WITH BAHARAT, YOGURT AND SESAME

SERVES 4

1kg raw beetroot, different varieties if possible

zest of 1 orange

1 tbsp toasted sesame oil

1 tbsp olive oil

1 tsp fresh thyme leaves

1 tsp baharat or mixed spice

FOR THE CRUST:

200g Greek yogurt

200g soft cream cheese

2 eggs, beaten

1 tsp honey

2 tbsp sesame seeds

Boil the beetroot in plenty of salted water until tender. It will take at least 1 hour, maybe more, depending on size. When cool, peel while wearing rubber gloves, then cut into 1cm-thick slices. This can be done ahead of time.

Put the beetroot in a bowl along with the orange zest, sesame oil, olive oil, thyme and baharat or mixed spice, tossing to coat. Season and arrange in a casserole.

Preheat the oven to 185°C.

Whisk the yogurt with the cream cheese, eggs and honey. Season, then spoon the mixture over the beetroot. Scatter the sesame seeds on top.

Bake in the oven for 25 minutes, until golden. Serve straight to the table.

SPICED CARROT, ALMOND AND CHICKPEA STEW
SERVES 4

2 large carrots (approx. 400g), peeled
200ml vegetable stock
juice of 1 orange
2 tbsp red wine vinegar
1 tbsp honey
½ tsp ground cumin
½ tsp nigella seeds
a pinch of chilli flakes
1 x 400g tin of chickpeas, drained and rinsed
50ml olive oil
80g whole salted almonds
a few sprigs of fresh mint

Slice the carrots thinly at an angle — if you have one, a mandolin is perfect for this job. Put them in a saucepan with the stock, orange juice, vinegar, honey, cumin, nigella seeds, chilli flakes and some salt and pepper. Cover tightly and cook over a gentle heat for 15–20 minutes, until the carrots are slightly softened.

Add the chickpeas, olive oil and almonds and warm through for a minute or two.

Serve warm with fresh mint leaves torn on top.

Feta, halloumi and Boursin – now that's what I call a party

05 MARCH 2022

Making cheese is akin to alchemy. Having cooked with and eaten a lot of cheese over the years, I'm still not completely au fait with the process. It's a bit like electricity. I'm not entirely sure how it works but I'd be upset if it didn't.

We had old friends at home recently. One came with her paramour, Mr C, a cheerful and affably posh bon viveur. He'd raided Morton's in Ranelagh for all their olives, truffle salami and stinky cheeses. The others came with cases of wine and high expectations. We know how to party, even if these days it only means sitting round a table with good food into the small hours.

We have an infamous downstairs loo with a dodgy lock. It's been that way for over 20 years. People have been stuck in there at parties, their absence unnoticed until they reappear covered in hedge, having climbed out the window. Only the most svelte make it.

Earlier in the evening, I heard the dreaded *click click* of the lock trying to find its way. It was Mr C. I'd forgotten to warn him. Thankfully he got out after a few more tries and a few nerve-wracking minutes. Disaster averted.

I slip cheese into my cooking when appropriate. These dishes are all enhanced by its presence in one form or another.

Where did all the lamb shanks go? There was a time you couldn't open a menu without them on it. This is a slightly Greek affair with the oregano and feta cheese. The cheese really cuts through the richness of the lamb to make it special.

Some of the best halloumi I've tasted is from the Proper Dairy Company in Clonmel. If you can get it, it really makes this simple gnocchi dish shine.

I love Boursin but hardly ever cook with it. I'm pairing it with apples to make a deeply flavoured and unusual tart.

LAMB SHANKS WITH FENNEL, OLIVES AND FETA
SERVES 4

4 lamb shanks

80ml olive oil

1 onion, cut into 2cm chunks

1 fennel bulb, cut into 2cm chunks

2 garlic cloves, crushed

1 x 400g tin of chopped tomatoes

200ml strong chicken stock

1 tbsp honey

1 tsp dried oregano

2 strips of orange peel

juice of 1 orange

100g mixed stoned olives

200g feta cheese

Preheat the oven to 200°C.

Put the lamb shanks in a roasting tin, drizzle over a little of the oil and season. Roast in the oven for 20 minutes to colour.

Turn the oven down to 150°C.

Tip the juices and oil from the tray into a casserole that will fit the lamb shanks snugly. Add the remaining oil along with the onion, fennel and garlic. Cook the vegetables over a medium-high heat on the hob for 10 minutes or so, until they start to turn golden.

Add the tomatoes, chicken stock, honey, oregano and orange peel, then nestle the lamb shanks in the casserole, bone side up. Cover and put back in the oven to cook for 2½ hours, until the lamb is soft and tender and almost falling off the bone. Check the sauce for seasoning and balance.

When serving the lamb shanks, tear the olives and crumble the feta over the top. Serve with your favourite pasta.

GNOCCHI WITH FRAZZLED SALAMI, HALLOUMI AND CHOPPED ROCKET

SERVES 4

4 tbsp olive oil

1 yellow pepper, cut into 1cm dice

1 x 200g packet of halloumi cheese, cut into 1cm dice

1 x 100g packet of sliced salami, shredded

1 garlic clove, sliced

a pinch of chilli flakes

1 x 500g packet of gnocchi

a handful of rocket, chopped

a drizzle of balsamic vinegar

a generous sprinkling of grated Parmesan cheese

Heat the oil in a large frying pan over a medium heat. Add the pepper, halloumi and salami and cook for 15 minutes, stirring periodically. Add the garlic and chilli halfway through to ensure the garlic doesn't burn. The mixture needs to be deeply coloured and charred around the edges but of course not burnt — this is the foundation for the flavour.

Meanwhile, cook the gnocchi as per the packet instructions. Drain but reserve half a cup of the cooking water. Add the gnocchi and cooking water to the pan, then fold in the chopped rocket, allowing it to wilt. Season.

Serve in warm bowls with a drizzle of balsamic vinegar and the Parmesan sprinkled on top.

APPLE, BOURSIN AND ALMOND TART

SERVES 4

1 x 320g sheet of ready-rolled shortcrust pastry, thawed

1 egg beaten with 1 tbsp milk

2 x 150g packets of Boursin cheese

2 red Gala apples

1 tbsp flaked almonds

1 tbsp butter

½ tbsp honey

Preheat the oven to 190°C.

Unfurl the pastry, keeping it on the parchment it's wrapped in, then brush lightly with the egg wash. Make a thin lip on the pastry by folding the edges back on themselves and egg wash the rim.

Crumble the Boursin over the base of the pastry. There will be big bits, little bits and gaps in between.

Quarter the apples and cut out the core. Slice the apples as thinly as you can – if you have a mandolin, it would be perfect for the job. Distribute the apples over the base of the tart, followed by the almonds.

Melt the butter and the honey together, then drizzle it over the apples. Bake in the oven for 20–25 minutes, until golden and crisp.

Serve with a green salad on the side.

Irish food has come a long way

12 MARCH 2022

With St Patrick's Day only a few days away, we have a chance to celebrate it like we used to: frostbitten children shifting their mottled legs, trying to keep warm. It always seems to be freezing. When our girls were small we braved the cold and rain to show them the local parade. It was never anything fancy but they always loved it despite the weather. Tractors pulled trailers with Irish dancers and a dolly-mixture of folk and drama groups in dodgy costumes. The fire brigade turned out to add a bit of pomp. Little boys stared wide-eyed at the size of the shiny red engines. It was all a bit cheesy, but it was ours. Recently arrived Syrian children clung to their parents and waved little Irish flags, all hoping that this bewildering new country would be kind to them. For them, we were a glimmer of hope.

Irish food has come such a long way. From a meagre smattering only a few years ago, Michelin has bestowed stars on us like delicious confetti. Gifted and committed chefs have been toiling for years to prove that there is so much more to Irish food than stew. Where once food was just fuel, necessary for our very existence and a grim legacy of our terrible past, it is now a sign of how far we have come. I am proud.

The hake dish is an example of simple fish cookery. The crème fraîche protects and lubricates the flesh of the hake while giving it a creamy texture. You can use another white fish, of course, but I can't resist the creamy goodness of hake. I'm blanching the cabbage to help keep the all-important colour.

The chowder in the title refers to the texture of this cream-free soup more than anything else. I adore wild garlic. For those of you who can get it, now is the time. Otherwise the leeks fulfil the brief admirably.

Springtime is all about green and this dish celebrates those wonderful verdant vegetables. The sourdough adds texture and soaks up their juices, while this simple goat cheese and apple dressing adds tang and creamy complexity.

BAKED HAKE WITH SAVOY CABBAGE AND PICKLED GINGER BUTTER

SERVES 4

4–6 Savoy cabbage leaves,

4 spring onions, trimmed

a drizzle of olive oil

4 x 180g hake fillets, skin on and deboned

2 tbsp crème fraîche or natural yogurt

FOR THE BUTTER:

100ml apple juice

150g butter, diced and chilled

1 sprig of fresh rosemary

25g pickled ginger, roughly chopped

Preheat the oven to 185°C.

Bring a pot of salted water to the boil, then add the cabbage and spring onions and cook until tender but still green — 2 minutes or so should do it. Drain and sit the vegetables in iced water until cool. This stops the cooking process and retains the colour. Drain again and dry on kitchen paper.

Brush the base of a grill tray with a little oil, then sit the hake on top, skin side down. Brush the fish with a layer of crème fraîche or yogurt, then drizzle the top with a little more oil and season. Bake in the oven for 10–12 minutes, depending on the thickness of the fish. Don't be afraid to take a small knife to gently prise the fish apart to see if it's cooked. You're looking for white, flaky flesh.

Meanwhile, to make the pickled ginger butter, bring the apple juice to a simmer in a small pan. Whisk in the butter bit by bit over a gentle heat, then add the rosemary. When all the butter been amalgamated, add the pickled ginger and remove the rosemary. Keep warm.

When the fish is nearly cooked, add the cabbage and spring onions to the tray with a little more oil and some salt and pepper. Turn them in the oil and cooking juices to make sure they are coated, then put the tray back in the oven to cook for just a minute.

To serve, carefully lift the fish off the tray onto warm plates. Arrange the cabbage and spring onions alongside, then spoon over the butter sauce. Eat with some boiled new potatoes.

ROAST CHICKEN, BUTTER BEAN AND WILD GARLIC CHOWDER

SERVES 4

80g butter

1 leek, halved lengthways and sliced

1 tbsp plain flour

2 bay leaves (fresh if possible)

800ml chicken stock

1 x 400g tin of butter beans, drained and rinsed

300g or so leftover roast chicken

½ tbsp Dijon mustard

a handful of wild garlic leaves, finely chopped

a squeeze of lemon juice

Melt the butter in a medium-sized saucepan over a gentle heat. When the butter starts to foam, add the leek, cover and cook for 10 minutes, until the leek softens without colour.

Add the flour and cook for 2 minutes, then add the bay leaves followed by the stock, little by little, making sure the flour is mixed in well. Bring to a simmer, then add the butter beans, chicken and mustard.

Allow all the ingredients to get to know each other gently for 5 minutes, then add the wild garlic, lemon juice and some salt and pepper.

Serve straightaway, before the wild garlic discolours.

ROASTED SPRING GREENS AND CRUNCHY SOURDOUGH WITH GOAT CHEESE DRESSING

SERVES 4

2 courgettes

1 bunch of asparagus

2 fresh red chillies, deseeded and halved lengthways

zest and juice of 1 lemon

1 slice of sourdough bread, roughly torn

80ml extra virgin olive oil

1 small packet of baby spinach

FOR THE DRESSING:

150g soft rindless goat cheese

80ml apple juice

2 tbsp natural yogurt

Preheat the oven to 185°C.

Trim and cut the courgettes into 1cm-thick pieces at a slight angle. Trim the bottom third from the asparagus spears and discard.

Put the veg on a shallow baking tray along with the chillies and the lemon zest and juice. Scatter the sourdough on top, season and pour over the olive oil. Mix everything together until coated, then cook in the oven for 20 minutes, turning once along the way.

When the vegetables are tender and slightly charred, remove the tray from the oven and add the spinach while the tray is still hot. Season once more and if you think it's a little dry, add a hint more oil.

Meanwhile, whisk the goat cheese, apple juice and yogurt together to make the dressing.

For best effect, serve the spring greens on a platter with the dressing drizzled over the top.

A trip to Milan was worth it for the lunch alone

19 MARCH 2022

Me and a friend of (gulp) 50 years went to Italy recently for a few nights. Crocker rang me to say he could get return flights to Bergamo for a tenner each. He, like me, has a built-in travel bug. We spend a lot of time talking about past and future travels.

The fact that I wanted to bring a bag was a bone of contention, as in his view it pushed the price up unnecessarily. A man only needs fresh jocks and a toothbrush to go on a short European escapade. 'No need to be encumbered with luggage, that's beer money,' he said as he tried to appeal to my base instincts.

There was an interminable pause on the phone as he waited for me to change my mind but I stood my ground. 'I need options,' I said. 'We are going to Milan, after all. I can't go schlepping round looking like a goatherd.' Me and my metrosexual ways.

I'm a bit of a restaurant list obsessive when it comes to a trip. I spend hours googling to find gastronomic nirvana. It doesn't always work. This time, though, we struck gold. After an anxious 20-minute walk from the Duomo, we entered my perfect Italian trattoria. We were the only tourists. The place buzzed with local families and businessmen. I can't tell you how relieved I was.

Vino de la casa was called for. I beamed as a jug was put in front of me. The staff were patient with our lumbering Italian. We ordered vitello tonnato, cacio a pepe, polpette and osso buco. I didn't want to leave so I ordered the most perfect tiramisu in an opulent little glass. The whole trip was worth it for that lunch alone. It was a great weekend but in retrospect I think I packed in too much.

This week I'm making an Italian feast. It's all based around this soft, spongy bread from Emilia-Romagna. Think Italian muffins that are opened, then stuffed with all the goodies. You don't have to make everything, of course, but this is a feast! The tigelle alone would suffice, but beware, it will make you crave your very own jug of wine.

Cooking is about the only gift I've been given. It comes naturally to me. I'm not sure where it came from but I'm glad I have it. I would be a terrible electrician.

TIGELLE WITH MOSTARDA GRAPES, BURRATA AND SALUMI

SERVES 6

150g lukewarm milk

150g lukewarm water

5g fast-acting dried yeast

500g '00' or strong white flour, plus extra for dusting

5g fine sea salt

25g olive oil

FOR THE MOSTARDA GRAPES:

500g black seedless grapes

50g Demerara sugar

100ml red wine

1 tbsp red wine vinegar

1 tbsp wholegrain mustard

TO SERVE:

salami, prosciutto, mortadella and mozzarella or burrata

The mostarda grapes can be done the day before. Pick and wash the grapes, then put them in a small pan with the sugar, red wine and vinegar. Bring to a simmer and cook for 15 minutes or so, until nearly all the juice has evaporated from the pan and the grapes burst and turn into a compote.

Add the mustard and cook for a couple more minutes, then remove the pan from the heat and allow to cool. Put in the fridge to chill.

To make the tigelle, combine the warm milk and water and stir in the yeast. Leave for 10 minutes to activate.

Put the flour and salt in a mixing bowl. Add the oil, then stir in the yeast mixture with a spoon. Once it starts to come together into a dough, knead it on a floured surface for 5 minutes, until smooth.

Put the dough in an oiled bowl, cover with a damp, clean cloth and leave somewhere warm to prove for at least 1 hour, until doubled in size.

Tip the dough out onto a floured surface and roll out to 0.5cm thick. Use an 8cm cutter to stamp the dough into discs. Re-roll the trimmings so you use all the dough.

Carefully arrange the discs onto a tray lined with greaseproof paper. Cover with the cloth and leave to prove again for another hour.

Put a non-stick frying pan over a medium heat and allow to come to temperature. Working in batches, cook the tigelle in the hot pan for about 4 minutes on each side, until puffed up and slightly charred.

Serve the tigelle with prosciutto, mortadella and salami and some burrata or mozzarella. Cut open the warm bread, then stuff it with whatever you fancy and add a spoonful of the mostarda grapes. Heaven.

SOFT POLENTA WITH ASPARAGUS AND MAPLE GREMOLATA

SERVES 6

250g asparagus

a good drizzle of olive oil

300ml milk

300ml water

2 strips of lemon peel

1 garlic clove, gently crushed

2 bay leaves (fresh if possible)

150g instant polenta

100g Parmesan cheese, grated

FOR THE GREMOLATA:

1 garlic clove, crushed

zest and juice of 1 lemon

100ml extra virgin olive oil

2 tbsp finely chopped fresh flat-leaf parsley

1 tsp maple syrup

Preheat the oven to 185°C.

Trim one-third from the bottom of the asparagus spears. If they are large you will need to carefully peel them too. Put them on a tray, drizzle with oil and season. Roast in the oven for 12 minutes or so, until they are tender and wilted slightly.

Bring the milk and water up to a simmer in a medium-sized saucepan, then add the lemon peel, garlic and bay. Let it infuse for a minute or two, then drizzle in the polenta, little by little, whisking all the time until you get a smooth, creamy texture.

Remove the lemon, garlic and bay leaves, then add most of the Parmesan, leaving some to sprinkle over the top. Season with salt and ground white pepper. Keep the polenta warm. It stiffens up pretty quickly but you can loosen it with a little more milk.

Meanwhile, mix all the gremolata ingredients together.

To serve, spoon a bed of polenta on the base of a platter, then top with the asparagus and any residual oil from the tray. Sprinkle with the remaining Parmesan and serve the gremolata on the side.

ARTICHOKE BALSAMICO AL FORNO
SERVES 6

2 x 280g jars of baby artichokes

40g butter

30g plain flour

1 garlic clove, chopped

200ml milk

1 sprig of fresh thyme

100ml cream

2 tbsp balsamic vinegar

1 tsp golden caster sugar

3 tbsp Parmesan cheese, grated

3 tbsp breadcrumbs

Preheat the oven to 185°C.

Drain the artichokes and pat them dry — you need to get rid of any excess oil.

Melt the butter in a saucepan over a low heat. When the butter starts to foam, add the flour and cook for 2 minutes. Add the garlic, milk and thyme. Whisk until smooth, then add the cream. When it's gently bubbling, add the balsamic vinegar, sugar and some salt and pepper.

Put the artichokes in a casserole, then pour the sauce on top. Sprinkle over the Parmesan and breadcrumbs, then bake in the oven for 30 minutes, until crisp and golden. Serve straightaway.

This week I just concentrated on making nice dishes

26 MARCH 2022

I devise these recipes by staring off into the distance and imagining what ingredients to put together and then how to cook them. The seasons are always the driving force. The method is, of course, crucial. Most of the time they work in my head but when it comes to testing the recipes, which also happens to be the day they are photographed, the odd time they don't work. It can be pretty hectic. There's a lot of feverish jotting down, cursing and adjusting.

This week was supposed to feature dishes to be cooked under the grill. Flaccid, unappealing meat and the smell of burning breadcrumbs alerted me to the flaws of two of the recipes. With the always-patient photographer, Harry Weir, I quickly abandoned the grill theme and just concentrated on making nice dishes.

The price of lamb has rocketed. I'm using the rack, which makes the dish quite expensive, but you could use gigot chops. It's my first time using aubergine this year and believe it or not, anchovies with lamb is a thing. I love its salty umami hit. Orange, rosemary and tomato bring the dish to the South of France, a lovely place to be at this time of year.

These were the burning breadcrumbs in question. This pepper dish is perfect for baking. The olive-laden breadcrumbs crisp as the peppers roast and sweeten and the crème fraîche provides the perfect foil for the fiery sriracha. This is perfect as a vegetarian main or as a side with a roast.

The next dish is for those who like simple seafood. The only snag is that I'm getting all forage-y and using sea beet for my set butter. It's also called sea spinach and can be found growing adjacent to most beaches, which I know won't be available to everyone. Don't fret, however, as there is good dried seaweed out there that you can substitute. Or just leave it out. That's the whole point of recipes — it's always a moveable, exciting feast.

You could use any fish instead of plaice with this method, but the cooking times will vary according to the thickness of your chosen fish.

LAMB CHOPS WITH AUBERGINE, ORANGE AND ANCHOVIES

SERVES 4

1 x 8-bone rack of lamb, cut into chops

1 aubergine, cut into 1cm-thick slices

3 garlic cloves, chopped

2 sprigs of fresh rosemary

1 tsp smoked paprika

½ tsp chilli flakes

100ml olive oil, plus extra to serve

cherry tomatoes on the vine

1 orange

1 x 50g tin of salted anchovies (Ortiz if possible)

Put the lamb chops, aubergine, garlic, rosemary, smoked paprika, chilli flakes and some salt and pepper in a large ziplock bag. Pour in the olive oil and scrunch everything together. Let it sit in the fridge for a couple of hours.

Turn your grill to high.

Spread the lamb chops and aubergine evenly over the base of a roasting tin, with the lamb on top. Grill for 6–7 minutes, until the chops start to colour, then turn them and the aubergine over. Add the whole cherry tomatoes to the tray and continue to grill for another 3–4 minutes.

Meanwhile, peel and slice the orange with a serrated knife, then punctuate the slices among the chops along with the anchovies.

Serve family-style with more olive oil drizzled on top, some boiled new potatoes and perhaps a rocket salad.

POINTED PEPPERS WITH OLIVE CRUMBLE AND SRIRACHA CRÈME FRAÎCHE

SERVES 4

8 pointed peppers, halved lengthways

FOR THE CRUMBLE:

120g fresh white breadcrumbs

100g mixed olives, stoned and chopped

zest and juice of ½ orange

50ml extra virgin olive oil

a few sprigs of fresh thyme, leaves picked and chopped

1 tbsp capers, chopped

FOR THE CRÈME FRAÎCHE:

200ml crème fraîche

3 tbsp sriracha

Preheat the oven to 185°C.

Mix the breadcrumbs with the olives, orange zest and juice, oil, thyme, capers and some black pepper.

Put the peppers in a roasting tin, cut side up, and stuff the breadcrumbs in the cavities. Bake in the oven for 25–30 minutes, until crisp.

Mix the crème fraîche with the sriracha and serve alongside so you can help yourself to as much as you want.

PLAICE WITH NEW POTATOES, LITTLE GEMS AND SEA BEET BUTTER

SERVES 2

4 tbsp olive oil

2 large plaice fillets, skin on

2 tsp crème fraîche or natural yogurt

2 heads of Little Gem lettuce

8 cooked new potatoes

FOR THE BUTTER:

225g butter, diced and softened

1 garlic clove, crushed

a handful of sea beet, shredded, or 1 tsp dried dillisk

zest and juice of 1 lime

2 tsp Dijon mustard

Put the softened butter in a bowl with the garlic, sea beet, lime zest and juice and mustard. Mix together with a spatula, giving it a good beating to make it light and creamy. Roll the butter in cling film or parchment to make a nice tight log, then chill for 1 hour or so. This will make more than you need but you can freeze it. It's very versatile, lovely with spuds or pasta.

Preheat the oven to 190°C.

Drizzle a little of the oil on a baking tray, then put the plaice on top, skin side down. Brush the fish with the crème fraîche, making sure you cover every part of it.

Halve the Little Gems lengthways and add them to the tray. Break up the potatoes and position them around the fish. Drizzle the remaining oil over the fish, lettuce and potatoes, then season. Bake in the oven for 10–12 minutes, depending on the thickness of the fish.

When cooked, transfer to warm plates. Cut slices of butter off the log and put on top of the fish. It will melt and release its aroma and flavour as it's put on the table.

A good salad is just the thing to restore your mojo

02 APRIL 2022

A good salad is a revelation, a breath of fresh air. When you're fed up cooking and eating the same old ding-dong week after week, it's refreshing to change tack and have something lighter. Is it the crispness of the ingredients or the zing of the dressing that elevates you? Or does your body crave a change?

I suspect (without judgement!) that most families have a revolving series of dishes that are tried-and-tested safe bets. I think it's normal to get a bit bored of cooking and eating the same thing. That's why a blistering salad is just the thing to restore your mojo.

Loving Salads Café on Academy Street in Cork City blows me away every time. You need sunglasses just to walk in there as the array of salads on display is so dazzling. Ottolenghi is undoubtedly an influence. Cavernous bowls twinkle, pop and glisten. Choosing can be fraught. It's an Aladdin's cave of deliciousness. Have a look online even if you can't get to it. It's inspiring.

I'm using leftover roast chicken for this elegant first salad. You can cook a chicken breast if you don't have any leftovers handy. It's mixed with lovely bits and pieces and sits on a creamy concoction called cervelle de canut, which literally translates as 'silk workers' brains' in homage to the Canuts, the silk workers of 19th-century Lyon. Fromage blanc is traditionally used but you can use crème fraîche as it can be hard to find. We sometimes use this as a dip in the restaurant. It's utterly fabulous.

I'm a big fan of petits pois. I'm shaving fennel and mixing them both with a mixture of baby spinach and kale and a punchy orange and chilli dressing, then topping the salad off with lots of tangy feta cheese.

There's a Middle Eastern accent to the next salad. Carrots are the star and the supporting cast are the bulgur and almonds. Dates bring their toffee sweetness and the yogurt gives the dish balance. It's a lovely change if you're up for it.

ROAST CHICKEN SALAD WITH CERVELLE DE CANUT
SERVES 2

2 tbsp extra virgin olive oil

a squeeze of lemon juice

a pinch of caster sugar

100g mixed salad leaves

¼ cucumber, peeled and thinly sliced

4 radishes, sliced

leftover roast chicken

FOR THE CERVELLE DE CANUT:

200ml fromage blanc or crème fraîche

1 small shallot, very finely chopped

1 tbsp chopped fresh chives

1 tbsp chopped fresh tarragon

1 tbsp white wine vinegar

1 tbsp walnut or hazelnut oil (optional)

1 tsp honey

For the cervelle de canut, simply mix all the ingredients together and chill.

Whisk the oil, lemon juice, sugar and seasoning together in a large bowl. Add the leaves, cucumber, radishes and chicken, tossing to coat.

Divide the cervelle de canut between two plates, then make a well in the centre with the back of a spoon. Put the salad in the middle and serve.

PEA, FENNEL AND FETA SALAD

SERVES 4

1 large fennel bulb, very thinly sliced

200g frozen petits pois, defrosted

1 x 150g packet of baby spinach and kale (spinach on its own will do)

1 orange, peeled and segmented

200g feta cheese, crumbled

FOR THE DRESSING:

75ml sunflower oil

75ml extra virgin olive oil

juice of 1 orange

1 small fresh red chilli, deseeded and diced

20g fresh dill, roughly chopped

1 tsp caster sugar

Get out a large bowl, one big enough to accommodate all the salad later on. Add the oils, orange juice, chilli, dill, sugar and some salt and pepper and whisk together.

Add the fennel, peas and the spinach and kale to the bowl, season and turn in the dressing. Transfer to a platter.

Cut the orange segments into smaller pieces and scatter them over the top along with the crumbled feta cheese.

This salad is lovely on its own but would also be delicious with roast lamb.

ROASTED SPRING CARROT SALAD WITH BULGUR, YOGURT AND DATES

SERVES 6

750g young carrots, halved lengthways

a generous drizzle of olive oil

200g bulgur wheat

200g stoned dates, chopped

80g whole salted almonds, chopped

1 tsp ground cumin

1 tsp ground cinnamon

1 tsp za'atar or ras el hanout

450ml hot vegetable or chicken stock

200ml natural yogurt

a few sprigs of fresh mint

Preheat the oven to 180°C.

Put the carrots in a large, deep roasting tin, drizzle with the oil, season and mix together so the carrots are coated in the oil. Roast in the oven for 30 minutes, turning once or twice.

Scatter the bulgur in among the carrots, then add the dates, almonds and spices. Season, then pour the stock over the top. Cover tightly with foil and put the tin back in the oven for 15 minutes.

Remove the foil and fluff everything up with a fork. Allow to cool, then transfer onto a platter.

Drizzle over the yogurt and tear the mint leaves on top before serving.

Food truck flavours straight from your kitchen

09 APRIL 2022

Even before food trucks became big, I was obsessed with them. My very first, and slightly terrifying, job, age 15, was in a travelling burger van at local summer festivals. We would wait for the lads to pour out of the tent at the end of the night and drunkenly descend on us. The little van pitched and rolled like a ship on a stormy sea, heaved by the hungry bodies and the funk of stale beer. As the chips fried in swirling fat, we narrowly avoided mutilation as it spat onto the floor.

So now I have my own food truck show coming out on RTÉ1. I even get my own vintage caravan to simulate another, freer life. What I came across astounded me. The sheer inventiveness of what people serve out of these tiny spaces is so impressive. I was a lucky man to get to do this.

The dishes today could all happily be served from a food truck but let's presume you don't have one.

I prefer sea trout over salmon any day. I appreciate it's not as widely available, so use salmon if you can't get it. The teriyaki sea trout is full of bold, punchy flavours nestling in a pillowy brioche bun, its stickiness foiled by the crunchy cucumber, deliberately made hot with lots of chilli and fragrant pickled ginger.

Coronation chicken was invented by the food writer Constance Spry while preparing the food for the banquet for Queen Elizabeth II's coronation in 1953. It originally consisted of cooked chicken in a simple curried mayonnaise but of course fellas like me have been messing with it ever since. I'm using crème fraîche to bind the chicken as it has to be wrapped in filo and baked. I must say I am quite pleased with the result.

I made this duck dish in my 28-year-old rice cooker. You don't have to have a rice cooker to make this but if I were to invest in a good kitchen gadget, this would be it. I'm giving simple instructions for an oven-baked alternative.

TERIYAKI SEA TROUT BUNS WITH CUCUMBER AND GINGER PICKLE

SERVES 2

2 x 150g portions of sea trout or salmon, skinned and boned

4 tbsp teriyaki sauce

1 tbsp toasted sesame oil

1 tbsp water

2 brioche buns

FOR THE PICKLE:

75g caster sugar

75ml rice wine vinegar

75ml water

1 cucumber, peeled and thinly sliced

1 fresh red chilli, deseeded and diced

50g pickled sushi ginger

To make the pickle, put the sugar, vinegar and water in a small saucepan and bring to the boil. Remove the pan from the heat and add the cucumber, chilli and sushi ginger. Mix everything together and allow to cool, then chill in the fridge for at least 1 hour. This will make more than you need but it will keep in the fridge for up to two weeks.

Preheat the oven to 180°C.

Put the sea trout in a baking dish and drizzle over the teriyaki sauce, oil, water and seasoning. Turn the fish around in the sauce, then bake in the oven for 12 minutes or so. It will need more time if the fish is thick. If it's very thick, cut it in half through the middle.

To serve, lightly toast the brioche buns. Put a portion of sea trout on the base along with any residual juices from the dish. Top with pickled cucumber, sandwich with the other half of the brioche bun and serve.

CORONATION CHICKEN SAMOSAS

MAKES 10

1 tbsp sultanas

300g approx. leftover roast chicken

1 small fresh green chilli, deseeded and finely diced

200ml crème fraîche

1 tbsp mango chutney

2 tsp curry powder

½ tsp ground cinnamon

1 x 270g packet of filo pastry, thawed

sunflower oil, for brushing

sesame seeds, for coating (optional)

Soak the sultanas in a bowl of just-boiled water for 15 minutes, then drain. Put them in a bowl with the chicken, chilli, crème fraîche, mango chutney, curry powder and cinnamon. Season and mix.

Lay a sheet of filo out on your countertop with the longest side going left to right. Brush lightly with oil then put another sheet on top, pressing down to stick both together. Add one more sheet on top and smooth all the pastry together with your hands. Cut the filo into four even strips from top to bottom. A pizza cutter is perfect for this.

Put a level tablespoon of the chicken mixture on the top corner of the pastry — it's important not to overfill. Fold the top right corner of the pastry over the filling to form a triangle and press down with your fingers to seal as best you can.

Continue to fold nice and tightly until you come to the end of the pastry. Make a tight seal and repeat the process with the rest of the filo and the filling. Look up 'how to make a samosa' on YouTube if you are struggling.

If using sesame seeds, brush the top of the samosas with a little oil and sprinkle on the seeds. Put the samosas in the fridge without touching each other to chill for an hour or two.

Preheat the oven to 180°C.

Bake the samosas in the oven for 25 minutes, until golden and crisp. Serve warm.

THAI RICE COOKER DUCK

SERVES 4

2 tbsp toasted sesame oil

1 red pepper, finely diced

1 red onion, finely diced

1 fresh red chilli, deseeded and finely diced

2 strips of lemon peel

8 green cardamon pods, lightly crushed

300g jasmine rice, rinsed

2 confit duck legs, skin and bones removed and meat diced

1 x 400ml tin of low-fat coconut milk

300ml chicken stock

2 tbsp Thai green curry paste

a few sprigs of fresh coriander

mango chutney, to serve

Put all the ingredients except the coriander and chutney in your rice cooker, stir and put it on to cook. When cooked, allow to rest for 5 minutes then fluff up with a fork. Garnish with coriander leaves and serve with mango chutney.

If you don't have a rice cooker, preheat the oven to 185°C.

Heat the sesame oil in a wide casserole over a gentle heat. Add the pepper, red onion, chilli, lemon and cardamon and cook for 10 minutes or so, until they soften. Add the remaining ingredients except for the coriander and chutney and bring to a simmer. Cover and cook in the oven for 20 minutes, until all the liquid has been absorbed by the rice.

Let the rice rest, then fluff it up with a fork. Garnish with the coriander leaves and serve with mango chutney.

Easter Sunday

16 APRIL 2022

After a two-year delay, my family and I are just back from what I hope will have been a life-affirming and special trip to New York.

My teenage girls are lucky. I was in my thirties before I went over the Williamsburg Bridge in a yellow cab, my face pressed against the window like a child. The familiar skyline loomed at first, then swallowed us up. I was happy to be eaten. New York City casts a spell on you.

I had a couple of restaurants booked but nothing like the usual extensive list. It was their holiday after all and I was going to end up in the Cheesecake Factory whether I liked it or not.

We've landed home straight into Easter so I'm going to cook lamb. I'm taking our Sunday lunch straight to the South of France. That's the thing about food. It allows you to dream. We'll hope for a sunny day so we can pretend we're in the lavender-scented, dappled sunlight of Provence.

Pissaladière is one of my very favourite things to eat — caramelised onions, olives and anchovies baked on a crispy dough base. I'd almost forgo pizza forevermore to immerse myself in its bold, salty flavours. I'm pairing the leg of lamb with these flavours to transport us. A chilled crisp rosé would take it to heaven.

I'm pairing the lamb and bulking it up with simply roasted potatoes, courgettes, lemon and pine nuts. The lamb needs some lubrication so I'm making a simple tomato and goat cheese sauce, laden with butter beans.

All in all, this is a lunch I would happily serve at home to a gang. It's well considered in that all the dishes are in harmony with one another and it's hopefully not difficult to make. Once Easter is past us, we'll have one eye on the summer. How the year is flying.

LEG OF LAMB PISSALADIÈRE

SERVES 8

1 x 2.5kg leg of lamb, bone in
a glug of olive oil
1 garlic bulb, torn apart and lightly crushed
3 sprigs of fresh rosemary
1.5kg onions, quartered
100g stoned black olives
100g stoned green olives
1 x 50g tin of salted anchovy fillets, chopped
3 tbsp red wine vinegar
1 tbsp honey
chopped fresh flat-leaf parsley

Pierce the lamb in numerous places with a small knife, then put it in a large bag (I use a bin bag) along with the oil, garlic, rosemary and some salt and pepper. Scrunch everything together vigorously, then wrap the bag in itself to form a seal for the marinade. Put in the fridge for a few hours or overnight if possible.

Preheat the oven to 185°C.

Put the lamb in a roasting tin with a little more oil and roast in the oven for 1 hour.

Add the onions to the tin and coat them thoroughly with the oil and lamb juices, then return the tin to the oven to cook for 45 minutes more. It's important to turn the onions periodically as they cook to get an even caramelisation.

A meat thermometer will take the guesswork out of cooking a roast. I'm cooking the lamb medium (pink), which is 65°C. If you would like it a little more cooked nudge it to 70°C, but above that you're in well-done territory.

Transfer the lamb to a tray and allow to rest under foil for 30 minutes.

Put the original roasting tin with the onions on the hob over a gentle heat. Add the olives, anchovies, vinegar, honey and parsley, season and keep warm.

Add any resting juices from the lamb to the onions. Carve and plate the lamb with the sticky onion mixture. This would be good with pilaf on the side.

ROAST POTATOES WITH COURGETTES, LEMON AND PINE NUTS

SERVES 8

1.5kg baby potatoes

50ml olive oil

2 sprigs of fresh thyme

2 courgettes, sliced into 0.5cm-thick rounds

2 garlic cloves, sliced

1 small fresh red chilli, deseeded and diced

60g pine nuts

juice of ½ lemon

Preheat the oven to 180°C.

Cut the potatoes into two or three, depending on their size, then put them in a roasting tin with the oil and thyme and season. Cook in the oven for 20 minutes, until they are nearly soft.

Add the courgettes, garlic, chilli and pine nuts. Cook in the oven for a further 15 minutes, keeping an eye on the pine nuts as they burn very easily.

Remove the tin from the oven, add the lemon juice and more salt and pepper, then it's ready to serve with the lamb on the previous page.

BUTTER BEANS IN ROASTED PEPPER AND GOAT CHEESE SAUCE
SERVES 8

2 garlic cloves, sliced

1 red pepper, diced

3 tbsp olive oil

1 x 400g tin of chopped tomatoes

zest of ½ orange

½ tsp dried oregano

200ml chicken or vegetable stock

150g soft rindless goat cheese

a squeeze of honey

2 x 400g tins of butter beans, drained and rinsed

Heat the oil in a large saucepan over a gentle heat. Add the pepper and garlic, cover with a lid and cook for 20 minutes, until the pepper is soft and sticky.

Add the tomatoes, orange zest, oregano and stock. Bring to a simmer and cook for a further 10 minutes, then crumble in the goat cheese and add the honey. Blitz with a hand blender, add the butter beans and season.

Serve warm alongside the lamb on page 565. This would also make a lovely vegetarian dish, perhaps with couscous, rice or gnocchi.

New York

New York is the one place that has left an indelible mark on me. There is something special about that city. Maybe it's because it seems so familiar — we grew up with it imprinted on our imaginations.

My wife and I have been several times but this time we had to consider our teenage daughters. I've annoyingly become a bit smug about the city and decided to stay in Brooklyn, where we could savour the vista and blend in with the hipsters of Williamsburg for the first couple of days. We'd all discussed at great length what we would eat long before we arrived.

Everything was split into the most important food groups: burgers, pizza, fried chicken, Chinese, Italian, Mexican, sushi, pancakes, waffles and doughnuts.

TikTok was their main reference point. Names of unheard-of restaurants were scattered about like confetti. In truth, I didn't like losing control. *What the hell?* I thought to myself. *What if they're rubbish?* But it was their holiday. I was going to keep schtum and play ball.

One full day in Brooklyn was enough, though. It was a bit scruffy and post-apocalyptic. It rained as we caught the ferry to gentrified Dumbo. We gratefully ducked into the Time Out indoor market, a collection of carefully curated food vendors with public areas for eating. It's Nirvana for the indecisive. You get whatever food group you fancy, eat up and people watch. We ate in Lilia that night, it was cool with heavenly pasta. I might be lifting a few of their ideas for my column in the future.

The next day we took a cab into the city and their eyes widened. This was the New York they expected.

Over the next few days I toned down my natural inclination to go to 'happening restaurants'. Thanks to my friend Tim Magee, we discovered Hectors, the world's most perfect diner which was right beside our hotel in the Meatpacking district. Burly men passed by the window with dead pigs curled over their shoulders. Horrified, the girls nudged their pancakes and bacon. I told them this area hadn't always been full of Tesla showrooms and designer stores. A few meatpacking businesses still remain in one stalwart corner. This area has a gritty past, and New York, more than any other city, is constantly regenerating.

We walked the Highline and went up the Edge in Hudson Yards, where we took in the magnificence of the city. I hadn't been to Times Square in years — too many tourists. However, over the four days I found myself there twice. I enjoyed the first visit. It was dark and the flashing monolithic signs consumed us, necks craned to the neon. The capital of consumerism was ready to gobble us up.

We queued in vain for Krispy Kreme doughnuts. Tantalisingly, we could see them being glazed before our eyes but the line wasn't moving. An M&M superstore beckoned from across the street. Patient parents with small children stood in more lines for their turn. I watched my excited girls become small again and felt a pang.

We found ourselves in Times Square again the next morning for a tour bus. The city is back with a bang but we could see the ghosts of businesses past. Not all have made it through.

We crawled downtown through the traffic. As we passed NYU one of the daughters wondered if any Kardashians went to college there. That worried me. We were told that we had to get off near Ground Zero, as a movie was being shot. We hopped off and thought of food once again but first we had to visit the site of the Twin Towers. It silenced us and quelled our appetites.

We turned towards Canal Street in the sun. Cumulus clouds of dope hung in the air as we walked. It turns out New York has legalised recreational marijuana and boy, do they embrace it. I got the munchies by proxy. We found Wo Hop, a charmingly raffish gem of an old Chinese restaurant in a basement on Mott Street, deep in the heart of Chinatown. Food always cheers us up and soothes any potential familial acrimony.

The afternoon was earmarked for shopping so we agreed to separate. The eldest is a good shopper, like her mother. It's like a military campaign to them. My youngest is more chilled. In time she'll probably be sent to keep an eye on me. I met a friend who lives there and we shopped for beer in some of New York's edgier bars. Later the family reunited in Arturo's on Houston for coal-fired pizza.

The next morning we took the subway intending to go to Central Park but overshot and ended up in Harlem. As we waited for a train to go back downtown we heard about a shooting in Brooklyn. Back above ground, we crossed through the park. It insulated us from the sirens.

Despite having tickets, a rather massive line at the Met museum almost put me off. I'm glad it didn't. It was exceptional. I saw some Vermeers and the girls saw the dress that Taylor Swift wore to the Grammys. Culture box ticked.

The daughters proved quite resourceful. We separated a couple of times and they always found us. One miscommunication saw us in a cab to go for an unplanned lunch. We'd had enough of the clamour of Fifth Avenue for one day but they wouldn't leave, consumed with shopping fever. Outraged at being abandoned, they followed us later. Yet they hopped out of the cab unfazed, laden with bags like the *Sex in the City* women.

I'm not sure whether we will ever be back again in New York as a family. Pretty soon they probably won't want to come on holidays with us. I'm glad we did this trip; it was special. Sometimes you have to store a memory, keep it warm and nurture it. In years to come I hope it will be a highlight of their young lives. We tried our best to help them fall in love with New York. I hope they did.

Chefs are magpies. We call on tradition to obtain our knowledge, then rely on observation for the rest.

29 APRIL 2022

Just dig in

23 APRIL 2022

As the summer approaches we lighten the food in the restaurant and at home. I also need this to happen as I'm in training again for the Camino next month. This time four of us are walking from Finisterre to Santiago. As usual, all of them are fitter than me but I'll be grand. The lure of the food in the next village always gives me an incentive.

I rarely cook stir-fries. In fact, I can be a bit judgey about them. I sometimes think they are the last resort of a chef with no imagination but I know that in the proper hands they can be wonderful. I've just never had an amazing one. In fairness they are a logical thing to cook for the family as it's easy to get pre-prepared meat and vegetables, and if it keeps the kids happy, everyone is happy. Maybe I'm just grumpy.

I recently cooked this one at home and everyone loved it. Kecap manis is a thick, sweet soy sauce from Indonesia and I'm a massive fan. It's available in Asian shops but if you can't get it, substitute thick teriyaki sauce instead. You can use pork or chicken or even omit the meat altogether and just use more vegetables. I really like the combination of pak choi and cashew nuts, though, and who doesn't like those crowd-pleasing Asian flavours?

I'm using hake for the next dish but you can use almost any fish. It's important to have a tight seal of foil over the tray or dish, as this ensures the fish will steam in the delicious gingery vapours. I'm serving this as one piece in the tray. No messing around, just dig in.

I'm sneaking a bit of my beloved Spain into this soup, which is full of nuance and depth. This is tomato soup's duskier, more interesting cousin. The chickpeas bulk it up but don't dominate. It's all about bringing out the best of simple ingredients. I know it's unusual but the quantities of these ingredients all add up to three healthy portions. What a rule breaker I am.

KECAP MANIS PORK WITH SWEET POTATO, PAK CHOI AND CASHEWS

SERVES 4

2 tbsp sunflower oil

1 tsp toasted sesame oil

300g pork loin chops, cut into 1cm strips

1 sweet potato, peeled and cut into 0.5cm-thick batons

2 red onions, sliced

2 pak choi, cut into quarters lengthways

2 garlic cloves, sliced

a thumb-sized piece of ginger, peeled and finely chopped

1 large fresh red chilli, deseeded and chopped

50ml water

100ml kecap manis or thick teriyaki sauce

100g cashew nuts

Heat the oils on a high heat in a wok until smoking, then carefully add the pork. Cook for 2 minutes, until it colours, then add the sweet potato, red onions, pak choi, garlic, ginger, chilli and water. Cover and cook for 5 minutes on the highest heat, turning the mixture once or twice.

Remove the lid and allow the water to evaporate, then add the kecap manis or teriyaki sauce, cashews and some salt and pepper. Turn the mixture together until everything is coated and glossy.

Serve straightaway with rice or noodles.

SOY-STEAMED HAKE WITH GINGERED VEGETABLES

SERVES 2

4 tbsp dark soy sauce

3 tbsp water

2 tbsp toasted sesame oil

1 garlic clove, peeled and grated

3cm piece of ginger, peeled and grated

1 x 350g hake fillet, skinned and boned

150g mangetout, halved

80g mixed mushrooms, sliced

1 small carrot, grated

4 spring onions, diced

a few sprigs of fresh coriander

Preheat the oven to 200°C.

Put the soy sauce, water and sesame oil in a bowl, then add the garlic and ginger and whisk together.

Spoon 2 tablespoons of the mixture on the base of a small roasting tin or casserole, then put the hake on top, moving it around the base to make sure it doesn't stick while cooking.

Mix all the veg together, then put them on top of the hake. Spoon the remaining soy dressing over the top.

Cover tightly with foil and bake in the oven for 15–20 minutes, depending on the thickness of the fish. It will be necessary to have a peek after 15 minutes – it's best to use a small knife to check. You're looking for white, flaky flesh. If in doubt, just cover tightly again and pop it back in the oven for a few more minutes.

Garnish with fresh coriander leaves and serve with boiled jasmine rice.

CHICKPEA AND SMOKY TOMATO SOUP

SERVES 3

3 tbsp extra virgin olive oil, plus extra to serve

2 garlic cloves, thinly sliced

1 x 400g tin of peeled plum tomatoes

200ml chicken or vegetable stock

1 sprig of fresh rosemary

1 tsp smoked paprika

1 tsp ground cumin

a squeeze of honey

1 x 400g tin of chickpeas, drained and rinsed

Heat the oil in a pot over a low heat. Add the garlic and let it slowly turn a light golden colour. It's important not to overcook it or it will go bitter.

Add the tinned tomatoes, stock, rosemary, smoked paprika and cumin, then bring to a gentle simmer for 15 minutes. Add the honey and some salt and pepper, then remove the rosemary.

Add the chickpeas and let them swirl around for a minute or two to absorb the flavours of the soup.

Serve in warm bowls with a slick of olive oil to anoint the top. A lovely addition would be a spoonful of hummus in the soup. Some people might say it's too much but I really don't think so.

An amalgam of French and Irish influences

29 APRIL 2022

For the most part, chefs are magpies. We call on tradition to obtain our knowledge, then rely on observation for the rest. Travelling, books, television and social media all influence us. We come back from our jaunts inspired by what we've eaten. We take note of who among our peers is doing something special and the news travels like Chinese whispers in the culinary community, who beat a path to their door.

I had a sublime experience recently at Chapter One although the word has been long out. This restaurant is a Mecca for those who love food cooked at the highest level. I have some skin in the game, as Mickael Viljanen came to work for me in the Tannery when he first arrived here from his native Finland. I taught him nothing. He is his own protégé as he is entirely self-made, driven by steely ambition, back-breaking work and the desire to realise his own remarkable talent.

We were invited by Ross Lewis, long-time owner and a gifted pot-slinger himself, to a boys' lunch at his chef's table. We drank wines way above my pay grade and ate food delivered with technique beyond my comprehension. Mickael's food is rooted in classic French style but made with a precision that would make Escoffier blush. The 'boys' were men of my trade, old soldiers of the stove. We settled back to absorb it all and marvel. We were all happy it wasn't us. The life is too hard at this level, always pushing. All we would do is get in the way as we shuffle around the kitchen.

My food this week is an amalgam of French and Irish influences. It's rustic, hearty and infinitely easier to make but it's definitely tasty. I have William Orbison to thank for the poulangère, a clever take on boulangère potatoes. I saw him make it on Twitter and stole it.

The other dishes are French with a little Irish influences twist. Young Buck cheese is an amazing Irish blue cheese. I've paired it with Highbank Orchard Syrup in the beignets, which is the nectar of the gods. Maple syrup or honey would be lovely too.

POULANGÈRE

SERVES 8

80g butter, plus more for the top

500g onions, sliced

3 garlic cloves, sliced

125g smoked bacon lardons

a few sprigs of fresh thyme, leaves picked

300g leftover roast chicken, shredded

2 tbsp Dijon mustard

2 tbsp red wine vinegar

500ml hot chicken stock

1.5kg potatoes, peeled and thinly sliced (on a mandolin if possible)

Preheat the oven to 180°C.

Melt the butter in a large saucepan over a medium heat. When the butter starts to foam, add the onions, garlic, bacon and thyme along with a splash of water. Cover and cook for 15 minutes.

Remove the lid and continue to cook for 5 more minutes, until the juices evaporate and the onions start to colour. Take the pan off the heat and add the chicken, mustard, red wine vinegar, some salt and lots of black pepper, then fold everything together.

Get out your largest casserole or a medium-sized, deep roasting tin. Add a ladle of stock to the base followed by one-third of the potatoes. Arrange them evenly over the base, then season the top. Add half of the chicken and onion mixture, then spread it out over the potatoes.

Put the next third of the potatoes over the top, pour over half of the stock and season.

Spread the remaining chicken and onion mixture over the potatoes, then carefully layer the remaining potatoes over it. Add the remaining stock and season. There should be three layers of potato and two layers of chicken and onion.

Dot some butter over the potatoes, cover with the lid or foil and bake in the oven for 1 hour. Uncover and put back in the oven for 20–30 minutes, until the top is crisp and the potatoes are tender.

Serve with a crisp green salad and perhaps some crème fraîche mixed with horseradish for a bit of a kick.

BACON CHOPS WITH PETITS POIS À LA IRLANDAISE

SERVES 2

a little sunflower oil

2 x 180g bacon chops, bone in if possible

100g black pudding, diced

1 tbsp butter

1 small red onion, sliced

1 sprig of fresh thyme

100ml cream

80ml apple juice

2 tsp Dijon mustard

100g frozen petits pois, defrosted

1 head of Little Gem lettuce, sliced, or a few handfuls of baby spinach

Preheat the oven to 185°C.

Heat a little sunflower oil in an ovenproof frying pan over a high heat until it's gently smoking. Carefully put the chops in the pan and cook for 3 minutes, until the bacon is golden. Turn the chops over and put the pan in the oven to cook for 20 minutes or so, until the chops are crisp and cooked through. Remove the pan from the oven. Transfer the chops to a plate, cover in foil and keep warm.

Meanwhile, heat a little oil on a small baking tray, turn the black pudding in it and cook in the oven for 10 minutes, until crisp.

Melt the butter in another saucepan over a gentle heat. When the butter starts to foam, add the red onion and thyme and cook for 5 minutes, until the onion softens. Add the cream and apple juice and bring to a simmer. Reduce by one-third, then whisk in the mustard.

Add the black pudding, peas and lettuce or spinach. Fold everything together over a low heat for 1 minute. The lettuce or spinach needs to wilt, not cook. Add any bacon juices to the pan and check the seasoning.

Serve straightaway with the bacon chops and some boiled new potatoes.

YOUNG BUCK BEIGNETS WITH HIGHBANK ORCHARD SYRUP DRIZZLE

SERVES 8

450ml water

170g butter, cut into pieces

1 tsp fresh thyme leaves

200g plain flour

5 medium eggs, beaten

150g Young Buck cheese or another blue cheese

500ml sunflower oil, for frying

Highbank Orchard Syrup, for drizzling

Put the water in a medium-sized saucepan with the butter and thyme, then simmer until the butter has melted. Tip in the flour and beat it as hard as you can until the mixture pulls away from the sides of the pan and is lump-free.

Transfer to a bowl and spread it up the sides to cool quicker (if you have a stand mixer, use this bowl). Add the beaten eggs little by little, until the mixture looks like a batter and becomes amalgamated. You may not need to add all the egg. Crumble in the cheese and fold everything together, then chill in the fridge for a little while.

Heat the oil to 180°C in a large, high-sided pan. If you have a deep-fryer, all the better. A sugar thermometer is invaluable if you don't have a deep-fryer. Always err on the side of caution when you are cooking with hot oil and keep the heat at medium at all times. To check if the oil is ready, drop a piece of bread in to see how quickly it colours. You're looking for a steady, even sizzle.

Working in batches, drop teaspoon-sized blobs of the mixture in the hot oil and cook for 3 minutes or so each.

Eat crisp and hot from the fryer with syrup drizzled over the top.

Small plates with big, bold flavours

06 MAY 2022

Small plates are big. People love the idea of having a little bit of everything, where the dishes keep coming until they greedily overwhelm the table. In the end, both your curiosity and your hunger are sated.

I love them myself. It's a much less formal way to eat. Everything is shared and it's not about getting a pile of spuds just to fill you up. In many ways a classic starter, main course and dessert format seems a bit, well, dull in comparison. There's great fun to be had in obliterating that staid structure. Today I'm giving you three fun dishes that you might make together or individually.

The polpette are based on an unusual but classic Italian dish, maiale al latte (pork braised in milk). I've made the original a few times over the years, being ignorantly sceptical at first. I could see the appeal of a whole joint of pork baked, semi-submerged, in a bath of milk. What emerged from the oven wasn't pretty, though. It was a worryingly split milky sauce but the pork was tender and succulent. It was ugly-delicous. The milk works its way into the pork to tenderise, then sets into a porky, cheesy custard. I'm scaling the classic dish down and making meatballs scented with sage, Parmesan and lemon. It's wondrously different.

The next dish is based on cod brandade, a Mediterranean stalwart. I'm using butter beans instead of potato in the mix and leaving everything a little lumpy. It's more of a crush, I suppose. Eat with toasted baguette smeared with shop-bought tapenade to give a bit of punch to the mellow flavour of the hake. The parsley is optional – it will still be lovely without it.

Chermoula is akin to a more interesting salsa verde. Its gentle spicing and slight heat take us to North Africa, its original home. It really lifts the subtle flavours of the asparagus. The ricotta joins the two together. You could use a mild, creamy goat cheese in its place or even Greek yogurt that you strain to make labneh, but only if you have time. I would never dare to impose.

PORK POLPETTE AL LATTE

SERVES 4

500g pork mince
100g Parmesan cheese, grated
100g fresh white breadcrumbs
2 garlic cloves, grated
8 fresh sage leaves, chopped
zest of ½ lemon
¹/₃ fresh nutmeg, grated
2 eggs, beaten
2 tbsp extra virgin olive oil, plus extra for drizzling
300ml milk

Preheat the oven to 185°C.

Put the pork, Parmesan, breadcrumbs, garlic, sage, lemon zest and nutmeg in a bowl. Add the beaten eggs and season, then scrunch everything together with clean hands. Form into eight even-sized balls.

Oil the base of a casserole, then add the meatballs. Drizzle a little more oil over the top, the pour the milk around the meatballs.

Bake in the oven for 30 minutes, until golden and crusty. You could serve this with your favourite pasta and plenty of Parmesan or just with crusty bread.

CRUSHED HAKE, BUTTER BEANS AND GARLIC (A SORT-OF BRANDADE)

SERVES 4

50ml olive oil

2 garlic cloves, sliced

1 x 250g fillet of skinless, boneless hake

2 bay leaves (fresh if possible)

1 x 400g tin of butter beans, drained and rinsed

120ml milk

100ml cream

a squeeze of lemon juice

black or green tapenade

toasted baguette slices

Heat the oil in a pan over a gentle heat. Add the sliced garlic and cook just until the garlic turns lightly golden. Remove the garlic with a slotted spoon before it burns.

Add the hake and bay leaves to the garlicky oil. Scatter the butter beans around the hake, then pour over the milk, cream and the reserved garlic pieces and season with salt and ground white pepper. Cover and poach gently for 10 minutes.

When the fish is cooked, add a little lemon juice, then crush everything with the back of a fork.

Meanwhile, smear the tapenade on the toasted baguette slices.

Check the seasoning, then serve the warm crushed hake and butter beans with the toast.

ASPARAGUS WITH RICOTTA AND CHERMOULA

SERVES 2

1 x 250g bunch of asparagus

100ml water

a drizzle of olive oil

150g ricotta or soft rindless goat cheese

FOR THE CHERMOULA:

50g fresh coriander

20g fresh flat-leaf parsley

1 garlic clove, peeled

zest of ½ lemon

40ml sunflower oil

40ml extra virgin olive oil

½ tsp ras el hanout

a pinch of chilli flakes

a pinch of caster sugar

a pinch of salt

2 ice cubes

To make the chermoula, put all the ingredients in a liquidizer or food processor and pulse until just blended. This makes more than you will need but the rest can be kept for a number of days in the fridge.

Trim the bottom third from the asparagus, then put the spears in a frying pan with the water, olive oil and seasoning. Cover the pan tightly and turn the heat on the highest setting. After 2 minutes or so you will hear a sizzle in the pan. This means the water has evaporated and the asparagus will be cooked.

Serve the asparagus with the ricotta and a tablespoon of the chermoula.

Satisfy your spice cravings

13 MAY 2022

I crave Indian food. I developed a love for it during my time in England. I'm not sure I ever had a curry other than a Vesta before I emigrated. It was the early 1980s. Those were grim times.

I was 18 and London was slightly terrifying. People didn't travel like they do now and I'd only left the country on two occasions: once on a Scouts trip to France, the other to chase a wayward brother to the bohemian ways of Amsterdam. My parents feared that I, too, might be lured but I had found my metier. My sights were set on London and Michelin stars.

The Indian subcontinent permeates London. I lived in Clapham before it became posh. Deliciously alluring but unfamiliar smells abounded. Every corner shop was a cornucopia of newness. At weekends the chefs gorged on late-night curries, fingernails stained until the next day from dredging naan through the remnants of a chicken tikka masala sauce. I loved every inauthentic mouthful.

Kahn's in Bayswater was my go-to, a cavernous, long-established, no-frills Indian that didn't serve alcohol. We gulped down mango lassi before heading to the Mean Fiddler for a slice of home and a big night out.

We get a takeaway from our local every now and then. I always order too much, as I get excited. The remainder gets put in the fridge for a sneaky little breakfast. Yes indeed, I am that classy.

There are days I crave spices in my cooking, the allure of cumin, coriander, cardamon. I'm giving three varied dishes today to satisfy your cravings.

A few things to note: I cut the monkfish across the bone, hence the 'chop'. As usual, though, it can be substituted for another fish. The biryani would be delicious either on its own or as an accompaniment to roast chicken or lamb. It's not the most colourful of dishes but the mango yogurt will cheer it up. The potatoes are a versatile and comforting dish, perfect with a salad.

FRIED MONKFISH WITH CURRIED SWEET POTATO BROTH

SERVES 4

80g dried red lentils

a generous knob of butter

1 onion, finely diced

2 garlic cloves, sliced

a medium piece of ginger, peeled and finely chopped

2 tsp curry powder

1 tsp ground turmeric

1 large sweet potato, peeled and cut into 0.5cm dice

60g dried apricots, sliced

850ml chicken or vegetable stock

8 x 1cm slices of monkfish from the thick end

a pinch of garam masala

sunflower oil, for cooking

a squeeze of lime

a few sprigs of fresh coriander

Soak the lentils in a bowl of cold water for 30 minutes, then drain.

Melt the butter in a large saucepan over a medium heat. When the butter starts to foam, add the onion, garlic and ginger. Cook for 5 minutes, until they start to soften.

Add the spices and cook for 2 minutes, then add the drained lentils, sweet potato and apricots. Turn everything together, then add the stock. Bring to a simmer and cook gently for 30 minutes, until everything is soft and melting. Season and set aside.

Put the monkfish on a baking tray, season and sprinkle lightly with garam masala.

Heat some oil in a non-stick frying pan over a high heat until it's gently smoking. Fry the monkfish in batches. It should take no more than a couple of minutes on each side. Keep the first batch warm and cook the second. Squeeze the lime over the monkfish.

Serve on top of the reheated broth with fresh coriander leaves on top.

CAULIFLOWER AND ALMOND BIRYANI
SERVES 4

100g butter

2 red onions, diced

1 medium head of cauliflower, roughly chopped

100g whole almonds

8 green cardamom pods, lightly crushed

2 tbsp garam masala

1 tsp ground cinnamon

300g basmati rice, rinsed

50g blonde raisins

peel of 1 lemon

850ml chicken or vegetable stock

FOR THE YOGURT:

250ml natural yogurt

1 ripe mango, peeled and diced

1 large fresh green chilli, deseeded and finely diced

chopped fresh coriander

Preheat the oven to 180°C.

Melt the butter in a large, wide, heavy-based casserole over a medium heat. When the butter starts to foam, add the onions and cauliflower. When the butter starts to brown and the cauliflower is slightly charred, add the almonds and spices and continue to colour for another 2 minutes or so. Add the rice, raisins and lemon peel and season generously.

Add the stock, bring to a simmer and cover. Cook in the oven for 30 minutes, until the rice is cooked and all the liquid has been absorbed.

Meanwhile, mix the yogurt with the mango, chilli and coriander.

Serve the biryani straight to the table with the yogurt on the side.

CHILLI AND COCONUT MASALA POTATOES

SERVES 4

1kg baby potatoes

2 tbsp toasted sesame oil

a thumb-sized piece of ginger, peeled and finely chopped

3 mixed fresh chillies, deseeded and halved lengthways

2 tsp garam masala

1 x 400ml tin of full-fat coconut milk

1 tbsp sesame seeds

Preheat the oven to 185°C.

Cut the large potatoes into three pieces and the small ones in half. Put them in a casserole or small roasting tin, toss them in the sesame oil, season with salt and pepper and roast in the oven for 20 minutes.

Remove the potatoes from the oven, then add the ginger, chillies and garam masala and pour over the coconut milk. Scatter the sesame seeds on top and bake for a further 20 minutes, until soft and golden. Serve straightaway.

Food is still our refuge

21 MAY 2022

I can't imagine having a partner who didn't care about food. It simply couldn't have happened. I spotted my wife's potential immediately but to be sure I took her out to my favourite restaurant at the time, Kensington Place.

Rowley Leigh, a highly esteemed cook and food writer — and my former boss — was the head chef. I loved the place. It was boisterous, perennially packed and super-cool. The food was modern British with inflections of Italian. There was none of the staidness of French haute cuisine with its whispering dining rooms.

A lunch there with friends was deliciously hedonistic. Hours passed in a flash, all laughter, gossip and clinking glasses. We all worked in the industry. KP, as we affectionately called it, made us feel as if we had achieved something simply by being there. Catering was never a profession for the academically gifted. The new Irish stuck together but this time not in Kilburn or Cricklewood. All of London was ours to be had. We were ambitious and we weren't afraid of hard work. Máire, my young, soon-to-be wife, embraced the food and our profession and moved over to London to be with me shortly afterwards. I'll always be grateful.

Many years later, food is still our refuge. After a hard week in the restaurant, there is nothing that soothes us more than a nice dinner at home and these dishes are some of my favourites.

The most technical thing here is the onion tarte tatin but really, it's not complicated once you put your mind to it. The reverse-sear steak is a revelation. It was my first time ever doing it this way. It's unconventional — the trick is to cook it backwards. First it's slowly cooked in a very low oven. This ensures minimum shrinkage and maximum tenderness. Then it's flash-fried to get a deep caramelisation. You will need a meat thermometer to get this right. And when you do, it will melt in your mouth like beautiful beefy butter.

The other dishes are rooted in Northern France and Spain with gentle, pleasing flavours that are bound to have you cooing like a pair of loved-up doves.

Running a restaurant is a vocation and cooking is what I still love to do.

25 JUNE 2022

REVERSE-SEAR CÔTE DE BOEUF WITH RED ONION TARTE TATIN AND HORSERADISH BUTTER

SERVES 2

1 x 850g côte de boeuf

3 tbsp sunflower oil

a knob of butter

3 garlic cloves, unpeeled and lightly crushed

1 sprig of fresh thyme

FOR THE TARTE TATIN:

3 red onions (350g)

a drizzle of sunflower oil

a few sprigs of fresh thyme

a good knob of soft butter

½ x 320g packet of ready-rolled puff pastry, thawed

1 egg beaten with 1 tbsp milk

FOR THE BUTTER:

100g butter, softened

1 tbsp horseradish sauce

chopped fresh parsley

Preheat the oven to 160°C.

For the horseradish butter, mix everything together, roll in cling film and chill.

To make the tarte tatin, cut the onions in half across the circumference. Drizzle the oil in a roasting tin, scatter the sprigs of thyme around, then put the onions in the tin, cut side down. Cover with foil and bake in the oven for 45 minutes.

Remove the onions and turn up the oven to 185°C.

Allow the onions to cool, then peel the outside layer off while keeping the shape of the onion.

Get out an ovenproof non-stick frying pan that's big enough to accommodate the onions in one layer. Smear the base and sides of the pan with the butter, season and add the onions to the pan, cut side down.

Cut out a circular piece of pastry the same size as the rim of the pan. It doesn't have to be too perfect. Drape the pastry snugly over the top of the onions and tuck it in. Brush the pastry lightly with the egg wash, put the pan in the oven and bake for 25 minutes, until the pastry is crisp and golden.

Allow to cool for no more than a minute or two. Nudge the pastry away from the pan with a spatula and overturn carefully. Put the tarte tatin on a baking tray to warm through when you're ready to serve.

For the beef, preheat the oven to 95°C.

Brush the meat with a little of the sunflower oil and season. Put on a wire rack in the oven for approximately 1 hour 45 minutes. The core temperature needs to be 60°C – this is at the cusp of medium-rare to medium.

To sear, heat a large pan with the remaining oil over a high heat until it's lightly smoking. Gently lower the beef into the pan and cook for 3 minutes or so, until the beef is dark and crusted.

Turn the meat over and add the butter, garlic and thyme to the pan. Baste the steak three or four times. When the crust has formed on the second side, transfer to a chopping board to rest while you warm the onion tarte tatin in the oven.

Carve the beef straightaway and serve with the horseradish butter and tarte tatin.

CHICKEN IN CIDER CREAM

SERVES 2

a small glug of sunflower oil

a knob of butter

1 x 1.2kg chicken, jointed into 8 pieces (ask your butcher to do this for you)

6 large shallots, peeled

3 garlic cloves, unpeeled and lightly crushed

1 sprig of fresh thyme

150ml chicken stock

150ml cream

100ml cider or white wine

1 tbsp Dijon mustard

4 slices of streaky bacon

1 x 200g packet of trimmed fine French beans

Preheat the oven to 185°C.

Pour the oil in a heavy-based casserole or pot, then add the butter and put it over a medium-high heat. When the butter starts to foam, add the chicken pieces and start to colour them. You may have to do this in batches.

When the chicken is almost coloured, carefully pour out any excess oil, then add the shallots, garlic and thyme. Season and continue to brown for 1–2 more minutes to glaze the shallots. Cover and cook in the oven for 20 minutes.

Remove the casserole or pot from the oven and add the stock, cream and cider or wine. Put back in the oven, uncovered, to cook for a further 20 minutes, until the chicken is fully cooked. Remove the chicken from the casserole or pot and keep warm. Whisk the mustard into the sauce and check for seasoning.

Meanwhile, cook the streaky bacon until crisp. Put the packet of unopened French beans in the microwave and cook on high for 2½ minutes.

To serve, divide the chicken between two warm plates and pour over the sauce. Add the crispy bacon and French beans on the side.

BAKED COD WITH BUTTER BEANS, OLIVES AND PIMENTON

SERVES 2

1 tbsp olive oil

2 x 150g cod fillets, skin on and bones removed

1 x 400g tin of butter beans, drained and rinsed

1 pointed red pepper, sliced

10 stuffed green olives in brine plus 2 tbsp brine

2 garlic cloves, sliced

1 piece of orange peel

1 tsp smoked paprika

1 sprig of fresh rosemary

150ml cream

Preheat the oven to 185°C.

Brush a small roasting tin or casserole with the oil. Put the cod in the tin or casserole and add the butter beans around the fish, then scatter the pepper, olives and garlic on top. Add the brine and orange peel, then evenly sprinkle over the smoked paprika. Nestle the rosemary beside the cod, then pour over the cream and season.

Bake in the oven for 20 minutes or so, until the cream is bubbling and the fish is cooked. Thicker pieces of fish will take a little longer.

Eat with some boiled new potatoes or rice.

Here's to all the Jimmys out there

28 MAY 2022

The extractor fan in the restaurant kitchen has broken down and terror runs through me. Is it electrical or mechanical? I ask myself. The red switch isn't lighting, so maybe that's a good thing. It could be a loose wire. I have no understanding of electricity. I understand sausages.

I have an image of an errant piece of metal just hanging there, teasing us, ruining our night. It's Friday, of course. It's always the weekend. These things never happens on a quiet day.

Cheffing is difficult enough without this and as we are an open kitchen with the dining room upstairs, everyone gets ratty. My stress levels are rising with the heat. Our stalwart electrician arrives even though it's 9:30 at night, climbs a ladder in the dark and in his own inimitable style proclaims the fan rightly f^*%#d. It wasn't a loose wire after all.

I'm trying to get hold of Jimmy, the fan guy, but he's away for a few days. I send him a begging text, apologising profusely. Gags (the electrician) says someone will have to go to Waterford to get a fan in the morning, I have a cookery course but I'll get a taxi to collect it if I have to. I anxiously await a call from Jimmy.

Early the next morning I'm out the road at his deserted warehouse, vainly peering in windows and knocking on neighbours' doors. I leave a note. Just when I'm losing hope, a text comes. The boys are on the way and will replace the fan. It looks like our extraction will be sorted. I unfrazzle and our weekend is saved. So here's to all the Jimmys out there, saving restauranteurs' skins every weekend.

Here are three very different dishes. The summer rolls are fresh, crisp and fun to make. There's no need for a dipping sauce, as the duck is coated in hoisin. The tart, easy and piquant, is for those who love that unique hit of Gorgonzola. The baked mozzarella is livened up by a little cheeky salami in the sauce.

DUCK SUMMER ROLLS

MAKES 12

2 confit duck legs

3 tbsp hoisin sauce

1 cucumber, peeled, quartered lengthways and deseeded

1 large carrot, peeled

2 heads of Little Gem lettuce, leaves separated

5 tbsp sushi seasoning

2 tbsp toasted sesame oil

1 x 340g packet of rice paper wrappers

pickled sushi ginger

fresh whole chives

fresh coriander leaves

Preheat the oven to 200°C.

Put the duck legs on a baking tray and cook them in the oven for 20 minutes, until they are very crisp. Keep any residual duck fat for roast potatoes another time.

Remove the meat and skin from the duck and chop it all, including the skin, into 0.5cm pieces. Turn it in the hoisin sauce and set aside.

Cut the cucumber quarters into thirds, then into thin batons. Put in a large bowl. Peel the carrot into thin strips with a vegetable peeler and add them to the cucumber. Tear the lettuce and add it to the mix. Add the sushi seasoning and sesame oil, then mix everything together.

Have all your ingredients ready in front of you. Line a baking tray with parchment paper.

Fill a wide, shallow bowl with hot water. One by one, immerse a sheet of rice paper in the water for 10 seconds or so, until it's soft. Shake any excess water off and lay it on a chopping board in front of you.

Taking care not to overfill it, put some vegetables along the centre of the roll. Top with a little duck, followed by pickled ginger, whole chives and coriander leaves. You need to divide the ingredients judiciously so you don't run out of anything for the last few rolls. It's easy to get carried away.

Fold the rolls as per the packet instructions. Put them on the lined tray but don't let them touch each other or they will stick together.

Eat as soon as you can, while they are crunchy and fresh.

COURGETTE, ALMOND AND GORGONZOLA TART
SERVES 4

1 x 320g sheet of ready-rolled shortcrust pastry, thawed

1 egg beaten with 1 tbsp milk

1 large courgette

2 tbsp olive oil

1 sprig of fresh thyme, leaves picked

200g Gorgonzola cheese

100g whole blanched almonds

Preheat the oven to 190°C.

Take the pastry from the fridge a few minutes before you start to use it, as it will be easier to work with. Unfurl carefully and put its parchment on a baking sheet, then lay the pastry on top. Brush the pastry lightly with the egg wash, then crimp the edges to form a lip.

Peel the courgette into strips using a vegetable peeler and put them in a bowl. Add the oil, thyme and some salt and pepper, tossing to coat. Cover the base of the tart with the courgette strips, then intersperse nuggets of Gorgonzola among them. Scatter over the almonds, then nudge everything down gently.

Bake in the oven for 25 minutes, until golden and crisp. Serve warm.

BAKED MOZZARELLA IN SALAMI PICCANTE SAUCE
SERVES 2

2 tbsp olive oil
2 garlic cloves, thinly sliced
1 x 400g tin of chopped tomatoes
½ chicken or vegetable stock cube
½ tsp smoked paprika
a pinch of chilli flakes
a drizzle of honey
juice of 1 mandarin
1 x 400g tin of chickpeas, drained and rinsed
80g sliced salami, shredded
2 balls of mozzarella
a few sprigs of fresh basil

Preheat the oven to 185°C.

Heat the oil in a saucepan over a gentle heat. Add the garlic and cook for 1 minute, just until it turns golden, then immediately add the tomatoes.

Crumble in the stock cube and add the smoked paprika, chilli flakes and honey. Bring to a gentle simmer and reduce by one-third.

Add the mandarin juice followed by the chickpeas and salami. Season, transfer to a baking dish and put the mozzarella on top. At this point, when cool you could put it in the fridge until needed. It will keep very happily until the next day — just give it an extra 5 minutes in the oven.

If cooking straightaway, put the dish in the oven and cook for 20 minutes.

To serve, tear the basil leaves on top and eat with crusty bread.

My less-meaty treaty with myself

04 JUNE 2022

We recently hosted a North American tour group at the Tannery. After breakfast one morning, a woman asked if we had any adapters. She had tried locally and there were none to be had, so she was in a pickle.

I told her we didn't have any American adapters. Clearly irked, she replied it was a Canadian one she was looking for anyway. It's amazing how things can go pear-shaped. All of a sudden she was annoyed and I was flustered. In fairness, I totally understand. There's enough ignorance around without me adding to it. I was made for the kitchen, not front of house. My life is full of Larry David moments like this.

That same morning, the radio was full of climate change doom. I always ask myself if I'm doing enough. I've certainly improved over the years. Now I'm the one at home giving out about recycling. The youth in our house are prone to all talk and no action. I'm also trying to eat less meat, so if anyone finds me gobbling a late-night burger, just move along and ignore me.

My recipes this week all feature meat in a supporting role. The steak salad is an equal combination of lovely things. I'm using Roquefort cheese for its addictive combination of pleasure and pain. Whoever put steak and Roquefort together was a genius, but if it's not your thing, use another cheese.

This soup is a riff on soupe au pistou except it's going south to Spain. The chicken butter is a brilliant tip, even if I say so myself. It can be spread on toast or put through pasta or mash. It's not my idea, I'm afraid. I have to give my head chef, Damien Derwin, all the credit for that one.

The roasted summer greens are a frequent visitor to our house. I just love creamy polenta and I'm on a mission to make other people love it too. The charcuterie is a lucky dip of whatever you fancy. Its porky pungency is a joy with the other two elements.

WARM STEAK SALAD WITH SHALLOT, PETITS POIS AND ROQUEFORT

SERVES 2

1 x 200g rib-eye steak
a little sunflower oil
100g frozen petits pois, thawed
1 large shallot, finely diced
10 seedless grapes, halved
100g mixed salad leaves
150g Roquefort cheese

FOR THE DRESSING:
1 tbsp Dijon mustard
½ tbsp golden brown sugar
80ml sunflower oil
2 tbsp olive oil
2 tbsp warm water
1 tbsp balsamic vinegar

Rub the steak with a little sunflower oil and season it. Heat a frying pan – or even better, a ridged grill pan – until it's lightly smoking and cook the steak how you like it. Remove from the heat and put it somewhere warm to rest.

Meanwhile, to make the dressing, put the mustard, sugar and some salt and pepper in a large bowl and slowly start to whisk in the oils. Once emulsified it will be quite thick, so add the water and vinegar to thin it down.

Back to the salad. Add the peas, shallot and grapes to the bowl, then slice the steak thinly and add it and its juices. Sit the salad leaves on top, then gently turn everything together, making sure the leaves are coated in the dressing.

Divide between two plates or put it all on a platter with nuggets of the Roquefort spooned on top to serve.

RED PEPPER AND BUTTER BEAN SOUP WITH CHICKEN BUTTER TOAST

SERVES 4

3 tbsp olive oil

1 large onion (350g), finely diced

2 pointed red peppers, sliced

3 garlic cloves, sliced

1 tsp tomato purée

1 tsp smoked paprika

1 x 400g tin of butter beans, drained and rinsed

2 strips of orange peel

850ml chicken stock

a few sprigs of fresh basil

FOR THE CHICKEN BUTTER TOAST:

100g butter, softened

½ chicken stock cube, crumbled

a little lemon zest

good bread, toasted

Heat the oil in a pot over a medium heat. Add the onion, peppers and garlic, cover and cook everything very slowly without it colouring for 15 minutes.

Add the tomato purée and smoked paprika and continue to cook for another minute or two, then add the butter beans, orange peel and chicken stock. Bring to a simmer and cook for 15 minutes, then season.

Meanwhile, put the butter in a bowl with the crumbled chicken stock cube and lemon zest, then whisk until fluffy.

Toast the bread and slather it with the butter. Any remaining butter can be used to put through steamed greens, pasta or mash another time.

Garnish with fresh basil leaves and serve the toast on the side.

ROASTED SUMMER GREENS WITH CREAMY POLENTA AND CHARCUTERIE

SERVES 4

1 bunch of asparagus

1 leek

1 courgette

50ml olive oil

2 garlic cloves, sliced

1 sprig of fresh thyme

a pinch of chilli flakes

1 large packet of mixed charcuterie

FOR THE POLENTA:

350ml milk

350ml water

1 bay leaf (fresh if possible)

2 strips of lemon peel

120g fine instant polenta

80g Parmesan cheese, grated

a good knob of butter

Preheat the oven to 190°C.

Trim off and discard the bottom third from the asparagus and put the tips on a baking tray. Slice the leek into 0.5cm-thick rings, wash if necessary and add to the asparagus. Slice the courgette the same way and add it to the tray too.

Pour the oil over the top, then add the garlic, thyme and chilli flakes. Season and turn everything together, then roast in the oven for 15 minutes.

Meanwhile, bring the milk, water, bay leaf and lemon peel to a gentle simmer, then slowly add the polenta. Cook for 3–4 minutes, until soft and creamy, then add the Parmesan, butter and seasoning.

Divide the polenta among warm plates and top with the roasted vegetables and a selection of the charcuterie. Serve straightaway.

A celebration of summer

11 JUNE 2022

I was at a loose end in East Cork recently so I gave my friend Ivan a call and got the much-coveted invitation for lunch in the Pink House in Shanagarry. The Midleton market was on, perfect to pick up a few bits so I didn't arrive empty handed. It was like being on holidays.

Regular readers might remember a lunch I wrote about almost two years ago where Ivan cooked a whole turbot under similar circumstances (see page 152). It was a perfect day. That time I stayed over but this time I was on dad duty so I could have all the food but none of the wine. I was a little bit sad but nevertheless, I was still steeped in luck to be there.

He pan-fried the perkiest fillets of red mullet that he'd got that morning from Pat O'Connell in the English Market. They sat ruddy and crisp in the buttery pan. Their unique, sweet, iodine-y aroma laced the air. It's not often I get to eat this precious fish, especially when it's cooked for me.

There were new spuds freshly dug and scrubbed from the Ballymaloe gardens. They are best boiled with plenty of salt, not steamed, according to Sinead, the chef– owner of the brilliant Crawford Gallery Café. Nasturtium leaves and flowers were gently chopped, then added to melted butter and spooned over to nestle in those craggy spuddy crevices. It was one of the prettiest things I've ever seen, in or out of a kitchen. Nasty butter, he had christened it. It was no such thing.

There was a brave, unconventional hollandaise, where more butter was stirred into bulging, luminous egg yolks over direct heat. They nearly scrambled but he added cold water and saved it. Nerves jangled, pots were banged, but soon a hungry calm returned. Asparagus appeared steamed with water, black pepper and more butter, then we sat out in the bucolic garden. There was gentle chiding about our different techniques, all of us cooks and inveterate food lovers who understood the rarity of perfect simplicity.

These three eclectic recipes are really a celebration that it's summer and time to eat fish as often as we can.

PRAWNS WITH CURRY CREAM, PEAS, CUCUMBER AND ALMONDS

SERVES 4

50g butter

1 onion, finely diced

2 garlic cloves, sliced

a thumb-sized piece of ginger, peeled and finely chopped

1 fresh green chilli, deseeded and chopped

1 tbsp medium curry powder

250ml chicken or vegetable stock

250ml cream

1 tbsp mango chutney

1 cucumber, peeled, quartered lengthways, deseeded and diced

200g large peeled prawns, halved lengthways

150g frozen petits pois, thawed

100g whole blanched almonds, toasted

a few sprigs of fresh coriander

Melt the butter in a large saucepan over a medium heat. Add the onion, garlic, ginger, chilli and curry powder and cook very slowly for 10–15 minutes, until the onion softens completely.

Add the stock, cream and chutney and bring to a simmer for 10 minutes, until the sauce starts to thicken.

Add the cucumber, prawns, peas and almonds, then simmer once more for 2–3 minutes, until the prawns are cooked. Season.

Garnish with fresh coriander leaves and serve with boiled basmati rice.

BAKED HAKE WITH SAFFRON, CHICKPEAS AND RAINBOW TOMATOES

SERVES 3

juice of 1 orange

a pinch of saffron strands

50ml olive oil, plus a little more for drizzling

1 large garlic clove, thinly sliced

1 x 400g tin of chickpeas, drained and rinsed

200g mixed baby tomatoes, halved

1 tbsp red or white wine vinegar

a drizzle of honey

1 x 400g hake fillet, skin on and bones removed

2 tbsp crème fraîche or natural yogurt

a few sprigs of fresh basil

Preheat the oven to 185°C.

Put the orange juice in a bowl and add the saffron strands to soak.

Heat the oil in a large saucepan over a low heat. Add the garlic and slowly colour just until it's lightly golden. Add the chickpeas, tomatoes, vinegar and honey followed by the saffron-flavoured orange juice. Continue to cook for a minute or two, until the tomatoes start to soften. Season and keep warm.

Drizzle a little oil on a baking tray and put the hake on the tray, skin side down. If you like you can pre-portion the fish but I like the effect of the whole fillet.

Brush the crème fraîche or yogurt thickly on the hake, then drizzle over a little oil. Season and bake in the oven for 12–15 minutes, depending on the thickness of the fish.

Divide the chickpeas and tomatoes among three warm bowls. Cut the hake into three using a fish slice, then put it on top and garnish with fresh basil leaves.

I made this a recipe for three as I don't like not using whole packets or tins. When I tested the dish it was intended for four but there wasn't quite enough, so three it became.

GRILLED MACKEREL WITH ORANGE FATTOUSH

SERVES 4

4 large mackerel fillets, bones removed

FOR THE FATTOUSH:

2 pittas, sliced into strips

1 tsp sumac or ras el hanout

1 small red onion, thinly sliced

1 packet of baby plum tomatoes, halved

½ cucumber, peeled, cut in half lengthways and sliced

2 heads of Little Gem lettuce, sliced

a few sprigs of fresh mint

a few sprigs of fresh flat-leaf parsley

FOR THE DRESSING:

1 garlic clove, crushed

50ml extra virgin olive oil, plus extra for the pitta

juice of 1 orange

a dash of red wine vinegar

a pinch of caster sugar

Preheat the oven to 185°C.

Put the pitta strips in a roasting tin and drizzle over a little oil along with the sumac or ras el hanout and some salt and pepper. Toast in the oven for 10 minutes, until crisp.

Put the garlic, oil, orange juice, vinegar and sugar in a large bowl and whisk together to make a dressing. Add the onion, tomatoes, cucumber in a bowl lettuce and torn fresh herbs, tossing to coat in the dressing, then season.

Switch the oven to the grill. Put the mackerel on an oiled tray, skin side up. Grill on a high heat for 3–4 minutes, until cooked through.

Serve the mackerel on top of the salad.

An enduring love affair with Italian food

18 JUNE 2022

I talk about Spain a lot. There is another country that vies for my attention just as much, though, and that's the wondrously delectable Italy. It's impossible not to be in love with it.

We have been there many times, from small hilltop villages in Umbria where it was so quiet the only thing that moved at night was the odd stray cat — it suited us perfectly when the girls were young, when all we did was watch them in the pool, cook and drink wine — to later visits to Garda and Como, which cemented our love of the country.

We always drove, and after the inevitable hairy start and predictable spectacular car hire row as we made our way from the airport to the motorway, the mood lifted as we edged closer to our destination and speculated on dinner. On arrival, once fed we were content in an instant. It was all spritzes and smiles after that.

Last year we were invited to a 50th birthday at La Posta Vecchia, a magical hotel about an hour and four pay grades up the coast from Rome. Formerly John Paul Getty's home impressed on the ruins of a Roman villa abutting the Mediterranean, it was impossible not to sense the history of the place and feel insignificant.

Romans still come to the area to escape the heat of the city, swim and eat in the numerous perfect beach restaurants that dot the lengthy coastline. We swam, then ate hot, crisp calamari and bowls of pasta washed down with cool, crisp jugs of wine. Generations of Laziale sat around us chattering, the nonnas wiping ice cream from children's faces as they gently scolded them before covering them with sunscreen and kisses. Did they know they were the luckiest people on earth, I wondered. And for one weekend, we were too.

I'm giving you three pasta dishes this week. The conchiglioni is made with a raw tomato sauce and bursting with crisp vegetables, perfect for a gang. Taking inspiration from tabbouleh, the orzo salad is laden with parsley and bursting with flavour. The bucatini has deep flavours and silky, porky strips of mortadella, one of my favourite things in the world.

CONCHIGLIE PRIMAVERA WITH GOAT CHEESE
SERVES 8

500g vine-ripened cherry tomatoes, halved

3 garlic cloves, sliced

1 fennel bulb

50ml extra virgin olive oil, plus extra for the top

juice of 1 orange

1 small bunch of fresh basil

150g soft rindless goat cheese

2 tbsp red wine vinegar

a pinch of chilli flakes

500g conchiglie or penne

1 courgette, halved lengthwise and thinly sliced

2 carrots, halved lengthways and thinly sliced

1 packet of radishes, halved

150g Parmesan cheese, grated

Put the tomatoes in a food processor along with the garlic. Thinly slice the fennel and put the tops in with the tomatoes. Reserve the bulb for later.

Add the oil and the orange juice. Pick the basil leaves and chop the stalks, then put the stalks in the processor with the tomatoes. Break the goat cheese into pieces and add it to the processor too, followed by the vinegar, chilli flakes and lots of seasoning. Blend everything together until it forms a thick dressing, not unlike a gazpacho.

Cook the pasta as per the packet instructions. When the pasta is nearly done, add the fennel bulb, courgette, carrots and radishes. Bring the pasta to the boil once more. After a minute or so, drain everything and put it back in the pot, then add the sauce. Season with salt and pepper.

Serve on a warm platter or individual plates with a generous scattering of Parmesan, a little more olive oil and the basil leaves torn on top.

ORZO SALAD WITH PARSLEY, CHILLI AND LEMON

SERVES 4

250g orzo

1 red onion, finely diced

2 garlic cloves, crushed

1 fresh red chilli, deseeded and finely diced

250g baby plum tomatoes, quartered

10 stoned green olives, chopped

1 x 50g tin of salted anchovies, chopped

1 large bunch of fresh flat-leaf parsley, leaves chopped

50ml good olive oil

zest and juice of 1 lemon

1 tbsp baby capers and 1 tbsp brine

1 tsp caster sugar

a pinch of ground cinnamon

Cook the pasta as per the packet instructions, then drain and mix with the rest of the ingredients. Serve chilled or at room temperature. A little Parma ham or salami would be lovely with it.

BUCATINI WITH LEEK, MORTADELLA AND PECORINO ROMANO

SERVES 2

80g butter

6 fresh sage leaves

1 tbsp sherry vinegar or red wine vinegar

200g bucatini or your favourite pasta

1 leek, chopped

4 slices of mortadella

Pecorino Romano or Parmesan cheese, shaved or grated

Put the butter in a saucepan over a low to medium heat. Let it melt and bubble. After 3 minutes or so it will start to foam and the colour will change to a golden amber. Immediately remove the pan from the heat and add the sage leaves. Carefully swirl the sage around, then add the vinegar. Set aside.

Cook the pasta as per the packet instructions. Add the leek for the last 2 minutes of the cooking time. Drain, leaving a little water in the pot.

Return the pasta to the pot with the sage butter, then season.

Serve straightaway with the mortadella on the side and the cheese sprinkled generously over the top.

Running a restaurant is a vocation

25 JUNE 2022

On the first of July, the Tannery will be open 25 years. In 1997 I was 32 and Máire was 28. I never thought we'd end up back in Dungarvan but we fell in love with the building. The place had history and I was smitten. My grandfather worked all his life in the leather factory on the very floor our restaurant now occupies. All it had back then were rusty remnants and gritty, stinking memories from when I was a child. I remember cycling down the lane as fast as I could, holding my breath so as not to inhale the bleach and death. Not the most obvious place to open a restaurant.

We wanted to quietly make a difference. After a few years, we bought one building around the corner for rooms as people were travelling to us, then another for more rooms and a cookery school. We were slowly evolving; there was no grand plan. On occasion it's been a turbulent path but the town was changing too. Then came the Greenway and it felt like the world discovered us.

How do you describe all those years in a few paragraphs? All those wonderful people who worked, and continue to work, for us? They all have a part in our story.

Running a restaurant is a vocation and cooking is what I still love to do. We've met all sorts of people along the way. Our locals who kept us open in the quiet winter months. Our summer people who have come every year since we opened, some no longer with us but we remember and treasure them all. They pulled us through and now their grandchildren keep the tradition going. It lifts our hearts to see them. There is a bond.

The spiced pepper bake is deep and flavourful, while the brioche adds crunch and luxury – it's perfect to accompany a barbecue.

I'm using gurnard to promote that fantastically underrated fish. You could use sea bass or any white fish in this gently spiced dish but adjust the cooking time according to the thickness of the fish.

I had a niçoise salad recently and it reminded me how good that classic is. I've condensed it down into a nifty potato dish, little flavour bombs of loveliness. I eat them with Heinz Turkish garlic sauce, it's wonderful stuff.

SPICED RED PEPPER, PIMENT D'ESPELETTE AND BRIOCHE BAKE

SERVES 4

a glug of olive oil, plus a little more for drizzling

1 onion, sliced

1 red pepper, sliced

1 green pepper, sliced

1 yellow pepper, sliced

2 garlic cloves, sliced

1 tsp piment d'espelette or smoked paprika

1 tsp ground cumin

1 x 400g tin of chopped tomatoes

1 chicken or vegetable stock cube, crumbled

1 tbsp honey

2 brioche buns

a few sprigs of fresh basil

FOR THE MAYO:

3 tbsp mayonnaise

1 tbsp olive oil

juice of ½ lemon

1 garlic clove, crushed

Preheat the oven to 180°C.

Heat the oil in a large saucepan over a medium heat. Add the onion, peppers and garlic, cover and cook for 10 minutes, until the peppers start to soften.

Add the piment d'espelette or smoked paprika and the cumin. Continue to cook gently for a few minutes, then add the tomatoes, crumbled stock cube and honey. The stock cube will dissolve in the tomatoes. Season and bring to a gentle simmer for 5 more minutes, until it starts to thicken, then transfer to a casserole.

Tear the brioche into chunks, then stud them on top of the pepper mixture and drizzle with a little olive oil. Bake in the oven for 25 minutes, until golden and crisp.

Meanwhile, to make the garlic mayo, whisk all the ingredients together. Serve it on top of the bake with torn fresh basil leaves.

GURNARD WITH SWEET AND SOUR ONIONS AND PINE NUTS

SERVES 4

4 tbsp olive oil, plus more for brushing

2 red onions, halved and thinly sliced

2 bay leaves (fresh if possible)

1 tbsp tomato purée

½ tbsp harissa

1 heaped tsp ras el hanout

2 tbsp red wine vinegar

1 tbsp golden brown sugar

300ml chicken stock

4 x 140g fillets of gurnard, bones removed

60g pine nuts, toasted

chopped fresh flat-leaf parsley

Preheat the oven to 185°C. Brush a casserole with a little olive oil.

Heat the oil in a large saucepan over a medium heat. Add the onions and bay leaves and slowly cook until softened. Add the tomato purée, harissa and ras el hanout and continue to cook for another minute or two.

Add the vinegar and sugar and bring to a bubble, then add the stock and some salt and pepper. Bring to a simmer and cook gently for 5 minutes to reduce a little. You can do this ahead of time, then warm the mixture up when you need it.

Season the fish, then put it in the casserole, skin side up. Spoon the onion mixture over the gurnard, then bake in the oven for 12–15 minutes, depending on the thickness of the fish.

Garnish with a scattering of pine nuts and parsley and serve with basmati rice.

NEW POTATOES NIÇOISE

SERVES 6

3 tbsp panko breadcrumbs

2 tbsp olive oil, plus extra for drizzling

3 large ripe tomatoes

800g new potatoes (3–4 per person), cooked and peeled

1 small red onion, finely diced

16 mixed stoned olives, chopped

1 x 50g tin of salted anchovies, chopped

2 tbsp chopped fresh flat-leaf parsley

1 tbsp small capers

juice of ½ lemon

Toast the panko breadcrumbs in the oil in a hot pan until golden, then set aside.

Cut an X in the top of the tomatoes. Plunge them into a pan of boiling water for 1 minute, then transfer them straight into a bowl of iced water. Peel, quarter, deseed and dice.

Put the cooked, peeled potatoes in a bowl with the diced tomatoes and the onion, olives, anchovies, parsley, capers and lemon juice. Season and add a little more oil to coat.

Transfer to a serving dish and top with the crispy breadcrumbs. Serve at room temperature. These are lovely with almost any fish, chicken or lamb, perfect for a summer day.

Let the seafood shine

02 JULY 2022

Driving along the Copper Coast on a summer day is when I'm at my happiest. Only a couple of years ago it was almost deserted, even in summertime, as if only the natives knew its craggy, undulating secrets. For those of you not in the know, it's a UNESCO global geopark in County Waterford comprised of 25 kilometres or so of spectacular coastline consisting of scalloped beaches and coves buttressed and enclosed by rocky headlands. Think Cornwall but with better-looking men.

It extends east from the dinky little village of Stradbally, ambling along the old copper mines of Bonmahon to the hurdy-gurdys of Tramore. You can almost smell the hot, salty chips as you approach. I've often mentioned to my family that I'd like my ashes to be scattered on this coast. They think I'm joking. I'm not, although I haven't quite decided where yet and I'm still working on the soundtrack.

I change my menu in the restaurant quite dramatically at this time of year. It seems natural to me that people visiting a seaside town want to eat fish as often as possible. The sea shimmers all around us, the ultimate flirt. Its ever-decreasing bounty always excites me but never more so than at this time of year. As I have got older, it's simplicity I look for in seafood cookery. Let the fish shine. Quality is the key.

The lobster dish is delicately Spanish. I never like anything shouty with lobster as it's important to pay homage and not overwhelm the flavour. This dish is essentially about the assembly of the very best ingredients.

The crab and watermelon is a bit of a showstopper. I've decided to serve it in one stunning piece like a cake to be portioned later. You already know I like a bit of drama.

Papa al pomodoro is a thick Tuscan bread soup. I'm serving it chilled with simply fried scallops. I admit the oil is a bit cheffy. You don't have to do it but along with the scallop shell, it does edge it up a notch.

LOBSTER WITH AJO BLANCO, CUCUMBER AND NEW POTATOES

SERVES 4

1 x 750g lobster, boiled in salted water for 10 minutes, then lifted from the water to cool

1 cucumber, skin removed then peeled into strips (excluding seeds)

12 new potatoes, boiled, peeled and halved

20 seedless grapes, halved

25g fresh chives, chopped

juice of ½ lemon

4 tbsp olive oil, plus a little more for drizzling

FOR THE AJO BLANCO:

180g whole skinned almonds

100g fresh white breadcrumbs

1 cucumber, peeled and thinly sliced

200ml ice-cold water

100ml olive oil

a drizzle of sherry, to taste

For the ajo blanco, put the almonds in a dry frying pan over a low heat. Shake them around for a minute or two to colour them very lightly, then tip onto a plate to cool.

Put the rest of the ajo blanco ingredients and a pinch of salt in a blender and purée until it's as smooth as possible, then pass through a sieve and chill in the fridge.

For the lobster salad, remove the cooked lobster meat from the shell and dice into 1cm chunks.

Put all the ingredients for the salad in a large bowl, then fold everything together gently so it's nicely coated in the oil and lemon.

To serve, divide the ajo blanco among shallow bowls, then put the lobster and potato mixture on top. Drizzle with a little more oil and serve straightaway.

SUMMER CRAB AND WATERMELON CAKE

SERVES 4

1 large seedless watermelon
250g of the best white crab meat possible
juice of ½ lemon
Maldon flaky sea salt
200ml natural yogurt
1 small fresh red chilli, deseeded and finely chopped
a pinch of piment d'espelette (optional)
a drizzle of extra virgin olive oil
fresh herbs and edible flowers (I used dill and chives)

Using a serrated knife, cut an even 3cm-thick disc from the centre of a large watermelon and put it on a platter or a cake stand.

Pick through the crab to make sure there is no shell, then spoon it evenly on top of the watermelon. Squeeze the lemon juice over the crab, then season with Maldon flaky sea salt and freshly ground black pepper.

Drizzle the yogurt evenly over the top with a scattering of chilli and a small pinch of piment d'espelette if you can get your hands on it. Drizzle over some good extra virgin olive oil and scatter with fresh herbs and edible flowers (if available). Chill in the fridge.

Serve and cut at the table for theatre.

SEARED SCALLOPS WITH PAPA AL POMODORO
SERVES 4

4 sprigs of fresh basil, leaves and stalks separated

100ml olive oil, plus a little more for the scallops

1 onion, sliced

2 garlic cloves, sliced

1 x 400g tin of chopped tomatoes

½ chicken or vegetable stock cube, crumbled

a little orange zest

a pinch of caster sugar

a pinch of chilli flakes

2 slices of good white bread, crusts removed

12 fresh scallops

For the basil oil, simply blend the basil leaves with 50ml of the oil and chill.

Heat the remaining 50ml of oil in a large saucepan over a low heat. Add the onion and garlic, cover the pan and cook for 15 minutes, until the onion is completely softened but not coloured.

Add the tomatoes, stock cube, orange zest, sugar, chilli and basil stalks. Slowly reduce by half, then remove the basil stalks.

Tear the bread into the tomatoes and mix through until it breaks up and amalgamates. Season and cool.

To cook the scallops, heat a little oil in a non-stick frying pan over a high heat and let it gently smoke. Add the scallops and cook for 1 minute on each side, until they caramelise lightly. Larger ones will take a little longer but do not overcook. Drain on kitchen paper when done.

To serve, divide the papa al pomodoro among bowls or plates. If you manage to get scallop shells, that's even better. Allow three scallops per person (or more if they are small). Set the scallops on top and drizzle the basil oil around. Serve immediately.

These condiments will dramatically change your cooking

09 JULY 2022

There's a lot I have yet to learn about cooking but thankfully I'm still curious. I recently found myself in Mr Bell's, purveyor of premium ingredients in the English Market in Cork, and swept the shelves. There were some I had used before, like the treacly, dark Lee Kum Kee brand of hoisin sauce. It's packed with so much more flavour than some of the more common brands that are weak and forgettable in comparison. This stuff is addictively top tier, the supermodel of hoisin sauces if you can get your hands on it. Asia Market on Dublin's Drury Street is your go-to place if you are in the capital.

I had used the Indonesian soy sauce, kecap manis, once or twice before. I was cross with myself that I had gone through 50 years of my life without its sticky, delicious sweetness. Now I always keep some at home for every eventuality.

I have two Murphys to thank for my gochujang enlightenment: Jess from Kai and Wade from 1826 Adare. One of Denis Cotter's books introduced me to sambal olek. I can't quite remember the exact dish as I was so captivated by his writing. It's often the case that people you admire lead you down a path you mightn't have trodden before. In my early days there was only French food in my world. I often had amazing Asian food but never dared to try cooking it myself. I was in a Francophile rut.

I enjoyed playing with my haul from Mr Bell's. I'm not sure any of these dishes are tremendously authentic but they are tasty and surely that's the point. It's good to be a little fearless when it comes to food.

The inspiration for the wraps came from crispy duck with pancakes. This is not food for a first date — or maybe it is. These noodles are so worthy, I almost feel like an earth mother. The buckwheat adds a nuttiness that beautifully complements the aubergine. The crunch of the peanuts are almost as important as the chicken in this drumstick dish, while the sour cream brings a necessary but unorthodox coolness.

BAKED SALMON AND SWEET POTATO WRAPS WITH KECAP MANIS

SERVES 4

1 bunch of spring onions

1 sweet potato

2 tbsp toasted sesame oil, plus a little more for drizzling

1 fresh red chilli, deseeded and sliced

4 tbsp kecap manis

2 tbsp water

2 tsp sesame seeds

2 x 140g salmon fillets

juice of 1 lime

½ cucumber, peeled and cut into batons

2 heads of Little Gem lettuce, leaves separated

Preheat the oven to 200°C.

Shred the spring onions as finely as you can at an angle. Cover with cold water and put in the fridge for a minimum of 30 minutes. This will crisp up the spring onions in true Chinese style.

Peel and slice the sweet potato ultra-thinly — a mandolin is perfect for this if you have one. Put the sweet potato in a bowl, add the sesame oil and chilli, then season. Turn everything together, then spread out on a baking tray in a thin, even layer.

Put the kecap manis, water and sesame seeds in a medium-sized bowl and mix together, then turn the salmon in the sauce so it's coated.

Put the salmon on top of the sweet potato, then scrape out the remaining sauce from the bowl and dot it around the tray. Add another drizzle of sesame oil over the salmon. Cook in the oven for 15 minutes, until the salmon is cooked through. Add a squeeze of lime.

Fork the salmon into chunks and wrap it in the lettuce along with sweet potato, cucumber batons and drained spring onions to serve.

BUCKWHEAT NOODLES WITH STICKY AUBERGINE AND SAMBAL OLEK

SERVES 3

50g raisins

1 tsp fine salt

1 aubergine, diced into 1cm pieces

4 tbsp olive oil

2 garlic cloves, sliced

4 tbsp sambal olek

50g salted cashew nuts, chopped

8 vine-ripened cherry tomatoes, halved

300g buckwheat noodles

a few sprigs of fresh mint

a few sprigs of fresh coriander

Put the aubergine in a bowl, sprinkle over the salt and leave to sit for at least 30 minutes. Rinse and gently squeeze dry before cooking. This both enhances the flavour and gets rid of any excess water.

Soak the raisins in a separate small bowl of just-boiled water for 15 minutes to plump them up, then drain.

Heat the oil in a large pan or wok over a medium heat. Add the garlic and cook without colouring for 1 minute.

Add the aubergine, then turn up the heat to high. Cook for 10 minutes, then add the sambal olek, cashews, tomatoes and drained raisins. Cook for another 15 minutes or so, until the aubergine almost completely breaks down into a spicy, thick, chutney-like consistency.

Meanwhile, cook the noodles as per the packet instructions. Drain but reserve half a cup of the cooking water. Add the noodles and reserved water to the aubergine and season.

Serve with a scattering of fresh mint and coriander leaves on top.

GOCHUJANG CHICKEN DRUMSTICKS WITH PEANUTS
SERVES 4

8 large chicken drumsticks

2 tbsp Korean gochujang paste

50ml water

1 tbsp sunflower oil

100g salted peanuts, roughly chopped

4 spring onions, finely chopped

a few sprigs of fresh coriander

a little sour cream

Put the drumsticks in a large ziplock bag. Add the gochujang, water and seasoning. Massage everything together and put in the fridge overnight.

Preheat the oven to 200°C.

Put the chicken in a roasting tin in one layer and cook in the oven for 25 minutes. Scatter the peanuts on top and turn them in the sauce, then return the tin to the oven to cook for another 5 minutes.

Serve with the chopped spring onions, fresh coriander leaves and sour cream.

The promise of lunch keeps me moving forward

16 JULY 2022

I'm recently back from another Camino with three old friends. Reflecting at the end of the trip in Santiago over a few crisp beers, one of the boys wondered what the hurry had been. Why power on from early morning through all kinds of weather just to get to our destination? He felt we had missed out on all the beauty by being in such a rush. Why not amble, make the most of the day and soak it all up?

One day we did 29 kilometres in the rain. I huffed, puffed and cursed up hills and vowed the next holiday would be by the pool. The lads blithely chatted as I struggled. They were fit and the man in question is contentedly retired. He walks, gardens and rides horses to fill his days at home. This Camino lark was like a stroll to him.

I spend my life rushing. Is it the nature of being in business or just my nature? I reflected on what he said and offered a meek excuse at the time. Lunch was always my objective. No matter what, I was getting there in time. To miss it was unthinkable. It was my reward for all the effort.

It was my fourth Camino and I have settled into a pattern over the years. Up at it early, get to the next village, have a beer to settle me, then lunch with Albariño, followed by a shower and a snooze. Later, a walkabout to explore our surroundings, another little beer, then dinner. I am a creature of happy habit. There's no changing me now.

We ate lots of different pastries on the road. I'm a sucker for the stuff. Here are three dishes using different types of pastry with very pleasing results.

In these spicy little puffs, the 'nduja seeps into and colours the pastry alluringly, perfect for when people are coming round or to make and put in the freezer.

This goat cheese, thyme and black grape tart is a little bit of a project if you have time but it's not difficult. The yeast pastry has a lovely texture that sets off the creaminess of the tart but if you don't want to make your own, you can buy shortcrust.

The trout tart is a stunner. The pastry is baked separately and the smoked trout is put on top. A nice change from smoked salmon.

RED PEPPER AND 'NDUJA PUFFS

MAKES 12

2 tbsp olive oil

2 red peppers, thinly sliced

2 garlic cloves, thinly sliced

75g 'nduja

75ml cream

100g Parmesan cheese, grated

2 x 320g rolls of ready-rolled puff pastry, thawed and chilled

1 egg beaten with 1 tbsp milk

Heat the oil in a large saucepan over a low heat. Add the peppers and garlic, cover and cook for 20 minutes or so, stirring once or twice, until the peppers thoroughly soften.

Add the 'nduja and break it up as best you can with a wooden spoon. Cook for another 5 minutes, then add the cream and reduce until it thickens and clings to the peppers.

Add the Parmesan and some salt and pepper. Take the pan off the heat and allow to cool, then chill in the fridge. The mixture needs to be thick so it doesn't seep from the pastry.

For best results the pastry needs to be a little chilled but not cold. Unfold one roll, keeping the parchment, and cut the pastry into six squares – a pizza cutter is perfect for this.

Brush the pastry lightly with the egg wash. Put 1 teaspoon of the filling in the centre of each square. Bring the four corners together to form a tipi and pinch the pastry deftly together to squeeze out any air. Lay the parchment out on a baking tray and put the puffs on top. Repeat for the remainder of this roll of pastry and the other roll. These can be frozen at this point for a later time.

To cook, preheat the oven to 185°C.

Brush all the puffs with the egg wash, then cook in the oven for 25 minutes, until golden and crisp. Serve straightaway.

GOAT CHEESE, THYME AND BLACK GRAPE TART
SERVES 8

FOR THE JAM:
500g seedless black grapes, halved
juice of 1 orange
2 tbsp golden brown sugar
1 sprig of fresh thyme

FOR THE PASTRY:
1 x 7g sachet of fast-acting dried yeast
75ml lukewarm full-fat milk
220g strong white flour
100g butter, softened
1 tsp golden caster sugar

FOR THE CUSTARD:
5 eggs
150g soft rindless goat cheese, crumbled
150ml milk
150ml cream
1 tsp fresh thyme leaves
a pinch of grated nutmeg

To make the grape jam, put all the ingredients in a pan and cook over a medium heat until all the liquid has evaporated and the grapes have become jammy. Allow to cool.

For the pastry, butter and lightly flour a 30cm loose-bottomed tart tin.

Dissolve the yeast in the warm milk in a small bowl. Let it sit for 10 minutes, until it's frothy.

Put the flour, butter, sugar and a pinch of salt in a food processor and pulse together. Add the milk and yeast mixture and pulse together again just until it all comes together into a dough. Tip out onto a floured board and knead a couple of times to make an even ball. Wrap the pastry in cling film and chill for 30 minutes or so to firm up.

Roll out the pastry into a round sheet, flouring it lightly as you go and rolling until the pastry is 2–3mm thick with a 2–3cm overhang around the edges of the tin. Gently press the pastry into the sides and edges of the tin, allowing the excess to overhang.

Preheat the oven to 200°C.

Cut a piece of parchment to go on the base and up the sides of the tin, then fill halfway with rice. Allow the tart to rest in the fridge for 20 minutes while the oven heats up.

Bake blind in the oven for 15 minutes, then lift out the parchment and rice, put the tart back in the oven and bake for another 5 minutes, until crisp.

Turn down the oven temperature to 165°C.

For the filling, blend all the ingredients and a pinch of salt and ground white pepper with a hand blender or liquidizer.

Spread the grape jam on the base of the tart, then carefully pour in the goat cheese filling. Bake in the oven for 30–35 minutes, until the tart is set but still has a gentle wobble in the centre.

Serve warm or at room temperature with a crisp green salad.

SMOKED TROUT TART WITH TZATZIKI

SERVES 4

1 x 320g sheet of ready-rolled shortcrust pastry, thawed

1 egg beaten with 1 tbsp milk

200g sliced smoked trout or smoked salmon

1 jar of trout roe (optional but lovely)

FOR THE TZATZIKI:

150g Greek yogurt

½ cucumber, peeled, grated and squeezed

1 small garlic clove, crushed

fresh chopped dill, plus extra to garnish

1 tsp mint sauce

a squeeze of lemon

Preheat the oven to 200°C.

Unfurl the pastry — it's easier when it's not too cold. Lay the parchment on a baking tray with the pastry on top. Crimp the edges of the tart, then brush the pastry lightly with the egg wash. Pierce with a fork a dozen times, then bake in the oven for 20 minutes, until crisp and golden. Allow to cool.

To make the tzatziki, mix the yogurt with the cucumber, garlic, dill, mint sauce and a squeeze of lemon.

Drape the trout over the pastry and artfully blob the tzatziki, roe (if using) and some extra dill over the top to serve.

It's good to be a little fearless when it comes to food.

09 JULY 2022

A Momofuku-inspired feast

23 JULY 2022

I love cookery shows. Of course, I have my favourites. Rick Stein will always be the king and I will always mourn the demise of Anthony Bourdain. Stanley Tucci's *Taste of Italy* was a feast for the eyes. His dapper travels made me want to get straight on a plane to Tuscany. John Torode is another favourite. I saw him make this yum yum sauce on the telly and went straight into the kitchen to reproduce it as best I could.

The recipes today are about another hero, David Chang. He is famous for popularising pork belly bao and on one visit to New York, I was determined to waddle my way around with a belly full of them.

One of my many idiosyncrasies is that while I may have a full and happy plate in front of me in a restaurant, I'm also eyeing up what other people are eating as I'm comprehensively riddled with FOMO. I had spotted a section on Chang's menu that said, 'Momofuku bo ssam … a pork shoulder for six or more, advance order necessary.' Sadly, we were only four.

Chang cooks his marinated pork for 6 hours at a low heat until it falls apart and serves his bo ssam with a ginger scallion sauce, ssam sauce, rice, lettuce, kimchi and optional oysters. Today's recipe is an updated version because I was transfixed by the yum yum sauce.

I couldn't decide what cut to use so I went to my local Polish shop to see what they had. I chose shoulder and belly as I was still prevaricating and decided to cook both. They also had a neck joint that would have been lovely too but I had enough pork for one day.

So I'm doing another version of a Momofuku porky feast. I never got to eat the real thing in the end and I'm still dreaming about it, hence the revisit. You can use shoulder or belly but I used belly because I love the wobbly nature of it.

The pickled vegetables are essential to lighten things up. This is good as it allows you to eat more pork. This twist on hasselback potatoes is, as Larry David says, 'prettaaay, prettaaay good'.

SLOW-COOKED PORK WITH YUM YUM SAUCE
SERVES 6

1kg pork belly or shoulder, off the bone

100ml dark soy sauce

2 tbsp golden brown sugar

1 tbsp five-spice powder or spice bag seasoning

1 garlic bulb, cut in half around the circumference and broken up

FOR THE SAUCE:

1 x 450g bottle of golden syrup

2 garlic cloves, crushed

2 tbsp gochujang paste

2 tbsp malt vinegar

Put the pork in a large ziplock bag with the soy sauce, brown sugar, five-spice or spice bag seasoning and garlic, then scrunch everything together thoroughly and leave to marinate for at least 6 hours but overnight is even better.

Preheat the oven to 160°C.

Wrap the pork in foil, put it in a roasting tin and cook in the oven for 3½ hours. Uncover and cook for 30 minutes more.

Pour off the juices carefully – this will include the rendered pork fat from the belly. Cover the meat once more and allow to rest.

For the sauce, melt all the ingredients together in a saucepan and put in a bowl for serving.

Serve the pork on a platter, cut or pulled, with the pickled vegetables and the hasselback potatoes on the following two pages and lettuce leaves for wrapping, with the bowl of sauce on the side.

PICKLED SUMMER VEGETABLES

SERVES 8

200g caster sugar

200ml rice wine vinegar

200ml water

3cm piece of ginger, peeled and finely chopped

1 tbsp coriander seeds

1 carrot, thinly sliced

1 fennel bulb, thinly sliced

1 red onion, thinly sliced

1 x 250g packet of radishes, halved

Bring the sugar, vinegar, water, ginger and coriander seeds to the boil in a small saucepan. Add the carrot, fennel and red onion and remove the pan from the heat. Allow to cool, then add the radishes and any green tops from the fennel.

Keep in the fridge until needed. You may have a little too much but the vegetables are lovely in a salad for another day.

SESAME AND SPRING ONION HASSELBACK POTATOES
SERVES 6

18 small new potatoes

2 tbsp toasted sesame oil

2 tbsp sunflower oil

6 garlic cloves, unpeeled and lightly crushed

1 tbsp sesame seeds

4 spring onions, finely chopped

1 tbsp malt vinegar

Wash the potatoes, then one by one make several incisions along their length two-thirds down the potato towards the base – this will help them become extra crispy. A little tip for cutting is to put the potatoes next to the handle of a wooden spoon as you slice, that way all the cuts will be even.

Put the potatoes in a bowl, cover with water and put in the fridge for an hour or so. This helps the potatoes to open up so they get extra crispy.

Preheat the oven to 190°C.

Drain and dry the potatoes, then put them on a baking tray, turn them in the oils and season. Roast in the oven for 30–40 minutes, depending on their size – they need to be just nearly done.

Add the garlic and sesame seeds, then roast in the oven for another 10 minutes. Add the spring onions and vinegar and they are ready to serve.

Summer salads for hot days

30 JULY 2022

We Irish need a decent summer to bolster us for what's ahead. Not getting one makes us glum and cranky. There has been chaos in the airports as unsurprisingly, people are keen to get away. War, soaring inflation and ever-lurking covid have curtailed the ebullient free-for-all we were told was going to happen when the pandemic eased and people got back to normal. Dungarvan is quieter than expected.

Damien Derwin, our head chef who started with us last summer, now has his feet well under the table. A Dub who wanted a lifestyle change, he has brought a zen-ness to the food and kitchen that we needed. I can be a bit high-octane, always wanting to try new things while I'm whizzing through, leaving confusion in my wake.

Professional cooking can be pressurised in a way that most people don't understand. We have to be on top of our game all day, every day, for every dish, no matter what. It takes a certain type of person to thrive in that environment. That's what hooked me when I first stepped into a kitchen. There's a certain frisson that becomes addictive. I was never going to be a librarian.

I know this sounds obvious, but you also have to love food and be continually curious about it. Doing the same thing over and over again can be tedious for the cook and the customer but repetition also brings consistency and an assuredness to an aspiring young chef. They master the dishes and learn to walk before they fly.

In theory I'm the calm, assuring mentor, the conductor of the orchestra. That gives me a certain freedom. Damien and I do the menus together and I taste everything but the most important component is the customers. If they are happy leaving, they'll come back. If they are not, they won't return and of course will tell twice as many people that we didn't live up to our reputation. So it's very much in our interests to impress them and there is never a day we don't try.

Sometimes dishes cross over and make it on the restaurant menu. This mozzarella and fennel dish has with simple aplomb. Mackerel is so under-rated. I'm slow-cooking mine in flavoured olive oil, then using the oil to make a unique sauce. I'm using gazpacho as my inspiration for the dressing for this salad that would be perfect for a barbecue.

MOZZARELLA WITH FENNEL, OLIVES AND RAISINS

SERVES 4

2 nice fresh green fennel bulbs
2 balls of buffalo mozzarella
a few sprigs of fresh dill, basil or thyme

FOR THE DRESSING:
50g raisins
zest and juice of 1 small orange
1 tsp Dijon mustard
50ml sunflower oil
50ml olive oil
12 stoned green olives, chopped
a pinch of chilli flakes

Soak the raisins in a bowl of just-boiled water for 15 minutes to plump them up, then drain.

Trim the tops and tough outer leaves from the fennel bulbs but be careful to leave the root intact. Cut into quarters and simmer gently in salted water for 20 minutes or so, until the fennel is soft and tender. Remove the fennel from the water and allow to cool.

To make the dressing, put the orange zest and juice in a bowl along with the Dijon mustard, then slowly whisk in the oils until you form an emulsion. Add the drained raisins, olive pieces and chilli flakes, then season. Chill the dressing for a little while.

When ready to serve, tear the mozzarella in half and sit it beside a piece of fennel, then spoon the dressing on top. Garnish with fresh dill, basil or thyme.

Eat with good bread to soak up the residual dressing. It's a perfect summer starter.

MACKEREL WITH NEW POTATOES, PEPPERS AND HARISSA DRESSING

SERVES 4

8 new potatoes, halved

2 pointed peppers, cut into 2cm strips

4 garlic cloves, unpeeled and gently crushed

2 strips of orange peel

1 sprig of fresh thyme

100ml sunflower oil

100ml light olive oil

2 large mackerel, filleted and pin-boned

FOR THE DRESSING:

2 egg yolks

juice of ½ lemon

1 tsp harissa

Preheat the oven to 150°C.

Scatter the potatoes, peppers, garlic, orange and thyme in a large roasting tin, then add the two oils. Season and cook in the oven for approximately 30 minutes, until the potatoes are tender.

Remove from the oven, then slip the mackerel into the tin and baste with the oil. Cook for 10 more minutes, then remove the tin from the oven and allow to cool.

Lift the mackerel, potatoes and peppers carefully from the tin and put on a large plate or dish to chill in the fridge. Strain the oil through a fine mesh sieve.

To make the dressing, put the egg yolks in a bowl with the lemon juice, harissa and a pinch of salt. Whisk the strained oil into the yolks in a steady drizzle, as if making mayonnaise. When it's all incorporated, it's ready.

To serve, artfully arrange the mackerel, potatoes and peppers on plates with the dressing on the side so everyone can help themselves.

CRUNCHY TWO-BEAN SALAD WITH A SORT-OF GAZPACHO DRESSING

SERVES 2

250g vine-ripened cherry tomatoes
1 garlic clove, sliced
4 tbsp olive oil, plus more for drizzling
½ tsp smoked paprika
a pinch of chilli flakes
1 x 200g packet of trimmed fine French beans
1 x 400g tin of butter beans, drained and rinsed
4 tbsp lightly toasted breadcrumbs

Put the cherry tomatoes, garlic, oil, smoked paprika, chilli flakes and some salt and pepper in a liquidizer or food processor and blend until smooth. If the tomato skins bother you, sieve the mixture into a medium bowl. Chill in the fridge.

Cook the unopened packet of French beans in the microwave on high for 2½ minutes. It's unconventional but it works. Allow to cool in the packet, then add to the tomato dressing along with the butter beans.

Season everything once more, then turn in the dressing so everything is coated.

Divide between two plates and top with the toasted breadcrumbs and an extra lick of olive oil to serve.

Favourite recipes for family holidays

06 AUGUST 2022

We've been going on holidays with my wife's sister and family for 10 years now. She has four children the same age as our two and I'm great pals with her husband, so everyone is happy. We always rent a house and being two families we get more bang for our buck, so luckily we always end up in pretty nice places.

In the early days I did a lot of cooking as taking a gaggle of smallies to a restaurant was never a great proposition. I explored local markets, often taking the car for hours, returning later laden with goodies and anticipation. They never missed me, really. They just got hungry.

One year in Mallorca, this time on foot, I came across a local co-operative where smallholders brought their produce to be sold. A group of men gathered round a pump, all holding plastic drums in various sizes. One by one, they hunched and pumped. *Whoosh ... whoosh.* I edged closer only to discover, to my joy, that it was the golden sound of flowing wine. I felt like Howard Carter the day he rummaged through the pyramids to find Tutankhamun's tomb. It was a wine pump – two whites, two reds, €1.70 for the regular stuff and €2.20 for the premium.

I ponied up for the good stuff and got 5 litres of each. Humping it home was no joke. I expected to be greeted with rapture. Instead, there was disinterest and withering accusations of cheapness. They preferred their wine out of bottles, whereas I considered myself a man of the people, a Bacchanalian Che Guevara. I spent the rest of the holiday working my way through the hooch just out of spite. I didn't manage all the red; it was rough. I left it to the flies.

These recipes are family holiday favourites. Feel free to chop and change, especially with the fish. Fillets of fish will work perfectly here, just adjust the cooking times. I always change this ratatouille—caponata hybrid depending on the location. The spices might give way for chorizo or 'nduja – the tone will always be determined by what's local. I've used lamb with this this Lyonnaise before, but this time I'm using crowd-pleasing chicken. I don't always make the tonnato sauce but there is always a tomato salad in one form or another.

BAKED WHOLE SEA BASS ON HOLIDAY RATATOUILLE

SERVES 6

2 whole sea bass (approx. 400g), gutted and cleaned

FOR THE RATATOUILLE:

100g raisins

100ml olive oil, plus more for drizzling

2 red onions, diced into 2cm pieces

2 red peppers, diced into 2cm pieces

2 courgettes, diced into 2cm pieces

1 yellow pepper, diced into 2cm pieces

1 aubergine, diced into 2cm pieces

3 garlic cloves, sliced

1 tsp ground cumin

½ tsp ground cinnamon

1 x 400g tin of chopped tomatoes

2 tbsp red wine vinegar

1 tbsp caster sugar

2 tsp tomato purée

a few sprigs of fresh thyme or rosemary, chopped

1 x 50g tin of salted anchovies, chopped (optional)

Soak the raisins in a bowl of just-boiled water for 15 minutes to plump them up, then drain.

Pour the olive oil in a large pot or frying pan, then add all the vegetables and garlic. Cook over a medium heat for 10 minutes, until everything starts to soften. Add the spices, mix together and cook for another 5 minutes.

Add the drained raisins along with the chopped tomatoes, vinegar, sugar, tomato purée and some of the herbs. Cook for another 10 minutes or so, until everything is soft and jammy. Season and add the anchovies (if using). This can be made earlier in the day.

Preheat the oven to 185°C.

Season the fish inside and out, then add the rest of the herbs to the cavity. Transfer the ratatouille to a roasting tin and put the sea bass on top. Drizzle the fish with a little oil and bake in the oven for around 20 minutes, until the flesh is firm, white and flakes easily.

Serve with rice or on its own with a chilled rosé.

CHICKEN AND FENNEL LYONNAISE WITH ROASTED GARLIC CRÈME FRAÎCHE

SERVES 6

1 x 1.9kg chicken, jointed into 10 pieces, including wings (this is a butcher's job)

4–6 large Rooster potatoes (850g), unpeeled and thickly sliced

a glug of olive oil

2 fennel bulbs

2 large onions

1 garlic bulb, cut in half around the circumference

1 lemon, quartered

a few sprigs of fresh thyme or rosemary

½ tsp chilli flakes

a drizzle of honey

FOR THE CRÈME FRAÎCHE:

12 garlic cloves, peeled

a drizzle of olive oil

1 sprig of fresh thyme

200g crème fraîche

juice of ½ lemon

Preheat the oven to 160°C.

To make the roasted garlic crème fraîche, put the garlic cloves on a piece of foil along with a drizzle of oil, the thyme and some salt. Bring the edges together to form a seal and roast in the oven for 20 minutes, until soft and golden.

Open the parcel and tip everything into a bowl. Remove the thyme stalks, then crush the garlic a little with the back of a spoon. Add the crème fraîche and lemon juice, then chill.

Turn the oven up to 190°C. Put the chicken pieces and potatoes in your largest roasting tin and pour over a good glug of oil. Season and turn everything together until coated. Cook in the oven for 20 minutes.

Meanwhile, halve the fennel and onions, then cut into thick slices. Add to the tin along with the garlic, lemon, herbs, chilli flakes and honey. Mix once more, adding a little more oil if necessary, then put the tin back in the oven for 30–40 minutes, turning everything once or twice, until the chicken is cooked.

Serve hot with the chilled crème fraîche. They go together like strawberries and cream.

TOMATO TONNATO

SERVES 4

2 egg yolks, at room temperature
juice of ½ lemon
1 large garlic clove, crushed
100ml sunflower oil
50ml olive oil
1 x 160g tin of tuna, drained
2 salted anchovies (optional but lovely)
500g mix of lovely tomatoes
fresh herbs of your choice

Put the egg yolks, lemon juice and garlic in a blender and blitz to combine. With the motor running, slowly drizzle in the oil until it comes together to make an emulsion.

Add the tuna, anchovies (if using) and a little salt, then blend until smooth. The texture shouldn't be thick like a mayonnaise, more like Caesar dressing. Add a little water if necessary.

Cut the tomatoes in a haphazard way. It always looks better.

Drizzle the dressing over the top of the tomatoes, then sprinkle with salt and a few twists of black pepper. Scatter the herbs on top. Serve chilled.

Keep summer cooking simple

13 AUGUST 2022

I had seafood rice for the first time only a few years ago, on the Costa Brava. I'm drawn to this type of food and its outward simplicity: one pot bursting with flavour, goodness and tradition. It's the culmination of a lifetime of the cook's knowledge.

The aroma is beguiling, the rice just waiting to be eaten, often without a thought to its complexity. When I ate that arroz caldoso in a perfect little restaurant by the twinkling sea, I was smitten. Cooking like this is all about building the flavours in layers. It's a skill that's acquired with practice. In the best hands, it can be powerful and transformative.

It's a soupy rice, laden with alluringly deep flavours. I'm using frozen calamari rings that I cut into small pieces. I wanted to push the boat out so I added squid ink for gentle mystery. Don't be afraid of it. Good fishmongers should have it in sachets. If you can't get it, don't worry, make this dish anyway.

In my test, I added the squid at the end of the cooking time. That's the rule with squid: cook it for a long time or a short time. It was a little bit chewy; not ideal. This time I'm giving it longer, which should do the trick. If you don't fancy squid, use small, uncooked, shelled prawns or a mixture of seafood, popped in 5 minutes before the end. But becoming a better cook is all about adventure.

This week, I want to make things as easy as possible. The chicken salad is as much about the vegetables as it is the bird. I pot roasted the chicken with the spuds. If you don't want to roast a chicken, buy a good pre-cooked one. Let it cool, but most importantly, save the precious juices. Add 100ml more chicken stock into the juices and continue to make the dressing as directed. Piment d'espelette is wonderful if you can get it, otherwise use smoked paprika.

Finding ripe peaches can be a challenge, but cooking slightly underripe ones can prove worthwhile. Halloumi's squeaky blandness previously left me unmoved, but in a friend's house one evening I began to see its warm, crunchy merits. Maybe I'm mellowing as I'm getting older.

ARROZ CALDOSO NEGRE

SERVES 6

100ml olive oil

500g squid rings, chopped into small pieces

1 large onion, finely diced

2 celery sticks, finely diced

3 garlic cloves, chopped

1 fresh red chilli, deseeded and finely diced

1 tsp smoked paprika

3 bay leaves (fresh if possible)

1 tbsp tomato purée

300g Bomba or Arborio risotto rice

150ml red wine (use white wine if you're not using squid ink)

1 litre chicken stock

2 sachets of squid ink

a squeeze of lemon (optional)

1 packet of prawn crackers

FOR THE DRESSING:

150ml cream

juice of 1 lemon

juice of 1 mandarin

½ tsp saffron strands or powder

For the saffron dressing, mix all the ingredients together and chill the dressing for an hour or so.

Put the oil, squid, onion, celery, garlic, chilli, smoked paprika and bay leaves in a pot. Cover and cook gently for 20 minutes, stirring once or twice. All the vegetables should be soft and tender. Add the tomato purée and cook for 1 minute more.

Rinse the rice under cold water, add it to the pot and stir everything together. Pour in the red wine, then after a minute or two, all the stock. Bring to a simmer and cook for 20 minutes, until the rice is tender.

Add the squid ink and lemon if you think it needs it, but keep in mind that the dressing contains quite a lot.

Season and serve with the saffron dressing and prawn crackers on the side.

AN IMPRESSIVE CHICKEN SALAD
SERVES 6

200ml chicken stock
2 tsp piment d'espelette or smoked paprika
2 bay leaves (fresh if possible)
1 good sprig of fresh thyme
1 x 1.4kg chicken
500g baby potatoes
a drizzle of olive oil
200ml sour cream
100ml natural yogurt
a drizzle of honey
a selection of salad leaves and vegetables
4 eggs, boiled to your taste, peeled and halved

Preheat the oven to 175°C.

Pour the chicken stock in a casserole that will fit the chicken comfortably. Add the spice and whisk it through, then add the bay leaves and thyme and sit the chicken on top. Tumble in the potatoes, season and drizzle everything with a little oil. Cover and cook in the oven for 1 hour, then uncover and cook for 1 hour more.

Remove the casserole from the oven and allow to cool. Remove the chicken and potatoes, then strain the cooking juices into a bowl and allow the fat to rise to the top. Skim the fat from the juices, then pat once or twice with a sheet of kitchen paper. This will ensure most of the fat is removed. Whisk the sour cream, yogurt and honey into the juices and season to make a dressing.

Put the chicken on a large platter and cut a few slices off for easy access. Arrange the salad, halved eggs, vegetables and potatoes all around in an artful way and serve the dressing on the side for everyone to help themselves.

ROASTED PEACHES WITH ZA'ATAR-CRUSTED HALLOUMI

SERVES 8

8 ripe peaches
olive oil, for drizzling and frying
1 tbsp golden brown sugar
1 sprig of fresh rosemary
2 packets of halloumi cheese (460g)
3 tbsp plain flour
1 tbsp za'atar
2 tbsp pumpkin seeds

Preheat the oven to 180°C.

Cut the peaches in half and remove the stones. Sit them in a roasting tin or baking dish, then drizzle a little oil over them. Scatter the sugar on top, then add the rosemary and a few twists of black pepper. Turn everything together, making sure everything is coated in the oil and the peaches are cut side up Bake in the oven for 20–30 minutes, until the peaches are tender.

Meanwhile, cut the halloumi into 2cm cubes, pat dry and put in a bowl with the flour and za'atar. Shake off any excess flour.

Heat some oil in a frying pan set over a medium heat. Fry the halloumi in hot olive oil, adding the pumpkin seeds when they're nearly golden.

Drain and serve warm with the peaches on a platter.

Let's go outside

20 AUGUST 2022

I love the idea of picnics. Secretly I see myself as Jane Austen's Darcy, louche and long-limbed, draped alluringly over a blanket, eyebrow arched for the next opportunity. All very chocolate boxy. The food never matters in my flights of fancy. It's all about the look and the accessories. I even have a proper picnic basket. It sits unused at home, pristine and glistening. I'm afraid to use it in case I lose any of its components. It's like a relic awaiting my retirement.

When I was small, picnics were warm tomato sandwiches laced with the crunch of sand on Clonea beach. I'd eat them without a care, plonked on a rock by my sisters with the promise of ice cream. Despite their best efforts, I was permanently sunburnt. We lived above our chemist in the Square so plenty of after-sun and sympathy were always available, the former tersely applied as I sucked on a stick of rock to placate me.

The dinkiest picnic item I ever saw, though, was at a recent fair in Ballymaloe. JR Ryall, the pastry chef there, professed his love of picnics and produced a loaf. Within its hollowed interior were the tiniest, most delicate sandwiches. The top of the loaf was replaced to cocoon them safely for a train journey he was taking later. He graciously donated a Lilliputian one from the top. It was deliciously ethereal, gone in a whisper. I felt lazy as I would never go to all that trouble for a sandwich, but it did inspire me.

So today I'm attempting to up my game and hopefully do a bit of inspiring myself. No more jamming chicken fillet rolls, crisps and biscuits into a backpack and heading off. From now on I will be accessorised to a T, complete with my shiny picnic basket brimming with perfectly formed goodies.

These dishes are of course all adaptable to different locations. I wouldn't judge you if you abandoned any schlepping and ate these in the comfort of your own home. Eat them outside, though, just as a gesture.

You can play around with the fillings for the large scone but I like this combination. My rough-and-ready stuffed loaf gets its inspiration from a panzanella. The chorizo imbues the bread with a deep savouriness. The pea and salmon salad is simple and transportable, perfect for the most elegant picnic baskets.

TEAR-AND-SHARE RED PEPPER, RED ONION AND FETA SCONE

SERVES 6

2 tbsp olive oil

1 red pepper, thinly sliced

1 red onion, halved and thinly sliced

10 stoned green olives, roughly chopped

275g self-raising flour

1 tsp bicarbonate of soda

½ tsp salt

60g butter, diced and chilled

210ml buttermilk

200g feta cheese, crumbled

1 egg beaten with 1 tbsp milk

a scattering of poppy seeds

Preheat the oven to 190°C.

Put the oil, red pepper and red onion in a pot and cook gently with a lid on for 15 minutes, with no colour. Season, then add the olives and allow to cool.

In a large bowl, mix together the flour, bicarbonate of soda and salt. Add the butter and use your fingers to work it in until it's crumbly.

Add the buttermilk, feta and the pepper mixture. Mix quickly to combine but do not overwork the dough or it will become tough.

Tip the dough out onto a lightly floured countertop and pat it into a circle about 18cm in diameter and 2cm high. Transfer to a baking tray lined with parchment. Cut into six triangles. Pull each triangle out ever so slightly so they are still in a circle but with 1cm between them.

Brush the top with the egg wash and sprinkle with poppy seeds. Bake in the oven for 20–25 minutes, until risen and golden.

Eat warm or at room temperature.

MY STUFFED PICNIC LOAF

SERVES 3

1 tbsp raisins

1 whole small white loaf of bread

50ml olive oil, plus more for drizzling

100g chorizo slices, shredded

1 red onion, sliced

1 garlic clove, thinly sliced

½ tsp ground cumin

a pinch of chilli flakes

1 tsp red wine vinegar

6 vine-ripened cherry tomatoes, quartered

a few sprigs of fresh basil, leaves torn

Preheat the oven to 180°C.

Soak the raisins in a bowl of just-boiled water for 15 minutes to plump them up, then drain.

Carefully cut the top off the loaf (set it aside for later) and tear out the inner filling, leaving the crust as a shell. Cut out the centre of the loaf as best you can. Tear into 3cm chunks and put on a baking tray along with the bread that you tore out of the top of the loaf, drizzle with oil and toast in the oven until golden – about 10 minutes or so.

Meanwhile, put the 50ml of oil in a pot with the drained raisins, chorizo, red onion, garlic, cumin and chilli flakes. Cook gently for 10 minutes, until the onions have softened and the chorizo has released its oil. Add the red wine vinegar, then the cherry tomatoes and season.

Add the mixture to the roasted bread along with the torn basil and fold it all together. Stuff the salad back into the loaf and replace the lid, pressing it down gently, then wrap in foil for travel. Put it in the fridge until you're ready.

To serve, portion out the filling to eat it as a salad, then tear up the now-empty shell to eat along with it. A little bit of aioli wouldn't go astray here either.

PEA AND POACHED SALMON SALAD

SERVES 2

1 x 250g piece of fresh salmon

200g frozen petits pois, thawed

50ml olive oil

1 shallot, finely chopped

1 small fresh red chilli, deseeded and diced

2 tbsp chopped fresh dill

a squeeze of lemon juice

a pinch of caster sugar

a pinch of Maldon flaky sea salt

a few twists of black pepper

To poach the salmon, bring a medium-sized pot of water to the boil. Add some salt and lower the salmon into it. Immediately remove the pot from the heat and set aside to cool.

Blanch the peas in boiling salted water for 30 seconds, drain and refresh under cold water, then drain well once more.

Put the peas in a bowl and crush them lightly with the back of a fork or potato masher, then flake the salmon into the peas. Add the remaining ingredients and mix gently, then chill until needed.

Kitchen disco

At this time every year I would be excited at the thought of next weekend's Electric Picnic. I started going there when I was over 40. Before that I always thought I was too old. There was a burgeoning food scene at festivals and John and Sally McKenna were in charge of running the Theatre of Food, so they invited some chefs and producers along to give talks in a wonky little tent with a table and a few chairs. It's come a long way since that weekend 14 years ago.

Back then it was always hard to get away from the restaurant. Normally someone would have to die to get a day off but I swung it and invited Robert, one of my Dublin pals, as my plus one. It rained most of the time. I remember endless tramping through mud punctuated by joy when we came upon an undiscovered band that we loved. Pockets of light would appear in the dark as we followed the thrum of the music through the woods to the Salty Dog stage. It was like a decadent, carefree spaceship in the middle of nowhere.

It was all very informal in those days. We got our wristbands and the best fun was seeing how far they could get us through security. It was a thrilling and addictive disaster. Our little two-man tent sank underneath the weight of the rain. Water poured in and swamped us. Robert's car keys drowned along with his phone so he had to be towed out of the field the next morning. We were sodden but invigorated, vowing to return every year to reclaim our fleeting youth.

I've hung up my EP boots but I haven't given up festivals. I just want a quieter one with plenty of room to roam. So instead of EP next weekend, I will be working. We have friends coming on the Sunday night, so I'll cook. If I'm lucky there might be a kitchen disco, just to remind us we're not over the hill yet.

I'm roasting the monkfish whole and placing it on an Italian vegetable stew. It's big and dramatic. Get your fishmonger to prepare it. This pepper dish is the essence of cool restraint. The creaminess of the butter bean brandade is perfectly offset by the pepper and the Fergus Henderson-inspired green sauce. I love Ummera smoked chicken. Its silky butteriness and gentle flavours lift all the other ingredients.

ROASTED MONKFISH RIBOLLITA

SERVES 6

50ml olive oil, plus extra for drizzling

2 red onions, diced into 2cm pieces

1 fennel bulb, diced into 2cm pieces

1 large carrot, diced into 2cm pieces

2 garlic cloves, sliced

1 tsp smoked paprika

a pinch of chilli flakes

1 x 400g tin of chopped tomatoes

1 x 400g tin of butter beans, drained and rinsed

750ml chicken or vegetable stock

2 pieces of orange peel

1 sprig of fresh rosemary

½ loaf of ciabatta

1 x 850g–1kg piece of whole monkfish, skin removed and trimmed

100ml crème fraîche

a few sprigs of fresh thyme, leaves picked

Preheat the oven to 185°C.

Pour the oil in a medium-sized pot and add the vegetables, garlic, smoked paprika and chilli flakes. It's important that all the veg are cut the same size. Cook over a low heat for 15 minutes so, until the vegetables soften without colour.

Add the tomatoes, butter beans, stock, orange peel and rosemary and bring to a simmer. Cook gently for a further 15 minutes, season and remove from the heat.

Meanwhile, tear the ciabatta into chunks and put them on a baking tray. Drizzle with oil, season and toast in the oven for 10 minutes or so, until golden and crunchy.

Drizzle a little more oil in a large roasting tin and sprinkle with salt and pepper. Put the monkfish on top, then brush generously with the crème fraîche, making sure it's completely covered. This will stop the fish from drying out. Drizzle the fish with a little more oil, sprinkle over the thyme and roast in the oven for 20–25 minutes. The flesh should be coming away from the bone down the centre. It's okay to make an incision to have a little peek if you're not sure.

Remove the rosemary from the ribollita and reheat. Add the toasted bread to the stew and fold everything together.

Serve straightaway on a dish with the monkfish on top.

ROASTED PEPPER AND BUTTER BEAN BRANDADE WITH GREEN SAUCE

SERVES 6

1 x 150g hake fillet, skin and bones removed

½ tbsp salt

1 tbsp olive oil

2 garlic cloves, sliced

150ml cream

1 x 400g tin of butter beans, drained and rinsed

a squeeze of lemon

1 x 650g jar of roasted red peppers

FOR THE GREEN SAUCE:

1 bunch of fresh flat-leaf parsley

½ bunch of fresh dill

1 sprig of fresh mint

a few sprigs of fresh tarragon

3 garlic cloves, peeled

1 x 50g tin of salted anchovies

50ml sunflower oil

50ml olive oil

1 tbsp capers

a squeeze of lemon

a few twists of black pepper

a pinch of caster sugar

Put the hake in a baking dish, cover with the salt and put it in the fridge for 1 hour. Rinse the fish under cold water and cut it into chunks.

Heat the oil in a small saucepan over a low heat. Add the garlic and cook gently for 1 minute, until lightly golden. Add the hake and cream. Bring the cream to a gentle bubble and allow to cook for 1 minute, then add the butter beans. Continue to cook gently for 5 minutes, mashing the butter beans into the hake all the while until the mixture forms a creamy paste. Add a squeeze of lemon, check for seasoning and set aside.

When cool, remove the peppers from the jar and drain. Stuff the hake mixture into the peppers. I used a piping bag but you could also cut them open, fill them and fold them over again. Put them in the fridge.

Everything for the green sauce would normally be hand chopped but for ease you can put everything in a blender and blitz until smooth. The mixture needs to be a little loose so it may need more oil – you can be the judge.

Serve the peppers warm or at room temperature with the green sauce on the side.

UMMERA SMOKED CHICKEN WITH ROASTED SQUASH, CREAMED BUTTER BEANS AND PARSLEY

SERVES 4

1 butternut squash

a drizzle of rapeseed oil

a pinch of grated nutmeg

1 sprig of fresh thyme

1 crown of Ummera smoked chicken (400g), removed from the bone and diced

1 x 400g tin of butter beans, drained and rinsed

100g baby spinach

150ml cream

½ tbsp horseradish sauce

Preheat the oven to 190°C.

Trim, peel, halve and deseed the squash and cut into 2cm chunks. Put in a deep roasting tin and drizzle with the oil, making sure all the squash cubes are glistening and coated. Season, then add the nutmeg and thyme. Roast in the oven for 25 minutes, until the squash is soft and lightly charred.

Remove the squash from the oven, then add the remaining ingredients to the tin. Fold everything together and put the tin back in the oven to cook for a further 5–10 minutes to warm everything through, then check for seasoning. The spinach shouldn't be allowed to wilt too much, it needs to stay nice and lively.

Serve warm.

Sticking to the seasons

03 SEPTEMBER 2022

It's September and straightaway I change my cooking. Yes, there will be amazing tomatoes for another few weeks, but aside from that I abandon all the Mediterranean influences of summer. I start to swap olive oil for butter and the occasional dollop of rapeseed oil.

I'm doing three mushroom dishes this week because it's only now that I feel I can reintroduce them on the menu in the Tannery. I know it's all a bit pedantic but it's this kind of rigour of sticking to the seasons that still keeps me excited about food. I impose a sense of monastic abstinence in my refusal to use ingredients out of season. It's as close to religion as I come. The appearance of a strawberry garnish beside a Christmas pudding can send me into paroxysms of apoplexy. I almost have to be tied down, foaming at the mouth with indignation. The anticipation of using an ingredient you haven't cooked with for months is akin to looking forward to a chill in the air so you can put on your favourite coat. That feeling is always worth the wait.

Mushrooms can be divisive though. There's definitely a textural thing with some people, while others can take them or leave them. The true mushroom lovers, however, are besotted with the myriad varieties and idiosyncrasies of fungi. I've been on a few mushroom hunts but the tramping never seemed worth the meagre reward. I'm not a forager. I prefer the comfort and warmth of the kitchen but I do admire people's passion for them. That, and the fact that mushrooms can kill you. They have my respect.

Of course, you can buy packets of mixed cultivated mushrooms that are interesting for the curious. Old-fashioned button mushrooms are so timid in flavour that I think they are hardly worthwhile. On an ordinary day I veer towards chestnut mushrooms or my very favourite, flat caps or field mushrooms. They never let me down. Full of earthy flavour and meaty texture, they give as much pleasure as the fanciest of mushrooms.

The bacon dish is deeply autumnal. One-pot dishes are my happy place. The flavours marry as if they were destined to be together.

Mushrooms, cream, tarragon and crisp pastry — if this tart doesn't make mushroom lovers happy, nothing will.

Field mushrooms are almost beefy in their richness. I've added mortadella for interest and a mild Cambozola for creamy Italian flair.

POT ROAST BACON WITH MUSHROOMS AND THYME CREAM

SERVES 6

1 x 1.2kg joint of back bacon

350ml chicken stock

1 cinnamon stick

1 sprig of fresh thyme

2 bay leaves (fresh if possible)

1 x 400g tin of butter beans, drained and rinsed

250g chestnut mushrooms, halved

250ml cream

1 small apple, peeled and diced

1 tbsp Dijon mustard

2 tbsp golden brown sugar

80g baby spinach

Preheat the oven to 165°C.

Put the bacon in a casserole with the chicken stock, cinnamon, thyme and bay leaves. Cover and cook in the oven for 1 hour 45 minutes.

Remove the casserole from the oven and turn the heat up to 185°C. Add the butter beans, mushrooms, cream and apple around the side, then turn together so everything is coated in creamy juices.

Brush the top of the bacon with the Dijon mustard and coat evenly with the sugar. Put the casserole back in the oven, uncovered, for 20 minutes, until the bacon is nicely glazed.

To serve, remove the bacon from the pot and allow to rest under foil for 10 minutes or so. Add the spinach to the casserole and wilt it a little in the sauce. Once seasoned, it's ready to serve with the carved bacon.

MUSHROOM BÉARNAISE TART
SERVES 4

1 tbsp rapeseed oil

1 large shallot, chopped

2 garlic cloves, chopped

300g mixed mushrooms, sliced

1 tbsp sherry vinegar or red wine vinegar

150ml cream

a few sprigs of fresh tarragon, chopped

1 egg yolk

1 x 320g sheet of ready-rolled shortcrust pastry, thawed

1 egg beaten with 1 tbsp milk

Preheat the oven to 185°C.

Heat the oil in a frying pan over a gentle heat. Add the shallot and garlic and cook for a couple of minutes without colour, then add the mushrooms and vinegar. Turn up the heat a little and cook for 2 minutes or so, until the mushrooms start to soften, then add the cream. Let the cream bubble and reduce until it forms a thick sauce around the mushrooms.

Remove the pan from the heat and allow to cool, then add the tarragon, egg yolk and some salt and pepper.

Unfurl the pastry. Keep the parchment and put it on a baking tray, then put the pastry on top. Brush lightly with egg wash, then spread the mushroom mixture over the pastry, leaving a 3cm rim all around. Fold the edge in on itself to form a crust, then brush with egg wash.

Bake in the oven for 25 minutes, until golden. Eat warm with a green salad.

FIELD MUSHROOM, MORTADELLA AND CAMBOZOLA BUNS

MAKES 4

3 field (flat cap) mushrooms (250g)
2 garlic cloves, thinly sliced
a few sprigs of fresh thyme
a drizzle of olive oil
4 brioche buns
4 slices of mortadella
100g Cambozola or Gorgonzola cheese

Preheat the oven to 180°C.

Check the mushrooms for any dirt. Brush or rinse it off and pat the mushrooms dry. Slice each mushroom across in three. Some pieces might break off but that doesn't matter. Put on a baking tray, scatter over the garlic and thyme, season and drizzle with oil. Bake in the oven for 10–12 minutes, until the mushrooms are soft and giving.

Toast the brioche buns, then put a layer of mushrooms on the base of each along with any residual juices, followed by the mortadella and the cheese. Eat warm.

Tried-and-tested autumn salads

10 SEPTEMBER 2022

I do love a good salad. I'm not talking about a few random leaves tossed in a ubiquitous dressing, an amalgam of apathy. We've all had them. Simplicity is appropriate when the produce is really fresh and the dressing is muted. Sometimes it can be just good oil, a squeeze of lemon and a little salt.

One of my older cookery books is by Édouard de Pomaine, a French cookery writer of Polish heritage who died in 1964. He was a big influence on the career of the young Elizabeth David. He wrote a simple recipe that still influences me to this day. I have done adaptations of it in this column, notably for a cheat's Caesar salad (page 309).

LETTUCES WITH CREAM

The hearts of 3 lettuces, 5 tablespoons double cream, 1 tablespoon vinegar

Wash and dry the lettuces carefully, separate the leaves and put them into a salad bowl. Mix the cream and vinegar in a small bowl with a little salt. Pour this over the lettuce and scarcely toss it using a very delicate movement.

Serve this salad with a white meat such as chicken or roast veal.

You get an indication here for his reverence for the ingredients. It's good to look back once in a while to ground ourselves.

The salads today are all different. The first two are a bit cheffy. Indeed, since writing the recipe they have made an appearance in the Tannery. I made a version of tarator, a Balkan walnut sauce, to go with the carrots. On its own it might take a moment or two to love, but with the carrots it's divine. Whipping the goat cheese with the cream makes it light and ethereal. The amazing balsamic vinegar really makes a difference along with the first of the blackberries.

One-pot dishes are my happy place.

03 SEPTEMBER 2022

BUTTER BOY

I've recently become a massive fan of Burren Balsamic if you can get it. If not, just use the best vinegar you can find. A little bit of quality goes a long way in this sophisticated salad. This is a jumble of deliciousness. The mild chilli dressing gives courgettes an unexpected lift.

The last recipe is a risky riff on panzanella. I really wasn't sure about it right up to the last moment when it came together, real seat-of-the-pants stuff. There were lessons learned. Buy good, dark, treacly brown bread and pat the chickpeas dry. I make the mistakes so hopefully you won't have to. Roasting the carrots sweetens and magnifies the flavour. I used fancy heritage carrots for a little extra drama.

ROASTED CARROT SALAD WITH TARATOR AND CRESS
SERVES 4

8 medium carrots
a drizzle of olive oil (enough to coat)
3 tbsp water
1 tbsp coriander seeds
a small handful of cress

FOR THE TARATOR:
2 slices of white bread
80g roasted walnuts
1 garlic clove, grated
50ml olive oil
4 tbsp natural yogurt
1 tbsp red wine vinegar
1 tsp honey

Preheat the oven to 200°C.

Peel and top the carrots, then cut them into quarters lengthways and put in a roasting tin. Add enough oil to coat them along with the water, coriander seeds and some salt and pepper. Roast the carrots in the oven for 25 minutes or so, depending on their size. They should be slightly charred.

Meanwhile, remove the crusts from the bread and cut it into chunks. Soak the bread in a little cold water and allow to sit for a few minutes, then squeeze it out gently and put in a blender. Add the remaining ingredients to the blender, blitz until smooth and season with salt and ground white pepper.

To serve, spoon the tarator onto plates. Make an oval well in the centre, then put the carrots on top, followed by some cress. Drizzle any residual carroty cooking juices over the top. If there are none, use a little olive oil instead. Serve warm.

BITTER LEAVES WITH WHIPPED GOAT CHEESE AND BURREN BALSAMIC VINEGAR

SERVES 4

4 tbsp rapeseed oil

3 tbsp Burren Blackberry and Thyme Balsamic Vinegar

mixed bitter leaves, such as frisée and radicchio

a handful of fresh blackberries

1 tbsp toasted mixed seeds or pumpkin seeds (optional)

FOR THE WHIPPED GOAT CHEESE:

150g soft rindless goat cheese

150ml cream

1 tsp honey

a squeeze of lemon

Put the goat cheese in a bowl or a stand mixer (I prefer to use an electric whisk). Add the cream, honey, lemon and a little salt. Start off slowly to amalgamate the cream, then turn up high to whisk into a mousse. When the mixture is stiff but not over-whipped, put it in the fridge to chill.

Mix the rapeseed oil and balsamic vinegar together. Wash the leaves and pat them dry.

When ready to serve, bring some water to a simmer in a small saucepan. Take the biggest tablespoon you can find — I have an old-fashioned silver one for such purposes. Dip it in the hot water and pat it dry. Immediately scoop out the goat cheese cream onto a plate — the hot spoon will give you a rounded surface. The French call this a quenelle. There is an art to this so don't worry if it takes a while to get it right. Repeat the process for all the plates.

Put the leaves beside the mousse, drizzle over the dressing and scatter the blackberries around. The seeds are nice to scatter on top for crunch, but if you don't have them the salad will be lovely all the same.

COURGETTE, SPINACH AND BROWN BREAD SALAD

SERVES 4

4 small courgettes, cut into 0.5cm rounds
½ loaf of dark brown bread (about 4 good slices)
1 x 400g tin of chickpeas, drained and rinsed
50ml olive oil
1 x 200g bag of baby spinach

FOR THE DRESSING:
juice of 1 lemon
juice of 1 mandarin
50ml olive oil
50ml sunflower oil
2cm piece of ginger, peeled and grated
1 fresh red chilli, deseeded and finely diced
1 tsp caster sugar

Preheat the oven to 190°C.

Put the courgette slices in a roasting tin. Trim the crusts from the bread, tear the bread into rough chunks and add to the courgettes. Pat the chickpeas dry and add to the tin along with the oil. Season and turn everything together to ensure it's all coated in the oil. Roast in the oven for 20–25 minutes, turning once or twice, until everything is golden and crunchy.

Meanwhile, whisk all the ingredients for the dressing together.

When the courgette mixture is done, add the spinach to the tin as soon as it comes out of the oven. This will wilt the spinach.

Add the dressing to the tin and gently fold everything together. Season and spoon onto a platter. Serve at room temperature.

Transform the bland into the beguiling

17 SEPTEMBER 2022

When I was growing up, the closest thing to culinary excitement was when Vesta curry mix came on the market. I was my mother's guinea pig for all things new in the 1970s as I was the youngest of eight and she was thoroughly fed up cooking. I embraced it, though, lapping up everything that was put in front of me, always crunching it down afterwards with a few bourbon biscuits and a glass of milk. I was a pudgy little fella.

My very first foray into cooking was sausages boiled up in that curry sauce, a sort of Indian fusion coddle. It wasn't the best idea. But it was a sign that I was never afraid to try out new things, even if they didn't always work.

Even now, I often use a little gentle spice in my food. In my cookery courses, I always talk about how the simplest of dishes can be transformed from bland to beguiling by the addition of a cinnamon stick, star anise or a couple of cloves. I get heavier handed with the spices as Christmas approaches. You can smell the season in the kitchen.

Using spices doesn't mean chilli heat. There are a myriad of spices that have been used from antiquity and none of them will cause discomfort. Spice doesn't have to be dominant. It should be there for reassurance, complexity and fortification. Curiosity is an important part of cooking and I approach it with a sense of adventure.

A word of warning, though. I always compare the use of spices to perfume or aftershave. A little goes a long way. Too much, no matter how expensive, and you will ruin the desired effect. Be judicious in your application. You can always add but never subtract.

My love of one-pot cooking comes into its own at this time of the year. As soon as I sense an autumnal chill, my mind switches to stews, casseroles and slow cooking. My Aga at home gets cranked up in anticipation of the chilly nights ahead. These dishes today all have some mild spicing in one form or another, perfect for this time of year.

CREAMY CORN, CARROT AND MANGO CHOWDER

SERVES 2

a knob of butter

1 large red onion, diced the same size as the sweetcorn

1 large carrot, diced as above

2 bay leaves (fresh if possible)

200g tinned sweetcorn

400ml chicken or vegetable stock

150ml cream

1 tbsp spiced mango chutney (or use regular mango chutney and a pinch of chilli flakes)

a few sprigs of fresh coriander (optional)

Melt the butter in a large saucepan over a medium heat. When the butter starts to foam, add the onion, carrot and bay leaves. Let the vegetables cook very gently for about 15 minutes, until they soften.

Add the sweetcorn, stock and cream. Bring to a simmer, then add the chutney and cook for 5 more minutes. Season and it's ready to serve. Fresh coriander leaves would be nice on top if you like.

PORK AND SPICED ONION WELLINGTON WITH KHUBANI CHUTNEY

SERVES 4

2 large onions, thinly sliced

50g butter

50ml water

2 tbsp sunflower oil, plus an extra drizzle for the pork

½ tbsp garam masala

1 x 420g pork fillet, trimmed

1 x 320g sheet of ready-rolled shortcrust pastry, thawed

1 egg beaten with 1 tbsp milk

sesame seeds for the top (optional)

FOR THE CHUTNEY:

500ml water

200g dried apricots, sliced

2cm piece of ginger, peeled and grated

3 tbsp golden brown sugar

3 tbsp malt vinegar

1 tsp ground cumin

½ tbsp nigella seeds (optional)

First make the chutney. Put all the ingredients in a saucepan, then cook them down over a medium heat until all the water has evaporated and the mixture is sticky. Cool and put in the fridge. This can be done the day before.

Put the onions, butter, water, oil and garam masala in a saucepan, cover and cook over a medium heat, stirring once or twice, for 15 minutes, until the onions soften and collapse. Remove the lid, turn up the heat a little and cook for another 10 minutes or so, until the onions start to caramelise. You will have to scrape the bottom of the pan a few times to ensure even caramelisation and a nice golden colour. Check the seasoning, remove from the pan and allow to cool.

Season the pork, then heat some oil in a large frying pan until it's gently smoking. Put the pork in the pan and colour it on all sides on a high heat. Remove from the pan and allow to cool completely.

Unfurl the pastry, transferring the parchment to a baking tray. Put the pork on top of the pastry along its width, just a touch above the centre. Brush the pastry all around the pork with a little beaten egg, then spoon the onions along the top of the pork.

Fold the pastry from the bottom over the pork and seal the edges tightly, leaving no air in the pastry, then crimp the edges with a fork. Brush the top of the pastry with the egg wash and sprinkle over the sesame seeds (if using). Transfer to the lined tray.

The Wellington can be put in the fridge until you want to cook it but if you do, allow it to come to room temperature before cooking.

Preheat the oven to 185°C.

Cook the Wellington in the oven for 30 minutes, until crisp and golden. Remove from the oven and allow it to sit for 10 minutes before carving.

Serve with the chutney and something green.

BEETROOT, FIG AND ALMOND SALAD WITH BLACK PEPPER SYRUP
SERVES 4

6 medium beetroot, cooked and peeled
4 ripe figs, some halved, some quartered
80g salted almonds
2 tbsp natural yogurt
a small handful of cress or salad leaves

FOR THE SYRUP:
150ml red wine
2 tbsp golden brown sugar
1 tbsp red wine vinegar
6 twists of black pepper
50ml rapeseed oil

To make the syrup, bring the red wine, sugar, vinegar and black pepper to the boil in a small saucepan and reduce by half, then remove from the heat. Whisk in the rapeseed oil and set aside.

Arrange the beetroot, figs and almonds on a board or platter. Drizzle with the yogurt and scatter over some cress or salad leaves to garnish. Serve the syrup on the side for everyone to help themselves.

Loving food and cooking can be cathartic. At the end of a hard day, cooking dinner can be soothing and eating it can be comforting. Afterwards, the world feels just that little bit better.

Cooking for yourself can be a pleasure

24 SEPTEMBER 2022

Being on your own, for whatever reason, is sometimes difficult. Motivating yourself is often a challenge. The easiest option is to just put on a slice of toast or get a takeaway. Giving yourself a treat, no matter what the circumstances, is important. Loving food and cooking can be cathartic. At the end of a hard day, cooking dinner can be soothing and eating it can be comforting. Afterwards, the world feels just that little bit better.

These recipes are simple. I'm using tins where possible, not only to make them easier to cook but also to prove you don't have to make everything from scratch. At home I use my cupboard as often as possible. Sometimes you just don't have the time or the inclination to be soaking pulses.

These dishes can be worked up for two very easily as you will have leftovers. The lentils will happily sit in the fridge for another couple of days. They can be strewn over a salad or eaten on a crostini with crisp streaky bacon. The beans are so moreish that you might be tempted to come down in the middle of the night in your nightie, sit on the stairs like Nigella and polish them off.

I love corned beef. At the risk of coming across as a right old snob I'm talking, of course, about the real thing. If you're reading this in the real capital, spiced beef would be a wonderful substitution. The hipsters can use pastrami as a very worthy swap. The pappardelle is ready in literally minutes, perfect for a fast solo dinner.

My go-to fish is hake if I'm looking for a white fish but you can happily substitute cod, ling, plaice, pollock, haddock or even whiting. As ever, the cooking times will vary depending on the thickness of the fish. The English mustard packs a punch and goes wonderfully with the earthy lentils. Eat with floury potatoes.

I'm a massive fan of a big bacon chop. I'm not talking about a wimpy, flaccid cut off the loin, but a regal praetorian guard of a chop heralding 'Time for Dinner'. There is a deep, resonant bacony flavour to this meat than would stir the Irish in us. Before you know it you'll be on your feet, at attention, singing 'Amhrán na bhFiann'.

PAPARDELLE WITH CORNED BEEF, CABBAGE AND COOLEA

SERVES 1

80g cooked corned beef, thinly sliced

50g butter

1 tsp horseradish sauce

a drizzle of maple syrup

125g pappardelle

2 Savoy cabbage leaves, shredded

a grating of Coolea cheese or your favourite Cheddar

1 small red apple, cut into batons

Put the corned beef, butter, horseradish, maple syrup and some salt and pepper in a bowl.

Cook the pasta as per the packet instructions but after 2 minutes, add the cabbage.

When the pasta is cooked, drain it, keeping 1 tablespoon of cooking water to add to the bowl with the corned beef.

Turn everything together with tongs, then put in a warm bowl with the grated cheese and apple sprinkled on top to serve.

BAKED HAKE WITH ENGLISH MUSTARD AND THYME BUTTER

SERVES 1

1 x 400g tin of cooked lentils

1 garlic clove, finely crushed

2 tbsp olive oil

1 tbsp balsamic vinegar

1 tsp honey

1 x 160g hake fillet, skinned and boned

FOR THE BUTTER:

50g butter, softened

1 tsp prepared English mustard

½ tsp fresh thyme leaves

Preheat the oven to 185°C.

Put the lentils in a bowl with 2 tablespoons of the liquid from the tin. Add the garlic, oil, balsamic vinegar, honey and seasoning.

Put as many lentils as you feel like eating in a small baking dish and sit the hake on top.

Mix the butter with the mustard and thyme, then smear it over the hake. Season and bake in the oven for 12–15 minutes, depending on the thickness of the fish.

Transfer to a warmed wide, shallow bowl to serve.

GRILLED BACON CHOP WITH PARMESAN CREAMED CANNELLINI BEANS

SERVES 1

2 tbsp sunflower oil

1 x 220g bacon or pork chop on the bone

150ml cream

½ chicken stock cube

50g Parmesan cheese, grated

1 x 400g tin of cannellini or butter beans

a squeeze of lemon

kale or other greens

Preheat the oven to 185°C.

Heat the oil in an ovenproof frying pan over a medium-high heat until it's gently smoking. Carefully lower the chop into the pan and colour on one side for 2 minutes.

Turn the chop over, then put the pan in the oven for 15 minutes or so, depending on the thickness of the chop. If you don't have an ovenproof frying pan, just transfer the chop to a baking tray. Remove the pan from the oven, cover with foil and allow the chop to rest for a few minutes.

While the chop is cooking, bring the cream to a gentle simmer in a medium-sized saucepan. It has a tendency to boil over, so keep a watchful eye on it. Crumble in the stock cube and add the grated Parmesan. Whisk them through, then add the beans, lemon juice and seasoning. Warm the beans through gently.

I served this with kale simply cooked in a covered pan with half a cup of water and a hint of butter and seasoning.

Serve the chop with the beans and greens but don't forget the bacony juices in the pan — pour them over everything.

Irish cheese

I usually write these articles early in the morning before anyone awakes. I relish the quietness of the house. In summer I bounce out of bed but on these darker mornings I have to force myself up, my body creaking in a way it never used to.

No matter how quiet I am, the cat wakes up, looking for food. She's permanently ravenous. She yowls incessantly until she's fed. We have the hungriest feline in Ireland. She roughly nudges my hand away to get at the food, as desperate for attention as Donald Trump bullying his way to the front for a photo op.

I'm organised from the night before for the school lunches. All the snacks are lined up like soldiers. I finish the lunches before the girls get up although I've recently been informed via her mother that the youngest doesn't like wraps anymore. This means there are now about four things that she will actually eat. Frustrating doesn't even begin to describe it. I know I'm not alone. People mistakenly think children of chefs appreciate food like pampered gourmets. This is not the case. They devour chicken goujons but quietly push away something I've thoughtfully cooked for them on a dark, cold night after a long day at school.

I often wonder, when they are in college eating beans on toast night after night, will they be longing for the weekend at home and finally relish one of my big dinners? Then I stop and think of how empty the house will be without them and I give them breakfast. A dutiful tea is brought to my wife as she gets ready for work. There is a scurry for books and bits of uniforms. Skye, our Nervous Nellie of a Westie, is always underfoot, waiting for scraps as I squeeze in a few lines of my article and wait for the house to quieten. If I'm not on the school run I have some hope of getting the piece finished before my day starts properly.

Today I'm writing about Irish cheese crafted by passionate, committed people. Choose your favourites. As always, the cook is boss. The first recipe is an autumnal riff on the classic Basque piperade. The eggs and cheese meld together like a dream. I know not everyone loves celery, but for those who do, this gnocchi is a sophisticated dish that makes a star out of the unloved vegetable. These decadent little pots are simple to make and perfect for a dinner party. Just make sure you use a decent, crumbly mature Cheddar.

PIPERADE OF LEEK, MUSHROOMS AND COOLEA CHEESE

SERVES 3

1 tbsp raisins

1 medium leek

150g mixed mushrooms or chestnut mushrooms

50g butter

a splash of water

a few fresh thyme leaves

6 eggs, beaten

75g Coolea cheese, grated

Soak the raisins in a bowl of just-boiled water for 15 minutes to plump them up, then drain.

Trim the leek, cut it into thin rounds, wash and drain.

Trim and cut the mushrooms into an even size, making sure to brush off any soil as you prepare them.

Melt the butter in a wok or a wide-bottomed non-stick pan over a low heat. When the butter starts to foam, add the leek, water and thyme, then cook for 5 minutes or so.

When the leek starts to soften, add the mushrooms and increase the heat to medium. Cook for a further 2–3 minutes, then add the eggs. Move them around in the pan to amalgamate with the leek and mushrooms. I use a rubber spatula for best results, scraping the bottom of the pan every 30 seconds or so. Add the drained raisins and season.

When the eggs are nearly set but still soft, add the cheese. Fold everything together, season and serve immediately on warm plates. The eggs should still be soft and silky for best results.

GNOCCHI WITH VICHY CELERY, BLACK GRAPES, CROZIER BLUE AND CANDIED WALNUTS

SERVES 4

1 x 500g packet of gnocchi

150g Crozier Blue or another ripe blue cheese

100g seedless black grapes, halved

FOR THE CELERY:

1 small head of celery, peeled and cut into 3cm pieces

200ml water

50g butter

a few sprigs of fresh sage

juice of ½ lemon

FOR THE CANDIED WALNUTS:

50g walnuts

25g butter

1 level tbsp golden brown caster sugar

½ tsp mixed or allspice

pinch of salt

Put the celery in a pan with a tight-fitting lid along with the water, butter, sage and some salt and pepper. Cover and cook on a high heat until the water has almost evaporated and the celery is tender. This should take no more than 10 minutes. You will have to keep an eye on the pan towards the end so that it doesn't boil dry. Add the lemon juice and keep warm.

Meanwhile, put all the ingredients for the candied walnuts in a frying pan and cook over a medium heat, stirring carefully, for 3–4 minutes, until everything melts together, toasts, than finally glazes. Transfer to a piece of non-stick baking paper to cool.

Cook the gnocchi as per the packet instructions and drain.

To serve, intersperse the gnocchi and the celery on warm plates. Crumble the cheese on top along with the candied walnuts, grapes and celery pan juices.

MATURE CHEDDAR POTS WITH MALT VINEGAR RAISINS
SERVES 4

100g mature Cheddar cheese, grated

1 large egg

150ml cream

150ml milk

a small grating of fresh nutmeg (optional)

FOR THE RAISINS:

50g raisins

150ml water

2 tbsp malt vinegar

1 tbsp Demerara or dark brown sugar

½ tsp mixed spice

Preheat the oven to 120°C.

Put the cheese, egg, cream, milk, nutmeg (if using) and some salt and ground white pepper in a jug and blitz with a hand blender. There will be a few cheesy lumps but they will melt while cooking. Divide the mixture evenly among four ramekins and put them in a small, deep(ish) roasting tin. Pour boiling water in the tin until it comes halfway up the sides of the ramekins.

Bake in the oven for 40–45 minutes. There needs to be a slight wobble in the centre of the custards, then they are ready.

Remove the ramekins from the tin, allow to cool then chill. They will be perfect for up to 48 hours.

For the raisins, put all the ingredients in a small saucepan and reduce slowly until there is only about 2 tablespoons of liquid left. Allow to cool, then chill in the fridge.

When serving, let the custards sit in the kitchen for a half hour or so to come to room temperature. Serve with the raisins on top and toast on the side.

I am a
self-confessed Luddite

08 OCTOBER 2022

One of my favourite kitchen gadgets is my 25-year-old rice cooker. It has two settings: cook and warm. This is my kind of machine, for I am a self-confessed Luddite.

Of course, you don't need a rice cooker to make a satisfying rice dish. Rice is easy and affordable. All you need is to give it a chance. We used to be potato people and that is not a slight. As a nation we have embraced pasta but I still look in the window of our local Chinese and spot chips on virtually every table. Call me elitist for judging but I don't care. If you have rice you don't need chips and the ubiquitous school lunchtime three in one is a curse for our children. I know all about struggling with weight and this is the worst possible start.

Rice graciously absorbs whatever is introduced to it and that is its beauty. It is the ultimate blank canvas. It also evokes a sense of mystery, conjuring up far-flung places, spice, discovery and ancient traditions. Rice makes the potato seem like a newly arrived upstart by comparison.

I'm making three different pilafs today, all using basmati rice. Always rinse rice under cold water to eliminate excess starch, resulting in fluffy, even grains packed full of the flavours you immerse them with. Then the method is to use just enough liquid so that by the time the rice is cooked the liquid has been absorbed, thus maximising the flavour. I start the rice on the hob and continue to cook it in the oven for an all-round even heat. In the rice cooker, sauté the initial ingredients as if in a pot, then continue on as normal.

The first two are standalone dishes but the caramelised onion rice would be content beside roast lamb or chicken, in which case mint or coriander yogurt would be the perfect partner.

This duck rice is almost creamy. The pineapple and chilli lift it in a deliciously interesting way. Coronation chicken is full of gentle flavours that will warm up the coldest of nights. Cinnamon and rice are magical bedfellows. The caramelised onions give heft and a depth of flavour.

DUCK AND COCONUT RICE WITH PINEAPPLE AND CHILLI DRESSING

SERVES 4

2 tbsp duck fat from the confit legs

1 medium onion, finely diced

2 garlic cloves, sliced

1 tbsp spice bag seasoning

2 confit duck legs, skin, fat and bone removed and the meat cut into 1cm pieces

300g basmati rice, rinsed

50g desiccated coconut, toasted

1 x 400ml tin of light coconut milk

400ml chicken stock

FOR THE DRESSING:

1 x 567g tin of pineapple chunks or slices

1 fresh red chilli, deseeded and finely diced

2 tbsp toasted sesame oil

1 small bunch of fresh coriander, chopped

Preheat the oven to 185°C.

Remove the residual fat from the duck legs and put it in a large ovenproof saucepan over a medium heat. Add the onion and garlic and cook gently for 5 minutes or so. Add the spice bag seasoning and continue to cook for another 5 minutes, until the onion is soft and translucent.

Add the duck meat, rice and desiccated coconut and turn everything together, then add the coconut milk and the stock. Bring to a simmer, then cover with a lid and bake in the oven for 20 minutes.

Remove the pan from the oven and fork through the rice to make it fluffy. Drape a clean kitchen towel over the top of the pan, then replace the lid to form a seal. The cloth will absorb any excess moisture.

Meanwhile, drain the pineapple juice from the tin into a small saucepan. Add the chilli and simmer until reduced by half. Allow to cool, then whisk in the sesame oil.If the pineapple is in slices, cut it into chunks. Add the pineapple to the liquid along with the coriander.

Serve the rice with the pineapple on top so the juice seeps into the rice to counteract its richness.

CORONATION CHICKEN RICE WITH LIME AND CORIANDER CREAM

SERVES 4

50g butter

1 large red onion, thinly sliced

2 garlic cloves, sliced

2 chicken breasts (350g), diced

2 tbsp curry powder

1 x 400g tin of chickpeas, drained and rinsed

300g basmati rice, rinsed

100g dried apricots, sliced

1 fresh red chilli, deseeded and halved lengthways

800ml chicken stock

a pinch of caster sugar

shop-bought crispy onions (optional)

FOR THE CREAM:

1 x 35g bunch of fresh coriander, roughly chopped (including the stalks)

250ml cream

2 limes – zest of 1 and juice of both

Preheat the oven to 185°C.

Melt the butter in an ovenproof saucepan over a gentle heat. When the butter starts to foam, add the onion and garlic and cook gently for 5 minutes. Add the chicken and curry powder and cook for a further 5 minutes, until the onion softens and the chicken colours a little.

Add the chickpeas, rice, apricots, chilli and seasoning, then stir together. Add the stock and sugar. Bring to a simmer, then cover the pan, transfer it to the oven and cook for 20 minutes.

Remove the pan from the oven and fork through the rice, then drape a clean tea towel over the pan and replace the lid to form a seal. The cloth will absorb any excess moisture.

To make the lime and coriander cream, quickly pulse all the ingredients together with a pinch of salt, then chill. Be careful – if you blend too much it will get too thick.

Serve the rice in warm bowls with the cream drizzled over the top along with a scattering of crispy onions (if using).

CARAMELISED ONION RICE WITH CINNAMON AND PINE NUTS

SERVES 4

50g butter

2–3 large onions (700g), sliced

2 bay leaves (fresh if possible)

2 tbsp water

2 strips of orange peel

1 tsp ground cinnamon or 2 cinnamon sticks

a drizzle of honey

300g basmati rice, rinsed

700ml chicken or vegetable stock

60g pine nuts, toasted

chopped fresh flat-leaf parsley

Preheat the oven to 185°C.

Melt the butter in a heavy-based casserole over a gentle heat. When the butter starts to foam, add the onions, bay leaves and water. Cover and cook gently for 15 minutes, until the onions collapse.

Remove the lid, turn up the heat to medium-high and start to caramelise the onions. Stir the onions every 2 minutes or so, being careful to scrape any residue from the bottom of the casserole, until the onions turn golden brown.

Add the orange peel, cinnamon, honey, rice and seasoning, then turn everything together. Add the stock and bring to a simmer, then cover the casserole with a lid and transfer to the oven to cook for 20 minutes.

Remove the casserole from the oven and fork through the rice, then drape a clean tea towel over it and replace the lid to form a seal. The cloth will absorb any excess moisture.

Serve with the pine nuts and parsley scattered over the top.

Cabbage just makes me happy

15 OCTOBER 2022

Our cookery school dining room is not only for the students to relax and eat their culinary triumphs but also for private events and usually I am the cook. I enjoy the more sedate pace than the restaurant and I can interact with people and have a bit of fun as I'm cooking. It's a dinner party where I don't have to do the washing up.

Last week I cooked for a double birthday. The family is originally from Dungarvan but most of them are now scattered around the country and the world. Their mother was a great customer and they've kept the tradition of coming to us for family events. This loyalty is what keeps our restaurant and others going through thick and thin.

Drinks are poured in the kitchen while everyone greets each other. They marvel at how the younger generation has shot up in these last few very strange years. The room starts off slowly and as the evening grows it bubbles with laughter and stories. A grateful normality is back.

That day we received a delivery of our first pumpkins of the season from our local grower, a bag of cavolo nero beside it, so with dinner I put them together along the table. The pumpkin, peeled and roasted with cinnamon and thyme. The kale, torn and nestled among it, anointed with a pickled walnut dressing.

This is my last week writing for you. It's been three years and over 450 recipes. I've enjoyed pouring my heart out and hopefully I have given you some useful dishes and the odd giggle along the way. It's been cathartic, sometimes challenging but always enjoyable, especially when I got lovely feedback. My last week expresses my love for the humble brassica. You can keep your baby vegetables and microleaves. Cabbage just makes me happy.

This steak dish is fresh, vivid and simple to make. The hoisin gives it great depth of flavour. Eat it with simple steamed rice. I'm on a mission for people to embrace Brussels sprouts. It might sound eccentric but sprouts and smoked salmon go together very well.

Look out for kohlrabi, it's a wonderful, much-underused vegetable. Try your local Polish shop. I urge you make this crisp, fresh winter salad.

PEPPERED HOISIN STEAK WITH PAK CHOI, SPRING ONIONS, CHILLI AND GINGER

SERVES 2

1 x 250g rib-eye steak

a drizzle of sunflower oil

2 tbsp hoisin sauce

2 pak choi, quartered

1 bunch of spring onions, trimmed

1 garlic clove, sliced

2cm piece of ginger, peeled and finely chopped

1 fresh red chilli, deseeded and quartered lengthways

1 tbsp toasted sesame oil

a knob of butter

150ml water

1 tbsp sesame seeds, toasted

a sprinkle of shop-bought crispy onions

Season the steak with salt and lots of black pepper. Heat the sunflower oil in a pan over a high heat and allow it to smoke gently before adding the steak. I like to cook my steak medium-rare so I'll usually give it 3 minutes on one side and 2 minutes on the other, but this entirely depends on the thickness of the steak.

Remove the steak from the pan, put it on a plate to rest, cover in foil and keep warm. Put the hoisin sauce in a medium-sized bowl to await the steak.

Meanwhile, put the pak choi, spring onions, garlic, ginger, chilli, sesame oil, butter and water in a small saucepan with a pinch of salt. Cover and cook on a high heat for 3 minutes or so, until the pak choi is tender and the water has reduced down to a buttery emulsion.

Pour any meat juices into the hoisin sauce. Cut the steak into 1cm-thick slices then add to the sauce, turning to coat.

To serve, alternate the steak and vegetables in warm bowls, then scatter over the toasted sesame seeds and crispy onions (if using). Eat with simple boiled rice.

FARFALLE WITH BRUSSELS SPROUTS, SMOKED SALMON AND CRÈME FRAÎCHE

SERVES 3

100g smoked salmon, roughly chopped

3 tbsp crème fraîche

2 tbsp chopped fresh dill

1 tsp wholegrain mustard or horseradish sauce

a squeeze of lemon

300g farfalle or penne

6 large Brussels sprouts, thinly sliced

4 tbsp breadcrumbs toasted in a little butter

Put the smoked salmon, sour cream, dill, wholegrain mustard, lemon and some seasoning in a large bowl.

Cook the pasta as per the packet instructions, adding the sprouts for the last minute.

Drain the pasta and sprouts thoroughly, then add to the bowl with the smoked salmon mixture, tossing to coat.

Serve straightaway in warm bowls with the toasted breadcrumbs scattered on top.

WINTER VEGETABLE SALAD WITH CHERVIL AND HORSERADISH DRESSING
SERVES 4

1 large kohlrabi, peeled and very thinly sliced (a mandolin is perfect for this)
1 fennel bulb, very thinly sliced
a handful of cavolo nero or baby spinach, torn into pieces
1 red apple, cored, halved and thinly sliced
a handful of salted almonds

FOR THE DRESSING:
150ml apple juice
80ml rapeseed oil
50g chervil
2cm piece of ginger, peeled and chopped
1 tbsp horseradish sauce

Put all the vegetables and the apple in a bowl.

Blend all the ingredients for the dressing together, then add to the bowl and turn everything together.

Serve in bowls or on a platter with salted almonds scattered over the top.

Index

PAUL FLYNN

PAUL FLYNN

chipotle
smoked chipotle sloppy Joes 240

chives
buttered asparagus with crushed egg
and chive dressing 337
jerk potatoes with butterhead lettuce,
crispy bacon, sour cream and
chives 367

chorizo
baked eggs with chorizo, cream and
Parmesan 8
baked monkfish with smoky tomatoes,
rosemary and chorizo 387
baked pasta with chorizo and Parmesan
55
caldo verde 308
chicken and chorizo Bomba 413
chorizo and red onion hash 235
chorizo, chicken and butter bean bake 18
chorizo, orange and almond stuffing 35
crunchy potato, beef and chorizo
hotpot 516
orecchiette with chorizo, little tomatoes,
cream and Parmesan 74
smoky piperade with chorizo 336

chowder
chowder smokies 533
creamy corn, carrot and mango
chowder 663
roast chicken, butter bean and wild
garlic chowder 544
seafood chowder 78

chutney
a very easy chutney 215
baked Cooleeney Camembert with
crimson grape chutney 495
goat cheese and chutney pie 166
pork and spiced onion Wellington with
khubani chutney 664–5

cider
baked Cavanbert with cider-roasted
turnip and Black Forest ham 476
chicken in cider cream 592
chicken, root vegetable and barley stew
with cider and ginger cream 457
Christmas ham casserole with winter
greens and cider 499
cider-glazed turnip with Crozier Blue
and chard 22
cider roast turkey 36
one-pot chicken with cider 201

Cidona
steamed mussels with Cidona, curry
spice and crème fraîche 165

cinnamon
apple cinnamon butter 32
baked sausages with cinnamon onions
and crispy croissants 442

caramelised onion rice with cinnamon
and pine nuts 679
maple-drizzled bacon ribs with sour
cream and apple cinnamon sauce 241
parsnips with cinnamon and ginger
ale 493

clams
gochujang chicken drumsticks with
sweet and sour clams 406
mussels and clams in wild garlic broth 90

clementines
Goatsbridge trout, cucumber and
butterhead with clementine
dressing 487
mussels with clementine and ginger
butter and parsley crunch 251

coconut
chilli and coconut masala potatoes 587
curried sweetcorn and coconut soup 244
duck and coconut rice with pineapple
and chilli dressing 677
fragrant pork meatballs with coconut,
cucumber and cashews 381
meatballs with chilli, ginger and
coconut 47
noodles with butternut squash, sesame
and coconut 206
poached seafood in ginger and coconut
broth 433
spiced ling with fragrant coconut rice
and spring onions 339

cod
a seafood roast 131
baked cod with butter beans, olives and
pimenton 593
baked cod with spiced pepper rice and
saffron cream dressing 425
cod brandade with roasted fennel and
olives 396
creamy cod brandade on toast 136

Coolea cheese
field mushrooms and black and white
pudding with Coolea and kale
pesto 430
pappardelle with corned beef, cabbage
and Coolea cheese 669
Pedro Ximénez, caramelised onion and
Coolea quiche 146–7
piperade of leek, mushrooms and
Coolea cheese 673
spaghetti with cavolo nero, tomatoes,
Coolea and salami 426

coriander
coronation chicken rice with lime and
coriander cream 678
glazed carrots with coriander oil and
toasted almond yogurt 359
spiced tomato tart with hummus and
coriander 171

courgettes
baked whole sea bass on holiday
ratatouille 637
chicken schnitzel with buttered
courgettes, red onion and thyme 157
conchiglie primavera with goat cheese 607
courgette, almond and Gorgonzola
tart 596
courgette, spinach and brown bread
salad 661
Provençal vegetable crumble 333
roast potatoes with courgettes, lemon
and pine nuts 566
roast salmon with courgette and butter
bean salad 415
roasted courgette, rocket and Parma
ham salad 95
roasted courgettes with burrata, umami
dressing and Serrano ham 193
roasted spring greens and crunchy
sourdough with goat cheese
dressing 545
roasted summer greens with creamy
polenta and charcuterie 601
summer leaves and courgette with
gazpacho dressing and Manchego 141

couscous
lamb chops with ras el hanout tomatoes,
couscous and elderflower yogurt 421
roast lamb with prune, pepper and
saffron couscous 81
warm couscous, cauliflower and almond
salad 271

crab
a simple crab salad 427
buttered tomatoes on toast with
elderflower and crab 162
crab claws with orange, pomegranate
and rosemary butter 39
crab vol au vents with apple and
wasabi 264
fluffy crab and avocado flatbreads 120
old-fashioned broccoli with pine nuts
and crab and saffron butter 372
pea and bacon frittata with crab crème
fraîche 407
summer crab and watermelon cake 616

cranberries
parsnip, sesame and red onion cake
with minted cranberry yogurt 258–9
sage, onion and cranberry pudding 492
turkey and ham Yorkies with cranberry
and horseradish cream 500
whipped goat cheese and cranberry
pots 488

cream
a winter soup with horseradish cream 513
baked cod with spiced pepper rice and
saffron cream dressing 425
baked eggs with chorizo, cream and
Parmesan 8

gazpacho

a green and good gazpacho 409

crunchy two-bean salad with a sort-of gazpacho dressing 635

summer leaves and courgette with gazpacho dressing and Manchego 141

watermelon gazpacho 183

ginger

baked hake with Savoy cabbage and pickled ginger butter 543

chicken, root vegetable and barley stew with cider and ginger cream 457

confit duck with sweet potatoes, apples and ginger 13

grilled gammon with gingery cabbage and sweet sesame roasties 250

hake with lentils, baby spinach, ginger and chilli 504

meatballs with chilli, ginger and coconut 47

mussels with clementine and ginger butter and parsley crunch 251

peppered hoisin steak with pak choi, spring onions, chilli and ginger 681

poached seafood in ginger and coconut broth 433

skinny salmon with soy, ginger and cabbage 132

soy-steamed hake with gingered vegetables 574

steamed sea trout with peppered cabbage, soy, garlic and ginger 270

teriyaki sea trout buns with cucumber and ginger pickle 561

ginger ale

parsnips with cinnamon and ginger ale 493

gnocchi

fried gnocchi with cacio e pepe sauce 449

gnocchi with crispy chicken, peppers and 'nduja 505

gnocchi with frazzled salami, halloumi and chopped rocket 540

gnocchi with Vichy celery, black grapes, Crozier Blue and candied walnuts 674

ragù of lamb and sticky onions with gnocchi 48

roasted asparagus with buttered gnocchi and Parmesan 178

sausage, gnocchi and red onion roast 56

goat cheese

bitter leaves with whipped goat cheese and Burren balsamic vinegar 660

butter beans in roasted pepper and goat cheese sauce 567

caponata bread salad with goat cheese mousse 110–11

cheat's ravioli with goat cheese, sage, lemon and Parmesan 75

conchiglie primavera with goat cheese 607

fig and goat cheese galette 213

goat cheese and chutney pie 166

goat cheese and roasted garlic on toasted sourdough 211

goat cheese and tapenade with hot spiced chickpeas 389

goat cheese, thyme and black grape tart 624–5

penne with roasted butternut squash, goat cheese and hazelnuts 450

roasted spring greens and crunchy sourdough with goat cheese dressing 545

rösti with crispy bacon, honey and goat cheese 105

salad of goat cheese, French beans and peaches 182

spring salad with goat cheese and mint 89

sticky onion, fig and goat cheese croissants 284

sweet potato and spinach with spiced pumpkin seeds and goat cheese 197

whipped goat cheese and cranberry pots 488

gochujang

gochujang chicken drumsticks with peanuts 621

gochujang chicken drumsticks with sweet and sour clams 406

Gorgonzola

beetroot, Beaujolais and red onion stew with Gorgonzola and walnuts 435

courgette, almond and Gorgonzola tart 596

Medjool date, Gorgonzola and prosciutto poppers 255

pork chops with roasted pears, sage, red onions and Gorgonzola 98

warm pork chop, field mushroom and Gorgonzola salad 326

grapes

a very easy chutney 215

baked Cooleeney Camembert with crimson grape chutney 495

glorious greens with Velvet Cloud yogurt, nuts and grapes 319

gnocchi with Vichy celery, black grapes, Crozier Blue and candied walnuts 674

goat cheese, thyme and black grape tart 624–5

grape and Parmesan risotto 12

quail with bulgur wheat, almonds and grapes 445

smoked chicken, grape and Crozier Blue salad 79

tigelle with mostarda grapes, burrata and salumi 548–9

gratins

Brussels sprout gratin 37

gratin of parsnip, pear and mortadella 459

gratin of smoked mackerel and turnip with spiced pickled cucumber 77

gravy

potatoes stump, sausages and apple gravy 218

green beans

four seasons green beans with crispy duck 163

gremolata

soft polenta with asparagus and maple gremolata 550

Gruyère

French onion pappardelle with Gruyère pangrattato 293

gurnard

gurnard with sweet and sour onions and pine nuts 612

H

haddock

smoked haddock leek and smoked haddock lasagne with curry spices 475

smoked haddock with new potato, egg and spring onion salad 128

smoked haddock, leek and potato bake 94

hake

a seafood roast 131

baked hake with cauliflower and harissa orange dressing 307

baked hake with English mustard and thyme butter 670

baked hake with orzo, garlic cream and roasted pepper and olive dressing 370–1

baked hake with saffron, chickpeas and rainbow tomatoes 604

baked hake with Savoy cabbage and pickled ginger butter 543

crushed hake, butter beans and garlic 582

hake chops with chickpeas and wild garlic butter sauce 327

hake with asparagus, new potatoes and lemon 190

hake with garlic cream and black pudding 133

hake with lentils, baby spinach, ginger and chilli 504

soy-steamed hake with gingered vegetables 574

spiced lamb shoulder with roast
vegetable bulgur wheat and tahini
dressing 312–13

langoustines
poached seafood in ginger and coconut
broth 433

lasagne
leek and smoked haddock lasagne with
curry spices 475

leeks
baked leek, pea and Cheddar risotto 169
bucatini with leek, mortadella and
Pecorino Romano 609
chicken, leek and bacon soup 91
crispy chicken legs and potatoes with
leek fondue 454
grilled chicken with roasted spring
vegetables, lemon and chilli 321
leek and smoked haddock lasagne with
curry spices 475
leek fondue 323
maple smoked bacon with roasted
apples, leeks and wholegrain
mustard 214
piperade of leek, mushrooms and
Coolea cheese 673
roasted summer greens with creamy
polenta and charcuterie 601
smoked haddock, leek and potato bake 94
warm salad of Jerusalem artichokes,
leeks and Parma ham 23

lemon
cheat's ravioli with goat cheese, sage,
lemon and Parmesan 75
confit pork chops with garlic, fennel and
lemon 453
crusted summer greens with lemon,
artichokes and salami 137
grilled chicken with roasted spring
vegetables, lemon and chilli 321
hake with asparagus, new potatoes and
lemon 190
orzo salad with parsley, chilli and
lemon 608
orzo with mushrooms, spinach, lemon
and Parmesan 515
roast potatoes with courgettes, lemon
and pine nuts 566
whole monkfish with rosemary salt and
charred lemons 422

lemon sole
baked lemon sole with fennel, orange
and chilli 139

lentils
bruschetta of lentils, balsamic cream
and salami 210
Galician porky bits and lentils 521
hake with lentils, baby spinach, ginger
and chilli 504

lentil vinaigrette 61
spiced cabbage, borlotti bean and lentil
soup 431

lime
coronation chicken rice with lime and
coriander cream 678
lime grilled plaice with jalapeño, lime
and parsley crust 429
little ears with peas, lime and
Parmesan 129

ling
ling with chickpeas, orange and ras el
hanout 177
spiced ling with fragrant coconut rice
and spring onions 339

Little Gems
grilled mackerel with peas and Little
Gem 86
Little Gems with ajo blanco, grapes and
toasted sourdough 349
Little Gems with baby potatoes and
devilled egg and spring onion
dressing 414
oxtail with star anise, Little Gems and
sesame 126–7
plaice with new potatoes, Little Gems
and sea beet butter 555

lobster
grilled lobster with Ibérico butter and
sea beet 405
lobster with ajo blanco, cucumber and
new potatoes 615

M
mackerel
baked smoked mackerel omelette with
melted Cheddar 234
fresh mackerel with new potatoes, sage
and bacon 355
gratin of smoked mackerel and turnip
with spiced pickled cucumber 77
grilled mackerel with orange fattoush
605
grilled mackerel with peas and Little
Gem 86
mackerel tataki 410
mackerel with new potatoes, peppers
and harissa dressing 634
smoked mackerel and cabbage frittata
477
smoked mackerel bubble and squeak
with sweet mustard dressing 523
smoked mackerel niçoise with butter
bean aioli 375
smoked mackerel, beetroot and dill
tart 335
smoked potatoes with smoked mackerel
butter and cornichons 423

malt vinegar
malt vinegar chicken with mushrooms,
thyme and smoked bacon 205
mature Cheddar pots with malt vinegar
raisins 675

Manchego
summer leaves and courgette with
gazpacho dressing and Manchego 141

mangos
baked rice and spiced frizzled chicken
with chickpeas and mango yogurt 219
creamy corn, carrot and mango
chowder 663
mango and cucumber tarka 341
pulled lamb vindaloo with mango
yogurt 472

maple
maple-drizzled bacon ribs with sour
cream and apple cinnamon
sauce 241
maple smoked bacon with roasted
apples, leeks and wholegrain
mustard 214
roast kohlrabi with maple syrup and
sesame 288
soft polenta with asparagus and maple
gremolata 550

mascarpone
baked aubergines with harissa, orange
and mascarpone 145
mascarpone mousse with grape
compote and frosted almonds 300

mayonnaise
a simple crab salad 427

meatballs
baked meatball casserole with sweet
paprika beans 363
fragrant pork meatballs with coconut,
cucumber and cashews 381
meatballs with chilli, ginger and
coconut 47
pork polpette al latte 581
rigatoni with sausage meatballs, pepper
cream and thyme 399

milk
field mushrooms and barley with
smoked bacon milk 226
pork polpette al latte 581

mint
lamb chops with minty pea and mustard
mash 189
lamb souvlaki with roasted peppers and
minted yogurt 181
parsnip, sesame and red onion cake
with minted cranberry yogurt 258–9
spring salad with goat cheese and
mint 89

monkfish
a seafood roast 131
baked monkfish with smoky tomatoes, rosemary and chorizo 387
fried monkfish with curried sweet potato broth 585
poached seafood in ginger and coconut broth 433
roasted monkfish ribollita 649
whole monkfish with rosemary salt and charred lemons 422

mortadella
bucatini with leek, mortadella and Pecorino Romano 609
field mushroom, mortadella and Cambozola buns 655
gratin of parsnip, pear and mortadella 459
rigatoni with cabbage, sage and mortadella 217

mozzarella
baked mozzarella in salami picante sauce 597
heirloom tomatoes with buffalo mozzarella and elderflower vinaigrette 400
mozzarella with chickpeas, tomatoes and basil 119
mozzarella with fennel, olives and raisins 633
mozzarella with Parma ham, sticky aubergine and red pepper 73
roasted asparagus and fennel salad with Toonsbridge mozzarella 93
sticky shallots with mozzarella and Parma ham 170

muesli
Bircher muesli with hot blueberries 107

mushrooms
baked duck with barley, sherry and field mushrooms 198
celeriac with soused mushrooms, smoked bacon, cream cheese and apple 455
chestnut mushroom carbonara 503
chestnut mushroom, parsnip and sherry soup 483
chicken with bacon, mushrooms and sour cream 70
field mushroom, mortadella and Cambozola buns 655
field mushrooms and barley with smoked bacon milk 226
field mushrooms and black and white pudding with Coolea and kale pesto 430
frivole, mushroom and barley stew with Cáis na Tíre 289
malt vinegar chicken with mushrooms, thyme and smoked bacon 205
mushroom béarnaise tart 654

mushroom, roasted bread and spinach salad 60
orzo with mushrooms, spinach, lemon and Parmesan 515
piperade of leek, mushrooms and Coolea cheese 673
pork steak and friends 311
pot roast bacon with mushrooms and thyme cream 653
pot roast lamb with balsamic and porcini mushrooms 519
warm pork chop, field mushroom and Gorgonzola salad 326

mussels
a seafood roast 131
mussels and clams in wild garlic broth 90
mussels with clementine and ginger butter and parsley crunch 251
mussels with curried pea cream and crunchy breadcrumbs 376-7
mussels with fennel and Pernod 28
poached seafood in ginger and coconut broth 433
steamed mussels with Cidona, curry spice and crème fraîche 165

mustard
baked hake with English mustard and thyme butter 670
lamb chops with minty pea and mustard mash 189
maple smoked bacon with roasted apples, leeks and wholegrain mustard 214
roast rack of bacon with creamed cabbage, mustard and apple 114

N
'nduja
barbecued lamb shoulder with tomato and 'nduja sauce 330-1
gnocchi with crispy chicken, peppers and 'nduja 505
red pepper and 'nduja puffs 623
stuffed aubergines with fennel, quinoa and 'nduja 393

noodles
buckwheat noodles with sticky aubergine and sambal olek 620
chicken noodle salad with peanut and cucumber sauce 417
noodles with butternut squash, sesame and coconut 206
roast chicken noodle soup 243

nutmeg
crushed sprouts with nutmeg brown butter 493

O
oats
Bircher muesli with hot blueberries 107
Crozier Blue, roasted plum, fig and oat crumble 469

oil
glazed carrots with coriander oil and toasted almond yogurt 359

olives
baked cod with butter beans, olives and pimenton 593
baked hake with orzo, garlic cream and roasted pepper and olive dressing 370-1
cod brandade with roasted fennel and olives 396
goat cheese and tapenade with hot spiced chickpeas 389
halloumi with olives, tomatoes and cardamom 508
lamb shanks with fennel, olives and feta 539
mozzarella with fennel, olives and raisins 633
peperonata puff pie with feta and olives 391
pointed peppers with olive crumble and sriracha crème fraîche 554

onions
baked sausages with cinnamon onions and crispy croissants 442
baked whole sea bass on holiday ratatouille 637
beetroot, Beaujolais and red onion stew with Gorgonzola and walnuts 435
caramelised onion and aubergine pilaf 509
caramelised onion rice with cinnamon and pine nuts 679
cheese, onion and wild garlic frittata 116
chicken schnitzel with buttered courgettes, red onion and thyme 157
chorizo and red onion hash 235
cream of white onion, Cheddar and apple soup 99
French onion pappardelle with Gruyère pangrattato 293
grilled lamb chop, caramelised onion, butter bean and feta bake 274
gurnard with sweet and sour onions and pine nuts 612
ham hock, cheese, onion and apple pie 199
lamb chops with sweet and sour onions and raisins 122
parsnip, sesame and red onion cake with minted cranberry yogurt 258-9
Pedro Ximénez, caramelised onion and Coolea quiche 146-7
pickled summer vegetables 630
pork and spiced onion Wellington with khubani chutney 664-5

spaghetti with garlic, chilli and chopped prawns 292
spaghetti with yellow pepper sauce 185

peaches
French bean, peach and toasted almond crumble 401
roasted peaches with za'atar-crusted halloumi 643
salad of goat cheese, French beans and peaches 182

peanuts
chicken noodle salad with peanut and cucumber sauce 417
gochujang chicken drumsticks with peanuts 621

pears
a special autumn salad 468
croissants with hot apples, pears, brown sugar and cream 10
gratin of parsnip, pear and mortadella 459
pork chops with roasted pears, sage, red onions and Gorgonzola 98

peas
a green and good gazpacho 409
bacon chops with petits pois à la Irlandaise 578
baked leek, pea and Cheddar risotto 169
black and white pudding with crushed pea mash 285
grilled mackerel with peas and Little Gem 86
lamb chops with minty pea and mustard mash 189
little ears with peas, lime and Parmesan 129
mussels with curried pea cream and crunchy breadcrumbs 376–7
pea and bacon frittata with crab crème fraîche 407
pea and poached salmon salad 647
pea, fennel and feta salad 558
prawns with curry cream, peas, cucumber and almonds 603
rigatoni with smoky pea cream and white pudding 158
spiced pea and avocado soup 52
warm steak salad with shallot, petits pois and Roquefort 599

Pecorino Romano
bucatini with leek, mortadella and Pecorino Romano 609

peperonata
peperonata 151
peperonata pie 480
peperonata puff pie with feta and olives 391

peppers
baked cod with spiced pepper rice and saffron cream dressing 425
baked hake with orzo, garlic cream and roasted pepper and olive dressing 370–1
baked whole sea bass on holiday ratatouille 637
butter beans in roasted pepper and goat cheese sauce 567
chicken with red pepper and smoky Parmesan cream 191
chopped roast chicken with aioli and red pepper and anchovy dressing 276–7
confit calamari with cheat's aioli, peppers, orange and saffron 378
escalivada 348
gnocchi with crispy chicken, peppers and 'nduja 505
lamb souvlaki with roasted peppers and minted yogurt 181
mackerel with new potatoes, peppers and harissa dressing 634
mozzarella with Parma ham, sticky aubergine and red pepper 73
peperonata 151
peperonata pie 480
peperonata puff pie with feta and olives 391
pointed peppers with olive crumble and sriracha crème fraîche 554
potato, Parmesan and red pepper cake 109
red pepper and 'nduja puffs 623
red pepper and butter bean soup with chicken butter toast 600
red pepper, piment d'espelette and brioche bake 611
rigatoni with sausage meatballs, pepper cream and thyme 399
roast lamb with prune, pepper and saffron couscous 81
roasted pepper and butter bean brandade with green sauce 650
roasted pepper, bread and orange salad 419
root vegetable feast with harissa and butter bean hummus 535
smoky piperade with chorizo 336
socca with piment d'espelette, peppers and anchovies 395
spaghetti with yellow pepper sauce 185
spiced red pepper, piment d'espelette and brioche bake 611
tear-and-share red pepper, red onion and feta scone 645

Pernod
baked salmon with warm red cabbage, fennel and Pernod crème fraîche 497
mussels with fennel and Pernod 28

pesto
field mushrooms and black and white pudding with Coolea and kale pesto 430
pork steak and friends 311

pickles
a fab and easy cucumber pickle 231
baked hake with Savoy cabbage and pickled ginger butter 543
carrot and cucumber pickle 143
gratin of smoked mackerel and turnip with spiced pickled cucumber 77
pickled summer vegetables 630
prawn satay with pickled cucumber 525
roast loin of bacon with pickled rhubarb and Highbank Orchard Syrup 317
smoked potatoes with smoked mackerel butter and cornichons 423
teriyaki sea trout buns with cucumber and ginger pickle 561

pies
apple roly poly pie 71
Bolognese hand pies with jalapeño cream 221
cauliflower korma, raisin and almond pie 222
cock-a-leekie pie 223
coq au Riesling pie 357
goat cheese and chutney pie 166
Greek-style chicken pie 479
ham hock, cheese, onion and apple pie 199
peperonata pie 480
peperonata puff pie with feta and olives 391

piment d'espelette
red pepper, piment d'espelette and brioche bake 611
socca with piment d'espelette, peppers and anchovies 395
spiced red pepper, piment d'espelette and brioche bake 611

pine nuts
caramelised onion rice with cinnamon and pine nuts 679
gurnard with sweet and sour onions and pine nuts 612
old-fashioned broccoli with pine nuts and crab and saffron butter 372
roast potatoes with courgettes, lemon and pine nuts 566

pineapple
duck and coconut rice with pineapple and chilli dressing 677

piperade
piperade of leek, mushrooms and Coolea cheese 673
smoky piperade with chorizo 336

orzo salad with parsley, chilli and lemon 608
pea and poached salmon salad 647
pea, fennel and feta salad 558
potato, shallot and sausage salad 175
roast chicken salad with cervelle de canut 557
roast salmon with courgette and butter bean salad 415
roasted asparagus and fennel salad with Toonsbridge mozzarella 93
roasted carrot salad with tarator and cress 659
roasted courgette, rocket and Parma ham salad 95
roasted pepper, bread and orange salad 419
roasted spring carrot salad with bulgur, yogurt and dates 559
salad of goat cheese, French beans and peaches 182
smoked chicken, grape and Crozier Blue salad 79
smoked haddock with new potato, egg and spring onion salad 128
spring salad with goat cheese and mint 89
summer leaves and courgette with gazpacho dressing and Manchego 141
turkey and ham crunch with Christmas Caesar salad 501
Tuscan bread salad 155
warm beetroot salad with smashed feta, orange and pumpkin seeds 51
warm Christmas salad 265
warm couscous, cauliflower and almond salad 271
warm pork chop, field mushroom and Gorgonzola salad 326
warm salad of baby potatoes, smoked salmon, apple and broad beans 358
warm salad of Jerusalem artichokes, leeks and Parma ham 23
winter vegetable salad with chervil and horseradish dressing 683

salami
an autumnal salad 207
baked mozzarella in salami picante sauce 597
bruschetta of lentils, balsamic cream and salami 210
crusted summer greens with lemon, artichokes and salami 137
duck risotto with cabbage, salami and red wine 283
gnocchi with frazzled salami, halloumi and chopped rocket 540
roasted summer cabbage with salami and apple 161
spaghetti with cavolo nero, tomatoes, Coolea and salami 426

salmon
a very simple seafood stew 524

baked salmon and sweet potato wraps with kecap manis 19
baked salmon with warm red cabbage, fennel and Pernod crème fraîche 497
butter-poached salmon with sticky fennel jam 227
pea and poached salmon salad 647
poached seafood in ginger and coconut broth 433
potted salmon 41
salmon brioche rolls 173
salmon with courgette and butter bean salad 415
skinny salmon with soy, ginger and cabbage 132
smoked salmon and butterhead with wasabi, apple and dill 195
smoked salmon farfalle with Brussels sprouts, smoked salmon and crème fraîche 682
smoked salmon puff with princess beetroot 254

salsa verde
fennel risotto with roasted vegetable salsa verde 366

salt
salt-baked root vegetables with wild garlic aioli 314–15
whole monkfish with rosemary salt and charred lemons 422

salumi
tigelle with mostarda grapes, burrata and salumi 548–9

sambal olek
buckwheat noodles with sticky aubergine and sambal olek 620

samosas
coronation chicken samosas 562

sandwiches
beefy cheese melts 66
field mushroom, mortadella and Cambozola buns 655
my favourite grilled cheese sandwich 345
my stuffed picnic loaf 646
steak trencher with parsley, capers and shallots 209
teriyaki sea trout buns with cucumber and ginger pickle 561

satay
chicken satay lettuce wraps 305
prawn satay with pickled cucumber 525

sauces
baked mozzarella in salami picante sauce 597
barbecued lamb shoulder with tomato and 'nduja sauce 330–1

butter beans in roasted pepper and goat cheese sauce 567
chicken noodle salad with peanut and cucumber sauce 417
Coquilles St Jacques with smoked paprika butter sauce 296–7
fried gnocchi with cacio e pepe sauce 449
hake chops with chickpeas and wild garlic butter sauce 327
maple-drizzled bacon ribs with sour cream and apple cinnamon sauce 241
osso buco of beef and red cabbage with apple sauce and horseradish cream 64–5
roasted pepper and butter bean brandade with green sauce 650
slow-cooked pork with yum yum sauce 629
spaghetti with yellow pepper sauce 185
Tafelspitz steak 527

sausages
a family cassoulet 511
baked sausages with cinnamon onions and crispy croissants 442
kielbasa cassoulet with parmentier potatoes and sour cream 464
pot roast Italian sausages with spring cabbage and polenta 343
potato, shallot and sausage salad 175
rigatoni with sausage meatballs, pepper cream and thyme 399
sausage, gnocchi and red onion roast 56
sausage, sweet potato and red onion crumble 481
stump, sausages and apple gravy 218
Waterford coddle 236

scallops
Coquilles St Jacques with smoked paprika butter sauce 296–7
seared scallops with papa al pomodoro 617

scones
tear-and-share red pepper, red onion and feta scone 645

sea bass
baked whole sea bass on holiday ratatouille 637

sea beet
grilled lobster with Ibérico butter and sea beet 405
plaice with new potatoes, Little Gems and sea beet butter 555

sea trout
teriyaki sea trout buns with cucumber and ginger pickle 561

Serrano ham
roasted courgettes with burrata, umami dressing and Serrano ham 193

sesame

baked beetroot with baharat, yogurt and sesame 536

caramelised cauliflower, chickpea and sesame bake 507

grilled gammon with gingery cabbage and sweet sesame roasties 250

noodles with butternut squash, sesame and coconut 206

oxtail with star anise, Little Gems and sesame 126–7

parsnip, sesame and red onion cake with minted cranberry yogurt 258–9

roast kohlrabi with maple syrup and sesame 288

sesame and spring onion hasselback potatoes 631

shallots

pork rack chops with sticky shallots and sage and Cheddar mash 365

potato, shallot and sausage salad 175

steak trencher with parsley, capers and shallots 209

sticky shallots with mozzarella and Parma ham 170

warm steak salad with shallot, petits pois and Roquefort 599

sherry

baked duck with barley, sherry and field mushrooms 198

barbecued pork neck with sherry, garlic and rosemary 347

chestnut mushroom, parsnip and sherry soup 483

Pedro Ximénez, caramelised onion and Coolea quiche 146–7

sticky parsnips with sherry and smoked bacon 21

turkey crown with sherry cream 491

smoked paprika

baked cod with butter beans, olives and pimenton 593

Coquilles St Jacques with smoked paprika butter sauce 296–7

prawns with smoked paprika and rosemary butter 489

roast honey pimenton chicken and rice 531

socca

socca with piment d'espelette, peppers and anchovies 395

soufflé

soufflés twice-baked Cashel Blue soufflés 40

soup

a green and good gazpacho 409

a winter soup with horseradish cream 513

chestnut mushroom, parsnip and sherry soup 483

chicken, leek and bacon soup 91

chickpea and smoky tomato soup 575

cream of white onion, Cheddar and apple soup 99

curried sweetcorn and coconut soup 244

Little Gems with ajo blanco, grapes and toasted sourdough 349

lobster with ajo blanco, cucumber and new potatoes 615

pea and avocado soup 52

red pepper and butter bean soup with chicken butter toast 600

roast chicken noodle soup 243

roasted monkfish ribollita 649

spiced cabbage, borlotti bean and lentil soup 431

spiced pea and avocado soup 52

watermelon gazpacho 183

sour cream

chicken with bacon, mushrooms and sour cream 70

chilli calzones with smoked jalapeño sour cream 382–3

jerk potatoes with butterhead lettuce, crispy bacon, sour cream and chives 367

kielbasa cassoulet with parmentier potatoes and sour cream 464

maple-drizzled bacon ribs with sour cream and apple cinnamon sauce 241

Tafelspitz steak 527

souvlaki

lamb souvlaki with roasted peppers and minted yogurt 181

soy sauce

skinny salmon with soy, ginger and cabbage 132

soy-steamed hake with gingered vegetables 574

steamed sea trout with peppered cabbage, soy, garlic and ginger 270

spice bag

roast spice bag chicken with butternut squash, baby spinach and cashews 82

spice bag slaw 230

sticky spice bag chicken traybake 517

spinach

courgette, spinach and brown bread salad 661

hake with lentils, baby spinach, ginger and chilli 504

lamb chops with spinach, cumin, almonds and apricots 325

mushroom, roasted bread and spinach salad 60

orzo with mushrooms, spinach, lemon and Parmesan 515

roast spice bag chicken with butternut squash, baby spinach and cashews 82

roasted Jerusalem artichokes with bacon and spinach 287

sweet potato and spinach with spiced pumpkin seeds and goat cheese 197

spring onions

a green and good gazpacho 409

Little Gems with baby potatoes and devilled egg and spring onion dressing 414

peppered hoisin steak with pak choi, spring onions, chilli and ginger 681

sesame and spring onion hasselback potatoes 631

smoked haddock with new potato, egg and spring onion salad 128

spiced ling with fragrant coconut rice and spring onions 339

squid

arroz caldoso negre 641

sriracha

pointed peppers with olive crumble and sriracha crème fraîche 554

star anise

oxtail with star anise, Little Gems and sesame 126–7

stew

a very simple seafood stew 524

beetroot, Beaujolais and red onion stew with Gorgonzola and walnuts 435

chicken, root vegetable and barley stew with cider and ginger cream 457

frivole, mushroom and barley stew with Cáis na Tíre 289

spiced carrot, almond and chickpea stew 537

stroganoff

pork, parsnip and apple stroganoff 434

stuffing

chorizo, orange and almond stuffing 35

sultanas

saffron chickpeas with sultanas and orange 19

sweet potatoes

baked salmon and sweet potato wraps with kecap manis 19

baked sweet potatoes with feta and spiced pumpkin seeds 85

confit duck with sweet potatoes, apples and ginger 13

fried monkfish with curried sweet potato broth 585

grilled gammon with gingery cabbage and sweet sesame roasties 250

kecap manis pork with sweet potato, pak choi and cashews 573

Acknowledgements

THANK YOU

Thank you to Marie Claire Digby for that phone call that brought me back to the *Irish Times*. Without that call, this book wouldn't exist and those fateful, surreal years of covid would have passed without me having ever recorded them.

Thank you to Patsey Murphy, formerly of the *Irish Times*, who encouraged and nurtured me while all the time believing that I had a story to tell.

Thank you to Kristin Jensen. One day I called her wondering if she'd be interested in publishing a small book. 'No,' she said, 'but I would be interested in a big book.' That was the start of it. The journey was an incredibly easy one. Her professionalism and support convinced me that this was the right format in which to bring out the book. It's a chronicle of those weird and not-so-wonderful years, already written but needing a touch of love and imagination to bring it along.

Thank you to Harry Weir, my photographer and my partner in crime during the *Irish Times* years. He would rock up once a month to photograph and style the food, as I can be a bit agricultural at times. It was hectic but wonderful. We were some team. I still miss you, Harry.

Thank you to my wife, Máire, who as ever stayed by my side to edit, correct, steer and encourage and had the discipline it took to produce the goods week in, week out. We are, I think, a formidable team in the best way when we get going.

My girls, Ruth and Anna, grew up so much during this time. They and all their peers had years taken from them. Now it's time for them to bloom.

I want to thank my friends for the stories and all the good times that gave me such rich content. Hopefully there will be many more adventures.

I also want to acknowledge our staff at the Tannery, who are an integral part of our business. It is true that many hands make light work and they have always been there to support us through thick and thin. Thank you to our customers too. There is simply no point in having a restaurant without people to feed.

Lastly, thank you to Dungarvan. How fortunate we are to live in this beautiful part of the world.

About the Author

Paul Flynn is a chef, restauranteur, cookery school owner and teacher, TV presenter and personality. He co-owns the Tannery Restaurant and Townhouse in Dungarvan, County Waterford with his wife, Máire, which opened in 1997. In 2008, they opened the Tannery Cookery School.

Paul has been a regular on Irish and international television with numerous successful shows, including *Lords and Ladles* and *Paul Flynn's Food Truck Favourites*. Paul has also been the cookery writer for the *Irish Times* on two occasions: from 2000 to 2004 and from 2019 to 2022.

When Paul isn't in the kitchen or at a music festival, he's probably hopping on a plane for a new adventure. Who knows, he may even write more about his travels someday.

@paulflynnchef

Nine Bean Rows
23 Mountjoy Square
Dublin
D01 E0F8
Ireland
@9beanrowsbooks
ninebeanrowsbooks.com

First published 2023
© Paul Flynn, 2023

ISBN: 978-1-7392105-1-9

Editor: Kristin Jensen
Design and layout: Jane Matthews janematthewsdesign.com
Assisted by: Alan McArthur dexal.ie
Printed by L&C Printing Group, Poland

The author and publisher are grateful to Clodagh Beresford Dunne
for permission to reproduce her poem 'Ruminant' (pages 232–3),
first published in *Poetry Magazine*, Chicago.

The paper in this book is produced using pulp from managed forests.

All rights reserved.

No part of this publication may be copied, reproduced or transmitted in any
form or by any means without written permission of the publishers.

A CIP catalogue record for this book is available from the British Library.

10 9 8 7 6 5 4 3 2 1